Pilgrim's Progress, Puritan Progress

Pilgrim's Progress, Puritan Progress

Discourses and Contexts

Kathleen M. Swaim

University of Illinois Press
Urbana and Chicago

© 1993 by the Board of Trustees of the University of Illinois
Manufactured in the United States of America

C 5 4 3 2 1

This book is printed on acid-free paper.

Library of Congress Cataloging-in-Publication Data

Swaim, Kathleen M.
    Pilgrim's progress, Puritan progress : discourses and contexts /
Kathleen M. Swaim.
        p. cm.
    Includes bibliographical references and index.
    ISBN 0-252-01894-X (hard : alk. paper)
        1. Bunyan, John, 1628–1688. Pilgrim's progress.   2. Puritan
movements in literature.   3. Puritans in literature.   I. Title.
PR3330.A9S93   1993
828'.407—dc20   91-44385
                                                                 CIP

For Margo Culley

Contents

——◈——

ACKNOWLEDGMENTS

Portions of Chapter 6 appeared in *Studies in English Literature* (90.3[1990]) and in *Religion & Literature* (21.3 [1989]). Permission to reprint for the former has been granted by *Studies in English Literature* and for the latter by *Religion & Literature*, University of Notre Dame, Notre Dame, Ind.

I am grateful to the Graduate School of the University of Massachusetts, Amherst, for a University Fellowship that freed me from a year's teaching to work on this project, and for varied assistance to Robert Bagg, Elizabeth Swaim, Suzie D. Beans, and Margo Culley.

A NOTE ON TEXTS

The edition of *Pilgrim's Progress* used throughout is *The Pilgrim's Progress From This World to That Which is to Come*, edited by James Blanton Wharey, 2d ed. Roger Sharrock (Oxford: Clarendon Press, 1967). Insofar as possible Bunyan's other works are cited from Clarendon Press editions as well, including *Grace Abounding to the Chief of Sinners*, edited by Roger Sharrock (1962); *The Holy War Made by Shaddai Upon Diabolus*, edited by Roger Sharrock and James F. Forrest (1980); and *The Miscellaneous Works of John Bunyan*, general editor Roger Sharrock (1976–). For all works not yet available in this edition, I have used *The Works of John Bunyan*, 3 vols., edited by George Offor (London: Blackie and Son, 1862), except in the case of *The Life and Death of Mr. Badman*, where I have used the Oxford University Press edition of 1929, with introduction by Bonamy Dobree. The Clarendon Press volumes are cited within the text as volume number (where there is one) and page numbers; Offor's edition is cited within the text as "Offor" plus volume number and page numbers. Unless otherwise specified, I cite the King James Version of the Bible.

Pilgrim's Progress, Puritan Progress

Introduction

In the decades before the English lobbed cannon balls at each other, they bombarded their religious opponents with epithets. The targets of the moniker "Puritan" were people who looked with distress on the condition of their church and who covenanted together in groups of self-professed godly souls to reform what they considered an intolerable string of abuses. Considering themselves the leaven that would raise the lump of ignorant, indifferent, and false professors through constant pious endeavor, they earned their neighbors' enmity for divisive scrupulosity and hypocritical self-righteous zeal. To friends they seemed militant soldiers in the army of the Lord; to foes, officious busybodies disrupting village camaraderie, but on at least one point all observers could agree: to be a puritan meant living a life distinctively ardent.—Charles L. Cohen, *God's Caress*

FOR AT LEAST the first two centuries after its publication, John Bunyan's *Pilgrim's Progress* (1678) belongs among the most formative and beloved books England has contributed to the Western tradition, second only in popularity and influence to the English Bible and with it providing "the staple diet of all literate Englishmen."[1] It has been called "the prose epic of English Puritanism," "the epic of the poor," "the epic of the itinerant," and "the best *Summa Theologiae Evangelicae* ever produced by a writer not miraculously inspired." Its author has been dubbed "the Spenser of the people," "the Shakespeare of the Puritans," and the "poet-apostle of the English middle-classes imperfectly educated like himself."[2] It ran to two editions in its first year and to eleven editions and some one hundred thousand copies in John Bunyan's lifetime alone. There were at least thirteen hundred editions by 1938, of which the New York Public Library owns some eight hundred editions, and a Bedford County Council guidebook of 1972 cites translations into two hundred languages.[3] Little Nell, Maggie Tulliver, Adam Bede, and Huckleberry Finn read *Pilgrim's Progress; Jane Eyre, Little Women,* and in the twentieth century Margaret Drabble's *The Needle's Eye* borrow character and structure from it. Paul Fussell records that during World War I soldier after soldier articulated the waste, horror, loss, and fear of his experiences by invoking Christian's burden, the Slough of Despond, and the Valley of the Shadow of Death (99, 137–44). Indeed, Carolynn Van Dyke has recently suggested that even those who have not read Bunyan's allegory "carry a kind of template for it in their heads" (156).

The first part of *Pilgrim's Progress* (1678) traces the history of its hero Christian, in the words of the subtitle, *From This World to That which is to Come,* and discovers *The manner of his setting out, His Dangerous Journey; And safe Arrival at the Desired Countrey.* The second part (1684) proposes a similar journey, this time undertaken by the pilgrim's wife Christiana and their children. While the mythic and narrative force of part I has drawn consistent admiration, part II has often been ignored or treated as an afterthought. At a simple level the double text contrasts categories of gender and also radical differences between the aspirations and salvational strategies of the individual and those of the social group. Largely considered, it fictionalizes two profoundly differing worldviews, the first looking backward to Reformation theology and medieval certainties, the second looking forward to the more familiar and scattered parameters of the modern world.

Although millions of readers over three centuries have found *Pilgrim's Progress* transcending history and echoing universal truths, it is also a text that encodes and participates in history. Besides celebrating Bunyan's artistic practices and achievement, the present study examines *Pilgrim's Progress* as a mirror of late seventeenth-century Puritan culture. It considers both parts of *Pilgrim's Progress* in relation to Bunyan's threescore works, especially the sermon-treatises recording his theological principles, interpretive procedures, and instructional goals, texts massively documenting intersections between Bunyan and late seventeenth-century Puritanism and therefore Bunyan and theological, political, and cultural history more generally. To attend to the textual conjunctions and disjunctions between Bunyan's popular fictions and such contexts is to reconstitute a series of contemporary discourses and to bring forward some telling compounds of literature and history heretofore largely overlooked.

Behind the inquiry lies one of the most teasing questions of history and literary history: How did a literary century that began with the astonishing creativity and passionate energy of a Spenser, a Donne, a Raleigh, and a Shakespeare end up with a Dryden and a Pope "translating" into an acceptably polished idiom not just Virgil and Homer and their own Chaucer but even Shakespeare's *Antony and Cleopatra*, Donne's *Satires*, and Milton's very recent *Paradise Lost*? In terms of history, how did the great age of English exploration end up as the great age of English complacency, an age content, in Basil Willey's words, merely to consolidate the certainties of the previous century (264)?

The seventeenth century witnessed radically altered attitudes toward selfhood, society, politics, economics, religion, science, and taste that leave behind a medieval world and lay the groundwork for a modern one, even questioning such entrenched institutions as the Bible, the state church, the family, private property, and male superiority. It learned to solve political problems through discussion and argument, to prefer utility and expediency over historical precedent, and to pursue practical means for bringing about and nourishing peace, order, and prosperity to the commonwealth. For Hans Blumenberg, its underlying idea of progress derives from a displacement of the fixed authority of Aristotelian science by a cooperative science guided by method and a "modern" displacement of "ancient" hegemony in the arts and letters. For Michel Foucault, its emerging episteme deals in signs and perception not things, in analysis not a hierarchy of analogies, discontinuities not "conjuncture," order not interpretation. In telling reversals, the end of the century honored the goodness of the material world and the body and the pursuit of earthly happiness. In an atmosphere dominated by Latitudinarianism, empowering skepticism, and distrusting enthusiasm, it is no accident, as Gerald R. Cragg quips of the Restoration decades, that "an era which opened with the Act of Uniformity ended with the Act of Toleration."[4]

To speak of American colonization, or the defeat of the plague, or Descartes's legitimation of methodical doubt is to acknowledge some important ingredients of the public and philosophical change, but the seventeenth century brought a revolution in the accoutrements of life as well as in thought. Literary priority begins its shift from the theater to the novel, from an aristocratic to a chiefly middle-class audience, from hearing to reading.[5] Revolutions in domestic architecture and furnishings, costume, and diet, and innovations in tea and coffee, crockery, forks, mirrors, and chairs gloss a transformation of daily life. Christopher Hill indexes the sweeping changes by listing such end-of-century developments as "banks and cheques, budgets, the stock exchange, the periodical press, coffee-houses, clubs, coffins, microscopes, shorthand, actresses, and umbrellas." He extends Bunyan's vision to summarize the century's end: "Pilgrims who had set out for the Celestial City found themselves lingering in Vanity Fair, or the nearby village of Occasional Conformity."[6]

Contrary to expectation, political defeat—and the ensuing Restoration persecution—were not the demise but the essential creative condition of Puritanism's cultural achievement, according to N. H. Keeble's recent study *The Literary Culture of Nonconformity* (22), and the two parts of *Pilgrim's Progress* encode in two modes what preceded and what followed this huge cultural shift and illuminate its nature and implications. Written by the same author and using the same basic setting and plot, the two halves of *Pilgrim's Progress* nonetheless are grounded in radically different assumptions and goals. Scriptural and spiritual evidence predominates in the masculine part I; material culture, social organization, and nurturance claim priority for the feminine part II. The first half of the study that follows supplies the Reformation context, often drawing upon Bunyan's own theological corpus; the second half attends to the Restoration context, the cultural texture, social reorganization, and altered epistemology and value system that came to dominate.

Though just six years separated their publication, part I was in fact probably written a dozen years before part II, that is, by 1672 and perhaps even earlier. Richard Greaves assigns part I to the late 1660s on historical, biographical, and textual grounds: Part I addresses the specific needs of newly threatened Nonconformists in these years, the overlap with *The Heavenly Footman* supports this assignment, and Bunyan required some years prior to 1678, as the "Apology" makes clear, to circulate the text among friends and to overcome his reticence to publish a work whose entertainment values threatened more normative means of edification. Sharrock reaffirms 1666–72 as the dates of composition, adding to these grounds independent datings by Bunyan friends and contemporaries.[7]

Pilgrim's Progress transposes into allegory Bunyan's own life and era, but the life and era themselves encapsulate the Puritan culture they inhabit. G. M. Trevelyan equates Christian with Bunyan as "the representative Puritan of the English Puritan epoch" to "illustrate" English society of the era (173), and Q. D. Leavis similarly sees *Pilgrim's Progress* as produced as much by Puritan culture generally as by its particular author (97).[8] "A thinking and striving nation showered its intellectual and sentimental nourishment on Bunyan," writes his "inner" biographer Henri Talon: "To understand Bunyan is to penetrate the spiritual significance of Puritanism." In the only modern full length study of his theology Richard L. Greaves remarks of Bunyan's soteriological views what is also generally true: "What [Bunyan] said also was essentially representative of that which any Puritan or sectary in the seventeenth century would have heard from his own strict Calvinist minister on the subject of salvation."[9]

In his enormous appetite for religious ferment and publication, Bunyan is in many ways typical of his era, labeled by Donald Davie as "the heroic age of English Dissent," a century whose demand for sermons and religious discussion was almost insatiable. Douglas Bush records that in 1619 nearly three-fourths of the books printed in England were religious and moral and that in 1657–58 the number of works of divinity equaled the number of works published on all other subjects. For most people, including those who were not particularly devout, religion was a principal, often intense concern more than at any other time before or since.[10] From this context, Bunyan's centrally placed religious thinking and activities look both backward to the Reformation and forward to the Chapel and Evangelical traditions of later centuries.

Pilgrim's Progress is a late product of the Protestant Reformation in England, a movement miniaturized in the figure of a lonely reader of the Bible passionately seeking salvation. In small as in large matters, the Reformation was thus essentially grounded in the processes and goals of literary criticism. Part I at least participates fundamentally in the Reformation's profound reorganization of consciousness whose echoes continue to sound in the late twentieth century. Although Puritanism reaches both backward and forward in time, its basic principles were essentially stable and continuous, centering upon a piety understood as a resurrection of primitive Christianity and translated into formal theology eagerly embraced and gladly rehearsed. Perry Miller summarizes its more broadly cultural outlook in these terms: "Puritans lived in a fixed, limited, and unalterable universe, appointed by God and every part of it known; they were intellectual conservatives, who constantly denounced 'novelty' as a sin. . . . They were quite content with their universe, even though it had been the scene of man's fall; they believed that God had created it by perfect wisdom, and that it was just such a universe as men should live in. They had no conscious intention of disturbing its outlines or widening its horizons" (*New England Mind* 365–66). As Boyd M. Berry explains, having accepted an inherited framework of thought, they busied themselves to refine its positions and draw out its implications, finding novelty in Reformation breakthroughs and in systematic elaborations of biblical texts (86).[11]

Bunyan in particular was more systematic and explicatory than innovative, and centuries of readers agree that his chief originality lies in making theology psychologically appealing, experientially apt, and intellectually satisfying by translating abstraction into vitalized and memorably realistic form. He was not, like his Puritan literary contemporary John Milton, a theoretician or prophetic voice or definer of public policy. Greaves calls him "a Bedfordshire tinker with the vision of Paul, the conviction of Luther, and the commitment to freedom of Milton." Bunyan's was a hybrid theology that no single label will fit, manifesting sometimes the personalized and experientialized divine wrath-grace dichotomy of Luther and sometimes a more intellectualized Calvinistic concern with divine will and omnipotence. Between the options of a Lutheran private knowledge of and communion with God and a Calvinistic intellectualism and social and moral system, Bunyan leans toward the latter but overlays its terrors and anxiety with ardent assurance of divine love.[12]

Throughout the three decades of his publishing life, Bunyan's theology consistently urges the inner workings of the Holy Spirit, what *Grace Abounding* calls his "awakening and converting Work" (89), but it undergoes a significant shift of emphasis that indexes personal, professional, and historical changes as well. Successive editions of the basic theology of *The Doctrine of the Law and Grace Unfolded* in 1659 and 1685 remain surprisingly unchanged, while changes to *Pilgrim's Progress* part I, even in its first year, show Bunyan moving away from struggles of conversion and toward such failures of Christian practice as hypocrisy and greed. The early Bunyan preached the terrors of the law with vigorous intellectual conviction, while the late Bunyan proffered an invitational salvation to the willing with tolerant charity and wise humanity. Talon describes the change as Bunyan's heart speaking more loudly and urgently than his reason in his later life, and Cragg recognizes the norm of a beginning preacher denouncing sin while a man of greater experience and deeper human insight will expound divine mysteries and minister comforts.[13] The posthumous *The Saints' Knowledge of Christ's Love* "abounds with ardent sympathy for the broken-hearted, a cordial suited to every wounded conscience" (Offor 11:1).

These distinct phases of Bunyan's ministry mirror a general adjustment of English life in which, as Leopold Damrosch describes it, "Calvinism underwent an unexpected and astonishing collapse, reflecting a reaction both to its angry moralism and to its political behavior," a movement "from dogmatic clarity to ethical complexity."[14] A turning point for Bunyan occurs when, faced with the gallows, he makes the full leap of faith and is thereafter free to function fully in relation to others and the outside world, having left his own extreme self-analysis behind him (*Grace Abounding* 101). From a variety of angles the chapters that follow translate such differences between the early and the late Bunyan into the larger patterns of life and thought they miniaturize, and for the most part they see the two phases encoded in the disjunctive parts of *Pilgrim's Progress*.

Because this study projects Bunyan and his pilgrimage allegory against contemporary theology, it often generalizes about Puritanism, and it is appropriate to preface the argument with some basic understandings of *Puritan*, a word Christopher Hill speaks of as "an admirable refuge from clarity of thought."[15] With similar wryness, Patrick Collinson acknowledges "a secondary academic industry . . . devoted to the search for an acceptable definition" of the word *Puritan*.[16] In the later decades of the seventeenth century certain developments in Puritanism were imported from—not exported to—the American colonies, and I have filled out the English context by drawing advisedly upon some studies of American backgrounds, the more confidently because a number of key figures were active on first one and then the other side of the Atlantic throughout the century.

Puritans were defined by their emphasis on preaching, their high ideals and integrity, their religious intellectualism, their service to the community, their doctrine of spiritual equality, their commitment to Scriptures and to doing God's will (Hill, *Century* 68–69). Puritans were people of purposive and systematic activity whose emphasis on preaching and hearing the Word constituted an essentially clerical and evangelical movement. Greaves finds the essence of mid-century Puritanism not in matters of polity, theological dogma, principles of authority, or class orientation—as others have—but rather in the deeply spiritual but elusive personal experience of God, in evangelical piety, covenantalism, and the operations of the Holy Spirit. *Puritan* often can be equated rather simply with a desire for reform targeted especially against worldliness in the church and the court. What began as "purifying" the church from within broadened beyond Sabbatarianism, hostility to oaths, and especially anti-

Catholicism to become a dominant political and military force in the England of the mid-seventeenth century. "Puritanism," generalizes David E. Stannard, "was a reform movement within a reform movement," or in Milton's contemporary phrasing, it seeks "the reforming of reformation itself." [17] After enormous upheaval, what began as the "reform" of the Reformation had exhausted itself by the late century. But even its post-Restoration ebbing left behind radically altered power, economic, class, domestic, and gender relations.

On the one hand, *Puritan* refers to dogma and ecclesiastical politics, and from its Elizabethan beginnings Puritanism emphasized church re-organization and a vigorous preaching ministry. On the other hand and more generally, *Puritan* refers to evangelical Protestantism and the pious and practical conduct of public and private life. At the extreme it most widely bequeathed to later generations, it coincides with the Protestant work ethic, which David Leverenz summarizes as "internalized authority manifested as hard work and postponed leisure" (19). While *Puritan* is not to be simply equated with such combinations of killjoy, hypocrite, and self-righteous megalomaniac as depicted by Shakespeare and Jonson in Malvolio and Zeal-of-the-Land Busy, in fact zeal, piety, and busyness are indeed among its characteristics.

Charles H. and Katherine George describe Puritans as "those most intense of English Protestants" (108 and similarly 352), and in many ways Puritanism embodies English Protestantism in its ultimate and perhaps most dynamic form. Politically as theologically, Puritanism was ardently committed to principles of individual liberty. At the private level of devotion, according to Alan Simpson, "The essence of Puritanism . . . is an experience of conversion which separates the Puritan from the mass of mankind and endows him with the privileges and the duties of the elect. The root of the matter is always a new birth, which brings with it a conviction of salvation and a dedication to warfare against sin. . . . The whole object of the Puritan's existence was to trace its course in himself and to produce it in others. He develops it in his sermons, systematizes it in his creeds, charts it in his diaries." In Simpson's summary phrasing, Puritanism is a grand iconoclasm, sustained by a grand utopianism (2, 11, 19, 61). Puritanism is further defined by an insistent separation between nature and grace, as well as by discipline, self-accusation, and self-denial, the wish to establish a holy community, and an apocalyptic view of their place in history. In essence it relied on the Bible alone, worshiped only according to the explicit commands of Scripture, presumed man's sinfulness, and believed salvation derives only through Christ's grace, not human efforts—however extensive and meritorious. It encouraged the individual to think independently, but expected everyone to arrive at the same understanding founded upon Ramistic reasoning and axiomatic truth. Characteristically, Puritans interwove the private and the public, regularly projecting equivalents between the most private and the most inclusive realms, between the *domus* and the *polis* and even the apocalypse. They saw and regularly interpreted themselves as Hebrew patriarchs and England as the New(est) Jerusalem and America as Eden.

In general, my usage makes two claims for the term. Although before and after the English Revolution *Puritan* could be notably pejorative, I mean always to use it in a positive sense, and although it can refer to a variety of religiopolitical positions dating from the middle sixteenth century onward in America as well as England, I intend it to refer to those English post-Restoration decades when Puritanism and dissent coincide, specifically for Bunyan the years between 1656, the date of his first publication, and 1688, the year of his death. Even within these years, as Puritanism was waning from its earlier empowerment into a hardened provincialism, the category undergoes telling shifts that this study attaches to the two distinct parts of *Pilgrim's Progress*, the first reflecting Bunyan as agonized convert and jailed martyr, and the second reflecting the popular Bedford minister who had left behind his own conversion traumas in favor of carefully shepherding a needy flock less heroic than himself.

It is appropriate as well as convenient to speak of Bunyan as a Puritan for, although his thinking was often notably liberal, he shared Calvinistic emphases on such fundamental principles as man's fall, his natural corruption, his regeneration through grace, the peculiar privileges of the elect aristocracy, and the Christian liberty of the regenerate (Barker xxiii). *Puritan* is not a label he attaches to himself—he calls himself an Anabaptist if anything (e.g., *The Heavenly Footman* v:153—but cf. *Peaceable Principles and True* Offor 11:649)—but his rare uses of the term *Puritan* reference the life of heightened moral awareness and action generally understood in the term and contrast an earlier godliness with present deteriorations of faith. *The Life and Death of Mr. Badman* (1680) refers to a contemporary as "a godly old Puritan, for so the godly were called in time past" (233). *A Holy Life* (1684) evokes similar nostalgia: "Were but our times duly compared with those that went before, we should see that which now we are ignorant of. Did we but look back to the *Puritans*, but specially to those that but a little before them, suffered for the word of God, in the *Marian* days, we should see another life than is now among men, another manner of conversation, than is now among professors" (IX:345). The opening page of *The Church Book of the Bedford Meeting* (later called the "Bunyan Meeting") lays claim to a nonconforming fellowship "such as in those days did beare the name of Puritanes."

Bunyan's own religious profession, what I am calling his *Puritanism*, is especially marked by zeal, simplicity, and ardor for reformation, principles in line with the three governing graces of professors listed in *A Holy Life*: "*simplicity, innocency*, and godly *sincerity*" and later as "self-denial, charity, purity in life and conversation" and as "Faith, and Patience, and the love of God" (IX:329, 346, 347). Without invoking the word *Puritan*, Bunyan's summary advice in *Christian Behaviour* encompasses its meaning: "He that walketh *uprightly*, walketh *safely*; and they that add to *Faith, Virtue*; to *Virtue, Knowledge*; to *Knowledge, Temperance*; to *Temperance, Brotherly kindness*; and to these *Charity*, and that *abounds* therein, he shall neither be *barren* nor *unfruitful*; he shall never fall, but so an *entrance* shall be ministred to him abundantly, into the *everlasting Kingdom of our Lord and Saviour Jesus Christ*" (III:57). *A Holy Life* draws the edifying exhortation: "Singularity in godliness, if it be in godliness, no man should be ashamed of. For that is no more than to be more godly, than to walk more humbly with God than others: and for my part, I had rather be a pattern, and example of piety: I had rather that my life should be instructing to the Saints, and condemning to the world, with *Noah*, and *Lot*; than to hazard my self among the multitude of the drossie" (IX:346). Bunyan's life as it comes down to us is largely an acting out of such lofty principles of salvation and service.

After conversion in the early 1650s, Bunyan joined John Gifford's Bedford congregation in 1656. From 1655 or 1656 on he was an itinerant lay preacher at first in the Bedford vicinity, then in the counties of Cambridge, Hertford, Leicester, Huntington, Northampton, and Buckingham, and late in life in London itself. His first publication dates from 1656. He spent most of the twelve years between 1660 and 1672 and part of 1676 in Bedford jail—"the nerve centre for Nonconformity in the region" (III:xvi)—in a form of ministerial martyrdom that *Seasonable Counsel* shows he welcomed as confirming his divine calling (X:40–98). For his preaching and clerical influence his contemporaries sometimes dubbed him "the Bishop of Bedford," but he was remarkable too for his more personal ministry. In this he died at age sixty from a fever caught while riding long hours in the rain on a mission to reconcile a father and son.[18]

Puritanism permeated the very air Bunyan breathed in Elstow, the village of his birth, and in Newport Pagnell where he served as a member of the Parliamentary army from 1644 to 1647, from age sixteen to nineteen. Although little can be certainly known of his military service, referred to briefly in *Grace Abounding* (18), the Parliamentary army, and Newport Pagnell in particular, were centers of radical debate on issues of both church and state. Christopher Hill's recent biography of Bunyan details the arguments to which the Elstow youth was exposed in these impressionable years, declaring the new mode of open discussion by ordinary people an "overwhelming experience" and noting Bunyan's avowed interactions with fringe groups. It was an army of soldiers preaching to each other, of numerous visionaries, of religious services before battles and prayers of thanksgiving afterward. This army served also as Bunyan's "school of politics," and in Henri Talon's image "in the privacy of his heart the leaven of tomorrow's feelings and beliefs was already rising." [19]

Bunyan's history overlaps that of thousands of his English contemporaries who went to war under such medieval systems as Falstaff so enormously abuses in *Henry IV, Part I*, only to find later that the army, like the world generally, had turned upside down, specifically under the rubric of the New Model Army with its modern base in efficiency and meritocracy. Besides its preference for volunteers over impressed men and its new uniforms and drills, among other things it operated on the principle that "free men consciously motivated by a belief in their cause could get the better of mere professionals simply by superior morale and discipline," [20] and it thereby translated Reformation individuality into middle-class aspiration and appetite for success and for the uniquely Puritan compound of radical moral change and social stability.

The army served as a medium for the free spread of thought and spiritual exercise and thus made unprecedented learning opportunities available to Bunyan and thousands like him. Though only ordained ministers were authorized to preach formal sermons to the soldiers, in fact a great deal of godly instruction went forward unofficially through reading, biblical exegesis, prayer, and mutual instruction and edification (Haller, *Liberty* esp. 193). In an often-mentioned analogue, Cromwell's army of visible saints formed itself into units rather like gathered churches. Fired by new knowledge and new capacity for thought, when such soldiers dispersed throughout the land, they brought home fresh zeal and opportunity as well as new doctrinal information and skill. Their chief lessons pointed in two complementary directions, on the one hand toward individual freedom of mind and life, and on the other toward congregate action and consensus politics. Even the most skeletal legislative record shows a frightened Restoration government responding to such empowerments by manipulating tolerance and intolerance for Nonconformists and Roman Catholics through the 1662 Act of Uniformity, the 1664 Conventicle Act, the 1665 Five-Mile Act, and the several Declarations and Repeals of Indulgence. Bunyan's works sometimes echo such public strife in a generalized way but do not react datably or sequentially to its details.

Like military service, other population and values shifts also index the contemporary English character and Puritan scheme of things. Much can be read from the raw numbers: Some twenty thousand people left England during the reign of Charles I, including, between 1629 and 1640, 132 graduates of Cambridge and Oxford who provided America with intellectual and political—and of course theological—leadership; some sixty thousand Nonconformists were prosecuted under Charles II, with five thousand dying in prison; fifteen hundred Quakers were imprisoned even during the first year and a half of James II's rule. Such statistics place Bunyan's incarceration in perspective. These forty years spawn such developments of the English character as Harry G. Plum recognizes:

> Men had lost their property and had been banished or had fled from the kingdom, had gone to prison, and in many cases had died there; yet they kept the faith and the purity of their lives. Charged with treason, rebellion, lawlessness, crime, and immorality, they had become respected for their integrity which gave such charges the lie. . . . If Puritanism put emphasis upon the spiritual and moral foundations of the individual life, it also led the way toward a grasp of the social possibilities in a religion which put little emphasis upon organization and much upon character.[21]

When the majority of a wearied nation relaxed into the stabilities of the Restoration, Bunyan persisted in religious zeal. When *Puritan* again became a name of opprobrium in general (urban) parlance, his faith drew strength from persecution.

To be a Puritan was to accept public accountability on such terms and privately to practice intensive reading and living. Although Bunyan disavows theological learning, we know from *Grace Abounding* that he minutely studied and passionately responded to a volume of Luther on Galatians that happened to come into his hands (40–41). We know too of his familiarity with the two books that constituted his first wife's dowry: Arthur Dent's *The Plain Mans Path-way to Heaven* and Lewis Bayley's *The Practice of Piety* (*Grace Abounding* 8, 134). Most of the reading he is assumed to have done remains unknown, but the few books he did read, he read with such wholehearted absorption that they became the foundation of an entire education. Large ranges of his life, principles, and context are epitomized in the two texts central to contemporary religion and variously empowered by and empowering to the English Reformation and Revolution. The first is, of course, the Bible, a work Bunyan held in absolute loyalty. The second was Foxe's *Actes and Monuments*, popularly called Foxe's *Book of Martyrs*. As the Bible informed Bunyan's views of reading, knowing, and expression, this second book with its lessons on personal sacrifice and English destiny informs his view of the right pattern of the Christian life.[22] During the dozen years in Bedford jail that so much shaped his vocation, Bunyan had both books with him. He was a Puritan in spiritual brotherhood with those sixteenth-century reformers whose Actes and Monuments Foxe celebrated and with those seventeenth-century exiles to what was to become the United States who devoted all their passionate intensity to newly defining or "re-forming" a world.

Bunyan became a Puritan, specifically a Particular Open-Communion Baptist, in this arena in the decades following general demobilization and took on the role of the mechanick lay preacher with its special social, economic, sectarian, and literary conventions and implications. William York Tindall has detailed Bunyan's place in the tradition of itinerant enthusiastic craftsmen along with their norms of social inferiority, "their economic discontent, the mockery and abuse to which they were subjected by society for their trade, illiteracy, poverty, and presumption, and their class-conscious campaign of preaching against the rich and the powerful in behalf of the oppressed." Although Bunyan was a relatively moderate enthusiast, like them generally he "depended upon inspiration and revelation, upon openings, trances, illuminations, visions, and celestial voices" and felt that "the mysterious direction of God exempted [him] from dependence on man and lent to [his] actions and speech an unquestionable authority" (vii, ix, 18, 13, and see 3–4).

Tindall's *John Bunyan: Mechanick Preacher* also proposes that *Grace Abounding to the Chief of Sinners* serve as the key work around which Bunyan's other productions distribute themselves as variant or ancillary expressions (41). Without discounting the importance of this autobiography, we may note that the publication date of 1666 does not allow at least its first edition to take into account developments in his theological thought and self-definition. In the course of the six editions of *Grace Abounding* published during his lifetime, Bunyan appended *A Brief Account of the Author's Call to the Work of the Ministry*, and it would perhaps be possible to distribute all of Bunyan's works under the conversional and biographical headings that emerge from this now-compounded text.

This study proposes not *Grace Abounding* but the two parts of *Pilgrim's Progress* as the central opus. Besides its important popularity, *Pilgrim's Progress* is the work that most fully and artfully integrates the pieces of Bunyan's thought. It is chronologically as well as otherwise central. Twenty-one of the works published during his lifetime were issued before the publication year of part I (1678), and twenty afterwards. It offers a comprehensive framework for understanding Bunyan's entire corpus, not just the half-dozen of Bunyan's sixty works familiar to readers and literary scholars—the two parts of *Pilgrim's Progress*, *The Life and Death of Mr. Badman*, *The Holy War*, *Grace Abounding*, and *A Relation of My Imprisonment*—but also the dozens of theological sermon-treatises, contributions to religious controversies, and edifying poems.[23] In it, earlier thinking crystallizes into full artistic representation, and it generates later treatises more thoroughly developing spiritual actions and thoughts here too concisely allegorized.

Bunyan's didactic and controversial prose and poetry variously illuminate these narratives. Insofar as *Pilgrim's Progress* recounts a Christian pilgrimage, for example, *The Heavenly Footman* provides a model and a set of rules for the journey. *A Mapp of Salvation and Damnation*, in more visual than verbal form, also supplies the travel metaphor. Insofar as part I invokes the military metaphor for the Christian life, *The Holy War* applies. This work's dramatizations of judicial trials also gloss the indictment of Christian and Faithful at Vanity Fair. *The Advocateship of Jesus Christ* develops the juristic metaphor fully. *The Life and Death of Mr. Badman* illustrates the Puritan fascination with individual life-histories in the extreme negative exemplum of its title figure and in a series of ancillary biographies. Its anecdotal (but not really allegorical) dialogue between an older sermonizing advisor, Mr. Wiseman, and an eager Puritan youth, Mr. Attentive, may well remind us of Christian's godly conversations with Help and Evangelist early in the narrative and with Faithful and Hopeful in the second half as they too anatomize the lapses of an absent third party. Much of Christian's pilgrimage passes as encounters with false professors, and modes of religious error listed in *The Strait Gate* and *The Barren Figtree* characterize much of the allegory's dramatis personae. As their titles suggest, *The Strait Gate* also glosses the doorways and gates of the Way Christian travels upon and *The Holy City* may be read as one long footnote on the climax of both parts of *Pilgrim's Progress* in the Celestial City.

Additional analogues solidly ground theological issues throughout the allegory. Part I begins by attending to contrasting covenants of grace and of the law and legal works, matters treated at length in *The Doctrine of the Law and Grace Unfolded*. An explicitly complementary work, *Christian Behaviour*, provides a guidebook for family relationships and thus glosses the travelers of part II. *Israel's Hope Encouraged*, a treatise on the relationship of Faith and Hope, thence explicates Faithful and Hopeful in part I, and its text, "For with the Lord there is Mercy" (Ps. 130.7), illuminates the character of Mercy in part II. By documenting Bunyan's way of handling a feminist uprising in his congregation, *A Case of Conscience Resolved* glosses the female base of part II, as part II's representations of the nature and practices of the Church are enriched by four interlocking works on church history and three pamphlets on baptism. Part II variously employs the Puritan tradition of meditation upon what *The Resurrection of the Dead* calls "the Book of the Creatures" with sometimes striking similarities to *A Book For Boys and Girls* (also called *Divine Emblems*). Emanuel's explication of the theory of riddles in *The Holy War* may be invoked behind the riddling games at House Beautiful in part II to the same purpose. Even such small points as "Remember Lot's Wife" from part I, the hen and chickens emblem from part II, and the invocations of Ecclesiastes for funereal purposes are explicated in the larger Bunyan corpus.

Glosses and analogues could well be multiplied, but the point need not be labored further. Bunyan's miscellaneous works contextualize his fictional persons, actions, and ideas within a range of theological categories and practice. Further, their implicit and sometimes explicit discourses clarify such Puritan categories as the sermon, conversion narrative, catechism, and meditations upon the Scriptures, the self, and the creatures. As the theory and practice of such discourses emerge from the incidental works, we not only recognize ways in which they have been encoded in the actions and goals of *Pilgrim's Progress* but also ways they reference whole systems of religious belief, practice, and expression in the encompassing Puritan culture.

Whatever the norms in earlier centuries, as Donald Davie has argued, it is no longer possible to study Bunyan's narrative without also studying Calvinist theology (7). Bunyan knew that highly developed reading energy and skills were the identifying characteristic of a post-Reformation audience, and the present study approaches the separate parts and the compound of the whole as narrative as well as theological art that will repay the closest attention to detail and resonance. Besides reading *Pilgrim's Progress* as an expression of Puritan culture, the present study seeks throughout to balance an interest in literary categories such as narrative, genre, and discourse, with an interest in the theological strategies and ends which these are made to serve. If *fiction* describes the literary form of *Pilgrim's Progress*, *allegory* describes its mode, or procedures, or atmosphere, or intention. In line with usual definitions of allegory, the following analysis concerns itself with ways in which tenor and vehicle, the concrete and abstract, the literary and thematic or theological categories are played off against and integrated with each other, in what Roger Sharrock, Bunyan's most devoted twentieth-century editor and commentator, calls "dramatised theology" (*Casebook* 16), a compact definition of allegory for Bunyan's dream similitude.

Allegory by definition grounds its theoretical and theological purposes in familiar and concrete reality. Secularly, part I of *Pilgrim's Progress* asks to be read against the norms of the mythic male hero, which I take to be representatively codified within Joseph Campbell's comparative psychological paradigm of *The Hero with a Thousand Faces*. The multilayered *Pilgrim's Progress* richly compounds the secularly monomythic and universal within the minor seventeenth-century genre the progress of the soul, a highly personalized literary form reflecting Protestantism's emphasis on applying the self to Scripture and Scripture to the self, and discovering scriptural paradigms and providential workings (Lewalski, "Typological Symbolism" 81). Heroic self, escape from self, redefinition of self, and edifying personal narratives and typological projections provide much of the content of Christian's narrative.

Readers read this book about a reader reading his book, and as they see him drawing lessons from the Bible's every phrase and learning to process and discuss it with his friends, they are pressured into imitative behavior and discourse. Chapters 1 and 2 examine the setting, action, and characters of *Pilgrim's Progress* part I, while Chapters 3, 4, and 5 study the Puritan processes of reading and interpreting the Bible and the Puritan discourses of sermon, meditation, and self-history underwriting these activities and variously incorporated in the allegory. Textual openings, progressive revelation, exemplary history, typological projections, and a priori faith and "progress" give shape to Bunyan's characterizations and plot. Finally, Christian turns into an edifying text to be read by his extended family in part II. Because the Puritan Word and Christian dogma are often recalcitrant and paradoxical, Bunyan's narrative enactments are sometimes cryptic, but the theological positionings in his minor works help to sort out the complexities.

The second part of *Pilgrim's Progress* feminizes the masculine or heroic mode of part I, and Chapter 6 examines its secular evidence with an eye to such critical positions as gender studies, psychology, sociology, social history, material culture, cultural anthropology, and the like. As part I records the conversional history of the unique, isolated, anxious individual believer, so part II enfolds within its family metaphor the nature, practices, and developing comforts of the church community. Chapter 7 unfolds this ecclesiological argument, while Chapter 8 defines the epistemology and expressional principles underwriting these changes, variously a matter of Puritan "declension" and generation(s) displacing the prioritized regeneration of part I. Christiana's narrative may lack the mythic intensity of her husband's, but compensates by a full participation in history.

As the concluding chapter argues, "progress" from the theological to the chronological makes visible some radical shifts of emphasis within seventeenth-century culture and intellectual history and some radical adjustments of Bunyan's own life from the persecuted convert of the 1660s to the industrious and thriving minister of the 1680s. Where the early convert, and the Puritan theology he epitomizes, harks back to the Reformation, the late ministerial Bunyan—foregrounding good works rather than an absolute scriptural Word—anticipates the modern and variously secularized world of ensuing centuries. Part I enacts the first and part II the second of these schemes. Narrative by definition refers to serial events in time, and taken most largely, the two parts of *Pilgrim's Progress* function not just as sequential stories but as an encoded record of the author's life, and as the progressive pilgrimage of Puritanism into and within history.

CHAPTER ONE

The Allegorical Way

> Bunyan so intensely presents the Christian life, so urgently
> wishes to communicate actuality to the reader, is such a
> psychological realist and didactic in so evangelical a fash-
> ion, that the convention of mediaeval allegory is given new
> shape and new pressure, losing its point by point applica-
> bility, shifting rapidly, passing from figurative representa-
> tion to actuality and back again as easily as scripture does
> and making each episode mean the whole. There are in-
> congruities but there is complete unity of theme, inten-
> tion, plot, characters, ornaments, illustrations, biblical ref-
> erences, and allegory. Every character may be the reader.
> —Roy Daniells, *Milton, Mannerism and Baroque*

DIFFICULT TO CATEGORIZE, *Pilgrim's Progress* has been much praised for
its form, much honored for its content. It has been labeled a child's story,
a dream vision, a picaresque novel, a social document, and a Puritan treatise. Generically, it is sometimes claimed for the epic, sometimes for the
novel; sometimes praised for its fantasy, sometimes for its realism. Roger
Sharrock has called it "a literary hybrid" compounded of "the forms and
language of religious allegory, the early novel, popular sermons and moral
dialogue, romance and folk story," and similarly ten years later "this mix-
ture of Calvinist theology, folk-tale reminiscence, personal psychology
and realistic thumbnail sketches."[1]

From such a range of descriptors, reflecting the varied needs this narrative has answered through several centuries, I wish to explore two literary
categories that articulate not so much the story's form as its process and
power. Thus, *allegory* will focus a review of some basic narrative evidence
in this chapter, as *myth* will govern the argument in the next. Analy-

sis of *Pilgrim's Progress* properly begins by deconstructing the dominant similitude of pilgrimage and setting forth the issues relating to the Way, the travelers, and "progress," or in literary terms the setting and context, the hero and character interactions, and the plot and narrative structure. This chapter applies theoretical definitions of allegory and the allegorical transaction to evidence of setting, character, and horizontal narrative "progress" (or lack of it) in *Pilgrim's Progress*. Given Bunyan's materials and purposes, literary considerations cannot exclude the theological even when, as here, the intention is chiefly secular. The Puritan context makes all such categories problematic, and thus rewarding in unexpected ways.

From its title-page invocation of Hosea 12.10, "I have used Similitudes," Bunyan's pilgrimage is constantly overlaid with equations of narrative data and Protestant thematics; in other words, it is an allegory. Few discussions of *Pilgrim's Progress* avoid its allegorical foundations, as few discussions of allegory can ignore the sometimes inconvenient evidence of this work. *Allegory* means literally "other-speaking," or saying one thing and meaning both the thing said and also something else. In Coleridge's famous formulation, allegoric writing employs "one set of agents and images with actions and accompaniments correspondent, so as to convey, while in disguise, either moral qualities or conceptions of the mind that are not in themselves objects of the senses, or other images, agents, actions, fortunes, and circumstances, so that the difference is everywhere presented to the eye or imagination while the likeness is suggested to the mind; and this connectedly so that the parts combine to form a consistent whole." For Coleridge elsewhere, allegory manifests "mechanic" rather than "organic" form.[2]

The narrative allegorist fleshes out a dominating idea by creating a complex imaginative system, field, or environment of correspondence between the ideational and the concrete in what handbooks call an "extended metaphor" or "continuous similitude," Spenser's "dark conceit" and "pleasing analysis." The allegorical system contains flexibly linked narrative clusters or subsystems of evidence, themselves made up of varied tropes, especially personifications, equations of person and place, and externalizations of inward traits of character. Gay Clifford outlines allegory's analytic procedures as "separating out various aspects of a concept or process into a multiplicity of persons or personifications . . . [and] placing related notions in sets or categories or in more or less self-contained dramatic units . . . [and] us[ing] visual detail and thematic and symbolic images." For Clifford, allegory is a kinetic combination of the familiar and the elusive communicating urgency and mystery (94, 12, 2). One of the greatest literary allegorists, Dante Alighieri, specifies his method as "poetic, fictive, descriptive, digressive, and transumptive, and it as well consists in definition, division, proof, refutation, and the giving of examples" (100).

Allegory handles its narrative data and its controlled environment in distinctive ways. As a linguistic procedure of encoded and reciprocating speech, allegory appeals, says Maureen Quilligan, "to readers as readers of a system of signs" (24). Angus Fletcher's booklength analysis equates allegory with "symbolic power struggles" and specifies its symbolic mode as ornamental, obsessive, hierarchic, didactic, and paratactic, a matter of daemonic agents, cosmic imagery, symbolic acts and rituals, and thematic ambivalence. Fletcher explains the environment thus: "The typical personified agent can 'act' only in consort with other similar agents, a combination which limits each work to a given problem or set of problems. The highly controlled interaction of ideas requires a corresponding definition of the limits of each." Allegory is, for Fletcher, "the manipulation of a texture of 'ornaments' so as to engage the reader in an interpretive activity," a technique fostered by Christianity which "sees the creation of the world as an establishment of a universal symbolic vocabulary." Its "openness of purpose" is in tension with "an opposite encapsulating tendency"; it simultaneously simplifies and complicates, clarifies and deliberately obscures. Allegories translate culturally viable moral assumptions into metaphor, and are thus both monuments to ideals and ideological instruments, agencies of power and propaganda, vehicles for expressing (and sometimes critiquing) traditional ideas.[3]

For the most part the narrative evidence of *Pilgrim's Progress* part I to be considered in the present chapter operates out of such basic understandings of the nature of allegory, but because later chapters on the written and expressive Word and on the self employ allegory's richer operations it is appropriate to lay some foundations for later, more complex inquiry. Thus allegory is a matter of both form and content; it is both a product and a process, both a mode of expression (Lewis, *Allegory* 48) and a mode of thought (MacCaffrey 25–26). Edward A. Bloom captures much of the nature of allegory within the metaphors of lamination and foliation (173). Allegory is, then, both a homogeneous construct made up of multiple, parallel, superposed, and bonded layers, and also a system of lateral outgrowths of branches, stems, and leaves, literally a "ramification." The layered model recognizes allegory not just as a form but also as a complexly interactive process involving text, the author's purposes and context, and the reader's participation. Allegory thus viewed can be highly convoluted and self-reflexive, centripetal rather than centrifugal.

Since allegory produces literary works dominated (some would say overwhelmed) by themes, it participates in a very special transaction with its readers. By attaching ideas systematically to a literary structure, allegory "releases a counterplay of imagination and thought by which each becomes an irritant to the other, and both may grow through the irksome contact" (Edgar Wind quoted in MacCaffrey 51). Speaking particularly of Bunyan's practice, Brian Nellist calls allegory a trap whose customary privilege is to present selective obsessions as if they were universal laws (139). Out of a dialectic between the literal and the metaphorical, the analytic reader of allegory produces meaning. To some extent, all literary commentary is allegorical interpretation, but in formal allegory the author deliberately creates structures that guide, even dictate how interpretation of a particular work must proceed. Commenting on the invitational component in allegory, Fletcher says: "The silences in allegory mean as much as the filled-in spaces, because by bridging the silent gaps between oddly unrelated images we reach the sunken understructure of thought" (107). Allegory is both the creation and interpretation of ambiguous or polysemous signs that instruct in what to believe (*quid credas*) and how to act (*quid agas*). Allegory is also didactic (*quo tendas*); it projects an ideal, a worthy goal of vitalization and/or renewal.

The reciprocating nature of allegorical data helps break down our understanding of objects and meaning so that allegory's "dark conceit" can initiate a process of gradual enlightenment and progressive self-discovery. Gregory the Great's definition of allegory, enfolded within a discussion of the Song of Solomon, contextualizes the aspirational process:

> Allegory serves as a kind of machine to the spirit by means of which it may be raised up to God. Thus when enigmas are set before a man and he recognizes certain things in the words which are familiar to him, he may understand in the sense of the words what is not familiar to him; and by means of earthly words he is separated from the earth. Since he does not abhor what he knows, he may come to understand what he does not know. For the things which are known to us from which allegory is made are clothed in divine doctrine, and when we recognize the thing by an exterior word, we may come to an interior understanding. (quoted in Robertson 57–58)

As an analytic mode well adapted to deal with our epistemological dilemma, allegory imitates "the process whereby we analyze, categorize,
and give names to the opaque realities, both 'external' and 'internal,'
of experience" (MacCaffrey 37, 39). The chief characters in an allegory,
themselves enacting truth-seeking, are thus exemplary and didactic for
the reader. Allegories are also often attended by instructional and interpretational apparatus—Dante's letter to Can Grande, Spenser's letter to
Raleigh, Bunyan's verse "Apology" and marginal glosses—so that both
the explication and the reader's self-consciousness reenact the allegorical
content.

An allegory is thus a complex linguistic and epistemological adventure, a matter at once of self-consciousness and heightened consciousness,
proceeding from exterior signs to interior illumination. In the most recent comprehensive commentary, Maureen Quilligan calls the allegorical
mode "the most self-reflexive and critically self-conscious of narrative
genres" whose purpose is to make readers correspondingly self-conscious
and to teach us "what kind of readers we are, and what kind we must
become in order to interpret our significance in the cosmos" (24). Allegorical narratives or "self-reflexive fictions" *read* the reader as well as
vice versa in a process Quilligan calls "collusion," for they require the
reader's active participation in order to be perfected, and that perfection
will occur primarily in realms outside the fictional environment (226).
In a context of the priesthood of all believers, such reading has a marked
hieratic function.

Allegory's convolutions of consciousness multiply because the allegorical transaction not only contains whole series of such attachments to data
but because allegories are characteristically referenced to texts outside
themselves; they offer "a twice-told tale" (Honig 12). Allegory regularly
"echoes" (Fletcher's word) a specific, sometimes specified, precedent cultural pattern or written text outside itself, what Quilligan labels the pre-
text (also a pretext). The gulf between text and pre-text forces readers of
allegory to reflection, re-collection, and discovery of the prior truths that
lie concealed behind or beneath the textual surface. *Prior*, as we shall see,
has some very special meanings for the reading action of *Pilgrim's Progress*
part I, for that narrative depends heavily, as did Puritanism generally,
upon a priori truth and texts. The original and authorizing pre-text of all
Christian allegory is of course the Bible, functioning not as a source of
ideas so much as a source of power, authority, and the truth the allegorist

reinvigorates. Indeed many writers of prophetic allegory so far privilege the Bible as to threaten the autonomy of their narratives (Quilligan 122).

Through its various codes and structures, allegory blends text and commentary and guides reader interactions with both the largest and smallest units of evidence. Both inside and outside the narration, *Pilgrim's Progress* regularly references the Bible for individual words but also as its controlling authority. The chief biblical authorization of allegorical transactions between reader and text, the distinction in 2 Corinthians 3.6 between the letter that killeth and the spirit that giveth life, is itself highly self-conscious. Even in the biblical context, St. Paul equates believers with texts to be read: "Forasmuch as ye are manifestly declared to be the epistle of Christ ministered by us, written not with ink, but with the Spirit of the living God; not in tables of stone, but in fleshy tables of the heart" (3.3). For Paul interpretive sufficiency derives not from the reader but from God (3.5), and what the reader reads is himself and God in himself. In Puritan thinking, the experience of conversion capacitates such reading skill. Such convoluted reflexivity can create a reading experience rather like tracing a Möbius strip with its improbable progression along planes of thought and imagery that fold back upon themselves endlessly.

Because allegory is simultaneously a creative and an interpretive procedure, because it is at root a quest for intellectual enlightenment as well as spiritual growth, in important ways all allegorical writings may be said to take their readers on journeys. The metaphor applies to *Pilgrim's Progress* with special force, however, for Bunyan launched his enterprise with the hope that "This Book will make a Traveller of thee" (6). As its brief title indicates, it concerns itself with both forward movement—that is "progress"—and with "pilgrimage"—that is movement toward a holy site. At the literal or narrative level *Pilgrim's Progress* variously develops the evidence of traveling, travelers, and the road, and the remainder of this chapter reviews that dominating similitude with an eye to allegorical forms and transactions.

Edwin Honig has proposed two possible re-creative relations between the Bible and an allegory: "prophetic" and "apocalyptic." The former looks backward to reinforce the Bible and the Law, while the latter offers more personal, more forward-looking and mysterious vision; the former attaches to history, the latter to poetry; the former describes such allegory as Bunyan's, the latter those of Dante and Spenser (107–8). The prophetic mode dominates *Pilgrim's Progress*, and much of the basic and least self-

conscious textual evidence supports this assignment. The "Kings High-
way" to the Celestial City on which Christian travels "was cast up by the
Patriarchs, Prophets, Christ, and his Apostles, and it is as straight as a
Rule can make it" (59, 27). The ultimate goal of Christian's pilgrimage
is "an *Inheritance, incorruptible, undefiled, and that fadeth not away;* and
it is laid up in Heaven, and fast there, to be bestowed at the time appointed, on them that diligently seek it" (11, quoting 1 Peter 1.4). The goal
is variously identified as Mount Sion or Zion, the heavenly Country or the
heavenly Jerusalem, the Celestial Gate or Celestial City, the Paradise of
God. The starting point and destination of the journey and the role of the
traveler as stranger and pilgrim, moving from rejected to idealized sites,
are essentially founded upon Hebrews 11.13–16:

> [The cloud of patriarchal witnesses] all died in faith, not having
> received the promises, but having seen them afar off, and were per-
> suaded of them, and embraced them, and confessed that they were
> strangers and pilgrims on the earth. For they that say such things
> declare plainly that they seek a Country. And truly, if they had been
> mindful of that country from whence they came out, they might
> have had opportunity to have returned. But now they desire a better
> country, that is, an heavenly: wherefore God is not ashamed to be
> called their God: for he hath prepared for them a city.

At Vanity Fair Christian and Faithful identify themselves as "Pilgrims
and Strangers in the world [who are] going to their own Countrey" (90,
and see *Saints' Privilege and Profit,* Offor 1:681).

Allegories characteristically begin with a striking representation of
their narrative world, with a particularized spiritual and psychic environment, a comprehensive problem to be addressed, and an implicit goal
to be striven for. Early static emblems and symbolic acts give way to later,
more dynamic fictional, thematic, and interpretational interactions. At
the outset *Pilgrim's Progress's* isolated and desperate hero reading in his
book quickly enacts the governing question of the fiction, What must I
do to be saved? That question shapes an answer implying the journey
ahead and its ultimate goal and rationale. To be saved, Christian must
travel from the City of Destruction to the Celestial City, a matter of travel
and reading, of outward and inward "progress," a process collapsing the
spatial into the nonspatial.

The allegorical purpose thus launched in *Pilgrim's Progress* is in many
ways characteristic of the genre. Its settings, characters, and actions real-

istically and even charmingly image familiar physical, psychological, and social experience and often achieve the evocative power of a symbolic and suprarational overlay of the familiar. The varied and flexible environment is engagingly and copiously detailed. As is characteristic of allegory, the sites are occasionally and paratactically rather than causally sequenced, challenging the reader to seek an underlying logic or controlling order. Whether we find or create such an order or fall back upon the Puritan expectation of an arbitrary world and a mysterious divine purpose, a large proportion of the reader's processing of this text depends upon an increasingly confident sense of the Way, as traveler after traveler adds a new layer of fresh coloration upon the basic grids.

Cumulative reinforcement or incrementation is characteristic of allegory—also of course the principal given of the narrative of part II—and sometimes topography is personified into threats, visions, or voices. Sites regularly function as externalizations or projections of the hero's psychic nature or present circumstances. In an often-remarked narrative feature, the geography in *Pilgrim's Progress* varies with the spiritual condition of those who encounter it. It is also true that an apparently supportive site, such as the arbor on Hill Difficulty, can surprise the reader and the hero by harboring unsuspected kinds of danger. As By-path Meadow literalizes "trespass" so the Delectable Mountains literalize "pastoral," two samples of the plays on words so typical of allegory's awakening or reorganizing of the reader's epistemology.

The characteristically discontinuous nature of allegorical imagery sustains its illustrative purposes. The sites of Christian's journey are for the most part notably discrete units, what unity there is deriving from what U. Milo Kaufmann identifies as the historically refined wholeness of consensus Puritan religious experience (*Pilgrim's Progress* 114). Only rarely is a new allegorical setting dictated by its predecessor, nor does a thoroughgoing step-by-step progression of the topographical, physical, psychological, or spiritual emerge. Data are in marked isolation from each other, and Fletcher speaks of the objects within an allegorical world as "all lined up, as it were, on the frontal plane of a mosaic, each with its own 'true,' unchanging size and shape" (87, 104–5). Such discontinuity applies to the allegorical population as well as to setting, and Fletcher notes the characteristically "segmented" nature of the allegorical hero's life (35).

Allegories normatively feature reciprocity of persons and places. The details of place externalize character traits, while the actions of characters put abstract concepts into motion and into relationships. The characters Christian encounters, like the places he visits, map the allegorical environment of *Pilgrim's Progress* part I and test the hero's strength, perception, and faith. Some characters interact directly and intensely with Christian; others extend his character traits or project his options from a greater distance; still others attach to his story only tangentially. Such widening circles highlight both the central figure and the complexity of the narrative world. Allegories regularly proceed by generating multiples, "secondary personalities," or "chips of composite character," and these fractionated extensions of the main character interact with the hero in what Fletcher describes as a "syllogistic" manner. They also multiply the symmetries of plot (35, 38, 195).

The usual base of symmetry in *Pilgrim's Progress* is the pathway along which travel and plot occur. When characters project the hero's choices they occur in multiples of course, but it is a point of some interest, especially by contrast with the general conversation in part II, that Christian seriously converses almost exclusively with only one other person at a time. The sisters at House Beautiful, for example, speak only serially, and late in the story, Christian drops back so that Ignorance and Faithful may interact only with each other. Christian's social development may be seen in a "progress" from monologue to dialogue, and these categories of discourse translate into a progress from Puritan self-involvements to Puritan godly conversations, from a conversion crisis to witnessing and works.

The principal characters in allegories are often devices for including the reader—an Everyman or a Christian—or containing arenas for psychic display—Red Cross Knight or again Christian. Within the terrain of both the universal and the particular inhabited by allegorical characters, names signal meaning, sometimes subtly, sometimes not. A series of Christian's fellow pilgrims receive full characterization, including humanizing as well as idealizing features, but a great number function merely as reflections of their names, as "real persons with nicknames," according to Coleridge (*Coleridge* 475). Quilligan has remarked of personification allegory generally that it reifies language, that by animating nouns, it subjects their concepts to close, sometimes etymological scrutiny (115–16). Specifically in *Pilgrim's Progress* part I, names tend to be adjectival, not nominal, to exemplify rather than incarnate qualities (Quilligan 128), or in Kaufmann's distinction they hint at attribute rather than essence (*Pilgrim's Progress* 90). Wolfgang Iser proposes, especially in relation to Faithful and Hopeful, that "the numinous is allegorized by nouns when it is concerned with the human soul; the self is allegorized by adjectives when the only impulsion is a longing for the transcendental world beyond" (17).

The population of Vanity Fair miniaturizes Bunyan's allegorical technique, arraying the details of failed community in the figures of Hategood, Envy, Superstition, Pickthank, Old Man, Carnal Delight, Luxurious, Desire of Vain-glory, Lechery, Having Greedy, Blind-man, No-good, Malice, Love-lust, Live-loose, Heady, High-mind, Enmity, Lyar, Cruelty, Hate-light, and Implacable. These figures are, in Vincent Newey's phrase, "presences in a phantasmagoric festival of malice" ("Bunyan" 29). A smaller similarly satiric list is invoked with Byends's former schoolfellows (101). Deft portraits capture individuals within a single word, behavior, speech, or personality trait rather than by invocations of traditional visual iconography or expansive physical detail. It is an art that Rosemary Freeman traces to the emblem tradition on the basis of the characters' singularity, centripetal energy, and stasis (225). Interestingly, these radically concise externalizations of personal natures are aural rather than visual. Vanity Fair is Bunyan's only detailed depiction of a site more inclusive than a single dwelling or single topographical feature, and the larger scale invites painting with a more satirical and comprehensive brush. The combination of rabble, hubbub, judicial proceedings, biblical base, and a cataloguing style and glancing wit make Vanity Fair one of the great set pieces of *Pilgrim's Progress* part I and indeed of English literature. Stylistic distancing sets the episode off from the text, the more so as Christian shows no residual effects of his experiences here.

Christian's encounters with others normally occur not as psychomachy or debate but in linear sequence in an attraction-repulsion model. Allegorical characters and settings are morally valenced or in Fletcher's suggestive word "daemonized," that is, acting out, or acting out of, a particular moral energy or compartmentalized function: when "a man is possessed by an influence that excludes all other influences while it is operating on him" and thereby he "has no life outside [its] exclusive sphere of action" (47, 40, 49). As is usual in allegory, the dramatis personae divide into representations of either vice or virtue, seventy-three evil and seventeen virtuous ones by Monica Furlong's count.[4] Bunyan also groups characters according to their relations to the Way and the traveling process.

The virtuous characters fall into two distinct categories, three if we include the several Shining Ones or angels as a separate group. In the first half of the story, older advisors and instructors—Evangelist, Help, the gatekeepers, and Interpreter—demarcate psychic stages of the journey, impel the traveler forward, and perform "ministerial" and "congregational" functions. At House Beautiful, the questioners Discretion, Prudence, Piety, and Charity—the only female characters with whom Christian directly interacts—signal the community and catechism of a church. The shepherds, Knowledge, Experience, Watchful, and Sincere, both literally and liturgically, fulfill a "pastoral" role.

The majority of the second half of the narrative consists of "godly conversation." The visual, topographical, externally active, and descriptive data that dominated the first half drop away in favor of edifying dialogue, sometimes between two visible saints, sometimes between a saint and a false professor. The most important other saints are Faithful, a chronological peer, and the younger Hopeful. We expect Bunyan's Christian hero to interact importantly with the traditional Christian virtues, but we might not expect that he would give as well as receive the strengths these characters embody. We also might not expect a humanizing, even comedic dimension to relationships among such sober concepts, but when Faithful refuses to tarry, Christian rushes to catch up: "Putting to all his strength, he quickly got up with *Faithful*, and did also over-run him, so the *last was first*. Then did *Christian* vain-gloriously smile, because he had gotten the start of his Brother: but not taking good heed to his feet, he suddenly stumbled and fell, and could not rise again, until *Faithful* came up to help him" (66). Readers easily gloss the charming moment as "Pride goeth before a fall." Christian's later condescending, rather grumpy correction of Hopeful again strikes a comedic note (127). Together Christian and Faithful and later Christian and Hopeful sort through the claims of a series of false professors, refining individual points of belief, knowledge, motive, and expectation.

Where we expect Christian to become increasingly like such allegorical companions, Bunyan highlights differences. Both Faithful and Christian began as citizens of the City of Destruction, but they have been differently challenged by the same terrain. Dorothy Van Ghent describes Faithful as an unburdened man without "shadows," with "little imagination and a relatively meager sensibility," who throws Christian "into relief as a man who has suffered and been afraid and wallowed in mud, a man of complex and difficult temperament, vainglorious at times in his strength, at other times doubtful or despairing."[5] Faithful's history is ontological rather than teleological; it reflects the past, essential natures, and the foundations of action. Evangelist's prophetic reappearance confirms Christian's fully achieved Faith. The happy transcendence of Faithful's martyrdom generates Hopeful, the second of the three Christian virtues, as Christian's companion in his stead and redirects the hero's experience toward future action and ultimate ends. "Thus one died to make Testimony to the Truth, and another rises out of his Ashes to be a Companion with *Christian*" (98). Bunyan's commentary on Genesis remarks how, similarly, Seth takes the place of the murdered Abel and Peter the place of James (Offor 11:453–54). Christian's interactions with Hopeful, "his own better self" (Newey, "Bunyan" 28, 23), are marked by experience rather than hearing, patience rather than external enemies, anticipations of heavenly reward rather than justification or doctrine or the Bible.

Faithful and Hopeful allegorize the substance of Bunyan's treatise on Ps. 130.7, *Israel's Hope Encouraged; or, What Hope Is, and How Distinguished from Faith: With Encouragements for a Hoping People*, and its major arguments directly illuminate the evolution of Faith[ful] into Hope[ful] in Christian's experience in *Pilgrim's Progress*. In essence, for Bunyan Hope is born of Faith, and though secondary can do what Faith cannot:

> Faith comes by hearing . . . hope by experience. . . . Faith comes by hearing the Word of God, hope by the credit that faith hath given to it. . . . Faith believeth the truth of the Word, hope waits for the fulfilling of it. . . . Faith lays hold of that end of the promise that is next to us, to wit, as it is in the Bible; hope lays hold of that end of the promise that is fastened to the mercy-seat. . . . Faith looketh to Christ, as dead, buried, and ascended; and hope to his second coming. . . . Faith looks to him for justification, hope for glory. . . . Faith fights for doctrine, hope for a reward. . . . Faith for what is in the Bible, hope for what is in heaven. . . . Faith purifies the heart from bad principles. . . . Hope from bad manners. . . . Faith sets hope on work, hope sets patience on work. . . . Faith looks through the word to God in Christ; hope looks through faith beyond the world to glory. . . . Faith saves by laying hold of God by Christ. . . . Hope saves by prevailing with the soul to suffer all troubles, afflictions, and adversities that it meets with betwixt this and the world to come, for the sake thereof. . . . It is hope that makes the soul exercise patience and long-suffering under the cross, until the time comes to enjoy the crown. (Offor 1:578)

This treatise glosses Hopeful and Christian's successes against despair at both Doubting Castle and the River of Death, and of course Bunyan's own decades of struggle recorded in *Grace Abounding*. Despair is the sense of

God's desertion and of the self as incapable and unworthy; it is the failure of hope for future betterment, felt as irreversible stasis and incapacitating confinement within present circumstances, the inability to move not only forward but in any direction. *Israel's Hope Encouraged* provides this definition: "For what is the ground of despair, but a conceit that sin has shut the soul out of all interest in happiness? and what is the reason of that, but a persuasion that there is no help for him in God?" (Offor 1:593). *Good News For the Vilest of Men* describes despair as the devil's chains, as a contradictor of Christ, as undervaluing the Promises, and as making man God's judge: "It drives a man to the study of his own ruine, and brings him at last to be his own executioner" (xi:65, 66).

Pilgrim's Progress part I variously "realizes" the motifs of despair in the Man in the Iron Cage at Interpreter's house with his deep sadness, downcast eyes, heart-breaking sighs, and hardened heart. God, he claims, by denying him repentance, has locked him in an iron cage. His testimony shows that the condition is one chiefly brought upon himself (35, similarly *Grace Abounding* 49). When we first meet Bunyan's hero, originally named "Graceless" (46), he is in a "desperate" stasis in the City of Destruction. The early Slough of Despond and the late dungeon of Doubting Castle compound personal helplessness and psychic confinement. The Giant Despair, after sound cudgelings, pressures his victims to commit suicide. As seen from the vantage of Mount Caution, Despair usually leaves his victims blind and wandering among tombs.

In such settings Bunyan's Hopeful indeed proves to be what *Israel's Hope Encouraged* analyzes as a soul-encouraging grace, a soul-emboldening grace, and a soul-preserving grace. The treatise presents hope as turning the mind away from difficulties and toward faith and patience and lists the ways to exercise hope as: to look well to your faith, not to stumble or doubt at the sight of your own weakness, to call to mind what God has done for you in earlier times, and to look to the end of this and the beginning of the next world (Offor 1:582–83). Even as late as the crossing of the River of Death, Hopeful helps Christian master the sense of unworthiness that temporarily overwhelms him and enact the advisories of *Israel's Hope Encouraged*: "Hope is the grace that relieveth the soul when dark and weary. Hope is as the bottle to the faint and sinking spirit. Hope calls upon the soul not to forget how far it is arrived in its progress towards heaven. Hope will point and show it the gate afar off; and therefore it is called the hope of salvation. Hope exerciseth itself upon God" (590). The references here to progress, to heaven, and to distant gates sharpen to a fine point the parallels between treatise and allegorical pilgrimage.

Christian's responses to the linked despair occasions in *Pilgrim's Progress* trace a somewhat different line. Doubt, we may note, is a process of perception, despair a product. The *doubt* of Doubting Castle for him marks an expected stage in the Puritan sequence of conversion and salvation, but the site's agent Despair achieves only a limited control over him. The psychodrama here empowers Christian to rely upon his own resources. The presence of Hopeful and the key of promise in Christian's bosom help him process spiritual threats into spiritual victories by means that are at once logical and theological. Because Christian remains subject to despair even in the River of Death, some commentators deplore his lack of "progress," but in fact these late occasions, though intense in their terrors, serve to vitalize and magnify, to "illustrate," faith against enormous odds and thus demonstrate not only spiritual achievement appropriate to a moment of challenge but also spiritual endurance, not only a qualitative or subjective progress but also a quantitative or temporally linear one.

Whereas Christian's positive encounters comfort, instruct, or accompany him upon the Way, his negative encounters, such as these with forms of Despair, also fall into distinguishable groups and patterned relations to the travel similitude. The stasis of nonhuman or superhuman enemy figures, such as Apollyon, Despair, Demas, and Pope, essentially represents the nature of evil by contrast with Christian's varied "progress."[6]

With the exception of the citizens of Vanity Fair, the negatively valenced human figures in part I are ordinarily entering or traveling either forward or backward along the Way. Character groupings in the first half illustrate the characteristic feature of allegory in which, as Roger Sharrock phrases it, particular traits of the soul are drained away from the hero and projected onto personified temptations and incentives (*John Bunyan* [1966] 54). In the second half, they crowd the Way as what Bunyan here and elsewhere calls "false professors." Pairs or triads of peer figures make character traits and choices situational, the options screening the hero's mind and marking progress or decision points. Christian's early psychic conflict, projected onto Obstinate and Pliable, illustrates this allegorical operation. The former shows us a newly converted Christian who might have been "obstinate" in his despairing residence in the City of Destruction or in the way he would allow himself to be saved. The character's rigid insistence upon his own will signals stasis. Pliable is only ostensibly less stubborn about having his own "Way." So long as it is easy to move he will keep company, but his character cannot sustain any real challenges to the status quo or consent to the loss of selfhood Christianity requires.

Several later sets of interlocking characters of this sort situationalize allegory more complexly. After leaving his burden at the sepulcher, Christian comes upon the options of Simple, Sloth, and Presumption, who do not now threaten him, but immediately thereafter he is fully engaged by Formalist and Hypocrisy. The first three represent what may happen to the new convert after the moment of spiritual triumph fades; the second pair, who have tumbled over a wall into the Way, signal a bypassing of the conversion experience of changed selfhood: "And besides, said they, so be we get into the way, what's matter which way we get in? if we are in, we are in: thou art but in the way, who, as we perceive, came in at the Gate; and we are also in the way that came tumbling over the wall: Wherein now is thy condition better than ours?" (40). We shall return in a moment to the slippery word *Way*. Here the "simplified" and "slothful" "presumption" that recurs in Formalist and Hypocrisy allows Christian an opportunity to distinguish between his disciplined spiritual service and their self-indulgent fancy, between his covenant of grace and theirs of works (here keeping the "Laws and Ordinances" [40–41]). Like Pliable they have no capacity to sustain challenges. They chiefly provide Christian with an opportunity to affirm, in the words of Ephesians 1.13, that he is one who has been "sealed with the holy Spirit of promise."

The allegory compounds, however, when Formalist and Hypocrisy pass to the left (Danger) and to the right (Destruction), while Christian climbs up the narrow Way of Hill Difficulty. To refresh himself against increasing "difficulties" during the climb, Christian pauses but falls asleep, a sleep that loses him his roll and requires that he retrace his steps thrice over.[7] This sleep reactivates and internalizes the condition of Simple, Sloth, and Presumption, and with Christian this time indeed subject to their force as he earlier was not. Moments later Timorous and Mistrust tell Christian that they turned around when they "had got up that *difficult* place" (43; Bunyan's italics). These two represent not just alternate responses to a particular Hill but also aspects of himself, literally "reflections," that Christian overcomes easily within the narrative, but can overcome thematically only with greater effort. The discourse with them obliges him to remember, return for, and thereby reempower his lost roll of promises. These "reflections" of Christian's character oblige him to psychic "reflection" which he translates into action by traveling backward on the Way.

The word *reflection* expresses what Quilligan defines as central to the genre, that is "the generation of narrative structure out of wordplay" (22).

"Reflection" signals both layered interactions of character and layered meanings of physical and psychic action. Another differently layered, generating word for *Pilgrim's Progress* part I is *Way*, whose compound meanings in both text and pre-text richly vary the narrative's radical travel metaphor. At the narrative level, *Pilgrim's Progress* calls frequent attention to the primary setting, the pathway upon which the hero and others travel, but even in its simplest usage *Way* often glances at the pre-text of Matthew 7.13–14, the straight and narrow Way that leads to life by contrast with the wide and broad Way that leads to destruction. At first Christian does not know how to put himself in the Way: "Yet he stood still, because, as I perceived, he could not tell which way to go" (9 and similarly 10). Later and more normatively, his "narrow way lay right up the Hill" (41). Upon occasion, *Pilgrim's Progress* lingers over the authorizing text, Matthew 7.13–14, for example, when Christian parts from Formalist and Hypocrisy to follow the path that is "steep and high," whereas they choose the easier byways called "Danger" and "Destruction" (42). Christian's pathway through part of the Valley of the Shadow of Death is exceedingly narrow between a deep ditch on one side and a dangerous quagmire on the other. The Way is also "here so dark, that oft times when he lift up his foot to set forward, he knew not where, or upon what he should set it next" (62).

The narrative often interweaves realistic detail with other authorizing texts to generate variously polysemous meanings of this key word. At By-path Meadow we are told that Christian and Hopeful "durst not go out of the way" and that "*The soul of the Pilgrims was much discouraged, because of the way*" and that "still as they went on, they wished for better way" (111, quoting Numbers 21.4). One must go "out of the World" to go "out of the Way" in avoiding Vanity Fair (89). As a "Caution" to pilgrims, however, Lot's wife errs even though she never steps out of the Way (109). A mysterious voice cites Jeremiah 31.20 to guide Christian and Hopeful: "*Let thine Heart be towards the High-way, even the way that thou wentest, turn again*" (113), and the shepherds attach Proverbs 21.16 to the occasion of Despair and Doubting Castle: "*He that wandereth out of the way of understanding, shall remain in the Congregation of the dead*" (121). In general, we may say, again with the shepherds, the Way is "Safe for those for whom it is to be safe, *but transgressors shall fall therein*" (119, quoting Hosea 14.9).

The Way is a linear set of topographical features by or through which a traveler passes. The usual understanding of "progress" in Bunyan's narrative assumes a direct correlation between physical and spiritual place, which measures pilgrimage by relative positionings upon the graduated scale of a linear and shared Way, what Christian means when he says he walks "by the Rule of my Master" (40). Stanley Fish analyzes traveling of this sort in *Pilgrim's Progress* to include: "(1) the negotiation by one or more pilgrims of a fixed and graduated set of obstacles (2) a direct and progressive relationship between the number of obstacles negotiated and the piling up of spiritual 'points' toward a definite goal (3) a growing sense of accomplishment and self-satisfaction (in the reader as well as in the characters) which accelerates as the pilgrims draw nearer to the Heavenly City" (*Self-Consuming Artifacts* 228, 231, 229). It is difficult to isolate, even temporarily, the physical Way from its spiritual coordinate, for reasons that Bunyan's *The Holy City* explains: "It is usual in the holy *Scripture* to call the transformation of the sinner from Satan to God, *a holy way*, and also to admonish him that is so transformed *to walk* in that way, saying, *Walk in the Faith, Love, Spirit, and newness of Life*, and *walk in the Truth, Wayes, Statutes and Judgments of God*" (iii:151). This work also calls the street of the New Jerusalem "the way of Holiness, even the way in which men learn to fear God, and to believe in, and love the Lord Jesus" (iii:151).

The linear Way is thus also a complex, biblically endorsed metaphor for the spiritual journey, the traveler, and the process or even style of the traveling. In distinguishing between two meanings of *Way* as "the outward profession of Christianity" and as "the inward and spiritual grace," Coleridge took occasion to complain of Bunyan's "degeneration" into a pun (*Coleridge* 479). Similarly, but without complaint, Philip Edwards identifies three ideas of the journey as "(a) the vicissitudes of a Christian's life, arising from external threat and inner disturbance, (b) obeying the strict demands of the true faith, and (c) advancing in the understanding and practice of the Christian life." Within the qualification that keeping to the path means keeping to the *whole* path, Edwards generalizes: "Christian's journey charts the progressive attainment of spiritual understanding and proficiency and the never-lessening danger of losing one's way, or one's determination, right up to the last mile" (115, 116). In such usage, *Way* equates with *end*, an ambiguous term evoking traditional logic's distinction between "the end of which" and "the end for which," that is, between terminus and informing purpose or perfection. Puritans defined themselves as Wayfarers, and Bunyan's *Way* is at once the universal life-journey and the journey of Christian commitment; it is "the path of all Christians through the wilderness of the world . . . and simultaneously the inner way of faith of the individual believer."[8]

The Way, so often acknowledged within the narrative, is at once the figure, example, and mediation of Christ and also the mode of procedure appropriate to his followers and imitators. As such it is governed primarily by John 14.6, "I am the way, the truth, and the life: no man cometh unto the Father but by me," a text buttressed by such Pauline passages as Romans 4.12 advising that the Christian "walk in the steps of that faith of our father *Abraham*," and 2 Corinthians 5.7 observing that "we walk by faith, not by sight." Bunyan cites Job 14.6 and Matthew 7.14 to describe Christ as "the way to God the Father" in *Grace Abounding* (20, and see *Christian Behaviour* III:13). Fish enfolds an inclusive range of meanings of "Way" in a formulation at once crisp and suggestive: "Being in the way, then, is paradoxically independent of the way you happen to be in, for you will be in the way only if the way is in you" (*Self-Consuming Artifacts* 228).

Christians are advised not just to honor the Way but to walk in it. The minutes of Bunyan's Bedford congregation regularly use the phrase *walking with us* as synonymous with church membership. *Walking* here also means conduct, in individual incidents and also as a general practice. At its simplest, travel or *progress* upon the Way means: forward movement in space; continuous improvement; and "going on to a further or higher stage, or to further or higher stages successively" (OED 4b). As the narrative unfolds, the first of these senses of *progress* as *journey* gives way to the more modern sense of *progress* as *improvement* or *movement toward* (Keeble, *Literary Culture* 278). For Bunyan and his contemporaries more than for us, "progress" included a political dimension (or the Puritan translation of such politics within the context of the late seventeenth century) and meant a state journey or official visitation or circuit made by royal, noble, or church personages or other public figures (OED 2a).

From the earliest literary records, travel has served as an organizing principle of narrative as well as a metaphor for growth. Like many authors, Bunyan exploits it for allegorical and nonallegorical purposes. His treatise *The Heavenly Footman* particularly develops the simple metaphor nonallegorically to teach readers exactly how to travel. It glosses both the similitude and the text of *Pilgrim's Progress*. At its simplest, *footman* means someone traveling on foot, but *footman* is also a lowly military status, and it is in this sense that Christian contrasts himself and Hopeful with the gloriously armored King's Champion (131). Of course,

England's recent history included spiritually minded soldiers on very real battlefields.[9]

Prefatory verses explain that *Pilgrim's Progress* came upon Bunyan unawares when he had almost finished writing a different work, by general agreement *The Heavenly Footman*,[10] whose subtitle might serve as subtitle for *Pilgrim's Progress* as well: *A Description of The Man that gets to Heaven. Together, With the Way he Runs in, the Marks he Goes by: Also some Directions, how to Run, so as to Obtain.* The verses develop the allegorical principles of both projects:

> This Book it chaulketh out before thine eyes,
> The man that seeks the everlasting Prize:
> It shews you whence he comes, whither he goes,
> What he leaves undone; also what he does:
> It also shews you how he runs, and runs,
> Till he unto the Gate of Glory comes. (6)

The Heavenly Footman expands the metaphor of 1 Corinthians 9.24: "So Run, that ye may Obtain" (v:147), the text also of a brief sermon Evangelist delivers to Christian and Faithful in *Pilgrim's Progress* (86). Milton's *Areopagitica* develops the same text to encourage wayfaring Christians toward "the race where that immortal garland is to be run for, not without dust and heat" (*Poems* 728). Bunyan enjoins: "Arise Man, be *slothful* no longer, set Foot, and Heart and all into the way of God, and *Run*, the Crown is at the end of the Race; there also standeth the loving forerunner, even *Jesus*" and concludes with a similar exhortatory peroration: "But be sure thou begin betimes, *get* into *the way*, Run apace, and hold out to the *end*. And the Lord give thee a prosperous Journey" (v:140, 178). The treatise defines "Way" as "Christ the Son of Mary, the Son of God" (152), citing John 14.6.

The Heavenly Footman follows the usual format of Bunyan's sermons, and Puritan sermons in general. After 1 Corinthians 9.24 has been "laid down," Bunyan "opens" its individual words. It considers three definitions of the word *run*, that is fly, press, continue, with reference to the related texts of Hebrews 12.1 and Philipians 3.14: "Let us run with patience the race that is set before us," and "I press toward the mark for the prize of the high calling of God in Jesus Christ." Bunyan then "clears" the doctrine, that is explores some of its implications, such as that not every runner obtains, that the way is long and the time uncertain, and that the gates may be shut shortly. The remainder of the treatise considers nine directions of how to run, nine motives for running, and nine uses.

Its nine directions make explicit the principles that govern *Pilgrim's Progress* and provide a procedural rulebook for pilgrimage, most concisely in this passage:

> First, *get* into the way. 2. Then *Study* on it. 3. Then *strip*, and lay aside every thing that would hinder. 4. *Beware* of By-Paths. 5. Do not *gaze* and stare too much about thee, but be sure to ponder the Path of thy Feet. 6. Do not *stop* for any that call after thee, whether it be the World, the Flesh, or the Devil; for all these will hinder thy Journey, if possible. 7. Be not *Daunted* with any discouragements thou meetest with as thou goest. 8. Take heed of *stumbling* at the Cross. And 9. *Cry hard* to God for an *enlightened* heart, and a *willing* mind, and God give thee a prosperous Journey. (165–66, and similarly 152–64)

The directives tellingly gloss virtually every unit of *Pilgrim's Progress*, sometimes individually, sometimes as compounds, but the treatise's sometimes wooden alignments of a simple metaphor contrast markedly with *Pilgrim's Progress*'s complex, multiply referential, and self-conscious artistry in the fully allegorical mode.

The Heavenly Footman secures guidelines for what, at one level, *Pilgrim's Progress* consists of: a *progress*, a forward movement toward a goal. It enacts a programmatic allegorical quest, one of the ritual plots Fletcher finds to be characteristic of allegory (184). Viewed within a straightforward novelistic design, Bunyan's pilgrim progresses from the self-bounded to the self-transcending. "The more violent, and dramatic assaults on Christian's faith come early," as John Knott reminds us, while more subtle temptations founded in fraud and deceptive appearances later predominate (*Sword* 142–43). Christian's terrors of destruction gradually abate; a regular rhythm of positive and negative encounters emerges; abstraction increases; battles give way to restorations; and anticipations of transcendent glory become increasingly empowered. Vincent Newey describes "the earlier hurried, hesitant, fearfully eager" pilgrim developing into a stable, capable, self-reliant, self-sufficient personality, his wise passiveness supplanting paralysis and disorientation and his personal deciphering of inscriptions and cautionary spectacles replacing passively received explanations ("Bunyan" 35–37). In Newey's formulation, experience gives way to words, "life-and-death confrontations to conversation, psycho-drama to psychological example" (39). In addition, as part I progresses, descriptions and encounters become decreasingly visual and increasingly aural, a development backgrounded in the basic Protestant preference for teaching by the ear over teaching through the eye.

Generally speaking, Christian's travel moves away from problematic sites and toward edification and solace, and the growth of his percep-tive capacities indexes his spiritual progress (Knott, *Sword* 149). The early landscape is aggressively inhospitable though occasionally broken by way stations or other refuges, while late in the story horticultural beneficence in a spiritually reciprocal landscape sustains the pilgrims. What begins as a journey of escape and desperate alienation develops into a quest for a progressively clear destination, a migration to the Heavenly City. The in-door locations dominating the first half of the story—Interpreter's house, House Beautiful—provide relief against generally difficult travel, whereas those in the second half occur as evil and notably confining—Vanity Fair, Doubting Castle. Outdoor sites and encounters tend to threaten until Christian is relieved by a spring of water and pastures that anticipate the blessed horticulture of Beulah Land.

Like allegory generally, Bunyan's travel metaphor is not, however, simply straightforward. The technique is contrapuntal (N. Frye 90); some of its units dissolve where we expect them to resolve. It is true that Chris-tian's forward travel is reinforced by such devices as the proleptic Armed Man tableau at Interpreter's house, the companionate forward move-ment of Faithful, Evangelist, and Hopeful, Evangelist's prophecy before Vanity Fair, and anticipatory views of the Delectable Mountains from the top of House Beautiful and of the gates of the Celestial City from Hill Clear. But this latter event includes Christian and Hopeful's reflec-tive backward visions of an analogue of their recent experiences with Despair and Doubt from the same vantage. Although most of the pilgrims Christian encounters on the Way are traveling in the same direction as he is, a number of others are "misguided." Some are going backward on the Way as are Timorous and Mistrust, two "children of the Spies" (gloss 61: characterized as "Children of them that brought up an evil report of the good Land" [61]), Turnaway, and Atheist. The Flatterer leads Chris-tian and Hopeful around in a circle so that they are themselves turned the wrong way, and entangled in a net to boot. The reverse movement of such figures may actually aid the story's forward thrust, but also signals a counterenergy operating within the text. Many readers are troubled by

Ignorance's lapse into a byway to Hell "even from the Gates of Heaven" (163) in the penultimate sentence of part I. Although the previous travel has followed the dominant horizontal line, with only minor fluctuations of terrain, our final glimpse of Ignorance secures a vertically dimensioned terrain, and his damnation enforces the dominant transcendence. Ignorance's fate heightens the Puritan view that every moment is potentially damning or salvific and therefore recommends constant self-examination and vigilance.

At least two spatial designs operate simultaneously beneath such "progress," one quantitative, the other qualitative. The first accords with normal narrative expectations, and proportions positive increases of spiritual energy against negative decreases. The second exploits Puritan epistemological preferences for dichotomies in a sorting-out process that can occur only in retrospect, a model running counter to normal narrative development. *Pilgrim's Progress*'s references to the Way normally distinguish between the right Way, which the text instructs in, and such alternatives as the non-Way or the wrong Way, which must be actively rejected. Wolfgang Iser draws the distinction as between a directly described objective, exemplary road to salvation and a dialogically developed, increasingly subjective certitude of salvation: "Salvation is an a priori precondition for all events in the book; certitude must be gained a posteriori. Man's destiny—the search for salvation—is clear from the beginning; the certainty of finding—the fulfillment of this destiny—is identical with death. The objective goal can only be reached through subjective 'self-experience,' and this process is communicated to the reader by the alternation between dream vision and dialogue and the respective tensions arising from this alternation" (9–10). In religious terms, Kaufmann sees the a priori Word and the a posteriori achieved unity of Puritan experience as natural coordinates and speaks similarly of *Pilgrim's Progress*'s "conspicuous superimposition of stasis and linear movement" in which "events only seem to be happening" and its "saving *non sequitur* of faith" (*Pilgrim's Progress* 107, 198n., 112, 116). We shall see more fully in later chapters that Puritans particularly honored the a priori, repetitiousness, and the progressive revelation that reprocesses spiritual openings into the illuminations they contain.

The Valley of the Shadow of Death marks the middle and turning point of *Pilgrim's Progress* part I as narrative, but it signals the epistemological shift as well. The mouth of Hell, situated in its midst, provides a hinge or "dead center" for the change of character and emphasis. Two unnamed men warn Christian: "We were going that way as you are going, and went as far as we durst; and indeed we were almost past coming back, for had we gone a little further, we had not been here to bring the news to thee" (61). Christian faces the same crisis: "Somtimes he had half a thought to go back. Then again he thought he might be half way through the Valley; he remembered also how he had already vanquished many a danger: and that the danger of going back might be much more, then for to go forward; so he resolved to go on" (63). Morning signals a new day and new awakening. Christian is not just delivered from nocturnal hobgoblins but enacts the "reflection" noticed earlier. Literally, a *reflection* is a "turning backward" or a "looking again" as well as seeing oneself in a mirror. "Now morning being come, he looked back, not of desire to return, but to see, by the light of the day, what hazards he had gone through in the dark" (64). Here Christian is also delivered "from all the dangers of his solitary way" (64) and joins pilgrimage with Faithful and then Hopeful. Verbally, when dialogue replaces the earlier occasional monologues, it externalizes "reflection." Surprisingly, dialogue increases rather than decreases subjectivity (Iser 9), and when what are discussed are earlier events of the story, dialogues model the study of the self, God's creatures, and the providences characteristic of Puritanism. The reader is likewise regularly held responsible for re*interpretation along the lines of a substructure Fish traces in *Pilgrim's Progress*, the pattern of a premature interpretation followed by a later emerging "*revelatory* stage of the episode," and thus a pattern of *de*interpreting, *de*signifying, and "delayed revelation, which has the effect of widening a perspective that had been assumed to be full and adequate" (*Self-Consuming Artifacts* 226, 228, 237, 238; Fish's italics).

Fish argues the case for *Pilgrim's Progress* as "antiprogressive," for the illusion or at least tension of "progress" in it (233, 229, and 250). For him Christian's spatial situation is not linear but cyclical or even static, and he sees three contravening intentions within the narrative subverting normal expectations of progress: "(1) a route whose landmarks and dangers vary with the inner state of those who travel it (2) no direct relationship at all between the point (in space and time) one has reached and the attainment of the ultimate reward, and (3) a pattern of backslidings and providential rescues that works to subvert the self-confidence of pilgrim and reader alike" (232, 229). Fish is correct in calling attention to an illusory dimension to the pilgrim's progress and to the reader's necessary awareness of the problematics of the narrative, but he goes too far I think in concluding that Bunyan therefore intended to "disqualif[y] his work as a vehicle of the insight it pretends to convey" (224–25).

Because allegories assume multiple interpretations, the allegorical transaction is not so much self-consuming as self-reflexive, and Bunyan participates in it primarily to further his Puritan agenda. Theoretically, the two levels of allegory will evoke balanced attention, but in practice one or the other level predominates. While an emphatic literal level restores reader security—sometimes much needed—dissolutions of the literal level stimulate further thematic and abstract pursuits. Thus Quilligan can speak of allegory's plots as evaporating and of its reader's experience of vertigo (68). Such disorientations underwrite the growth and participation that allegory exists to impose. For allegory, the model of action ceases to be a dialectic or carom and becomes instead a spiral, aimed progressively and simultaneously forward, backward, and upward on a three-dimensional continuum (Honig 179).

Søren Kierkegaard formulates the philosophical principle behind the anticlimactic features of *Pilgrim's Progress* part I: "Though life is lived forwards . . . it is only understood backwards" (quoted in Talon, *John Bunyan* 89). Necessarily, anticlimax underlies allegory's mimetic, thematic, and interpretational layering, for generically, allegories will look to the past for the values they affirm, for the biblical authority they serve, and for the representational definition of the good place which is also their narrative goal. They will also progressively and incrementally unfold their inaugural emblem, action, and question, and they are characterized by inconclusive endings (Quilligan 53, Fletcher 174–75). Christianity itself is complexly transtemporal, a matter of remembering the promises, of looking backward to what looks forward, looking backward in order to be redirected forward. Allegory is at once temporal, sequential, atemporal, and countertemporal, all in the service of each other and of a process of provoked and rewarded illuminations and "reflections."

CHAPTER TWO

The Mythic Pilgrim

Dreaming, we are heroes. Waking, we invent them. Conscious, unable to recreate the universe according to the patterns of desire, we require heroes to redeem a fallen world.
Seductive figures, bold and daring, heroes promise power to
the weak, glamour to the dull, and liberty to the oppressed.
Their thoughts and actions cut channels into custom's rock.
They cross borders, advance into new territory, inspire re-
volt. Dreamers' agents, necessary fictions, heroes enact our
sleeping visions in the world, in daylight. We dream our
heroes. In exchange, our heroes alter us.—Lee R. Edwards,
Psyche as Hero

WHILE NEARLY ALL CRITICS comment on the allegorical mode of *Pilgrim's Progress*, most ignore the codes of myth that give access to some
not otherwise available operations within Bunyan's art. As we shall see,
the schematic stages of Puritan conversion and salvation through which
its hero progresses overlie an ancient and universal heroic paradigm. Its
verse "Apology" introduces a work that is mythic in the sense of inherited
story, at once simple and profound. When Bunyan speaks of details delivering themselves to him and multiplying as fast as his pen could write
them down (1), he describes a work mythic too in the sense of deriving
from particular depths of his own psyche as that psyche was furnished by
the Reformation Protestant and Puritan ethos of his time. As we shall see,
the later part II resolves what were mythic pressures in favor of history,
secularity, and the novel.

To examine the evidence of *Pilgrim's Progress* as myth rather than as
allegory is to move from one radical epistemology, expressional mode,
and literary and spiritual design to its opposite. Like allegory, myth

—along with the symbols conveying its power and vision—operates within elusive and multivisioned parameters. *Myth* derives from the Greek *mythos*—meaning word, speech, talk, tale—especially as compounded with the etymologically related *mysterion* 'close-mouthed or unspoken'. As allegory treats *logos* or the *word* as rational construction, so this other Greek word for *word*, *mythos*, deals with "the word as the most ancient, the most original account of the origins of the world, in divine revelation or sacred tradition, of gods and demi-gods and the genesis of the cosmos, cosmogony." Literary students are most familiar with the term from Aristotle's *Poetics* where *mythos* equates with plot, "the first principle and, as it were, the soul" of a literary work. Like allegory, myth in this sense can serve as an organizing structural principle of literary form and relate to both temporal sequence and causally linked, linear action.[1]

I am using *symbol* as a subset of myth, a perhaps confusing usage because some commentators speak of symbols as foundational to allegory as well. In so doing, they define *symbol* as an isolatable literary object, person, or event standing for something other than itself, especially for something ideational.[2] The key word in this definition is, of course, *isolatable*. Although allegory's components may be symbolic, they are not isolated; they function dialectically through point-by-point correlations between mimetic data and an interpretational overlay. Allegory aligns its numerous components in a mimetic environment at once strictly controlled and dynamic. Both the mythic whole and its parts are vertically rather than horizontally meaningful, aspirational rather than caught in rhythmic and equational allegiance to both the concrete and the abstracts of its extended metaphor. Mimesis is based—as Aristotle insisted—in the natural and the probable, and seeks concrete expressive form with reference to the norms of common human experience. The primary, even exclusive allegiance of myth, however, is to a transcendental and archetypal realm. If myth overlaps with allegory it is only at the level of anagogy, as Angus Fletcher has suggested, for by its very nature anagogy supplies a visionary structure that transcends strict correspondences (322).

In the traditional sense, a myth tells a recurrent and inherited story embodying the truths of its particular culture. It treats the origins of life and the deeds of human or supernatural heroes so as to explore the whys and wherefores of natural phenomena and to provide an implicit rationale for customs, conduct, and belief. It is "an anonymous, non-literary, essentially religious formulation of the cosmic view of a people who ap-

proach its formulations not as representations of truth but as truth itself,"
the product of a culture rather than a single author (Thrall and Hibbard
299). Primitive in its impression and popular in its reception, it evokes
deep emotional responses and arouses belief. In Terry Eagleton's summary, "myths have a quasi-objective collective existence, unfold their
own 'concrete logic' with supreme disregard for the vagaries of individual
thought, and reduce any particular consciousness to a mere function of
themselves" (104).

A series of key contrasts between *myth* and *allegory* will map the literary critical terrain and bring forward some points to be sorted out more
precisely in the following pages. Where allegory foregrounds the reader
and the various self-reflexive elements in the reading transaction, myth
foregrounds the hero and society. "The poles of truth for amphibious
mankind" are embodied in what Isabel MacCaffrey calls the "this temporal" of allegory and the "that eternal" of myth. The former presents "invented truths," as the latter puts forward "the achieved truths of vision"
(61, 65). Although authors of allegory are tied to their chosen traditional
values and pre-texts, they are free to, indeed obliged to, generate their
fictional environments and furniture out of their own art, whereas the
writer who deliberately redeploys inherited myth risks compromising the
sacred quality of its truth if his or her individuality becomes apparent.
Authorially as epistemologically, although allegory is conscious and self-
conscious, the symbols through which myths find expression may arise
unconsciously in the writer's mind.

While allegory emphasizes the compound formula, the mythical mode
highlights the individualized integer, and exploits different sources of
power and aspirations and very different reader expectations. Edwin
Honig recasts Coleridge's alignment of narrative allegory with reality and
myth with symbol by observing that allegory deals with things and symbolism with qualities of things. Allegory targets the realistic and myth
the deepest levels of felt experience. Where denotative and reflective allegory expresses traditional ideas dialectically, connotative and affective
myth expresses mood or emotion and practices transcendence of form,
content, and purpose. "It is the seeing mind which authorizes symbol,"
according to Brian Nellist, "where[as] allegory takes its authority from
what the mind sees." Myth projects the expression of emotion into an
image and thereby redefines the dimness and subjectivity of feeling into
an active process.[3] Where allegory is fueled by analysis and intellection,
myth models a quest for synthesis. This view of ancient myth adapts

readily to such modern systems as Freud's where a systematic code also captures and reveals otherwise elusive mysteries.

Myth and symbol position themselves differently toward the universal and particular as well as toward the mimetic and visible. Where allegory begins with immaterial fact and invents expressive *visibilia*, the mythic or symbolic mode—what C. S. Lewis calls the "sacramental"—begins with the material and reaches for the invisible, begins with the sensible imitation or copy and reaches for the archetype.[4] Allegory equates two things of which we have direct knowledge as redeployments of the familiar, but symbol promises to convey knowledge not obtained previously and not available by other means. The first retains, the second transcends, things. Its multiple dimensions require that allegory be apprehended by at least two attitudes of mind, whereas to cite Coleridge once again: "The advantage of symbolic writing over allegory is, that it presumes no disjunction of faculties, but simple dominance." Myth and symbol can thus target ultimate paradoxes in an epistemology that "refuses to admit that reason or perception provide the highest wisdom" (quoted in Fletcher 17, Fletcher 322).

Coleridge explains—insofar as he can explain—such mysteries through images of light. He quotes Goethe that "true symbolism is where the particular represents the more general, not as a dream or a shadow, but as a living momentary revelation of the Inscrutable." The Coleridgean symbol is "characterized by a translucence of the special in the individual, or of the general in the special, or of the universal in the general; above all by the translucence of the eternal through and in the temporal. It always partakes of the reality which it renders intelligible; and while it enunciates the whole, abides itself as a living part in that unity of which it is the representative" (quoted in Fletcher 16). Although allegory seeks *illustration* in the usual sense of using a pictorial example, symbol uses *illustration* in the light-related sense of making lustrous. Myth illuminates the datum itself rather than the activity of apprehension.

Symbol and myth build not upon the mechanic form Coleridge finds in allegory but upon his organic form; they present unmediated vision, not the "picture-language" of Coleridgean allegory (*Coleridge's Essays* 46). Allegory is explanatory and analytic, while myth is synthetic both in its forms and in its effects. A literary work, according to Northrop Frye, owes its variety, clarity, and intensity to identification *as*, but it owes its unity to this process of identification *with* (123). In contrast to the distinguishing feature of seventeenth-century verse, T. S. Eliot's "dissociation of sensibility," myth and symbol seek an association or a reassociation of sensibility. Coleridge puts forward the epistemological principle in *Anima Poetae* as a quest for synthesis: "In looking at objects of Nature . . . I seem rather to be seeking, as it were *asking* for, a symbolical language for something within me that already and forever exists, than observing anything new" (115). The symbolical language Coleridge here *asks* for puts its questing participants in touch with the large and unifying patterns of nature, cosmos, and history. It is the essence of myth that such content, wherever else it originates, also exists already and forever *within* the asker.

Like their different uses of *illustration*, universality, and "isolation" of images, the modes of allegory and myth rest upon radically different senses and uses of trope. The defining trope of allegory is the continuous similitude, while the radical trope of symbol and myth is synecdoche. In relating part to whole myths abandon realistic vehicles in favor of mysterious tenors. Grounded in an inaugural likeness, they leave behind the corporal forms in favor of "what surmounts the reach / Of human sense" (*Paradise Lost* v.571–73). The idea is not that the part can capture, reduce, or control the whole, but that its microcosmic representation can free and guide the mind to apprehend the large and unknown.

Myth and symbol occur at a unique juncture of nature, psyche (and therefore psychology), and religion to achieve a multivalent and transtemporal signifying value. Where pagan myth imitates nature not as structure or system but as cyclical process, Christian myth is also historical and affirms singularity (Ross 11). Its expression absorbs the biological and the psychological, and in Jean Danielou's nice term, it *assumes* the cosmic and makes pagan symbols signs of its own realities. Moreover, Christianity's systematic salvational reenactments retain the singularity of particular events within a linear and teleological design, and Christian reading promotes progressive revelation, especially through typological compounds of history and prophecy, past and future (Danielou 436, 438, 439). Typology—a matter returned to in Chapters 3 and 8—provides transtemporal expression that allows both powerful ancient universals and aspiring modern particulars to have their say.

Bunyan's narrative inhabits a unique nexus of the allegorical and the mythic, the cosmic and the historical, the typological in this sense. Where traditional mythology projects itself as theology (N. Frye 64), readers of *Pilgrim's Progress* part I can observe theology in the process of becoming mythology. For centuries Bunyan's myth has served countless readers as the most powerful literary expression of the essence of Puritanism. Myth characteristically targets the hero's character and the patterned nature of his career, and Aristotlean *ethos*—that is expression and action growing out of and reflecting moral purpose—exists primarily as a function of plot or *mythos*. It is in the sense of *myth* as compounded with *ethos* that E. M. W. Tillyard can speak of Bunyan as "the true interpreter, I should even say poet, of the Puritan myth" (392). For Bunyan, Puritan *mythos* and *ethos* are deeply interknit in the two senses of *ethos* Aristotle recognized, that is in the character of the individual and in the rules and ideals of conduct within a society. His hero Christian enacts both traditional and Puritan myth, both the common character, wisdom, and goals of Western culture and Puritanism's re-presentation of it.

One of the most basic synecdoches of traditional myth and of epic literature aligns the hero with a culture and its ideals. The hero is by definition exceptional, in gifts or promise, in good or bad luck. Elevated above his peers as the most strong or courageous or wise or educable or disciplined or otherwise advanced of his people, the hero aspires to his culture's ideals and acts out the solutions of its dominant problems. Kenneth Burke develops a paradigm of the epic hero as "a recurrent configuration of cultural processes": "A charismatic leader of men, the epic hero . . . magnifies and makes socially acceptable the actual conditions of men living under stress or in a primitive condition. The hero is a repository for all the virtues the group needs to believe in to survive. Other men live vicariously in his deeds, his courage, and self-sacrifice, and thus share in a communion (or community), both social and religious, of the heroic body. The mediator between men and gods, the epic hero humanizes divinity by his flaws and sufferings no less than by his miraculous exploits" (Burke, paraphrased in Honig 156–57). In the literary—specifically epic—tradition the hero's acts are celebrated in written records, myth masked as history. The hero is didactic both in action and in story, and when his action is psychic growth, that story itself collapses back into allegorical self-referentiality. In *Pilgrim's Progress* part I, the hero as reader becomes the hero as read about, and travelers in part II regularly read inscriptions of Christian's progress in markers along the way. For his family as for the reading audience, the hero himself authorizes future reading and enfolds these audiences into the dominant heroics.

In enacting universal, generalized, normative human patterns, the hero participates in myth as Aristotelian *ethos* enacted on the stage of history, and also in *myth* in the sense of *mythology*, the collective body of human stories with deep cosmic and psychic resonances. Joseph Campbell analyzes the thousand faces of this heroics, what he calls "the universal adventure," in a paradigm of departure, initiation, and return. Bunyan's mythic and symbolic hero acts out Campbell's "morphology of the adventure," in separating from the familiar but symbolically deficient world, penetrating to a source of mysterious power, interacting victoriously with supernatural forces, losing his selfhood and dying to the world of the everyday, and achieving a rebirth for himself and a restoration of his society. As a rule, the adventure includes solitary wanderings, recognition of a mission, initiations, awakenings to new vision, and new integrations with nature and cosmos.[5] Within the parameters signaled by his name, Christian's psyche conflates with an allegorized landscape of the rural England of the later seventeenth century.

Bunyan's Christian is a hero of this universal sort as well as a specifically Puritan hero inhabiting a specifically Puritan myth. The story elements of Campbell's psychological radical translate directly into the categories of Bunyan's theology. What Campbell calls "a morphology of adventure" is simultaneously an acting out of the traditional Puritan codification Edmund S. Morgan dubs "a morphology of conversion." Both *morphologies* refer to series of recognizable signs of change in one's spiritual condition. As an heir of the Reformation, Christian's heroism encompasses the Bible and the actions of reading and professing. It follows the stages codified, for example, by the Elizabethan Puritan William Perkins as Effectual Calling, Justification, Sanctification, and Glorification, or in Bunyan's formulation Vocation, Justification, Preservation, and Glorification (*Israel's Hope Encouraged* Offor 1:600). In keeping with the Puritan passion for stability, each of these categories, as Boyd Berry remarks, "turn[s] a potentially transitive act into a solid, manageable noun."[6]

Whether as Puritan paradigm or traditional myth, *Pilgrim's Progress* part I presents, or re-presents, "a universal quest, realized individually," variously combining *mythos* with *ethos*, plot with character, ancient story with cultural repository. Puritans deliberately reduced experience to manageable pattern and meaning and were characteristically fond of secured derivatives from the Bible and early Christianity, fond too of repetitiousness and typicality. Richard Baxter affirms the common *ethos* Puritans expected to share: "God's dealings are much what the same with all his servants in the main, and the points wherein he varieth are usually so small, that I think not such fit to be repeated; nor have I anything extraordinary to glory in, which is not common to the rest of my brethren, who have the same spirit, and are servants of the same Lord." What may look to us reductionist and mechanical, however, impressed Puritans themselves as expansive and transcendent, a noble rising above the self rather than a denial of individuality.[7]

It is difficult to overemphasize the extent to which conversional morphology interpenetrated the thinking and daily life of the seventeenth-century Puritan, and Joan Webber captures the essence of Puritanism in calling attention to "the painful day-to-day experience of learning to conform to the will of a mysterious God, and then attempting to find out whether grace has been granted" (33). The codified stages of the morphology, so often repeated in Puritan writings of the sixteenth and seventeenth centuries, enter *Pilgrim's Progress* in Faithful's explanation of how a work of grace discovers itself to the believer:

> It gives him conviction of sin, especially of the defilement of his nature, and the sin of unbelief. . . . This sight and sense of things worketh in him sorrow and shame for sin; he findeth moreover revealed in him the Saviour of the World, and the absolute necessity of closing with him, for life, at the which he findeth hungrings and thirstings after him, to which hungrings, &c. the promise is made. Now according to the strength or weakness of his Faith in his Saviour, so is his joy and peace, so is his love to holiness, so are his desires to know him more, and also to serve him in this World. But though I say it discovereth it self thus unto him; yet it is but seldom that he is able to conclude that this is a work of Grace, because his corruptions now, and his abused reason, makes his mind to misjudge in this matter; therefore in him that hath this work, there is required a very sound Judgement, before he can with steddiness conclude that this is a work of Grace. (82–83)

Awakened from an initial indifference, converts gradually leave behind blind confidence in the covenant of works and progress to humiliation at their self-deception and depravity. Moving through intensifications and alternations of self-consciousness, self-deception, moral sensitivity, terror, alienation, and despair, they arrive at an overwhelming sense of God's benevolence, the imputed righteousness and justification by faith alone that Bunyan's prose so often celebrates. Despite reviving fears and temptations, thereafter they persevere in promise and hope, though never achieving salvational certainty. This denial of closure forces converts constantly to review the origins of their hopes. Various stages require the believer's interactions with Scriptures as mediated by the Holy Spirit to awaken doubts, assurances, and saving knowledge. Progress toward salvation—if it can be called that—is both logical and psychological, at once biblically rooted, universally prescribed, and uniquely enacted by the individual who feels that his destiny depends upon his ability to recognize this shared pattern of divine illumination within his own mind (Ebner 38). Clearly, the process implies intense drama, repeatedly reenacted even within the individual life.

The most curious work in the Bunyan canon, *A Mapp Shewing the Order and Causes of Salvation and Damnation* (c. 1664), codifies his version of the Puritan myth by visually deploying circles, boxes, and ribbons in what resembles a modern flowchart or genealogical tree, starting from God, then the trinitized God, at the top and ending with a final bottom circle divided between heaven and hell. A division down the middle separates the lefthand tracing of the line of grace and election from the righthand tracing of the line of justice and reprobation, both arrayed in circles containing exhortations and biblical verses and adorned with floral and other ornamentation. Like *Pilgrim's Progress*, *A Mapp* is governed by an advisory introductory poem that collapses the reader into the reading process:

> When thou dost read this side, then look
> Into thy heart, as in a book.
> And see if thou canst read the same
> In thee from God by Christ his name;
> If not, then fear the other side,
> Which not to life but death doth guide.[8]

The shepherds of the Delectable Mountains present Christian with a "note of direction for the way," perhaps resembling this *Mapp* (134, similarly 123).

The left side of the *Mapp* arrays Bunyan's version of the Puritan morphological sequence in twenty-four circled stages that accumulate into a single sentence:

Election, upon which standeth . . . The Covenant of Grace . . . To the Elect comes by the Covenant Effectual Calling . . . By which is given the Holy Ghost and the operations of it . . . Which causeth sound convictions for sin . . . Where at the soul is cast down . . . Which occasioneth Satan to tempt to despair . . . Which driveth the soul to the promise . . . Which strengtheneth faith . . . Which encourageth to pray . . . Which causeth God to hear . . . And in mercy to Christ's righteousness . . . Which increaseth confidence . . . Working true love to holinesse . . . Humility at the sight of sin . . . Watchfulness against it . . . And patience under the Cross . . . Which brings more experience of God's goodness . . . Which worketh strong hope in an unseen world . . . Which begets much sweet soul contemplation . . . Which bears them up in faith above their sufferings . . . Whereby they overcome the world . . . And have an enterance into the kingdom of Christ . . . Wherein it dwelleth to ETERNITY.

A biblical text authorizes each item, and a supplementary array along the left margin translates each of the circled stages into verse. Bunyan's chart literally "maps" the Puritan myth's spiritual stages and principles. It belongs to a no-longer-familiar tradition of such items, of which William Perkins's *A Golden Chain, or The Description of Theology Containing the Order of the Causes of Salvation and Damnation According to God's Word* (1590) provides another popular example. Like Perkins and Bunyan, thousands of believers in intervening years were passionately devoted to such systematized arrays of theological principles, especially where the influence of Peter Ramus was felt in England and America.

The Puritan morphology of election overwrites the departure stage of Joseph Campbell's secular paradigm. Theologically, calling is brought about by effectual preaching and hearing, the mollifying of the heart, and faith (Perkins 168). What Campbell describes as initiation occurs as Puritan justification—remission of sin along with imputation of righteousness (Perkins 168)—in other words, rebirth. Bunyan's hero variously enacts the mortification, vivification, repentance, and new obedience that constitute sanctification. Campbell's return coincides with Puritan glorification and with Christian's achievements of Beulah and the Celestial City. Both Campbell's departure and initiation and Puritan initial awakening and dedication include a rejection of the past and an affirmation of future goals, and both mythic schemes often stage awakening in a dream format. Both morphologies press toward universalizing and toward synecdochic reenactments of the recurrent cultural inheritance so foundational to the mythic mode, and in both, late stages emphasize myth's psychic and emotional transformation and empowerment, its pressures toward transcendence and synthesis, its aspirations toward vision and redemption, fulfilled by the story's end. Both morphologies are weighted in favor of

the initial stages, and the structure of *Pilgrim's Progress* part I in line with
key Puritan principles likewise makes much of beginnings, perhaps to the
subversion of narrative climax.

We first view Bunyan's hero in a memorable static, even statuesque,
tableau: "I dreamed, and behold *I saw a Man, cloathed with Raggs, standing in a certain place, with his face from his own House, a Book in his
hand, and a great burden upon his Back.* I looked, and saw him open the
Book, and Read therein; and as he read, he wept and trembled: and not
being able longer to contain, he brake out with a lamentable cry; saying,
what shall I do?" (8). The figure then acts out effectual calling, defined by
Bunyan as an awakening to the evils of sin and unbelief, an awakening
to the world to come and the glory of unseen things, and a sanctifying
virtue (*A Confession of My Faith* Offor II:599). Christian is troubled in
the expected ways: "The night was as troublesome to him as the day:
wherefore instead of sleeping, he spent it in sighs and tears. . . . He began
to retire himself to his Chamber to pray for, and pity them; and also to
condole his own misery: he would also walk solitarily in the Fields, sometimes reading, and sometimes praying: and thus for some days he spent
his time" (9). He experiences legal fear and "Conviction of the necessity
of flying" (gloss 10), is dramatically reborn with the loss of his burden at
the sepulcher, and is variously tossed between awakenings and backslidings, and generally fulfills the later stages of the conversion schema that
The Doctrine of the Law and Grace Unfolded outlines as pardon for sin, the
gifts of faith, hope, righteousness, strength to do God's works, comfort or
consolation, and the Spirit and its fruits (II:86–87).

Bunyan places this initially symbolic figure, obsessively reading in his
book, into motion as a traveler on the allegorical Way. His autobiography
glosses such imagery in presenting himself as "a man driven by a tempest
across a bare landscape" and as "a fleeing sinner who pauses upon occasion to glance back over his shoulder" at the merciful God shouting after
him.[9] Reading forces Christian to assume the burden on his back (18) and
to see himself as caught between the City of Destruction and the wrath
to come. He responds with lamentation, restlessness, social and familial
disorientation, and perplexity, knowing himself "Condemned to die, and
after that to come to Judgment" and unwilling to do the first and unable
to do the second (9). According to Bunyan's *Doctrine of the Law and Grace
Unfolded* (II:18), those who do not answer to such convictions become
"more hard, more senseless, more seared . . . and hardened in their con-
sciences," but Christian does not yet know how to translate his awakened
perception into positive action.

Christian's book and the later ministrations of Evangelist clarify how the spoken and written Word helps a sinner to apprehend spiritual danger. As Perkins advises, in Christian's turmoil where the devil seeks to separate him from the Word, he should exercise himself in: "premeditation of the power and use of the word; diligent attention of the mind; a hungering desire of the heart; integrity of life; the casting away of evil affections; the inward consent and agreement of the heart with the word preached; an hiding of the word in the heart lest we should sin; a trembling at the presence of God in the assembly of the church" (239). The individual needs the assistance of the minister, but even on his own Christian is able to make textual progress, from the simpler question of Acts 2.27, "What must I do?" to the more precise question of Acts 16.30–31, "What must I do to be saved?" (10, 11, and *Mapp* #6). Since five of his minor works rehearse this same question, it apparently focuses spiritual crisis in Bunyan's thought.[10]

The Christian we meet has just accepted his role in covenantal theology, the system of Puritan contracts between God and man wherein believers are promised eternal life on condition that they fulfill their part of the bargain. Christian finds himself to be elected, called, covenanted to God as in *Mapp* #1, 2, and 3. As in 2 Samuel 23.5, his whole desire is toward God, and he has turned against his house which is ungodly. But as the conversion sequence anticipates (or dictates), he knows himself to lack the perfect obedience required by a covenant of works, but also feels cut off from the second covenant of grace.

These covenants rest upon the principle of Hebrews 7.19: "The Law made nothing perfect, but the bringing in of a better hope did; by the which we draw nigh to God." *The Doctrine of the Law and Grace Unfolded* (1659) assumes that knowledge of the covenants is the duty and absolute concern of every believer and that the first covenant is foundational to the second (11:13). A two-stage procedure brings sinners into the covenant of grace: "[God] doth first kill them with the Covenant of *Works*, which is the Morall Law, or Ten Commandments," by opening their minds to divine and infinite justice and their own lack of righteousness and great need for an alternative covenant. Death to sin then opens to them a vision of "a most glorious, perfect, and never-fading life" imputed through Christ and makes them eager for Christ at whatever sacrifice (11:146–47, 137–38).

The early pages of *Pilgrim's Progress* situate Christian primarily with reference to the covenant of works. He must encounter representations of Old Testament reason and justice before being relieved by a thorough New Testament orientation. As Christian's departure from home and family enacted his election and the earliest stages of the morphology sequence, so three early encounters on the journey enact covenantal trials. First, the Slough of Despond dramatizes legal fears: "This *Miry slow*, is such a place as cannot be mended: It is the descent whither the scum and filth that attends conviction for sin doth continually run, and therefore it is called the *Slow of Dispond:* for still as the sinner is awakened about his lost condition, there ariseth in his soul many fears, and doubts, and discouraging apprehensions, which all of them get together, and settle in this place: And this is the reason of the badness of this ground" (15). At this stage Christian is totally circumscribed by the psychological fact of his burden: "This burden upon my back is more terrible to me than are all these things which you have mentioned: nay, methinks I care not what I meet with in the way, so be I can also meet with deliverance from my burden" (18). The burden on his back—more precisely his new awareness of the burden on his back, in other words his guilt and fear in the face of the old covenant—sinks him in the mire. He wallows in and is "grievously bedaubed with the dirt" (14) of his sin. The phrase "conviction for sin" locates this occasion precisely within the morphology sequence, and as *The Strait Gate* urges, "Be thankful therefore for convictions, conversion begins at conviction, though all conviction doth not end in conversion. It is a great mercy to be convinced that we are sinners, and that we need a Saviour" (v:121).

In his second trial, Mr. Worldly Wiseman temporarily deceives Christian into believing in a covenant of works. This plausible figure advises removing Christian's burden by the means named in his adjunctive villages and associates—Carnal-Policy, Legality, Morality, and Civility. He promises safety, friendship, and content (19) instead of the dangers of Christian's chosen travel on the Way, and in acceding to such options Christian enacts the subterfuge Bunyan warns against in *Doctrine of the Law and Grace Unfolded*. But increased terrors quickly displace such temporary self-deceptions. In the third of Christian's trials, Mount Sinai itself embodies topographically as well as typologically the chief limitations of this first covenant. Its towering height, threatening overhang, and terrifying flashes of fire serve only to stymie the traveler and make his burden even heavier. It puts Christian into "dumps" (27). As Good Will later explains, "That Mountain has been the death of many," and Christian is lucky to have "escaped being by it dasht in pieces" (27).

Bunyan's theoretical account in *The Doctrine of the Law and Grace Unfolded* illuminates in detail Christian's legalistic trials and the urgent need for a relieving gospel. "To be under the Law . . . is, *to be bound upon pain of eternal damnation, to fulfill, and that compleatly, and continually, every particular point of the Ten Commandments, by doing them*" (11:30). "I tell thee also," says Bunyan, "that these ten great guns, the Ten Commandments, will with discharging themselves in justice against thy soul, so rattle in thy conscience, that thou wilt in spite of thy teeth, be immediately put to silence, and have thy mouth stopped" (49). The law does not allow for deviation or repentance and indicts and destroys even the righteous when they seek justification merely by the law (36, 54). Man cannot remove sin from himself or himself from sin by his own efforts however intensive or extensive, but only by a knowledge of the law can "the freeness and fulness of the Gospel" be had (14). Grace does not make void the law, nor can the law be established without the gospel *mingled with* (Bunyan's verb) the covenant of works. The goal of enlightenment is to speak of the law so as to "magnifie the Gospel; and also, to speak of the Gospel, so as to establish (and yet not to idolize) the Law, nor any particular thereof" (16).

The "terrour, horrour, and thundering Sentences" of the law prepare the convert, like Bunyan's hero, for ministerial instruction. As the treatise explains, "honest preaching" should aim not to terrorize with the law but to discover grace through the gospel (15). The Puritan minister and his secular equivalent, Campbell's herald figure, both guard and guide the initial steps of the hero's adventure.[11] As Campbell outlines the norm, they demand the hero's trust and mediate his acceptance of the call to adventure. They may also personify the hero's destiny or mirror his psychic responses to the prospect of transformation and often also supply an essential amulet or piece of advice.

Three appearances of Evangelist mark him as precisely such a figure. Initially, he gains Christian's trust and willingness to leave behind all that has been familiar and safe in favor of a dangerous unknown future. Christian is isolated, lost, diffusely anxious, socially and psychically disoriented until his herald's catechizings force him to articulate his contradictory feelings, reenvision his predicament, and transmute his negative motivations to a positive one. Evangelist supplies an amulet, "a *Parchment-Roll*, and there was written within, *Fly from the wrath to come*" (10), a text inscribing Christian's psychic impulsion and replacing his earlier interrogatives with its imperative syntax. It is a text drawn from Christian's book, specifically the words of John the Baptist to the Pharisees and Sadducees, "a generation of vipers" (Matthew 3.7).

This flight from wrath modulates into the affirmation, "Life, Life, Eternal Life" (10). The second parchment roll Christian receives from the Shining Ones at the sepulcher records the very different message that is his ticket to the Celestial City: "This Roll was the assurance of his life, and acceptance at the desired Haven" (44).

By definition, the Puritan minister's role was "to give good example; to exhort; to comfort; to admonish" but especially to mediate Scripture, to deliver the Word and also to instruct his audience in their private processing of the written Word (Perkins 246, 214). Evangelist extends these tasks by answering Christian's question "Whither must I fly?" with a pair of questions that stimulate Christian to perform the valiant act of faith: "Do you see yonder *Wicket-gate*? The Man said, No. Then said the other, Do you see yonder shining light? He said, I think I do. Then said *Evangelist*, Keep that light in your eye, and go up directly thereto, so shalt thou see the Gate; at which when thou knockest, it shall be told thee what thou shalt do" (10). Thereafter, his fingers in his ears and crying out for eternal life, Christian embarks fully on his heroics, and as S. J. Newman remarks, "to venture and to adventure are always read in their root sense of putting at risk, making a trial of one's chance" (239). Readers are similarly positioned in uncertainty and like the hero must learn to take risks and become not just learners but relearners (Quilligan 227).

Under Evangelist's guidance Christian's difficulties may transmute into faith as here. Christian moves toward unseen goals by trusting to the evidence of things not seen (Hebrews 11.1). *Justification By an Imputed Righteousness, Or, No Way to Heaven But by Jesus Christ* articulates this fundamental Christian principle with particular force and clarity: "[Faith] is the most submitting act that a man can do; it throweth out all our righteousness; it makes the soul poor in itself; it liveth upon God and Christ. . . . It is a receiving of mercy, an embracing of forgiveness, an accepting of the righteousness of Christ, and a trusting to these for life." It is, in sum, "a believing, a trusting, or relying act of the soul" (Offor 1:326, 328). Stanley Fish calls it "an inverse relationship between invisibility and reliability" and finds in *Pilgrim's Progress* a reader and hero "refus[ing] to accept as final the perspective that validates a problem" and affirming the possibility of solution *against* the available evidence: "Christian never more surely perceives than when he refuses to be paralyzed by his inability to perceive."[12] The occasion recalls the differentiating principle offered Christian at Interpreter's house between carnal sense and things to come (32). Faith is reenacted in similar terms at the Slough of

Despond, when Pliable asks him where he is, and Christian reverts to the answer, "Truly . . . I do not know" (14); when Worldly Wiseman (echoing Evangelist) asks Christian if he sees "yonder high Hill," meaning Mount Sinai, and Christian confidently answers, "Yes, very well" (20); and when Christian and Hopeful look through a perspective glass toward the Celestial City (122–23). The alternative is literalized in Atheist's confidence that if there were any Heavenly City he would have seen it in his extensive travels (135).

Evangelist's second and third appearances further clarify the ministerial role. Christian's assessment of Evangelist as "a very great and honorable person" is enhanced rather than subverted by Worldly Wiseman's view of him as "dangerous and troublesome" in the ways of the world (18). Evangelist appears for the second time when Christian is again stymied into inaction, at Mount Sinai. From "a severe and dreadful countenance," Evangelist reasons with Christian, skillfully catechizes him, and then delivers a sermon on the text of Matthew 7.13–14: "*Strive to enter in at the strait gate, the gate to which I sent thee; for strait is the gate that leadeth unto life, and few there be that find it*" (22). Evangelist reconstitutes Christian's faltering conversion; he redeems him as *Isreal's Hope Encouraged* defines the term: "To redeem is to fetch back, by sufficient and suitable means, those at present in an enthralled, captivated, or an imprisoned condition" (Offor 1:604). At his third appearance, in the middle of the book, Evangelist preaches to Christian and Faithful on the text of *The Heavenly Footman:* "The Crown is before you, and it is an incorruptible one; so run that you may obtain it. . . . and believe stedfastly concerning things that are invisible." Christian gratefully acknowledges Evangelist's ministerial activities as "ancient kindness, and unwearied laboring for my eternal good" and calls him a Prophet (86–87).

Threshold imagery demarcates the transition between departure and initiation in the careers of both Bunyan's Puritan hero and Campbell's monomythic hero. At the point of entering "the zone of magnified power" (77), Campbell's secular hero encounters custodians or gatekeepers who provide access to new dimensions of possibility. Theologically, at both the Wicket Gate and the door to Interpreter's house, Christian knocks in keeping with the gate's inscription from Matthew 7.8: "Knock and it shall be opened unto you" (25). In typical Puritan parlance *The Doctrine of the Law and Grace Unfolded* equates "all your knockings at our fathers door" with prayer (11:19), and a *Pilgrim's Progress* gloss explains, "The Gate will be opened to broken-hearted sinners" (25). In response to his knock at the gate, Good Will pulls him over the threshold and "discovers" the straight and narrow Way that lies ahead for Christian and "An open Door [that] is set before thee, and no man can shut it" (26). Inside the Interpreter's house the proleptic Valiant Man successfully battles through the door of a palace and is welcomed with the verse: "Come in, Come in; / Eternal Glory thou shalt win" (33). The gatekeepers, along with the porter of House Beautiful, are contained within *The Strait Gate*'s proposition that "God hath porters at the gates of his temple, at the gate of heaven . . . to look that none that are unclean in any thing may come in thither." Through their watchfulness, diligence, and valor, they prevent the entry of the unsanctified or unprepared, as do the porters at Solomon's Temple. They generally function as "types of our gospel ministers, as they are set to be watchmen in and over the Church, and the holy things of God" (v:77, 77–78, and Offor III:477; see also III:xliii and vI:279).

Bunyan's theological works variously background thresholds as well. The doors of Solomon's Temple provide the governing model, "represent[ing] Christ, as he is the way to the Father, as also did the door of the Tabernacle, at which the people were wont to stand when they went to inquire of God" (*Solomon's Temple Spiritualized* Offor III:478). *The Strait Gate* acknowledges Christ as "the gate or entrance . . . without whom no man can get thither . . . the very passage into heaven" (v:75). The authorizing text of this work is Luke 13.24: "Strive to enter in at the strait gate, for many, I say unto you, seek to enter in, and shall not be able." In a related metaphor in *Grace Abounding*, Bunyan long felt himself excluded from membership in the Bedford church community by a great wall, but he was at last able to squeeze in through a narrow doorway (19–20).

In Campbell's monomyth and in Christian vision, the threshold signifies rebirth (J. Campbell 90). Specifically, for Bunyan it is a threshold between the legal and the evangelical or between "meer moral principle" and "the spirit of adoption" into the gospel (*The Doctrine of the Law and Grace Unfolded* II:71, and similarly *I Will Pray With the Spirit* II:254 and Colossians 2.13). In an autobiographical passage, *The Doctrine of the Law and Grace Unfolded* describes Bunyan's personal analogue of Christian's experience at the sepulcher, where he too was relieved of his burden of sin and experienced what the new covenant offers generally: a new heart, a new spirit, faith, the love of God, a promise and assurance of life, and love (II:158–59, 186). To achieve new knowledge and mystery, the hero of Puritan as of secular myth must abandon the self as previously known, in Christian terms must lose his life in order to save it (Mark 8.35, and see also John 3.3, 1 Peter 1.23 and 2.2). Bunyan's *The Greatness of the Soul* and *The Strait Gate* develop the principle underlying Christian's experience at and just beyond the gate, where he begins to "walk in the newness of life" (Romans 6.4). His rebirth is completed when he arrives at a cross and his burden falls from his back into the sepulcher. Here three Shining Ones offer him peace and forgiveness of sins, exchange his rags for new raiment, set a mark upon his forehead, and provide him with a sealed parchment roll. Christian's radical change at the sepulcher, "the place of Deliverance" (28), is treated with surprising brevity and with only the barest mention of Christ (38, and see 49), perhaps because, as Leopold Damrosch notes, to the Puritan mind "the death of the immortal and un-changing God . . . is literally unimaginable and should be kept free of physically limiting imagery" (168, and see *The Heavenly Footman* v:159; *The Doctrine of the Law and Grace Unfolded* 11:84; and *The Water of Life* Offor iii:549).

In Campbell's universal secular myth as in Bunyan's Puritan variant, the threshold serves a particular purpose. It demarcates past negatives from future promises and fulfillments and models choices of self and arenas of action. Crossing it signals the hero's ability to take risks and to accept transformation. It looks both backward and forward, focusing the hero's initiation and forecasting the ultimate attainment of what is for now only tasted and longed for, synthesis, vision, redemption. In the final phase, after he has negotiated a series of alternating ordeals and prom-ises, reorientations of his relationship to himself, to the Word, and to his community and culture, Christian passes through the climactic analogue of these earlier manufactured gates and doors, also a threshold of a sort, but now the boundary between nature and transcendence. Beulah's land-scape typologically foreshadows the divine reality of the Celestial City, and the River of Death marks the threshold between them and between Old and New Testament visions of blessedness (Knott, *Sword* 151, 153).

The dissolving endings of *Pilgrim's Progress* provide a varied vehicle for Christian transcendence, and indeed one commentator has discov-ered as many as five distinct endings (Fish, *Self-Consuming Artifacts* 260). This layering underscores Puritan warnings against too great spiritual assurance, a lesson enacted in Ignorance's damnation even after cross-ing the River of Death. From another angle, the Puritan need for active uncertainty about salvation destabilizes the reader's confidence and gen-erates the textual reprocessing so central to the cyclical nature of secular myth and to the writing and reading of part II of *Pilgrim's Progress*. At a key point, the Old Testament model for Christian's heroism shifts from the initiate and traveler Jonah to Job, "the honest, courageous, horizon-searching sufferer" (J. Campbell 147), whose Almighty shatters familiar categories to provide the unique Job with a luminous revelation far beyond the capacity of his societal norms or "friends."

Generically, the revelation with which *Pilgrim's Progress* concludes is a passage into anagogy or myth. It marks the point where the synecdoche of myth collapses in favor of the whole for which the part had stood. In this transcending enactment, the aspirant becomes enfolded into that which is aspired toward and "nature becomes, not the container, but the thing contained, and the archetypal universal symbols, the city, the garden, the quest, the marriage, are no longer the desirable forms that man constructs inside nature, but are themselves the forms of nature" (N. Frye 119, and see also 120–21). The culminating event of the myth, this anagoge, achieves the goals toward which the preceding action and ethos have been directed; it dissociates itself from lesser levels of meaning and measurement; and it "realizes" the state of perfection that was supposed unattainable. Speaking specifically of the mythic endings of both parts of *Pilgrim's Progress*, MacCaffrey sees such acts as representations of that moment when "the figurative intimations of our lives are absorbed into the actualities that stand behind them" (65).

The final or return phase of the monomythic heroic journey translates directly into Puritan myth. What Campbell describes as the hero's reorientation to his father and mother readily adapts to Puritan rebirth metaphor, as for example in David Leverenz's Freudian reading of Puritanism's "Family Romance fantasy: a rebirth into the higher family of God as good father and good mother combined."[13] Where the secular hero characteristically is initiated into the techniques, duties, and prerogatives of his vocation through a radical readjustment of his relationship to the representations of his parents, Christian must wrestle with the mysterious and apparently self-contradictory nature of Bunyan's paternal deity, a mythic/psychic Father knowable through his book. Both kinds of hero work through aspects of the Father in which their ego reflexes contrast with assurances of ultimate salvation. After a series of purgings, the hero must himself become the mystagogue or Father, able to enact the role of initiator and guide (J. Campbell 136–37, 145, 129); as in Bunyan's own life, Christian progresses from his own achieved salvation into the role of Puritan minister for the final third of *Pilgrim's Progress* part I.

In Campbell's composite myth, the metaphoric male represents the initiating principle or method and the metaphoric female the goal to which initiation leads, a synthetic resolution of apparent divisiveness within a higher unity. In the secular tradition, the inevitable image for this union or reunion is marriage (J. Campbell 109), and in the theological one, the fact that in Hebrew "Beulah" means "marriage" provides a metaphor for Bunyan's dramatization of heroic interaction with the Word:

> For in this Land the shining Ones commonly walked, because it was upon the Borders of Heaven. In this Land also the contract between the Bride and the Bridgroom was renewed: Yea, here, *as the Bridegroom rejoyceth over the Bride, so did their God rejoyce over them.* Here they had no want of Corn and Wine; for in this place they met with abundance of what they had sought for in all their Pilgrimage. Here they heard voices from out of the City, loud voices, saying, *Say ye to the daughter of* Zion, *Behold thy Salvation cometh, behold his reward is with him.* Here all the Inhabitants of the Countrey called them, *The holy People, the redeemed of the Lord, Sought out,* &c. (154–55)

The Geneva Bible's gloss on Revelation 19.7 amplifies the range of meaning: "God made Christ the bridgrome of his Church at the beginning, and at the last day it shalbe fully accomplished when we shal be ioyned with our head" (see also *Profitable Meditations* VI:27). In Bunyan as in Campbell's paradigm (J. Campbell 116), through marriage "the one who comes to know" attains an heroic mastery of life by uniting with "the totality of what can be known."

The very high priority Puritans assigned to family life further contextualizes the metaphoric marriage at the conclusion of *Pilgrim's Progress* part I. Whether out of convenience, immediacy, or heightened consciousness and valuation of such relations, or whether because of the frequent incidence of such imagery in the Bible, Puritans regularly regarded the believer's union with God as appropriately metaphored in the highest relation between mortals, marriage. Edmund Morgan's study *The Puritan Family* identifies marriage as the favorite metaphor for the relationship of God and man in Puritan sermonizing, a metaphor "dominat[ing] Puritan thought so completely as to suggest that the Puritans' religious experiences in some ways duplicated their domestic experiences." The believer as a bride of Christ and a child of God implied a networking at once familial and parabolic.[14]

The return phase of the hero's career, though fraught with difficulty, is the most important from the society's point of view, "indispensable to the continuous circulation of spiritual energy into the world" (J. Campbell 36). The startled world may reject the great boon the hero intended for it, or he, who has won through to ultimate enlightenment, may lose all connection with his earlier community or be so altered by his adventure that the community cannot receive his return (J. Campbell 36–37). Initially, Christian's family and neighbors reject the salvation he models and offers them, but the close of part I finds other means to reconcile the hero's transcendence with the community's salvation. Since Bunyan's return threshold between the divine and the human equates with death, recrossing is precluded, but in the monomyth sometimes heroes can be brought back even from this extremity by external assistance or device.

Within the dominating Puritan hermeneutic, when Christian is born again after passing through the River of Death, he is reconstituted in service to others as a series of edifying texts read by his family and community. The basic precedent for reading and for later similar inscribing occurs in the first wayside marker Christian and Hopeful encounter, a statue engraved "Remember Lot's Wife." Labeled "a Caution and Example," this biblically derived text provokes thought and discourse: "Let us take notice," says Christian, "of what we see here, for our help for time to come" (108–9). A later gloss supplies the principle: "A remembrance of former chastisements is an help against present temptations" (135). The a priori base of Puritan thought promotes the memory as the most important of faculties requiring disciplined development.

Learning to read and to remember fueled Christian's earlier heroism, and as an apt conclusion, he must instruct others in reading, in their own imitative acts, and in exercises of memory. Character collapses into action when Christian becomes a memory locus through which others affirm the promises. From the vantage of part II, he provides a variously "realized" text of his dangers and triumphs, his cautions and examples, which his family "read" more or less as they open riddles at Gaius's inn (263, 264). For them a sign explicates the deaths of Simple, Sloth, and Presumption (214); a stage bearing "a broad plate with a Copy of Verses Written thereon" records the site of Timorous and Mistrust (217); a "Scheme," a pillar, some battle debris including some of Christian's blood, and later a monument engraved with verses memorialize Christian's fight with Apollyon (236–40). It is of hermeneutical interest that this last item casts its message in the first person: "a Monument I stand, / The same to testifie"

(240). These markers are established about Christian but not by him. In their turn, however, in imitation of their forebear, the family deliberately erect similar markers to ease the passage of later pilgrims and to record their notable and edifying accomplishments (276, 245, 267). When they defeat Giant Despair (283), they set their marble marker with its new verses directly over Christian's warning pillar and thus publicize their correct interpretation. In a miniature of differences between parts I and II examined later, their reinscription deals not with a crisis of conversional psychology but with the novelistic history of their own community.

Part II of *Pilgrim's Progress* completes the transfer of the meaning of the hero's unique achievement on behalf of his society. The heroic or mythic boon for this culture is faith, choosing against this world and in favor of the unknown, and faith requires individual salvational action. Each person must make that choice and follow the Way independently. Insofar as he can teach, Christian will do so by signs and open-ended provocations to spiritual exercise, and insofar as others can learn they will do so by imitating the hero's example and hermeneutical dynamic. In such matters Christian is witnessing to his name and titular role, matters glossed by Bunyan's *Justification By an Imputed Righteousness*. There when Christ took upon himself flesh and blood, he "took not upon him a *particular* person, though he took to him a human body and soul; but that which he took was, as I may call it, a lump of the common nature of man; and by that, hold of the whole elect seed of Abraham. . . . Hence he, in a mystery, became *us*, and was counted as *all* the men that were or should be saved" (Offor 1:304; Bunyan's italics). It is in such a spirit that Gaius in part II can cite Christian's family heritage as deriving from the Ancestors at Antioch, Stephen, James, Paul, Peter, Ignatius, Romanus, Policarp, and the like (260). All are absorbed into the character of Christian as Christian himself is absorbed into the role of the savior whose name he bears. Through membership in such a line of inheritance, Christian transcends into the myth he himself inscribes.

Himself a follower of Christ's example, Christian's proper function is to multiply by generation and regeneration the community of the blessed. The narrative of Christian's pilgrimage becomes a text for study by his family, by other pilgrims encountered in part II, and by various stationary figures with whom Christian interacted during his passage. His biography inscribes an exemplary life along the lines of the advisory implicit in Puritan biography, "to emulat[e] the man insofar as he emulated Christ."

Christian has become a legendary figure by part II, not because the later pilgrims have a false sense of his history but because, as N. H. Keeble puts it, "the dross of circumstance has slipped away and the pure example remains."[15] Through such sectarian equivalents of the saint's life, the lives of extraordinary Puritan "visible saints" make their way into meditative spiritual exercise and into history.

CHAPTER THREE

The Scriptural Word

For the worde of God is an euident token of Gods loue
and our assurance of his defence, wheresoeuer it is obe-
diently receyued: it is the trial of the spirits: and as the
Prophet saieth, It is as a fyre and hammer to breake the
stonie heartes of them that resist Gods mercies offred by
the preaching of the same. Yea it is sharper then any two
edged sworde to examine the very thoghtes and to iudge the
affections of the heart, and to discouer whatsoeuer lyeth hid
vnder hypocrisie and wolde be secret from the face of God
and his Churche. So that this must be the first fundacion
and groundworke, according whereunto the good stones of
this building must be framed, and the euil tried out and
reiected.—Prefatory Epistle, *The Geneva Bible* (1560)

THE FOUNDATIONS of the Puritan worldview and of the individual Puritan's knowledge and action were the Scriptures, his own history, the
church community and ordinances, and meditation upon the experiential
world. Each of these categories has its own history, and each is the subject of a chapter below. The foundation of them all, as of the Reformation
itself, is a particular view of and use of the Bible, and this background
will launch the next stage of inquiry into Bunyan's *Pilgrim's Progress*, a
work both implicitly and explicitly about the Bible and the reading skills
and processes appropriate to it. Such an inquiry must also attend closely
to *Grace Abounding* because biblical texts provide not only much of its
activity and expression but its structuring principles as well.

Puritanism in the middle of the seventeenth century carried to the
extreme certain Reformation principles, particularly what one commentator calls "rigorous and systematic Bibliolatry."[1] At the core of existence

for believers such as Bunyan was the absolutely authoritative Scripture. It was an inexhaustible storehouse of wonders and revelations, the target and touchstone of all knowledge, human and divine, and the foundation of all principles of politics, church practice, and even of literary criticism. It was also each person's unifying and redemptive agency. Seventeenth-century Puritans sought to integrate the whole of their lives with the teaching of Scripture and to bring the Bible to bear on virtually every intellectual, practical, social, and experiential occasion. While submitting reason to the Word, they relied heavily on rational process to draw spiritually enlightening insights from it. Theirs was a theocentric and logocentric world, indeed a theologocentric one, and for them the logical is more than wittily embedded in the theological.

Puritans participated in three compelling textual activities, a reading of the Bible, a thoughtful, energetic, and creative processing of biblical texts, and a thoroughgoing application of the advantages thus acquired to the conduct of daily life, activities backgrounded in the Reformation emphasis on the Bible as the embodiment of divine truth, in the progressive dissemination of a vernacular Bible and a responding literacy throughout the later sixteenth and seventeenth centuries, and in the radical shift toward Protestant subjectivity and spiritual understanding and defiantly away from various religious representations associated with Roman Catholicism. In the absence of such traditional comforts as confession, penance, and sensuous rituals, they were thrown upon their own resources as Bible readers and interpreters to make sense out of their internal and external worlds. With the passage of time, it is not just literacy but the literary that becomes privileged. The system placed a high premium on unifying the personality, methodically ordering one's conduct, controlling the surrounding world, and in general leading an acutely alert, intelligent existence (Weintraub 231).

As U. Milo Kaufmann has thoughtfully explained, Puritan readers characteristically reduced *mythos* to *logos*, events to doctrine, the numinous to the logico-biblical. Their hermeneutics divorced exegesis from devotion and married it instead to homiletics.[2] They left behind Aristotelian *logos* as the thought, speeches, universal principles, and systematically philosophical dimension of a work, in favor of the scriptural *logos*, the text of the Bible as mediated by the Holy Spirit. Such a *Word* is authorized by John 1.1 ("In the beginning was the Word, and the Word was with God, and the Word was God"), John 1.14 ("And the Word was made flesh and dwelt among us"), and John 10.35 ("The scripture cannot be broken"). Moreover, the Puritan Word collapses the read and written Word into the delivered sermon, authorized by the Protestant principle that faith comes by hearing (Romans 10.17).

John S. Coolidge calls attention to Puritanism's dynamically Christocentric interactions with the Bible. It saw the Bible as existing to exalt participation in Christ's life and death and Paul's epistles as illuminating its unity. Characteristically, biblical meanings were centripetal not centrifugal for the Puritan, and in the principle developed by Calvin, the Word is *autopistos*, that is self-validating or self-authenticating, "sufficient in itself to convince one of the truth of its message."[3] For Puritans, the Scriptures, like so much else, were referenced to the Scriptures themselves, especially the Old to the New Testament, and their processings of the text took the form of analysis and synthesis, parsing texts and concording contexts. In terms of faculty psychology, although the imagination—that is the creative, participatory, and progressively illuminated component of the mind—helps in textual understanding, from whatever angle we view the matter, it is the memory that is of greatest importance within the Puritan psyche.

The Art of Prophesying by the Elizabethan Puritan William Perkins concisely formulates the basic Reformation views that the Bible so completely presents the truth and wisdom of God that "nothing may be either put to it or taken from it, which appertaineth to the proper end thereof" and that it "abideth inviolable and cannot pass until all that which it commandeth be fully accomplished." By its nature and operation, the truth is both discovered and examined (333–34). The authoritative 2 Timothy 3.15–17 speaks of "the holy scriptures, which are able to make thee wise unto salvation through faith which is in Christ Jesus. All scripture is given by inspiration of God, and is profitable for doctrine, for reproof, for correction, for instruction in righteousness: That the man of God may be perfect, throughly furnished unto all good works." Reading the Bible served as a compelling and defining discipline for the Puritan, and many, like Bunyan and Milton, had essentially memorized it.

Repeatedly, Bunyan pronounces his allegiance to the Bible's "perfect instruction" in all that is necessary for salvation, for the conduct of daily life, and for the judgment of all points of theology. *A Confession of My Faith* rehearses 2 Timothy 3.15–17 (Offor ii:601), and *A Few Sighs From Hell* ratifies Perkins's principle:

> The Scriptures spoken by the holy men of God, are a sufficient rule to instruct to salvation, them that do assuredly believe and close in with what they hold forth. . . . The Scriptures hold forth Gods

mind and will, of his love and mercy towards man, and also the
creatures carriage towards him from first to last. . . . Would thou
know what thou art, and what is in thy heart, then search the Scriptures, and see what's written in them. . . . The Scriptures I say, they
are able to give a man perfect instruction into any of the things of
God necessary to faith and godliness, if he have but an honest heart,
seriously to weigh and ponder the several things contained in them.
(1:323–25)

The Fear of God defines the written Word as synonymous with its title and
claims that "every jot and tittle thereof is for ever settled in Heaven, and
stands more stedfast than doth the world." As a corollary, "want of reverence of the word, is the ground of all disorders that are in the heart, life,
conversation, and in Christian Communion," and "all transgressions be-
ginneth at wandring from the word of God" (IX:16, 19, 20). *Grace Abounding* lists what Bunyan believes in as Faith, Christ, and the Scriptures and
again as God, Christ his Son, and the Scriptures (31, 32). 1 John 5.7 supports Bunyan's implanting of Scripture within the traditional Trinity by
listing "the Father, the Word, and the Holy Ghost."

Like Puritans generally, Bunyan devoted a great proportion of life to
the energetic pursuit of the counsel, rule, and enlightenment of the Bible.
Indeed, speaking of his early spiritual development, his autobiography
claims: "I was then never out of the Bible, either by reading or meditation,
still crying out to *God*, that I might know the truth, and way to Heaven
and Glory" (17), and *A Confession of My Faith* speaks of reexamining his
principles "a thousand times, by the word of God" (Offor II:593). His
works repeatedly prove the validity of even such extreme claims.

He captures many of his biblical attitudes in the verb *gospelize*, by
which he means thoroughly interweaving statements with the biblical
texts that support them or from which they are drawn.[4] The title-page
phrasing of *The Resurrection of the Dead*—"Asserted, and proved by, Gods
Word" (III:201)—signals such an intent. In an extreme case, *The Saints'
Knowledge of Christ's Love* makes at least 440 distinct references to the
Bible in its thirty-eight pages (Offor II:1). In *A Confession of My Faith*,
Bunyan avers that his principles and practice "stand and fall to none but
the word of God alone" (Offor II:593), and he calls any religious views
without direct scriptural backing "fictious, scriptureless notions" (607).
This allegiance confirms him in a number of controversies, against re-
quired baptism (*A Confession of My Faith*), against separate prayer meet-

ings for women (*A Case of Conscience Resolved*), against attendance at his parish church and use of the Book of Common Prayer, and in favor of his right and duty to preach despite civil laws (*A Relation of My Imprisonment*, and see *Grace Abounding* 87–88).

Bunyan's works constantly practice the logocentric inheritance of the Reformation, but *Of the Trinity, and a Christian* also lays down two rules for how to wrestle with difficult biblical questions. Its first "Preparative" expresses the absolute and a priori empowering of the Bible that is the most essential Puritan tenet: "Suffer thyself, by the authority of the word, to be persuaded that the scripture indeed is the word of God; the scriptures of truth, the words of the holy one; and that they therefore must be every one true, pure, and for ever settled in heaven" (Offor II:386). And again: "Be sure thou keep close to the word of God; for that is the revelation of the mind and will of God, both as to the truth of what is either in himself or ways; and also as to what he requireth and expecteth of thee, either concerning faith in, or obedience to, what he hath so revealed" (386). *The Doctrine of the Law and Grace Unfolded* extends this insistence: "thou must give more credit to one syllable of the written Word of the Gospel, then thou must give to all the Saints and Angels in Heaven and Earth" (II:191). Some biblical places are "more pregnant and pertinent" than others (*Some Gospel Truths* 1:48), but the overall wish is "that Scripture comes to be fulfilled on thy soul" and that the believer "not be contented untill he find his soul and Scripture together (with the thing contained therein) to embrace each other, and a sweet correspondency and agreement be between them" (*A Few Sighs From Hell* 1:267, 358).

The second "Preparative" in *Of the Trinity* dictates the faith and obedience implicit in the first. For Christians, "every thought, or carnal reasoning," is to be made "captive into obedience to Christ; that is, be made to stoop to the word of God, and to give way and place to the doctrine therein contained, how cross soever our thoughts and the word lie to each other" (Offor II:387). "To come to the word of God, as conceiting already that whatever thou readest, must either by thee be understood, or of itself fall to the ground as a senseless error" is "great lewdness, and also insufferable arrogancy" (Offor II 386). The authority for such a position is Romans 14.23: "Whatsoever is not of faith is sin." *Some Gospel Truths Opened According to Scripture* proffers the governing and humbling principle: "If thou wouldst not be deceived then, beware of slighting any known truth that thou findest revealed, or made known to thee in the Gospel; but honour, and obey it, in its place, be it (as thou thinkest) never so low" (1:27). Elsewhere Bunyan asserts that "in many points the gospel is above reason, but yet in never a one against it" (*Reprobation Asserted* Offor 11:350). To counterbalance threats from such pride, *Of the Trinity* registers the ideal: "To understand all mysteries, to have all knowledge, to be able to comprehend with all saints, is a great work; enough to crush the spirit, and to stretch the strings of the most capacious and widened soul that breatheth on this side glory, be they notwithstanding exceedingly enlarged by revelation" (Offor 11:386). His autobiography shows that Bunyan himself ran the risks of "put[ting] an *if* upon the allseeingness of God" (76) and sometimes supposing that Christianity, like other religions, could be but "a Fable and cunning Story," could be "but a think-so too" (31).

Grace Abounding describes how "the holy Mr. *Gifford*," the Bedford minister who aided Bunyan's conversion, taught him to discipline himself to the Word by refusing to trust any human explanation of theological matters, and instead always "to cry mightily to God, that he would convince us of the reality thereof, and set us down therein, by his own Spirit in the holy Word." Bunyan translates this principle into practice by praying "that in nothing that pertained to Gods glory and my own eternal happiness, he would suffer me to be without the confirmation thereof from Heaven." He finds himself immediately, fully, and often rewarded: "Truly, I then found upon this account the great God was very Good unto me, for to my remembrance there was not any thing that I then cried unto God to make known and reveal unto me but he was pleased to do it for me, I mean not one part of the Gospel of the Lord Jesus, but I was orderly led into it" (37). From this, he later generalizes that those whom "the Scriptures favour" will inherit bliss, but those they oppose and condemn perish for evermore (76).

Several dangers lurk behind extreme allegiance to the reformers' assumption that absolute truth inheres within the words of the Word. Even in their earliest history, Anabaptists differed from Lutherans and Calvinists in their more drastic search of the Scriptures, and of this danger the Anabaptist Bunyan, specifically the Particular Open-Communion Baptist Bunyan, would seem to be at risk (Bainton 95; Tindall 3–4). When William Foster accused him of taking the Scriptures too literally, Bunyan distinguished pronouncements the Bible intends to be taken literally, such as "He that believes shall be saved," from those that are to be understood through active endeavor (*A Relation of My Imprisonment* 110). When Foster complained that Bunyan could not fully understand Scripture because he knew no Greek, Bunyan cited Jesus' remark in Matthew 11.25 that to babes is revealed that which remains hidden from the wise and prudent (111). As pointed out by Perkins and Luther before him, the Word of God is true through both its nature and its operation, and Bunyan is saved from lapsing into this fundamentalist extreme by the thoroughness and range of his mastery of the Bible, by his personal flexibility and sincerity.

Bunyan himself was even less in danger of the other interpretational extremity, but many contemporaries carried too far the possibility invited by Reformation theology of substituting the individual experience of the Spirit for the discipline of the Word. Bunyan voices his objections in what is for him the strongest of terms. *Some Gospel Truths Opened* inveighs against such "Unstable Souls" as deluded Quakers, "loose Ranters, and light Notionists, with here and there a Legalist" and later against "the Ranters, Quakers, Drunkards, and the like." Such extreme "experiential" attitudes as the "inner light" opened the way to abuses and mutiplying sectarian division.[5] Bunyan required that the "opened" interpretation be always disciplined by the text and context of the Bible. Like other Puritans, he distinguished between "notional" knowledge and "spiritual" knowledge, the former relying on the self, the latter on the Word rightly processed and understood. *Saved by Grace* equates *notions* with "Fancies, Delusions, or meer *Thinkso's*" (VIII:206), and *Some Gospel Truths Opened* describes a Notionist as one who is "puffed up in his fleshly mind, and [who] advanceth himself above others, thinking but few may compare with him for religion and knowledge in the Scriptures."[6] The opposite are those who, like Bunyan himself, "receive truth in the love of the truth" and in whom "the more the head and heart is filled with the knowledge of the mysterie of Godlinesse, the more it is emptied of its own things" (1:16).

Bunyan is aware that unauthorized interpretation may arise because of the Bible's occasionally opaque or enigmatic surface. *Of the Trinity* assumes the possibility of harmonious reconciliation of all biblical statements no matter "how obscure, cross, dark, and contradictory soever they seem" to the deficient human intelligence (Offor II:386), and *Israel's Hope Encouraged* invokes the most benign of images to describe such scriptural occasions: "There is no single flower in God's gospel-garden, they are all double and treble" (Offor I:596). *An Exposition . . . of Genesis* sees Satan's temptation of Eve as a questioning of the simplicity of the Word's meaning and her fall as a failure to rely on the Word (Offor II:429–30, 428). Eve's example advises questioners to be suspicious of their assumptions and capacities and to be willing to pursue exhaustive textual inquiry, no matter how arduous, and concord all relevant passages. To do otherwise is to mangle the truth and be content with "notional" knowledge.

To the initiate, sound interpretation is possible because conversion entails the linguistic and literary transformation described in Bunyan's *Reprobation Asserted:* "Whoever receiveth the grace that is tendered in the gospel, they must be quickened by the power of God, their eyes must be opened, their understandings illuminated, their ears unstopped, their hearts circumcised, their wills also rectified, and the Son of God revealed in them" (Offor II:350, and similarly *The Desire of the Righteous Granted* Offor 1:749).

Conversion into the Spirit as well as the Word leads one to speak and understand what Puritans referred to as "the language of Canaan," that is to use familiar words with new and illuminated sense that takes into account not just words but grace, not just law but gospel. More technically, the language of Canaan is "the prophetic and metaphorical language used by God's chosen people when they talk of the kingdom of God and its realization in the last days" and "the mode of discourse to be enjoyed by those saints when the Scripture promises are fulfilled." An initiate into this language has undergone not merely a change of condition but a radical difference in kind: "When the gospel broke on a man it brought such a reorientation that all previous understanding appeared to have been inadequate and superficial, to have been going on mainly at an intellectual or 'notional' level only. For all the time the convert was 'under the law' he was certainly hearing about justification by faith and the promises of the gospel—only he did not really apply them to himself!" At its extreme, conversion amounts to a reversal of meaning as of values, even a "belief that the spiritual sense is normative and that socially constituted proper meaning is derivative."[7] The citizens of Vanity Fair accuse Christian and Faithful, among other things, of speaking "the language of *Canaan*" so that few understand them (90), and in *Pilgrim's Progress* part II, upon her spiritual awakening, Christiana "stunds" her neighbors by speaking this "new language" (gloss 181).

Bunyan's own conversion models less a reversal than an advance. Outward godly conduct, legal fears, and "notional" knowledge characterized Bunyan before he was "gospelized," before he encountered the faith of the women of Bedford (*Grace Abounding* 15). The early signs of his conversion were "a very great softness and tenderness of heart, which caused me to fall under the conviction of what by Scripture they asserted" and "a great bending in my mind to a continual meditating on them, and on all other good things which at any time I heard or read of" (15). As his conversion progresses, Bunyan experiences a newly enlivened, personalized, and transtemporal sense of the Scriptures and a new kind of participation in spiritual community. These changes reflect a growing preference for the "sweet and pleasant" gospels and Pauline epistles over the historical parts of the Bible.[8] They also reflect his gradual progress from mere convert to minister and the heightened reading skills and confidence required by such a calling.

It was not the Puritan reader alone who was active in the experience; the Bible itself was "kinetic" and "dynamic," showing, in John R. Knott's words, "the energy of the Spirit manifest[ing] itself in a continuing Reformation" (*Sword* 40, 4, 39). The Word functions both as construct and as process. As Bunyan explains, it both "stands by itself" and is "seconded with saving operation from heaven" (*The Acceptable Sacrifice* Offor 1:694). His *Saints' Privilege and Profit* divides the Word into letters, words, and meanings, attaching the first to ceremonial law, the second to Christ, and the third to processing an issue with relation to Christ (Offor 1:671). The usual agency for this third stage is, of course, the third person of the Trinity, for "the Holy Ghost must needs have a further reach, an intention of more glorious things" (*An Exposition . . . of Genesis* Offor 11:490). If Puritans were expected to close with the Word, they also anticipated the Word as spiritually opening itself to them, and in the ontological or anticlimactic emphasis so characteristic of Puritanism, it is initial textual awakenings that provide the greatest intensity of feeling and action. Textual openings, like the effectual callings they attend, are synonymous with "quickening, awakening, illuminating, and the bringing forth darkness into light" (Greaves, *John Bunyan* 61).

Bunyan eagerly courts the influx of the Word in what Puritans generally spoke of as "openings." Although no text is there involved, Christian models a spiritual opening when he escapes from Despair's dungeon by remembering the key of promise in his bosom. After a night of prayer has put him fully in touch with his own spiritual resources, he is able literally to "open" a series of doors to achieve physical and psychic freedom. *A Relation of My Imprisonment* dramatizes spiritual opening compactly in such observations as "God brought that word into my mind. . . . it came so fresh into my mind, and was set so evidently before me, as if the Scripture had said, Take me, take me" (115). God makes the Scriptures shine before Bunyan, dwell with him, and comfort him over and over (39). On one occasion he is "filled with admiration at the fitness, and also at the unexpectedness of the sentence," at "the rightness of the timing of it," and also at "the power, and sweetness, and light, and glory that came with it also" (59). The effects of the opening reach beyond illumination, refreshment, and laughter at destruction, to sometimes extraordinary insight into the power of the Word of God: "I have had sweet sights of the forgiveness of my sins in this place, and of my being with Jesus in another world. . . . I have seen that here, that I am perswaded I shall never, while in this world, be able to express; I have seen a truth in that Scripture" (96). As generally for Puritans "Faith comes by hearing," so for Bunyan on these occasions, "Tis the spirit in the word that is Gods ordinance" (115n.), and "it is the spirit that worketh Faith in the heart through hearing" (116).

Grace Abounding is made up of scores of occasions when the Word presented itself in these ways and compelled Bunyan's active responses. Typically, we see Bunyan as the passive receiver, even the victim, of the energetic Word, and the Word as "a strange, almost personified force" (Watkins 110). Texts may be supportive, even gentle, or assaultive, but always the arriving Scriptures are extraordinarily appropriate to immediate situations and his deepest needs. A verse will "fasten" or "drop" or "bolt in upon" him or "kindle fire" in him or "glance sweetly" at him or "visit his soul"; it may also trample upon or pinch him. Sometimes Bunyan feels a verse from Scripture so chasing after him or calling so loudly behind him that he looks over his shoulder expecting to see or meet it (52, 30–31). Brainerd Stranahan speaks of such textual "events" in *Grace Abounding* as "spring[ing] like wild animals or plummet[ing] like heavy weights" or "appear[ing] unexpectedly as welcome or unwelcome guests . . . endowed with individual personality." He generalizes that the events occur as "quick and irresistible inspiration, interrupting and even changing the direction of [Bunyan's] conscious intention."[9] Perhaps because at several points the voiced message can be described as an echo (59, 60), Kaufmann sees in Bunyan an "aural approach to a 'speaking' Word," the Scripture functioning as a voice to the inner ear and the voices of the Scripture and the self either merging or joining in dialogue (*Pilgrim's Progress* 240).

The familiar *Grace Abounding* presents surprising arrivals of spiritual openings to the convert, while the epistle "To the Godly Reader" prefaced to the unfamiliar *The Holy City* details the sort of opening that became possible for the experienced preacher, now writing from Bedford

jail. This sermon-writing and treatise-rewriting "event" draws prophetic
energy from its Revelation text:

> Upon a certain *First day*, I being together with my Brethren, in
> our Prison-Chamber, they expected that, according to our Custom,
> something should be spoken out of the Word, for our mutual Edifi-
> cation; but at that time I felt my self (it being my turn to speak) so
> empty, spiritless, and barren, that I thought I should not have been
> able to speak among them so much as five words of Truth, with Life
> and Evidence: but at last, it so fell out, that providentially I cast
> mine Eye upon the eleventh Verse of the one and twentieth Chap-
> ter of this Prophecie; upon which, when I had considered a while,
> methought I perceived something of that JASPER in whose Light you
> there finde this HOLY CITY is said to come or descend; wherefore
> having got in my Eye some dim glimmerings thereof, and finding
> also in my heart a desire to see further thereinto; I with a few groans
> did carry my Meditations to the Lord JESUS for a Blessing, which he
> did forthwith grant according to his Grace; and helping me to set
> before my Brethren, we did all eat, and were well refreshed; and be-
> hold also that while I was in the distributing of it, it so encreased in
> my hand, that of the Fragments that we left, after we had well dined,
> I gathered up this Basket-full. Methought the more I cast mine Eye
> upon the whole Discourse, the more I saw lie in it: Wherefore set-
> ting my self to a more narrow search, through frequent Prayer to
> God, (what first with doing, and then with undoing, and after that
> with doing again), I thus did finish it. (III:69–70)

An accompanying image testifies to the inexhaustibility of scriptural
meaning for the now active recipient: "Much more then I do here crush
out, is yet left in the Cluster" (70).

The relation of the written Word to the reading mind enacts the relation of the second to the third person of the Trinity. Perkins epitomizes
much of Reformation theology in asserting: "The principal interpreter of
the scripture is the Holy Ghost (2 Pet. 1.20). Moreover, he that makes the
law is the best and highest interpreter of the law. The supreme and absolute mean of interpretation is the scripture itself (Neh. 8.8)" (338). "Oh!"
exclaims Richard Sibbes, "the Spirit is the life and soul of the word."[10]
As Milton poses the relationship in *Paradise Lost*, postgospel eras have
been provided with "those written Records pure" of the Old and New
Testaments, but those texts are "not but by the Spirit understood" (XII:

513–14). Hebrews 8.10 speaks of the new covenant written upon the hearts of believers; 2 Corinthians 3.3 of faith and grace as "written not with ink, but with the Spirit of the living God; not in tables of stone, but in fleshy tables of the heart"; and Romans 2.15 of "the law written in their hearts, their conscience also bearing witness." What has been written is available to be read, and that reading attains equivalent authority. As the contemporary Thomas Case puts it, "*Scripture-Inference, is Scripture; that is to say, That which may be inferr'd from Scripture, by natural and necessary consequence, is to be received as the Scripture it self.* The Word of God *rightly interpreted,* is the Word of God." Along these lines, Gordon Campbell can define Puritan exegesis not as teasing doctrines out of the Bible but rather as reading already-believed-in doctrines into it.[11] Such reading operates out of Puritan assumptions that all textual units, even single isolated ones, will be richly edifying and that readers' efforts will be fully and even specifically rewarded, if not immediately, at least eventually.

Bunyan often attaches the third person of the Trinity to the interpreting process. *Saved by Grace* speaks of "*the Spirit of Revelation*" (VIII:192), a figure able perfectly to describe things and complete our knowledge (*The Saints' Privilege and Profit* Offor 1:662; and similarly 1:160, III:69, and Offor II:599). The psychodrama of *The Holy War* allegorizes the Holy Ghost as the first and chief teacher, "a revealer of those high and supernatural Mysteries that are kept close in the bosome of *Shaddai* my Father." It contrasts with the other teacher, Conscience, whose domain includes "Moral Vertues," "Civil and Natural duties," and "all things humane and domestick" (140, 142). The Holy Ghost as teacher is a native of heaven, knows the mind of the Father, shows his good will toward mankind, brings lost things to remembrance, and tells of things to come (139).

Both as convert and minister Bunyan often experienced spiritual openings, and he expresses his great wish that his own writings, echoing the Bible, will allow readers similar illuminations and creative opportunities. The introduction to *The Strait Gate* urges his audience to "Reade me therefore, yea, read me and compare me with the *bible;* and if thou findest *my* doctrine, and *that* book of God concur; embrace it, as thou wilt answer the contrary in the day of Judgment: This awakening work (if God will make it so) was prepared for thee" (v:69). The treatise goes on to equate Bunyan's readers with the apostles as readers (v:73–74). *A Few Sighs From Hell* self-consciously comments: "I might enlarge upon these things, but shall leave them to the Spirit of the Lord, which can better by ten thousand degrees enlarge them on thy heart and conscience, then I can upon a piece of paper" (1:278). *The Doctrine of the Law and Grace Unfolded* invites readers to approach it "with an understanding heart" and to "make a pause, and sit still one quarter of an hour, and muse a little in thy minde thus with thy self" (11:16, 35).

When the introductory verses of *Pilgrim's Progress* part I invite the reader to "lay my Book, thy Head and Heart together" (7), they argue that because Bunyan's works depend so heavily in inspiration and execution upon the Bible, the reader should accept Bunyan's equivalent authority. A concluding poem reinforces the distinction between successful and unsuccessful interpreting. Right interpretation by an honest mind seeks and sees "the substance of my matter" and "do[es] good," but "misinterpreting," which plays only "with the *out-side* of my Dream," leads to self-hurt, evil, and dross (164; Bunyan's italics). Bunyan's marginal glosses confirm these interactions. Text and gloss work together, as do reading and interpreting, prevenience and grace, especially within the recommendation of 1 Corinthians 14.26, "Let all things be done unto edifying," a biblical context where "all things" include a psalm, a doctrine, a tongue, a revelation, and an interpretation. The seeker after understanding, as in Isaiah 40.31, properly waits upon the Lord in order to receive new strength.

Puritans reached beyond faithfulness to biblical truth in the direction of progressive illumination. They welcomed Luther's insistence that Scripture should be interpreted by Scripture and that interpretation should follow the rule of faith. "God's word was never glimpsed as a pure intelligible," as Georgia B. Christopher explains: "It was not 'heard' at all until applied to some palpable heart." When God's words take hold in the believer's heart, in Luther's view, "the Word imparts its qualities to the soul": "The soul which clings to them with a firm faith will be closely united with them and altogether absorbed by them that it not only will share in all their power but will be saturated and intoxicated by them. If a touch of Christ healed, how much more will this most tender spiritual touch, this absorbing of the Word, communicate to the soul all things that belong to the Word." For Luther too, faith is a de facto sacrament; it "consummates the Deity . . . creat[es] the Deity, not in the substance of God but in us."[12]

Reformation Protestantism by definition cast the believer in the role of literary critic, and Puritan experiences of the Word reach beyond literacy and literalness into the arena of the distinctively "literary" just at that point where the Word gives way to interpretation, where the second person of the Trinity gives way to the third. Christopher uses the word "syntactical" to describe this epistemology or aesthetic on the grounds that the same vocabulary, as for example *sermo*, describes "the God who speaks, the language that conveys the divine word, the Spirit who underlines it, and the heart (or faith) that hears the word." For Puritans, Christopher judges, "Spiritual mystery resided, not in *being*, but in grasping, via words, the *relation* between beings" (21; Christopher's italics).

The believer succeeds not just in reading but in literary experience conceived more broadly as the fresh illuminations of individual tropes and the reordering of interrelationships (i.e., syntax). In both these formats, the Bible produces lively spiritual adventures, exploiting what we saw earlier as the metaphorics of allegory and the metonymics of myth. While the metaphoric implies analogy or transfers meaning from one arena of experience to another, the metonymic substitutes cause for effect, effect for cause, sign for thing signified, container for thing contained, and the like. In a telling instance in Interpreter's house, an initial metaphorical equation for the oil of grace soon deepens into a metonym (32). Through literary play the reader discovers clear and relevant meanings in dark Scriptures as text and interpretation energize each other under the influence of the Holy Spirit (Christopher 21, 127, 126). Both the tropes and the textual fluidity conduce not to idiosyncratic indulgence but to disciplined discovery of truth, and as his theological treatises often show, Bunyan was comfortable handling figurative Scriptures not just as *logos* but also as *poesis*.

Through complex interactions of text and reading process, Word and Spirit, Puritans lived within a dispensation not only of revelation but also of progressive revelation. They insisted upon both a solid systematic reading of an authoritative and unalterable Word and the individual believer's pursuit of increased cognitive understanding at each stage. As Maureen Quilligan observes relative to *Pilgrim's Progress*, "the proper way to read is to go on reading" (122). In a continuous and inconclusive meditational process, each newly achieved insight discards its predecessors and paves the way for its successors. Milton's *Areopagitica* images the dynamic action as "To be still searching what we know not, by what we know, still closing up truth to truth as we find it" (*Poems* 741–42).

Spiritually enlivening textual interactions are properly backgrounded, as we have seen, in Luther. They are also and more simply backgrounded in the contemporary Ramistic educational system favored by Puritans in

England, America, and the Continent. The key to study, the mind, and reality itself for Ramus's followers lay in their version of the two activities of logic, invention and disposition. Invention or discovery aligns with spiritual openings. In traditional or Aristotelian logic and rhetoric, the student examines a thing in order to find its arguments—cause/effects, subject/adjuncts, and the like. Collapsing rhetoric into logic, Ramistic logic views the thing as itself an argument voicing its own meanings, and its student seeks the nature of reality as well as a perfected understanding. To know something is to know its causes, for all knowledge is a knowledge of causes, and for the Ramist the first or efficient and the final or end causes equate with the deity. To know a thing is therefore to know God's creativity and purposes for it as well. Such lessons Ramists believed to inhere in the thing itself, and their task was therefore to sufficiently open their postlapsarian selves to achieve that revelation. It is a small matter to adjust this system so that the thing studied, the argument, the logical place, is also the biblical text or place. The student's task remains the same: Discovery is the alert receptivity to a priori reality which is also and therefore revelation.

Ramistic assumptions of inherent meaning also explain the Puritan transformation of fourfold medieval allegory and underlie their views of "literary" experience. Milton's position is characteristic: "Each passage of scripture has only a single sense, though in the Old Testament this sense is often a combination of the historical and the typological."[13] Despite the belief in one single sense of Scripture, actual interpretations could in fact be tropological or anagogical or otherwise multivalent or polysemous on the assumption that what is discovered actually exists as part of or within the unit itself not as an applied or derived overlay imposed externally. In this as in other matters the Puritan not only read but also "experienced" the text.

In the second half of Ramistic logic, disposition or arrangement also turns in upon itself. Where the Aristotelian student deployed the arguments earlier "invented" so as to develop and present a persuasive case, the Ramist's task is to "dispose" or align his discoveries with what was already known, and for the Puritan the a priori attaches to divine purposes and, of course, texts. The system assumes that the axiomatic compels assent, and it allows for doubtful cases to be resolved by way of the syllogism, especially the disjunctive syllogism (a category not admitted in Aristotelian logic): X is either a or b; but X is (or is not) a; therefore X is not (or is) b. The whole system is designed to confirm old truths, not discover new ones. As its careful students Perry Miller and Walter Ong have shown, it is a logic for dogmatists rather than original thinkers. Under the rubric of Method, the system arranges and rearranges known data in prioritized arrays running, for example, from generals to specifics.[14] When the Bunyan of the late theological treatises assumes full responsibility for guiding his flock toward helpful and memorable prioritizings in matters of faith and salvation, he is practicing Ramistic disposition, whereas the younger Bunyan of *Grace Abounding* and *Pilgrim's Progress* part I, the private rather than the public man, is more concerned with discovery, heightened awareness, Ramistic invention. In both the autobiography and the allegory, an inarticulate and uncomprehending but willing reader gives way to a highly articulate and authoritative bearer of the Word for the comfort and edification of those around him.

◄◙| I |◙►

Pilgrim's Progress at once gospelizes human experience and literalizes biblical metaphor. I am not presently concerned with the practice, often apparent in *Grace Abounding*, of retrospectively attaching a biblical parallel to an experience or sprinkling the text with biblical snatches, but rather with the allegory's presentation of *logos* as *mimesis*, its translation of the Word into narrative actions. This takes many forms from the simple act of reading in a book to complex reifications of internal conflict. *Pilgrim's Progress* backgrounds the Way (esp. John 14.6), Christian's rags (Isaiah 64.6), Christian's burden (Psalms 38.4), and so on, with biblical citations and presents a hero who is definitively a reader—of a book, parchment rolls, and a map. Because a number of characters share their experiences of reading, interpreting, and applying the Bible to their lives, the narrative as a whole becomes a layered reenactment as well as a progressively revealed commentary upon it. It also develops a homology between narrative action and the audience's reading activity. Bunyan's allegory "make[s] the action of the narrative parallel the process of reading, so that as readers read the action, they are, in reality, reading about their own reading experience" (Quilligan 254).

In an enactment of this layering, the most striking visual feature of *Pilgrim's Progress*, its marginal glossing, provides a strategy for taking advantage of Puritan uncertainty, self-consciousness, and biblical allegiance, and also for keeping the reading process itself fluid and therefore open to progressive insights. Glosses guide, regulate, and ensure proper interpretation of the actions and doctrines they accompany and high- light. Bunyan borrows the device from the Bible to pressure his readers to practice the compounded reading he himself found so enriching. His allegory's glosses are briefer and more scattered than those of the 1560 Geneva Bible, where each page allows half an inch of glossing for every two inches of the double-columned text. Bunyan seeks similar results by supplying additional information, interconnecting books of the Bible, and generally invigorating the texts to which they are attached. *The Holy War* images marginal glosses as windows (5), and a number of his minor works explicitly refer readers to their own marginal data (e.g., *The Life and Death of Mr. Badman* 181, 264, and see also 216; *The Saints' Privilege and Profit* Offor 1:657; *Of Antichrist and His Ruin* Offor 11:53; *An Expo- sition . . . of Genesis* Offor 11:448–49, 454, 474, and 496; *Of the House of the Forest of Lebanon* Offor 111:520; *A Holy Life* 1X:283, 316; and *The Advocatship of Jesus Christ* X1:174, 190).

The glosses of *Pilgrim's Progress* are not a reliable index to the content they attend. They are sometimes descriptive, sometimes moral and inter- pretive, sometimes exclamatory, and sometimes merely biblically refer- ential. We expect glosses to encapsulate memorable instruction especially by enfolding it within a cited biblical text, but Bunyan often subverts such expectations. He sometimes cites the Bible excessively, sometimes— when such citation is called for—not at all; sometimes he errs in both extremes in the same paragraph. Not only do some of the marginal notes not provide keys to their episodes, but instead some episodes seem to ex- plicate their glosses.[15] The energy flows from text to gloss but also from gloss to text as the occasional marginal index fingers literally point out. The double flow of energy accommodates the conflicting Puritan goals of affirming familiar doctrine already securely registered in the memory, but also provoking new insights. The goals are both stability and progress, both a retreat to faith and a fresh illumination.

Because a single sentence may be compounded of a half-dozen glances at Scripture, and because the narrative so often interacts with its biblical glosses, *Pilgrim's Progress* part I contains literally hundreds of "actions" of the Word. It generally embodies defeats and victories, embattlements and restorations, with regard to texts, interpretations, and applications of the biblical Word, and its hero develops clear and increasing skills in resolv- ing difficult matters by achieving biblical texts. Although many narrative and Puritan elements in this work may be judged as "antiprogressive"

and anticlimactic, Christian's interactions with the Bible show identifi-
ably cumulative skill and success, even though the Bible is taken to be a
collection of implosive single sentences, each independently decisive and
unpredictably connected to the overall narrative design (Damrosch 154).
To the relatively unscriptural modern reader, the interplay between allegorical text and these fragmented biblical pre-texts may at first appear
random, but within Bunyan's larger design that randomness creates its
own kind of unity. Through acts of concording and typology, textual
fusions supplant confusion. One signal of Christian's heroic progress is an
ability to collate, concord, apply, and generally to unify his understanding of the book by which he is identified at the outset and into whose
marriage, feast, and transcendent community he is absorbed at the end
of part I.

From the opening paragraph, Christian defines himself as one who
has accepted the absolute authority of the Bible over his immediate and
ultimate fate. Bunyan's *Questions About the Nature and Perpetuity of the
Seventh-Day Sabbath* supplies the motto of such an emblem: "Reading, I
mean, of the divine testimony, is ordained of God, for us to find out the
mind of God, both as to faith and our performance of acceptable service
to him" (Offor II:363). The effects of Bunyan's "closing" with the Word
show up almost at once in his ability to add *saved* to his initial cry of
lamentation. *The Strait Gate* calls this key addition "a word of worth and
goodness and blessedness" (v:72). Christian's questions are gospelized by
Mark 10.17 where the rich man asks, "What shall I do that I may inherit
eternal life?" (and similarly Matthew 19.16, Luke 3.10, 12, 14, 10.25, and
18.18). Acts 2.37–38 answers "Repent, and be baptized," and Acts 16.30–
31 presents Paul and Silas's advisory to the keeper of the prison, "Believe
on the Lord Jesus Christ, and thou shalt be saved, and thy house" (and
see Acts 9.6, 22.10). *Pilgrim's Progress* glosses both references. Bunyan's
glossing is partial rather than exhaustive, but he expects his readers to
draw upon the fuller range of reference. That range here includes both
the parabolic rich man and the apostle Paul whose story as chronicled in
Acts provided the model for Puritan life history and whose conversion,
ministry, and writings supplied their most essential enactments of both
doctrine and uses.

A network of gospelized reading undergirds *Pilgrim's Progress*. Christian's addition of the word *saved* coincides precisely with the arrival
of Evangelist, whom Kaufmann equates with the gospel and later with
"the divine Word, peripatetic, seeking men out where they are, and guid-

ing them aright in their Christian walk" (*Pilgrim's Progress* 17, 68, and see 106–7). On their initial meeting, Evangelist's gift of the Parchment-Roll with its inscription, "Fly from the wrath to come" (Matthew 3.7—gloss 10), gospelizes Christian's impetus for flight from the City of Destruction, but the initially terrifying inscription is itself translated into the language of Canaan when the scroll message becomes redemptive at the sepulcher: "This Roll was the assurance of his life, and acceptance at the desired Haven" (38, 49).

A sequence of textual openings signals Christian's spiritual progress. In the early and insecure stages, he tends to be overwhelmed by embodiments of Old Testament threats. A gloss to Exodus 19.18 and 16 reminds us, should the referencing be necessary, that the flashes of fire from Mount Sinai are the Ten Commandments (Exodus 20, and see the first half of *The Doctrine of the Law and Grace Unfolded*). On a more encouraging note, a miniature spiritual opening on the way up Hill Difficulty awakens the sleeping Christian and speeds him on his way with the text *"Go to the Ant, thou sluggard, consider her ways, and be wise"* (42–43, and Proverbs 6.6). When experiencing an opening, the believer may pause as Christian does when he regains his scroll to "g[i]ve thanks to God for directing his eye to the place where it lay" (45). *Place* as elsewhere in *Pilgrim's Progress* is both topographical and textual *locus*.

Reading and interpretational processes are foregrounded too when Christian and Hopeful "read" the opening *"Remember Lots Wife"* (108). This memorial icon invites the traveler-readers to remember or "discover" the biblical context from which the advisory is drawn, specifically that although Lot's wife escaped one judgment or destruction, she soon succumbed to another and more subtle one. In *Pilgrim's Progress*, Lot's wife is linked to the preceding Demas, a biblical figure who forsook Paul, as recorded in 1 Timothy 4.10, "having loved this present world." Since the negative example of Lot's wife occurs frequently in his works, we must assume Bunyan found this opening particularly rewarding. *Solomon's Temple Spiritualized* likens a covetous minister to Lot's wife (Offor III:475); *The Barren Fig-Tree* invokes her precedent to admonish the graceless professor who will not or cannot repent (v:58, 104); and *The Heavenly Footman* contrasts her with Lot himself who "did [not] so much as once look where she was, or what was become of her, his Heart was indeed upon his Journey, and well it might" (v:177, and see also v:147).[16] The icon thus compounds reading, memory, travel, and autobiography.

Christian's last and most definitive opening occurs in two phases as he is crossing the River of Death. "Then I saw in my Dream that *Christian* was as in a muse a while; to whom also *Hopeful* added this word, *Be of good cheer, Jesus Christ maketh thee whole:* And with that, *Christian* brake out with a loud voice, Oh I see him again! and he tells me, *When thou passest through the waters, I will be with thee, and through the Rivers, they shall not overflow thee.* Then they both took courage, and the enemy was after that as still as a stone, until they were gone over" (158). The first exhortation, mediated by Hopeful, begins by concording Christ's encouragement at Matthew 9.2, Matthew 14.27, Mark 6.50, Acts 23.11, and especially John 16.33: "In the world ye shall have tribulation: but be of good cheer; I have overcome the world." Paul's cheering of his shipmates amidst the tempest in Acts 27.22 and 25 is particularly apt as well. It ends by recalling the various persons to whom Christ says "Thy faith hath made thee whole" in Matthew 9.22, Mark 5.34, Mark 10.52, Luke 9.48, Luke 17.19, and similarly Acts 9.34. The second exhortation, deriving from Christian himself, interweaves the historical and experiential data of an Old Testament place with the more theoretical and aural New Testament promise. The text quotes Isaiah 43.2, and a marginal gloss interprets: "When thou passest through the waters, I will be with thee; and through the rivers, they shall not overflow thee: When thou walkest through the fire, thou shalt not be burned; neither shall the flame kindle upon thee." The typologically initiated reader will "re-collect" not just the text but also the context, specifically that Isaiah 43.1 expresses the New Testament promise in the strongest of terms: "Fear not: for I have redeemed thee, I have called thee by thy name; thou art mine." Such promise, ratified by Christian's typologizing, and thus going within and beyond the immediate text, signals his redemption.

As these late occasions show Christian responding to Scripture with the full and fruitful aid of the Spirit, so his early openings assume the absolute authority of the Bible, but a Bible not yet adequately absorbed and "useful" to the recent convert. Early on the Way Christian offers Obstinate and Pliable a chance to read his book. The former responds "Tush . . . away with your Book," while Pliable—"the epitome of the practical man" (Knott, *Sword* 147)—takes enough interest to ask if Christian believes that "the words of [his] Book are certainly true." When Christian answers, "Yes verily, for it was made by him that cannot lye," together they rehearse the book's New Testament promises of a blissful community and saints and crowns of glory, "enough," says Pliable, "to ravish ones heart." In a hope that comes across as somewhat fragile they speak too of how to attain these desired goals (11, 13–14).

Fragile too is the conviction of the Christian who is unable to articulate his understanding of the book even to Pliable's friendly inquiry and who has to reply merely by reading further from the book itself. He is overwhelmed by his authority, and his heavy and mechanical reliance on the Bible, reflected in the marshaled glossings, places Christian at risk of, at one extreme, ignorance and, at the other, of notional knowledge, or of the combination of the two deriving from disproportional accidents of textual supply. Christian is emotionally and conversationally unstable, as well as intellectually so, impelled forward negatively from Destruction, then impelled forward positively by the opposite extreme of ultimate promise. In narrative terms, becoming heedless (14) in their conversation about the ultimate kingdom, Christian and Pliable fall suddenly into the Slough of Despond. Although the Evangelist can materialize to guide him away from such desperations, clearly Christian needs to develop his own interpretational skills, a matter to whose depiction *Pilgrim's Progress* devotes sharply focused and richly varied ingenuity.

⋅❦❘ I I ❘❧⋅

COMMENTARY ON *Pilgrim's Progress* never fails to highlight the importance of the Interpreter's house, a site that dramatizes textual supply and processing, the interaction of the Word and the illuminating Holy Spirit. In Joseph Campbell's terms this is the threshold, encapsulating the major action to follow. Because the house offers "a brief training in hermeneutical procedure" (Kaufmann, *Pilgrim's Progress* 61–62), it is a point of some importance that its scriptural glosses often cite either Acts or the Pauline epistles. St. Paul handed down the procedures for reading the Old Testament in the light of the New, and for later readers his mediating presence is itself a constant factor in the interpretive transaction. Indeed in *The Pauline Renaissance in England: Puritanism and the Bible*, John Coolidge generalizes that "a Pauline understanding of scripture is in fact the matrix of Puritan thought" and endorses Luther's view that the Epistle to the Romans is " 'a light and a way in unto the whole scripture.' " Bunyan is characteristically Puritan in identifying Paul as "the greatest proficient" in the knowledge of Christ (*The Saints' Knowledge of Christ's Love* Offor 11:23). He speaks elsewhere of "Sweet Paul" and "this blessed apostle . . . ready and willing always to embrace the cross for the word's sake." [17]

The Interpreter repeatedly takes Christian by the hand, an action seventeenth-century Puritans identified with faith (Kaufmann, *Pilgrim's*

Progress 62), and his house presents Christian with a series of "profit-able" (61) texts that differ from spiritual openings in being mediated by a guide. Christian's experiences here model reading and meditation. Access to the Interpreter requires patient effort and repeated knockings (i.e., prayer). The Interpreter's seven sites or sights, which Christian sees with the aid of a candle (i.e., "Illumination," gloss 28), divide between, on the one hand, mirrorings of the hero and his past and future roles and, on the other, various Christian polarizations that sort the religious mysteries into the traditional Puritan categories of promise and threat (Kaufmann, *Pilgrim's Progress* 68). Christian responds to most of the tableaux with what becomes a choric question, "What means [sometimes "meaneth"] this?" The rooms are deliberately "secret," opaque in surface, revelatory only to those who are in the house or have the Interpreter at hand, in other words the Elect. The first site/sight layers secrecy and revelation as a picture behind and beyond a door within a private room. It occurs as a portrait, the others as emblems or parabolic dramas, "univocal statements in deed" or "holographs projected from the invisible world teach[ing] not merely doctrine but also perception," quickly transgressing empiri-cal limits to define the nature of apprehension.[18] The secret truths, in Kaufmann's words, "must be searched out, emptied from riddles and mys-teries, drawn up from the deeps, and in every case sought in pureness of intention" (*Pilgrim's Progress* 63).

Several of the Interpreter's scenes invoke the metaphor of pilgrimage, and since "the Way" is at once a topographical route, a conduct of life, a metaphor for Christ, and an encompassing reading process, here Chris-tian integrates the elements of his pilgrimage, his past and his future alter-natives, and in general "gird[s] up his loins" for the journey ahead. Since the integrative interpretational process is also always self-transcending, new sights and insights obliterate preceding lesser awarenesses and both embody progressive revelation and open the future to creative insecuri-ties. The Interpreter deposits important lessons in Christian's memory for later retrieval and application, and from the vantage of House Beautiful Christian later recalls the fourth, sixth, and seventh tableaux, specifi-cally "How Christ, in despite of Satan, maintains his work of Grace in the heart; how the Man had sinned himself quite out of hopes of Gods mercy; and also the Dream of him that thought in his sleep the day of Judgement was come" (48).

The text and interpretational process of the first scene reverberate alle-gorically within the narrative. Christian is shown "a brave Picture" of "a very grave Person": "It had eyes lift up to Heaven, the best of Books in its hand, the Law of Truth was written upon its lips, the World was behind its back; it stood as if it pleaded with Men, and a Crown of Gold did hang over its head" (29). At first glance, the answer to Christian's question, "What means this?" is that the figure presents Christ, but the glossed Scriptures interiorize both portrait and process. The Interpreter's explication—"the meaning of the Picture" and "Why he shewed him the Picture first" (glosses 29)—collapses Christic rebirth into the interpretative act. "Unfold[ing] dark things to sinners" (29), the Interpreter summarizes: "the man whose Picture this is, is the only Man, whom the Lord of the Place whither thou art going, hath Authorized, to be thy Guide in all difficult places thou mayest meet with in the way" (29). That "authorized" guide conflates Christ and the Holy Ghost (i.e., Interpreter) working with and within Christian in the Protestant paradigm of each individual wrestling salvation from interaction with the Bible. Finally, when the compound figure, who despises the things of this world and loves "his Masters service" and future glory, is targeted upon the Way, emphasis shifts from doctrine to uses.

Three biblical glosses foreground the interpretational process rather than the visuals of the scene:

1 Corinthians 4.15: For though ye have ten thousand instructers in Christ, yet have ye not many fathers: for in Christ Jesus I have begotten you through the gospel.

Galatians 4.19: My little children, of whom I travail in birth again until Christ be formed in you.

1 Thessalonians 2.7: But we were gentle among you, even as a nurse cherisheth her children.

These glosses do not acknowledge biblical analogues or even verbal borrowings. Their role rather is to compound the interpretational transaction. Given St. Paul as the model of textual interpretation, these passages from his epistles highlight the literary and linguistic rebirths that accompany initiation into the language of Canaan and reward responsive readers.

This first static portrait gives way to succeeding tableaux vivants where action becomes more important than character. The first, fifth, sixth, and seventh center on a single more or less human agent. The second, third, and fourth depict the operation of opposites. The second takes place in a large unswept parlor where the Interpreter calls upon a male sweeper who creates choking dust but then calls upon a damsel who, by sprin-kling water on the dust, succeeds in cleaning the room. The Interpreter responds to Christian's question of meaning here by equating the parlor with "the heart of a Man that was never sanctified by the sweet Grace of the Gospel" (30), the dust with original sin, the male sweeper with Old Testament law, and the damsel with the gospel, a series of equations that instructs the inquirer in the nature of metaphor.

This tableau receives two sets of glosses. The first, focused on the law, translates Christian's recent trial at Mount Sinai into full and gospelized understanding. Here as there, "the Law, instead of cleansing the heart (by its working) from sin, doth revive, put strength into, and increase it in the soul, even as it doth discover and forbid it, for it doth not give power to subdue" (30). To *revive it* draws upon Romans 7.6: "But now we are deliv-ered from the law, that being dead wherein we were held; that we should serve in newness of spirit, and not in the oldness of the letter." To *put strength into it* draws upon 1 Corinthians 15.56: "The sting of death is sin; and the strength of sin is the law." To *increase it* draws from Romans 5.20: "Moreover the law entered, that the offense might abound. But where sin abounded, grace did much more abound." The first of these Pauline authorizations glances at the principle formulated more fully in 2 Corin-thians 3.6: "For the letter killeth, but the spirit giveth life," a principle governing the whole operation of interpretation.

The second set of glosses leaves behind the law in favor of the gos-pel whereby "is sin vanquished and subdued, and the soul made clean, through the Faith of it; and consequently fit for the King of Glory to inhabit" (30).

John 15.3: Now ye are clean through the word which I have spoken unto you.

Ephesians 5.26: That he might sanctify and cleanse it with the washing of water by the word.

Acts 15.9: And put no difference between us and them, purifying their hearts by faith.

Romans 16.25–26: Now to him that is of power to stablish you according to my gospel, and the preaching of Jesus Christ, according to the revelation of the mystery, which was kept secret since the world began, But now is made manifest, and by the scriptures of the prophets, according to the commandment of the everlasting God, made known to all nations for the obedience of faith.

John 15.13: Greater love hath no man than this, that a man lay
down his life for his friends.

The first three references "illustrate"—that is, make lustrous as well as
exemplify—the successful action of the tableau, the cleansing, and interiorize and "verbalize" its subject. The fourth functions differently, to
interiorize not the subject but the process and thus to highlight the comprehensive and unifying action of interpretation. Before this threshold
site, the Old Testament was exclusively real and compelling and the New
Testament elusive, but now Interpretation fully empowers the New Testament. This tableau, like the former one, applies its lesson to Christian's
recent experiences and encapsulates interpretation's re-vision of memory.

The third and fourth linked scenes sort out attitudinal options within
the individual heart, now "a little Room" not "a very large Parlor." The
third images the contrast through an elder boy representing discontented
Passion, who is attached to the immediate rewards of this world, and
a younger boy representing wise Patience, who is quietly awaiting the
glory of that which is to come. Both the Interpreter and Christian progressively expound this scene. Its visual data project moral polarities
and thus the expected, while its biblical texts feature Christian paradox
and the unexpected. By way of Luke 16, and the Dives/Lazarus contrast,
the first paradox—that the first shall be last and the last first—recalls
Matthew 19.30, Matthew 20.16, Mark 9.35, Mark 10.31, and Luke 13.30
(and see *A Few Sighs From Hell*, a full-length consideration of Dives and
Lazarus). The second paradox, by way of 2 Corinthians 4.18, teaches that
"*the things that are seen, are* Temporal; *but the things that are not seen,
are* Eternal" (32). This second authority augments the gospels with an
interpretative Pauline overlay.

The fourth scene similarly images a hearthfire on which the devil casts
quenching water but Christ secretly casts fueling oil. "This fire," explains
Interpreter, "is the work of Grace that is wrought in the heart" (32). The
Interpreter here teaches the secret—literally behind the scenes—workings of Christ to maintain the operations of Grace in the soul. This enacts
the radical or first cause of Christ himself fueling the interpretational
process and the deeper understanding toward which it reaches.

When Christian poses his question "What means this?" for the second
time, the Interpreter responds that "notwithstanding what the Devil can
do, the souls of his people prove gracious still," a proposition glossed with
2 Corinthians 12.9: "And he said unto me, My grace is sufficient for thee:
for my strength is made perfect in weakness. Most gladly therefore will

I rather glory in my infirmities, that the power of Christ may rest upon me." Readers of *Grace Abounding* (64ff.) will recall "My grace is sufficient for thee" as the textual opening that relieved Bunyan of years of anxious terror that he like Esau had betrayed his birthright and damned himself. Within the allegory, 2 Corinthians 12.9 deepens the paradox beyond the preceding tableau. Stanley Fish's explication of this scene supports his general view that the action at Interpreter's house is "delayed revelation, which has the effect of widening a perspective that had been assumed to be full and adequate" (*Self-Consuming Artifacts* 238, and cf. *Saved by Grace* VIII:203). Specifically, the revealed meaning of the water here controverts the metaphorical water that cleansed dust in the second tableau. Now fire turns out to be not the effect of hell and water not grace thrown upon it; in fact, fire equates with grace, and water with the devil. It is a case of interpretation imposed upon rather than generated by the visibilia of the tableaux (Fish, *Self-Consuming Artifacts* 239), and the reversal of expectation thus proves 2 Corinthians 4.18 on temporal visibilia and eternal invisibilia. The Interpreter teaches that persistence and openness to the unexpected create the context for realizing both instruction and faith.

As the first pair of scenes glance at Christian's past and the second pair at present attitudes, so the last three visualize future possibilities. They also break down interpretational barriers between the scene and the seer. In the fifth a valiant armed man battles his way into a beautiful stately palace, a role in which Bunyan projected himself in *The Life and Death of Mr. Badman* (10). As Christian and the Interpreter watch, one valiant man enrolls his name with the doorkeeper and battles the armed guard with sword and helmet until, much wounded, he achieves entry and is welcomed to eternal glory. From the Ephesians 6 armor to the golden raiment of transcendence, the details of this tableau encapsulate the Way and the means of *Pilgrim's Progress* part I and compound way-faring and war-faring, two favorite Puritan self-projections with Pauline roots.

Although this scene involves more space, more characters, and more activity than previous ones, Christian is able without his guide's help to interpret it as a mirror of his spiritual and narrative roles. His usual question of meaning is here replaced by "May we go in thither?" (33), a question that advances interpretation to an imitation of the vigorous effort here enacted. The only gloss to the scene is Acts 14.22: "Confirming the souls of the disciples, and exhorting them to continue in the faith, and that we must through much tribulation enter into the kingdom of God." This gloss encapsulates the textual event but does not proffer a metatextual commentary on interpretational issues, perhaps because textual understanding and application are now so fully integrated by and within Christian himself that self-consciousness about process gives way fully to eager forward motion.

The sixth scene also glances at the larger narrative shape, this time in the form of a caged man in a dark room, an emblem of the despair that threatens Christian from the beginning to the end of his travels. Here Christian so much "closes with" the text or "enters into" the act of interpretation that he actively questions not the Interpreter but the man himself (34–35). This inert and purposeless despair figure, expecting only an eternity of damnation, inverts the valiant warrior of the previous scene. He is a failed professor, and the gloss to Luke 8.13 shows that he is one who has "no root" and who, though once a believer, in time of temptation has fallen away. The biblical references here amplify the victim's self-accusation. The first, "I left off to watch, and be sober" (34), though unglossed in the allegory, echoes 1 Thessalonians 5.6 and similarly 1 Peter 4.7 to show the former professor's normal "godly" vocabulary and propensity. His similar later speech echoes and is glossed to Hebrews (6.6), Luke 19.14, and Hebrews 10.28, 29. The scene is indeed, as Interpreter says, "an everlasting caution" (35) for Christian to remember. That the sixth tableau is left unresolved when Christian and the Interpreter move on keeps alive familiar Calvinistic fears of predestinate damnation.

The seventh and concluding scene mirrors Christian's spiritual and future status in a trembling dreamer who awakens and dons new clothing. He recounts an apocalyptic dream with eschatological depictions of darkness, thunder and lightning, of trumpets and flaming heavenly hosts, of the joyful or terrified dead rising to judgment. To interiorize interpretation, the dreamer explicates his own enactment, and the biblical glosses again attach exclusively to the words of the tableau character, who amalgamates no fewer than eighteen references in an instance of what Kaufmann calls Bunyan's "agglutinative" practice (*Pilgrim's Progress* 239–40). A number of these references are to biblical books which the generally Pauline Bunyan rarely cites, such as Jude, Daniel, and Malachi. The series cites several texts twice. Unusually too, more than half refer to multiple verses, and indeed several to whole chapters. Motifs of others in the series are collected in the initial reference to 1 Corinthians 15, recounting Christ's resurrection and its necessity and manner and culminating in the mystery of the last trumpet when death is swallowed up in the victory of Christ.

Clearly the concentration of biblical glosses at this site bespeaks altered expectations for the author and reader. The hints at ultimate things, and the guidance into the mystery of individually suggestive scriptural verses, are appropriate to the eschatological content and motivation of this tableau. Bunyan's device for intensifying this climactic interpretational event presses toward two extremes: on the one hand, enfolding the lesson entirely within the data of the tableau-to-be-interpreted rather than within the Interpreter's or the converted Christian's processing, and on the other hand, reaching far and deep beyond the narrative into the authorizing pre-text. The scene completes Christian's supply of text and instruction for its use. When he leaves the Interpreter's house behind, a new mode of the peripatetic Word, now called "the Comforter" (37), travels forward with him, and signals a change in the nature of the interpreting Holy Ghost for the convert who has attained confident mastery over his identifying and authoritative book.

In the "propaedeutic to pilgrimage" of the Interpreter's house with its encouraging and admonitory examples (Kaufmann, *Pilgrim's Progress* 73), the dramatic tableaux array varied scenes and pairings of faith in a sequence that both defines the stages of the trip and educes Christian's gradually increasing skill at developing distinctions, interpretations, and anagogical drive for himself. As a review of the scriptural glosses shows, the process is both textual and metatextual, and the Scriptures are both exteriorized and interiorized. The sequence of tableaux moves narratively between past terrors and future promise and insists extra-narratively upon continuously energetic reading and moral distinctions.

The discrete units of the Interpreter's house resemble a memory theater, and two later series of visual edifications, the "Rarities" of House Beautiful and the "Wonders" at the Delectable Mountains, array lessons in similarly discrete repository formats for the traveler. If Interpreter's house is a theater, House Beautiful is a museum.[19] The "Rarities" housed in its "Study" (53) are, first, records of antiquity, that is "the Pedigree of the Lord of the Hill" and his acts and his servants' acts. The list of acts—"how they had subdued Kingdoms, wrought Righteousness, obtained Promises, stopped the mouths of Lions, quenched the violence of Fire, escaped the edge of the Sword" (53)—show the servants to be the cloud of witnesses from Hebrews 11.33–34 and 12.1 whose past achievements, through faith, may be made perfect under the Christian dispensation. The move from the "Records of Antiquity" to the "Records of the House" is a shift toward the future and promises, and we hear now of

"Prophecies and Predictions of things that have their certain accomplishment, both to the dread and amazement of enemies, and the comfort and solace of Pilgrims" (54). On a second day Christian and the citizens of the house review spiritual armor based both on Ephesians and Old Testament "Engines," and on a third Christian is shown the Delectable Mountains (i.e., "Immanuels Land"). The "engines" embed a set of Old Testament stories in experiential data and encode history with typological expectations. Instruction in the metaphorics of the armory does not enact interpretation, but does transmute biblical texts into typological armaments. Confirmation rather than reformation is now the goal (Van Dyke 174). Moreover, the site provides initiation into church community and ordinances as well as the Bible.

The third series, the "Wonders" of the Delectable Mountains, geographically inscribes the shepherds' warnings to Christian and Hopeful. When Christian asks, as he had at Interpreter's house, "What meaneth this?" (120), he is told that those who died by falling from Hill Error had held mistaken views about the resurrection of the body. When from Mount Caution he asks similarly about blind men stumbling among tombs, he is told of pilgrims crossing the stile into By-Path Meadow and being captured by Giant Despair who causes their blindness and graveyard wandering. When they visit a bottom, look into a door in the side of a hill, and sense fire and brimstone, Christian's question elicits a warning against hypocrisy. Hopeful's remark—"These had on them, even every one, a shew of Pilgrimage as we have now; had they not?" (122)—establishes this vision as an analogue of their pilgrimage. The shepherds deliver an interpreted meaning to be registered securely in the memory rather than creatively achieved; in other words, the Word here is more sermonic than scriptural, and interpreting texts less important for the pilgrims at this stage than uses or applications.

These negative lessons fully secured in topographical experience, the shepherds present a final more positive destination from Hill Clear, where a perspective glass allows at least some pilgrims to see the gates of the Celestial City. Christian and Hopeful prove to have sufficient visual skills. Though shaken by the negative "wonders," "yet," we are told, "they thought they saw something like the Gate, and also some of the Glory of the place" (123). Tentative vision modulating into faith recalls Christian at the outset, only *thinking* he saw "yonder shining light" and not seeing "yonder *Wicket-gate*" at all (10). When Christian and Hopeful leave the Delectable Mountains, the shepherds present them with a map and with warnings against the Flatterer and against sleeping on the Enchanted Ground. The scene interlocks the present with preceding and future stages of the journey. The map, "a note of the way" (123), signals the need for further reading at later points, but Christian and Hopeful forget to refer to it in the one crisis where it would have helped them. They also fall into the Flatterer's net.

Both these series recall the rooms at Interpreter's house in spatially representing meaning, doctrine, and guidance, and in explicitly glossing the Way and travel upon it. Their sequence depicts progress from the interpretational instruction of conversion, through the fortification of church membership, and finally to the motives and rewards of perseverance in pilgrimage. The more practical map relates to applications as the earlier magical scroll related to doctrines and gospelizing. The "Rarities" and "Wonders" present passive rather than interactive instruction, and thereby appropriately follow in the wake of Bunyan's and Puritanism's prioritizing of the immediate vitalizing and participatory Word and interpretational process.

◄❸| III |❸►

OTHER EVIDENCE moves beyond depicting reading and interpretation to present the heroism of unmediated interaction with texts. Given the heroic paradigm, we expect from Bunyan's narrative a trip to the underworld or other encounter with the dead, a metamorphosis or reoriented relationship with powerful figures and with the positive and negative fragments of selfhood, an assimilation of the opposites within the self, conquests, illuminations, promises of perfection and bliss and wish fulfillment alternating with primal threats, revulsions, temptations, perhaps annihilation, perhaps apotheosis, perhaps a sharing of the imperishable divine substance. In *Pilgrim's Progress* part I these events occur as interactions with the Bible. Christian's "trials" are sometimes a matter of survival, sometimes of reward. Like the tableaux in Interpreter's house, they often divide into halves which, like faith, look toward both what he is working free from and what he is striving to attain.

Two central trials are couched in military metaphor, the only occasions of warfaring in *Pilgrim's Progress* part I. In the first Christian battles Apollyon with a "two-edg'd Sword" (60) and in the second a few pages later, when besieged by diabolical and divine voices in the Valley of the Shadow of Death, Christian wields the defensive weapon "*All-prayer*" (63). Any valiant Christian drawing his sword reenacts the penultimate tableau at the Interpreter's house, itself enacting the army of 2 Samuel 24.9. Late in the narrative, Christian voices his military principles: "to go out harnessed, and to be sure *to take a Shield with us*" (132, quoting Ephesians 6.16). He also recommends traveling with the king's convoy, referenced to David's successful passage through the valley of the shadow of death, to which we shall return in a moment, as well as to Exodus 33.15, Psalms 3.5–8 and 27.1–3, and Isaiah 10.4. The king's champion Great-grace, whom Christian and Hopeful so much admire, is notable for his excellent offensive militancy (130–31).

The linguistic accident that the word *Word* is embedded within the word *Sword* is authorized by the metaphorics of Ephesians 6.10–17, which lists "the sword of the Spirit, which is the word of God," "the shield of faith," "the helmet of salvation," "the breastplate of righteousness," the shoes of "the preparation of the gospel of peace," and an unspecified item which girds about the warrior's loins with truth. Isaiah 59.17 embeds a similar list: "For he put on righteousness as a brestplate, and an helmet of salvation upon his head; and he put on the garments of vengeance for clothing, and was clad with zeal as a cloke." Christian departed from the armory of House Beautiful harnessed "from head to foot, with what was of proof" (55), including just such a sword, shield, helmet, breastplate, and shoes (54). The "furniture" of the House Beautiful armory also lists an unspecified weapon *All-prayer*. *Of the House of the Forest of Lebanon* explicates metaphoric weaponry, assigning swords to offense, and shields to defense. In particular, the sword is said to be "a Weapon that hurteth none, none at all but the devil and sin, and those that love it. Indeed it was made for Christians to defend themselves, and their religion with, against hell and the angels of darkness" (Offor III:526–27; see also *Some Gospel Truths Opened* 1:23).[20] The House Beautiful armory also houses such Old Testament engines as Moses' rod, Jael's hammer and nail, Samson's jawbone, David's sling, and many others.

In the equations of arms with categories of belief and action, "the Sword of the Spirit," equated with the Word of God, is the ultimate weapon, and Hebrews 4.12 develops both the vehicle and the tenor: "For the word of God is quick, and powerful, and sharper than any twoedged sword, piercing even to the dividing asunder of soul and spirit, and of the joints and marrow, and is a discerner of the thoughts and intents of the heart." Christian's sword, specified as a "two-edged" one (60), echoes the "sharp twoedged sword" of Revelation 1.16 and 2.12 as well as of Psalm 149.6. Revelation 19.15 and 2.16 and Psalm 59.7 similarly link swords with speech.

Against Apollyon, a fiend dominating the Valley of Humiliation, Christian wields a sword and defends himself with a shield. Apollyon calls himself a prince and a god, but the narrative presents a different picture: "The monster was hidious to behold, he was cloathed with scales like a Fish (and they are his pride) he had Wings like a Dragon, feet like a Bear, and out of his belly came Fire and Smoak, and his mouth was as the mouth of a Lion" (56). The account remains unglossed, but draws upon at least Job 41.15 and Revelation 13.2. Elsewhere in Bunyan's works Apollyon occurs as one of the council of Devils (Diablonians) in *The Holy War* (esp. 174–75) and as the captain and king of God's enemies in *An Exposition . . . of Genesis* (Offor II:454).

Apollyon claims Christian as one of his subjects and accuses him of unauthorized leave and treason. Christian's most forceful and faithful articulations to date of his position, choices, and hopes enrage Apollyon into full military attack with his chief weapon, flaming darts, the enemy's weapon in Ephesians 6.16. Despite his shield, Christian is weakened by wounds in his head, hand, and foot (glossed as his understanding, faith, and conversation [59]), wrestled to the ground, and nearly pressed (literally) to death. Late in the half-day combat, out of his despair Christian suddenly catches up his sword and mortally wounds the dragon. Not Christian but God through Christian achieves this victory in what Fish describes as really "a battle of words . . . [wherein] the syntax continually shift[s] the responsibility from verbs of physical action to a quotation" (*Self-Consuming Artifacts* 235). As Vincent Newey similarly explains, "The Lord's triumph is his triumph, dependence on *logos* self-dependence; and the defeat of Apollyon is the defeat of the devil within himself" ("Bunyan" 32). In a triumphant song, Christian credits "blessed *Michael*" with military assistance (60).

Apollyon's initial verbal attack sparks actions of reading and faith from the reader as well as the hero. The (s)Words of the Spirit which lead to victory concord Micah 7.8 ("Rejoice not against me, O mine enemy: When I fall, I shall arise; when I sit in darkness, the Lord shall be a light unto me"), Romans 8.37 ("Nay, in all these things we are more than conquerors through him that loved us"), and James 4.7 ("Submit yourselves therefore to God. Resist the devil, and he will flee from you"). Bunyan's deployment of these citations requires the reader to amalgamate Old and New Testaments. The first half of Micah 7.8 describes the textual opening, the catching up of the sword, while Romans 8.37, again quoted in the narrative, glosses the delivery of the mortal blow and the hero's deliverance. When Christian quotes only part of the Micah passage, Bunyan expects his readers to apply the whole verse and context, including Micah 7.7: "I will look unto the Lord; I will wait for the God of my salvation: my God will hear me." James 4.7 is not quoted in the text, and while it specifically glosses the dragon's flight, it also resolves the narrative occasion and registers the lesson the incident is designed to illustrate. Both texts require the reader's recourse to the Bible and memory to achieve the layered illumination. The kind of interplay here between Old and New Testament passages enacts the transtemporal and transtextual reading that is the very nature of typology.

During the battle with Apollyon, Christian is directly energized by a spiritual opening and various Bible verses to perform an act of faith, as defined in Hebrews 11.1, the substance of things hoped for, the evidence of things not seen. Commenting on this text in *Some Gospel Truths Opened*, Bunyan adds: "The things that are hoped for faith sees, layes hold upon, and embraces them, *Heb.* 11.13. as if they were present: yea, it seales up the certainty of them to the soule" (1:17). As the incident concludes, Bunyan's hero, like Spenser's, is healed by leaves from the Tree of Life proffered by a mysterious hand, and refreshed by bread and drink (i.e., Communion [60–61]). This special nourishment, a parting gift from the ladies of House Beautiful, complements the gift of armor. It also resolves the occasion of private turmoil within the refreshment and community of church ordinances. Although he is not later called upon to wield such weaponry, "Christian goes on his Journey with his Sword drawn in his hand" (gloss 61).

Christian's "rest in the Word" is brief indeed, for he at once finds himself in the even more dangerous Valley of the Shadow of Death. The two experiences represent complementary uses of the Word. The first discovers how to wield the Word's power over evil, while the second teaches Christian how to keep to the path by relying on the Word's illumination (Knott, *Sword* 148), differences imaged in the change from an offensive weapon actively wielded to a defensive weapon passively relied upon. In this second valley, Christian literally inhabits a biblical site where, drawing upon a series of Old Testament passages, he achieves the hero's typical success against the challenge of an underworld. As the former occasion enacted typology, this one enacts concordancing, the exhaustive collecting and careful reconciling of all related biblical verses.

The Valley of the Shadow of Death, we are told, is "a very solitary place" of Hobgoblins, Satyrs, Dragons of the Pit, and "discouraging Clouds of confusion [where] death also doth always spread his wings over it," a place "every whit dreadful" and "utterly without Order" (62), a place of terror, noisy affliction, and misery. All pilgrims to the Celestial City must pass through this valley (61), and its dangers are those that *The Saints' Privilege and Profit* describes as attending pilgrims to Zion: "Now the devil has lost a sinner; there is a captive has broke prison, and one run away from his master: now hell seems to be awakened from sleep, the devils are come out, they roar, and roaring they seek to recover their runaway. Now tempt him, threaten him, flatter him, stigmatise him, throw dust into his eyes, poison him with error, spoil him while he is upon the potter's wheel; any thing to keep him from coming to Jesus Christ" (Offor 1:677). The narrow dark pathway through the valley has a deep ditch on one side, a dangerous quagmire on the other, and the fiery mouth of Hell in its midst. Similarly in *The Holy War*, the Land of the Shadow of Death abuts the Land of Doubting on one side and the Land of Darkness on the other (227–28). Two men going backward on the Way indicate to Christian that the danger here is not so much with some specific evil embodiment as with the place itself, its assaults upon the ear, its darkness and confusions. The marginal glosses are to Job 3.5 and 10.22. In this valley, as against Apollyon, Christian encounters "the shadow side of the psyche—the darkness within, the vortex of deadly fears and imaginings" (Newey, "Bunyan" 32).

As before, the narrative evidence here depicts a reading experience and demands the reader's active participation. We expect the site to draw its name from Psalm 23.4, but instead Bunyan borrows from Jeremiah 2.6 to describe it as: "*A Wilderness, a Land of desarts, and of Pits, a Land of drought, and of the shadow of death, a Land that no Man* (but a Christian) *passeth through, and where no man dwelt*" (61). One side of its Scylla/Charybdis challenge threatens destruction from the blind leading the blind; on the other, the precedent is a fallen David who was divinely rescued; on the one hand, an error in belief and on the other, surrender to outward sin; on the one hand, "Antinomian disregard for the moral law" and on the other, "self-righteous reliance on works" (323n.). The first, though unglossed, references Matthew 15.14 and Luke 6.39; the second, glossed to Psalm 69.14, records David's call to be delivered out of the mire, a fall and salvation reconstituting Christian's Slough of Despond adventure. The exceeding narrowness of the passage between these dangers increases the challenge, and the exceeding darkness compels faith even for survival: "Oft times when he lift up his foot to set forward, he knew not where, or upon what he could set it next" (62).

Those who, like Christian, successfully negotiate the narrow path between ditch and quag confront the mouth of Hell (63) with its threatening flames and voices. The hero, "so confounded, that he did not know his own voice," echoes the Bunyan assaulted by texts in *Grace Abounding*:

> Just when [Christian] was come over against the mouth of the burning Pit, one of the wicked ones got behind him, and stept up softly to him, and whisperingly suggested many grievous blasphemies to him, which he verily thought had proceeded from his own mind. This put *Christian* more to it than any thing that he met with before, even to think that he should now blaspheme him that he loved so much before; yet, could he have helped it, he would not have done it: but he had not the discretion neither to stop his ears, nor to know from whence those blasphemies came. When *Christian* had travelled in this disconsolate condition some considerable time, he thought he heard the voice of a man, as going before him, saying, *Though I walk through the valley of the shaddow of death, I will fear none ill, for thou art with me.* (63–64)

The saving speech comes from the psalmist or, in Bunyan's case, perhaps from Luther, whose commentary on Galatians had been so influential in his conversion (Greaves, *John Bunyan* 155). After again posing the inaugural query of *Pilgrim's Progress*, "What shall I do?" (63), Christian wields the unspecified weapon "*All-prayer*" against assaults from voices, "sparks and hideous noises (things that cared not for *Christians* Sword)" (63). This weapon, glossed to Ephesians 6.18 ("Praying always with all prayer and supplication in the Spirit, and watching thereunto with all perseverance and supplication for all saints"), takes the specific form of Psalm 116.4: "Then called I upon the name of the Lord; O Lord, I beseech thee, deliver my soul." The psalm invocation is quoted within the narrative, while readers presumably remember Ephesians.

Bunyan explicates this weapon and enactment in *I Will Pray With the Spirit*, where prayer is a shield and buckler and also a defensive weapon as it was for David in Psalms 18, 27, and 28 (II:242). The treatise concisely defines prayer as "a sincere, sensible, affectionate pouring out of the heart or soul to God, through Christ, in the strength and assistance of the holy Spirit, for such things as God hath promised, or, according to the Word, for the good of the Church, with submission, in Faith, to the Will of God" (235). When Christian prayed after losing his scroll at Hill Difficulty, his relatively simple act involved "falling down upon his knees . . . [and] ask[ing] God forgiveness for that his foolish Fact" (43–44), an enactment of the two bases of prayer cited in the treatise, "a detestation to sin, and the things of this life" and "a longing desire after Communion with God, in an holy and undefiled state and inheritance" (II:271). But when Christian wields the weapon *All-prayer* in the Valley of the Shadow of Death, he compounds actions more complexly imaged in the treatise: "Right Prayer bubleth out of the heart when it is over-pressed with grief and bitterness" and "while Prayer is making, God is searching the heart, to see from what root and spirit it doth arise" (237, 248). Another treatise, *The Fear of God,* images prayer as "the *pitcher* that fetcheth water from the Brook, therewith to water the herbs" and as "*seasonable showers* of rain, to keep the *tillage* of thy heart in good order, that the grace of fear may grow therein" (IX:120, 123; Bunyan's italics; and see also Offor II:237).

According to *I Will Pray With the Spirit,* prayer derives from interaction with both the Bible and the Holy Spirit (II:243, 257). For Christian in the Valley of the Shadow of Death, as the treatise promises, prayer "brings those that have the Spirit of Supplication, into great familiarity with God; and . . . getteth of God, both for the person that prayeth, and for them that are prayed for, great things. It is the opener of the heart to God, and a means by which the soul, though empty, is filled. By Prayer the Christian can open his heart to God as to a Friend, and obtain fresh testimony of God's Friendship to him" (235). Insofar as it is a private matter it overlaps with meditation, but *I Will Pray With the Spirit* has much to say about public prayer as well. It particularly argues against use of the Book of Common Prayer and even against the Lord's Prayer as usually voiced on the grounds that one does not need "to look into a Book, to teach him in a Form to pour out his heart before God" (264, and similarly 252). Bunyan even goes so far as to call "anti-Christian" such "pretended Worship of God" (285).

Christian wields *All-prayer* "a great while" and "for several miles together" (63) against fiends who sometimes whisper blasphemy in his own voice. He reinvigorates himself by remembering his former successes, and by vehemently calling out *"I will walk in the strength of the Lord God"* (63), an assertion reaffirmed by the external voice quoting Psalm 23 back to him (64). In the doubling of Satanic and psalmic voices against Christian's own, the incident reenacts a major trauma of *Grace Abounding* when Bunyan felt himself to be not just a warrior but a battlefield for the warring of texts, the accusatory Scriptures of Esau's sale of his birthright battling against "My Grace is sufficient for thee" (43). The autobiography references the Esau story not from Genesis 25.29–34 but as mediated through Hebrews 12.16–17. Bunyan likens the Esau text to "a flaming sword, to keep the way of the tree of Life, lest I should take thereof, and live" and to "a Spear against me" (55, 71). The conflict is resolved when the Esau threat "began to wax weak, and withdraw, and vanish; and this about the sufficiency of Grace prevailed, with peace and joy" (66–67). Here, as in *Pilgrim's Progress*, voices of temptation create mimic openings and arrive from outside with great force (42).

This *Grace Abounding* parallel defines the spiritual "place" in which Christian now finds himself. The death whose shadow defines the site does not threaten the traveler's physical life—it is not an analogue of the River of Death between Beulah and the Celestial City. Rather it threatens spiritual death, despair, the temptation to abandon faith in the face of the mystery of loss or evil. The running subtext is the Book of Job, which ten times employs the phrase "Shadow of Death" and whose hero throughout enacts the trial which we are to understand that Christian is now passing through.[21] For this incident *Pilgrim's Progress* glosses five passages from Job (3.5, 10.22, 9.10, 12.22, and 29.3). Job 3.3–6 shows that Job's challenge, like Christian's, is extreme despair as articulated by the man who refuses to "curse God and die" (2.9).

Like the autobiographical Bunyan, Christian is saved by an alternate opening, and an altered format reflects a shift in interpretational method and purpose toward concording and typologizing. What Brainerd Stranahan calls "Bunyan's special talent" produces a third passage synthesizing the conflicting ones (334). In the Valley of the Shadow, Christian draws comfort from Hebrews, Genesis, and Joshua, but his central synthesizing text is, of course, Psalm 23.4, with its refusal to fear evil because of God's presence. This leads into such additional assurances as Job 9.10 and Amos 5.8. Given the characteristic Puritan preference for the security of the a priori, it is no accident that the text of greatest assurance derives from the most familiar of psalms, the twenty-third, the more so in absorbing a series of scattered scriptural echoes.

The arrival of daylight activates Job 12.22 ("He discovereth deep things out of darkness, and bringeth out to light the shadow of death" [64]) and fortifies Christian for the even more dangerous second half of the valley with its Snares, Traps, Gins, Nets, Pits, Pitfalls, deep holes, and shelvings (65). The daytime half of Christian's adventure literalizes his defeat of darkness and achieved illumination. He cheerfully applies Job 29.3 to the case, a verse paralleling *All-prayer* as a defense: "*His candle shineth on my head, and by his light I go through darkness*" (65, and see Offor III:520).

When his reading skills reach this point, the allegorical and autobiographical hero is able to array his arguments in the enumerated divisions featured in Puritan sermons, a format Puritan audiences would automatically equate with logic and the triumph of reason over "notions." The interactivity of biblical verses achieved from the ordeal of the Valley of the Shadow marks a new stage in the hero's relation to the Word and to his vocation, a change in spiritual state, illumination, and confidence, and also a shift from private to public expression. Specifically, Christian offers three numbered reasons for the comfort of Psalm 23.4, and arrives at an additional confirmatory text, Amos 5.8: "*He hath turned the shadow of death into the morning*" (64). The Amos affirmation fully resolves the Jeremiah query with which this narrative occasion began, demonstrating Christian's new skills in biblical synthesizing or concordancing. After this valley Christian shares his travel with Faithful and then Hopeful, and their interactions exteriorize the Word into the Puritan discourses of the sermon, prophesying, and controversy that make up much of the remainder of part I.

•◎| I V |◎•

THOUGH IN TONE and spiritual condition the episodes of the Valley of the Shadow and Beulah are antithetical, echoing formal meditations on hell and heaven, Kaufmann correctly describes both as "visualized myth based upon and inviting imaginative participation in the biblical metaphors" (*Pilgrim's Progress* 160, 162, 164). Scriptural enactment extends the biblical Word beyond the participation examined earlier. Now the Word literally dramatizes an individual unit of vocabulary. A brief instance of this practice registers the category when the whole Vanity Fair episode is enfolded within the reiterated judgment of Ecclesiastes: "Vanity, Vanity, all is Vanity" (see *Pilgrim's Progress* 88). The practice illustrates Henri Talon's generalization that "Bunyan thought in images," enriched his vocabulary with concrete biblical notation, and populated his universe with biblical metaphors without which he was not himself able to grasp his ideas (*John Bunyan* 182–83). Now the single word governs, the allegory enfolds into the or *a* Word, and the culminating word for our inquiry is one important to the mythic mode as well, that is *Beulah* (i.e., marriage). In its only occurence in the King James Bible, Isaiah 62, the prophet proclaims a new name and destiny for Zion within a prophetic metaphor: "Thou should no more be termed Forsaken; neither shall thy land any more be termed Desolate: but thou shalt be called Hephzibah, and thy land Beulah: for the Lord delighteth in thee, and thy land shall be married. For as a young man marrieth a virgin, so shall thy sons marry thee: and as the bridegroom rejoiceth over the bride, so shall thy God rejoice over thee" (4–5).

The layered endings of *Pilgrim's Progress* juxtapose Beulah against the New Jerusalem to augment an Old Testament vision of blessedness with the promises of the New (Knott, *Sword* 151). The Beulah data are typic, available, experiential; the Celestial City is atmospheric, anticipated, dissolving into inexpressibility. The texts authorizing Beulah draw upon the Song of Solomon and Isaiah; those authorizing the ultimate goal upon Revelation. Bunyan invokes the Song of Solomon 2.10–12 to describe Beulah's sweet air, flowers, singing birds, and "voice of the Turtle"; he also echoes Deuteronomy 23.24 as a long-desired site of notably ameliorative agricultural abundance and glances at Isaiah 62.4 (gloss 154) to mirror Christian's achieved righteousness and election. Both the Song of Solomon and Isaiah transfer meaning between persons and place within a vocabulary of marriage, and both the Song of Solomon and Revelation support the marriage of Christ with his church as well as of Christ with the elected individual. Moreover, the Song of Solomon provides a precedent for shifting the point of view between bridegroom and beloved.

Bunyan inherited the traditional view of the Song of Solomon as not merely a lyric celebration of Solomon's nuptials or Christ's love for his spouse the Church. For some, as Stanley Stewart has shown, "the true subject of the Song of Songs was the [inexpressible] wonder of the mystical state" and "the ineffable splendors of spiritual marriage."[22] Since, as Stewart also points out, any contemporary writer may use *church* to refer either to the whole congregation or to a particular member as a microcosm of the whole (19), we are in the realm noted earlier, where metaphor and metonymy weave into and out of each other to multiply the "literary" effects of the reading experience. We must take something of the same attitude toward Bunyan's figuration of Beulah as well.

When he set out, the terrified hero of *Pilgrim's Progress* carried his authority in his hands, but by the conclusion the Holy Spirit has thoroughly written it and its interpretations upon his heart. With his passage to the Celestial City, Christian transcends the Old Testament Song of Solomon in favor of the marriage supper of the lamb of Revelation 19.7, a progress that concords Christ's parable of the marriage in Matthew 22.3 as well and resolves conflicts between type and antitype that have troubled the hero since Interpreter's house. The narrative leaves behind a metaphoric expression of divine truth in favor of the differently elusive language of Revelation and the higher plane of reality it implies (Knott, *Sword* 152). What is rapturously described in the climax of the allegory is prosaically and exhaustively detailed in a Bunyan treatise on Revelation 21.10 to 22.4: *The Holy City: Or, The New Jerusalem: Wherein Its Goodly Light, Walls, Gates, Angels, and the manner of their standing, are Expounded: Also, Her Length and Breadth, Together with the Golden-Measuring-Reed, Explained: And the Glory of all unfolded. As also, The Numerousness of its Inhabitants And what the Tree and Water of Life are, by which they are sustained.* As is usual in Bunyan's homiletic practice, the treatise incorporates citations of all biblical analogues for each item. *Israel's Hope Encouraged* more briefly catalogues the inexpressible delights of the Heavenly Jerusalem as the innumerable company of angels, immortality, "mansion-houses, beds of glory, and places to walk in among the angels," along with "badges of honour, harps to make merry with, and heavenly songs of triumph," in sum "a knowing, an enjoying, and a solacing of ourselves with prophets, apostles, and martyrs, and all saints" (Offor 1:579).

Bunyan's presentations of Beulah and the Celestial City compound the biblical and the mystical and precisely mirror, or even deconstruct, the form and spirit of typology. The interwoven passages from Old and New Testaments enact the marriage of texts, erasing an earlier randomness of citation within a transcendent synthesis. Christian is absorbed into the biblical text that has defined his heroism throughout. The two layers sort out Old Testament and New Testament mimesis and transcendence even as they enact the ultimate fulfillment of inexpressible promise adumbrated in the preceding dispensation of time, space, and experience.

We have seen earlier that Pauline epistles make explicit Bunyan's interpretational and typological assumptions, procedures, and goals and that he often drew fervently from Pauline authority. It is not surprising, though I am not aware that the point has been remarked upon previously, that his treatment of Beulah and the Celestial City draws instead from prophetic and mystical Scriptures, Isaiah and the Song of Solomon in the Old Testament and Revelation in the New. Whereas Pauline texts sustain a superstructure of intellectually achieved and formulated interpretation, these prophetic books generate a suprarational atmosphere. The former looks backward from the New to the Old Testament, but the latter is anagogical, eschatological, ultimate. At the simplest narrative level, *Pilgrim's Progress* represents such vision through the frequent sleeping, dreaming, musing, and prophesying in Beulah, deriving from "the nature of the fruit of the Grapes of these Vineyards" (156). At the metaphorical level, in leaving the Pauline precedents behind in favor of the mystical and prophetic, Bunyan is locating not just his hero but also his reader inside the biblical text and interiorizing interpretational vantage so as to multiply its mystical rewards.

CHAPTER FOUR

The Sermonic Word

It is hardly possible to exaggerate the importance of the sermon in the seventeenth-century world.—Douglas Bush, *English Literature in the Earlier Seventeenth Century*

[Sermons were] the one literary type in which the Puritan spirit was most completely expressed.—Perry Miller, *The New England Mind*

IN PURITAN USAGE *the Word* refers not only to the Bible but also to the sermon, the biblical text as mediated, analyzed, interpreted, and applied from the pulpit. Authorized by Romans 10.17, "Faith cometh by hearing, and hearing by the word of God," and privileged by Reformation Protestantism, Puritan preaching served as perhaps the most important means of instructing, persuading, and working upon people's hearts, and thus of bringing them out of sin's bondage into grace and of calling together the saints.[1] For William Perkins, as for the Reformation before him and Bunyan and many other Puritan preachers after him, the aim of preaching was to allow the Bible to speak for itself, hence the essential overlap of Puritan hermeneutics and homiletics, inward understanding and outward expression, private devotion and public discourse.

Bunyan often articulates this Reformation equation of the sermonic and biblical Words. In *Grace Abounding* he combines the two senses to describe his ministry (29, 84, 89). More largely, *Some Gospel Truths Opened* speaks of preaching as "God's Ordinance to beget Faith" and as "Gods usual way to communicate of his spirit into the hearts of his Elect" (1:57). Prayer, Christian conference, reading, meditation, and the remembrance of former experiences may increase it, but it originates in "the holy Spirit of God, which is renewed through the hearing of the Word, preached by the Apostles or Minister of Jesus Christ." It brings about new birth in those that have sufficient righteousness to be persuaded: "Whoever has heard the Word preached, and has not heard the voice of the living God therein, has not as yet had their hearts broken, nor their spirits made contrite for their sins" (*Instruction For the Ignorant* VIII:32–33; *A Vindication of Some Gospel Truths Opened* 1:197, 198; *The Acceptable Sacrifice* Offor 1:694). The preacher is authorized by 1 Peter 4.11: "If any man speak, let him speak as the oracles of God" (and see Acts 10.44). In the metaphor of *The Holy War*, the divine military strategy recognizes "that unless they could penetrate [Eargate], no good could be done upon the Town" (50).

Doctrine, reasons, and uses so much dominated Puritan sermonizing, and sermons were themselves so pervasive, that various discourses and actions were assimilated to its model. As with so many Puritan matters, the border between spiritually based theory and biographically embodied practice is often blurred. By analogy, the doctrine, reasons, and uses pattern outlines the normative Puritan life history, very specifically so for Bunyan, whose life and work mirror progressive relations to the Word—from the exploratory to the expository and then the hortatory (J. Turner, "Bunyan's" 109, 108). *Grace Abounding* records Bunyan's hermeneutical development: When conviction of human depravity is uppermost, he makes initial halting attempts at biblical exegesis, but when he has been justified, he advances to a methodical, logical Ramistic hermeneutic arranged under numerical headings. A similar move from the scriptural Word to the sermonic Word, from convert to minister, formats *Pilgrim's Progress* part I, where Christian the heroic soul-searching and Word-searching isolate turns into Christian the participant in godly conversations with the true and false professors he meets upon the later stages of the Way. In typical Puritan fashion, in both Bunyan's and his hero's lives, the private becomes public, exegesis becomes homiletics, and preaching to the self through reading and meditation becomes edifying discourse and public homily (Kaufmann, *Pilgrim's Progress* 25–26, 20).

Such life history encodes increasing reflection and usefulness. As *Grace Abounding* records, a passive stance gives way to more aggressive textual positioning that empowers redemptive texts. Bunyan's procedure is "to take some measure of incouragement, to come close to them, to read them, and consider them, and to weigh their scope and tendence" (70). This allows him to understand troubling verses "*not against* but *according to* other Scriptures" (my italics), and he progresses from highly emotional, even intimate private applications of the Word to public, generalized, intellectual ones. We recognize his victory when he expresses himself through numbered headings (69ff.), when full celebration of the mystery of Christ replaces earlier trials and torments (72–73), when he can analyze the sources of his temptation and handle a scriptural verse as if preaching a sermon to himself or to an external audience—when, that is, he successfully translates the written into the sermonic Word (75, 76).

Bunyan progressed from preferring the historical parts of the Bible to preferring the Pauline epistles, and the autobiography records an analogous progress in sermonic emphases. His early preaching showed a preference for the operation of the law, for threatening, terrifying, personally felt lessons: "Now this part of my work I fulfilled with great sence; for the terrours of the Law, and guilt for my transgressions, lay heavy on my Conscience. I preached what I felt, what I smartingly did feel, even that under which my poor Soul did groan and tremble to astonishment" (85). While the early conscience-stricken and recently converted Bunyan threatened his audience, the later Bunyan emphasized the mercy, comfort, and welcome available to Christians. This more positive strain is also personalized: "After [two years], the Lord came in upon my own Soul with some staid peace and comfort thorow Christ; for he did give me many sweet discoveries of his blessed Grace thorow him: wherefore now I altered in my preaching (for still I preached what I saw and felt;) now therefore I did much labour to hold forth Jesus Christ in all his Offices, Relations, and Benefits unto the World, and did strive also to discover, to condemn, and remove those false supports and props on which the World doth both lean, and by them fall and perish" (86). George Offor, Bunyan's nineteenth-century editor, summarizes Bunyan's ministry within a distinction between "a Boanerges, or son of thunder, to awaken the impenitent" and "a Barnabas—a son of consolation—an evangelist to direct the trembling inquirer to Christ the way, the truth, and the life" (Offor III:538).

William Perkins's preaching manual, so much relied upon by seventeenth-century Puritans, attaches this distinction and sequence to the preacher's choice of sermon texts: "The law is thus far effectual as to declare unto us the disease of sin and by accident to exasperate and stir it up, but it affords no remedy. Now the gospel, as it teacheth what is to be done, so it hath also the efficacy of the Holy Ghost adjoined with it, by whom being regenerated we have strength both to believe the gospel and to perform those things which it commandeth. The law therefore is first in order of teaching and the gospel second."[2] Like the Bible itself, Bunyan progressed from an Old to a New Testament emphasis. In later years and increasingly, his theological works emphasize opportunities for salvation rather than condemnation, grace rather than rebuke. Typically in *Instruction For the Ignorant*, for example, he calls himself his audience's "affectionate Brother and Companion in the Kingdom and Patience of JESUS CHRIST" and pledges himself "to serve you by my Ministry (when I can) to your Edification and Consolation" (VIII:7). This shift of emphasis, by no means peculiar to Bunyan, reflects various larger historical changes to be considered in the Conclusion.[3]

For the world Bunyan inherited, the sermon rippled widely beyond its initial delivery into a series of cultural phenomena. Auditors were encouraged to take notes of sermons for subsequent repetition and discussion within individual households, purposes assisted by carefully subdivided and enumerated sermon organization. Offor describes the device as "enabl[ing] a ready writer, by taking notes of each part, to digest prayerfully in private, what he had heard in the public ministry of the word,—a practice productive of great good to individuals, and by which families may be much profited while conversing upon the truths publicly taught in the church" (Offor II:1). As publicly the role of preacher was widely distributed among the male population, so in the private sphere individual Puritan fathers led their families and servants in reading and expounding the Word. Bunyan's *Christian Behaviour* recommends that each father "ought diligently and frequently to lay before his houshold such things of God, out of his Word, as are sutable for each particular." He is to pray with and preach to his family, and, like the pastor of a church, he must himself be "sound and incorrupt in his doctrine"; "apt to teach, to reprove, and to exhort"; and "exemplary in Faith and Holiness" (III:22–23).

The seventeenth-century oral sermon was likely itself to be further developed into the theological treatise. No matter whether originally delivered from a fully written text, or from full or skeletal notes, or extemporaneously, the majority of Bunyan's threescore surviving works consist of sermon subjects reworked into treatises. The title page of *Greatness of the Soul* presents both the process and the hope: "First Preached at *Pinners*-Hall, and now Enlarged and Published for Good" (IX:135). The political accident of Bunyan's long years in jail magnified the importance of the written treatise to his career and provided the leisure and reflection for developing his subjects with sometimes extreme thoroughness. He did not, however, practice the "verbal giantism" of a number of contemporaries who multiplied a work to many times its original bulk in subsequent editions,[4] for although his treatises regularly ran to multiple editions, he seldom introduced changes.

Perkins's title *The Art of Prophesying* identifies *prophesying* as synonymous with preaching, but "prophesying" also stretched beyond the delivery occasion to the larger congregation. In contemporary practice, after hearing the Word preached, the congregation formally engaged in spontaneous exhortation and active debate on matters growing out of it. This activity marks *prophesying* as "little extempore sermons or speeches by members of the congregation" raising questions or resolving doubts. Geoffrey F. Nuttall summarizes such *prophesying* as "an activity of biblical exegesis, coupled with personal testimony and exhortation, after the preacher 'had donn his stuff' [George Fox] and was open to all." It was believed to reflect New Testament practice wherein "gifted brethren" expressed the conviction of the presence and activity of the Holy Spirit in their hearts.[5]

Another mode of the "speaking" Word, formal meditations upon Scriptures, combines reading, textual openings, and interpretation in allegiance to Protestantism's religious immediacy and interiorization. Sometimes spoken of as "inner oratory" or preaching to the self, scriptural meditation fuses homiletics and devotions. The preacher meditated on Scripture in preparing his sermons, and audiences meditated on both Scripture and his sermonic presentation of Scripture. Tracing the interchangeability of the words *sermon* and *meditation* to the Hebrew of Genesis 24.63, Barbara Lewalski has shown the virtual identification of purposes and component parts in the two and the virtual equation of prayer with meditation as well. Both sermon and meditation follow the distribution into doctrine, interpretation, and application; both rely heavily upon biblical annotation and phrasing; both involve illustration and analysis, argument and persuasion, including interrogatives and apostrophes to the audience—in written meditation an audience of either God or the author's self. Private meditation allows specific, even rigorous, personal application to the self.[6]

Seventeenth-century scriptural meditation was likely to be conducted along lines popularly codified by Joseph Hall (1574–1656) and eloquently practiced by Richard Baxter (1615–91). Hall's *Art of Meditation*, a Ramistic how-to book, defines "Divine meditation [as] nothing else but a bending of the mind upon some spiritual object." Where occasional meditations (see Chapter 8 below) arrive and reveal their lessons easily, the precious and more worthy spiritual meditations must be pursued with effort by those who are pure of heart, free to undertake, and constant to pursue the task. Hall recommends beginning with a biblical story intellectually considered and concluding with applications that appeal to the affections. Recommended subjects include God's essence, attributes, and works, "those matters in divinity which can most of all work compunction in the heart and most stir us up to devotion."[7] *The Saints' Everlasting Rest* puts forward the meditative theory Baxter so eloquently exemplifies. For him, meditation is "cogitation on things spiritual" or "the set and solemn acting of all the powers of the soul upon this most perfect object." It exercises the heart as well as the head "to make your thoughts of heaven to be piercing, affecting, raising thoughts." Baxter's own subject matter reaches toward ultimate goals, the "rest" of Hebrews 4.9.[8]

Both Hall and Baxter credit an influential meditative pattern derived from Johan Wessel Gansfort. Hall transcribes the pattern in chapter 16 of his *Art of Divine Meditation*, although he does not espouse it. Before starting to write, the meditator is to proceed through the Question (What I think/should think), the Excussion (A repelling of what I should not think), and the Choice or Election (Of what most: necessary/expedient/comely). Despite its unfamiliar vocabulary, this plan's "Degrees of Proceeding in the Understanding" analyze the stages of the cogitation Baxter recommends:

Commemoration An actual thinking upon the matter elected.
Consideration A redoubled commemoration of the same till it be
    fully known.
Attention A fixed and earnest consideration whereby it is fastened
    in the mind.
Explanation A clearing of the thing considered by similitudes.
Tractation An extending the thing considered to other points,
    where all questions of doubts are discussed.
Dijudication An estimation of the worth of the thing thus
    handled.
Causation A confirmation of the estimation thus made.
Rumination A sad and serious meditation of all the former till it
    may work upon the affections. (Hall 26, 27, 87, 88; Martz
    332–35)

Besides "cogitation," Baxter's meditation includes "soliloquy," that is "self-conference," "a pleading the case with our own souls," and indeed "a preaching to one's self" (163). It shares with preaching such verbs as

remember, study, compare, use, "convince, inform, confute, instruct, reprove, examine, admonish, encourage and comfort" and, generally, "rise
up from sense to faith" (179). Its goal is "to quicken thine own heart:
enter into serious debate with it; plead with it in the most moving and affecting language; use it with the most weighty and powerful arguments":
"First, explain to thyself the subject on which thou dost meditate, both
the terms and the subject matter; study the difficulties till the doctrine is
clear. Secondly, confirm thy faith in the belief of it, by the most clear, convincing Scripture-reasons. Thirdly, then apply it according to its nature
and thy necessity" (163). Such soliloquy reenacts the sermonic design of
doctrine, reasons, and uses, and in its highest stage, it advances from
speech to the self to speech with God, i.e., prayer (164).

Baxter's meditation again calls attention to the overriding importance
for the Puritan mindset of the faculty of the memory, what Baxter calls
"the soul-reviving part" of meditation (158). Meditation provides both
a strategy for accessing one's own memory and a repository, defined as
"the magazine and treasury of the understanding" (156) and, of course, of
the Word. Failure of memory, in Bunyan's words, "makes preaching vain,
profession vain, faith vain and all to no purpose" (*A Holy Life* IX:289,
288, and see *A Few Sighs From Hell* 1:292). Out of the memory, where
ideas and the shapes of things are retained, the reason or "cogitation" or
"consideration" chooses its subjects by an act of will and "opens" the door
between the understanding and the heart (153). Only when the biblical
text in both its expansive and contractive modes has been transferred into
the mind of the believer can it be sufficiently and salvationally processed,
only then can the memory become, in Stanley Fish's formulation, "the
repository of the master's rule, the source of the inner light, the pulpit
that the Holy Ghost preaches in."[9] As the double meanings remind us, the
repository is where things have been *at rest* as well as stored, and in such
terms the openings of the Word examined earlier are properly metaphored
as "awakenings."

Bunyan's textual recall is not at all rote learning, even when the
mnemotechnics such as Frances Yates describes give way to a Ramistic
methodized, mentally schematic equivalent. The classical art of memory
codified visiting the topoi, places, or commonplaces for logical and rhetorical purposes, a tradition with a Reformationist dimension for our era.
Place joins *opening* and *prophesying* as another of those multiply referential terms attaching to the Puritan Word, *place* meaning both a repository
of data and a biblical passage or locus. Within *Pilgrim's Progress*, sermons,

or "wholsom Instructions," are said to be "the best materials to make good ground of the place" (16), where rhetorical meanings of *ground* and *place* augment the specific designation of the Slough of Despond. In additional layerings, Bunyan's allegory thus redirects psychospiritual and textual places into topographical sites. James Turner's study "Bunyan's Sense of Place" sees his travel sites as first despatialized and then respatializing manifestations of texts, working like grids in the art of memory to recall images of things (*imagines*) (108, 107).

❦ I ❦

IN AN OFTEN-CITED outline, Perkins's *The Art of Prophesying* maps "*The order and sum of the sacred and only method of preaching*" in four steps:

(1) To read the text distinctly out of the canonical scriptures

(2) To give the sense and understanding of it being read, by the scripture itself

(3) To collect a few and profitable points of doctrine out of the natural sense

(4) To apply, if he have the gift, the doctrines rightly collected to the life and manners of men in a simple and plain speech. (349)

Nehemiah 8.4–6 divides the minister's role into opening and reading the book to his people, giving the sense of it, and causing them to understand the word within a ritual context of praising the Lord. The "art" of Perkins's title, like the "art" of Joseph Hall's, identifies both as Ramist works, typically as here gathering the rules of a subject and arranging them methodically for use and memorability (Perkins 332). In practice, this meant progressively bifurcating the large issues and smallest particulars of a subject matter.

The doctrines, reasons, and uses of the Puritan sermon norm collapse these four into three in a design that sifts texts and moral implications with remarkable precision. Normally, the preacher quotes his text and "opens" out its circumstances, contexts, etymologies, grammar, tropes, and schemes, developing an exact exegesis of individual words and a detailed exposition of the biblical context along with meticulous definitions and distinctions. He logically deduces and "proves" his doctrine through numbered sequences of reasons. Finally, he applies derived lessons in series of memorable uses. The sermon's most striking features are its numbered lists, compacted headings and subheadings, and positive/ negative bifurcations. It abounds in scripture references and contextualizings and, when printed, in textual glossing. Its written mode often includes questions and answers or objections and replies—devices that perhaps appropriate the "prophesying" discussions that followed the oral delivery and allow the preacher the last word in a controversy. Boyd Berry backgrounds doctrines and uses in the Puritan psychosocial situation: Doctrine, he argues, aims at stability because Puritans lived so much in a changing and "protesting" world, while uses aim to present programs for change.[10]

The majority of Bunyan's theological treatises follow the basic model of right interpretation, true exposition of doctrine, and sound application to life and judgment (Perkins 328), with the proviso that in Bunyan as in others the categories sometimes shade forwards and backwards into each other. As "the sum of the sum" of preaching for Perkins is to "Preach one Christ by Christ to the praise of Christ" (349), so Bunyan expresses his goal as "to exalt and advance the first born of *Mary*, the Lord of Glory, and to hold on his side" (*A Vindication of Some Gospel Truths Opened* 1:136). *The Acceptable Sacrifice* offers "the text opened in the many workings of the heart" and an organizational division into "The doctrine, assertion, demonstration, and conclusion" (Offor 1:688, 690). *Good News For the Vilest of Men* divides into "The Text opened," "The Doctrine," supported by "The Reasons of the Point," and finally "Application" (xi:9–11). In *The Holy War* Captain Boanerges's sermon, after laying down his text (the same as that of Bunyan's *The Barren Figtree*), "shewed what was the occasion of the words . . . what was contained in the sentence. . . . by whose authority this sentence was pronounced. . . . And lastly . . . the *reasons of the point*. . . . But he was very pertinent in the application" (158–59). Generally speaking, in his earlier works Bunyan concentrates on texts and in late works on applications.

The first stage in processing a scriptural passage, interpretation, consists of "the opening of the words and sentences of the scripture, that one entire and natural sense may appear" (Perkins 337–38). "Opening" now signifies textual analysis and exposition, as in the Bunyan title *Some Gospel Truths Opened According to the Scriptures*. Additional Bunyan phrasings for this activity include *multiplying* and *laying down* Scriptures (1:54, 65) or *clearing* a text (1:76 and Offor ii:25). This stage stabilizes the biblical text, subjects it to grammatical, rhetorical, and logical analysis and explicates its difficulties of sense, language, and historical reference. In

The Strait Gate he approaches the words of his text, Luke 13.24, "First by way of *Explication*, and then by way of *Observation*." Explication will proceed first "with reference to their *general scope*" and then with reference to four particulars:

> (1) An intimation of the kingdom of heaven
> (2) A Description of the entrance into it
> (3) An Exhortation to enter into it
> (4) A motive to inforce that exhortation. (v:71–73)

He considers the word *strive* in three questions: "What does the word *strive* mean?" "How should we strive?" "Why should we strive?" The observations subdivide into numbered series of the general and particular (v:102ff.).

The Saints' Knowledge of Christ's Love, on the text of Ephesians 3.18–19, lays out Bunyan's organizational practice with greater fullness and self-consciousness than usual and illustrates the norms of his and Puritan practice. It partitions its subject: "In my attempting to open these words, I will give you, some that are of the same kind. And then show you, First, The reasons of them; and then also, Secondly, Something of their fulness" (Offor 11:3, and similarly IX:143). It divides its text ("And to know the love of Christ, which passeth knowledge") thus:

> In the words we are to take notice of three things:
> *First*, Of the love of Christ.
> *Second*, Of the exceeding greatness of it.
> *Third*, Of the knowledge of it.
> *First*, We will begin with the first of these, to wit, *Of the love of Christ*. Now for the explication of this we must inquire into three things, *First*, Who Christ is. *Second*, What love is. *Third*, What the love of Christ is. *First*, Christ is a person. (Offor 11:15)

When he develops this third point, Bunyan similarly deconstructs his text:

> The love of Christ is made known unto us, as I said, First, By his dying for us. Second, By his improving of his dying for us.
> 1. His dying for us appears, (1.) To be wonderful in itself. (2.) In his preparations for that work.
> (1). It appears to be *wonderful in itself*, and that both with respect to the nature of that death, as also, with respect to the persons

for whom he so died. (Offor 11:17, and see similarly 1x:138 and Offor
1:577)

Detailed outlines precede some Bunyan treatises as a kind of table of
contents (e.g., *Good News For the Vilest of Men*).

2 Timothy 2.15–16 authorizes such practice when it speaks of "rightly
dividing the word of truth," but clearly it is vulnerable to abuse. Bunyan's
longest chain of enumerations runs to twenty-five items (*Come, and Welcome, to Jesus Christ* viii:377–79), and *Saved by Grace* carries enumera-
tion to another kind of extreme in listing in only two pages seven elements
of the place of salvation, four of the company there, four of raiment there,
and four of the continuance of the heavenly state (viii:181–82). Joseph
Glanvill's preaching manual of 1678, like the Epistle to Timothy, worries
about excesses, saying: "Of all the Vanities in Preaching there is none
less accountable than this, of dividing Texts into indivisibles; and minc-
ing them into single words; which makes them signifie nothing," and in
The Country Parson, even the gentle George Herbert describes such ministerial analysis of the Word as "crumbling a text into small parts" and
thus presenting "not Scripture, but a dictionary."[11]

The second stage of the Puritan sermon, reasons, provides an exposition of what lies behind the "opened" Scripture. It translates the Bible
into doctrines, draws positive proofs from Scripture, logic, and practical
observation, solves doctrinal doubts and questions arising from the text
and context, and delivers its meanings " 'in proper, significant, perspicu-
ous, plaine, vsually knowne words and phrase of speech, apt, and fit to
expresse the thing spoken of to the vnderstanding of the hearers without
ambiguity' " (v:xxviii; P. Miller, *New England Mind* 341).

Perkins lists three ways of attaining reasons, or three alignments of
an immediate text with the Scriptures at large: "the analogy of faith,
the circumstances of the place propounded and the comparing of places
altogether." The first of these reduces the Scriptures to the consistency
needed to support progressive dynamic reading exercises. It assumes an
ascertainable unity behind the sometimes diverse and even contradictory Scriptures. Bunyan outlines the principles upholding this assumption
when he insists that the meaning of an individual word "admit[s] of an enlargement or a restriction, according to the true meaning and intendment
in the Text. We must therefore diligently consult the meaning of the Text
by compareing it with other Sayings of God; so shall we be better able to
find out the mind of the Lord, in the Word which he has given us to know

it by" (*Come, and Welcome, to Jesus Christ* VIII:245–46, and similarly *Of the Trinity and a Christian* Offor II:386). At its best the analogy of faith encourages "the fruitful corroboration of Word by way," but it is also subject to "a kind of exegetical gerrymandering, carried out to authorize practice" (Kaufmann, *Pilgrim's Progress* 114, 108–9).

Perkins's other recommendations for achieving "true exposition of doctrine" call for the propounding of textual circumstances and the comparing of places. The compression implicit in the analogy of faith balances the expansion implicit in propounding and collating textual places to develop expansive understanding. To *propound* is to submit the place to a series of questions—"who? to whom? upon what occasion? at what time? in what place? for what end? what goeth before? what followeth?" (338)—in other words, to subject an item to the process of invention or visiting the topoi or commonplaces to "discover" its logical causes and subjects and adjuncts. Recent examples showed Bunyan "propounding" the words *love* and *strive*. The more sophisticated "collation of places" practices concordancing and typology. By *concordancing* I mean the actual or mental (i.e., memorial) recourse to a thorough index of biblical words and motifs to align an immediate text with its larger and largest biblical contexts. Typology marshals collected texts within a systematic recognition of the New Testament as reconstituting and transcending the Old. It rests upon the assumption that God authored the Bible so as to invite active reading and to offer progressive interpretations and applications to worthy readers.

Grace Abounding roughs out an early concordancing occasion when an opening presented Bunyan with a text and instructions for processing it and, by extension, other future texts.

I was greatly lightened and encouraged in my Soul; for thus at that very instant it was expounded to me: *Begin at the beginning of Genesis, and read to the end of the Revelations, and see if you can find that there was any that ever trusted in the Lord, and was Confounded.* so coming home, I presently went to my Bible to see if I could find that saying, not doubting but to find it presently, for it was so fresh, and with such strength and comfort on my spirit, that I was as if it talked with me. Well, I looked, but I found it not; only it abode upon me: then I did aske first this good man, and then another, if they knew where it was, but they knew no such place: at this I wondered that such a sentence should so suddenly and with such comfort, and strength seize and abide upon my heart, and yet that none could find it, (for I doubted not but it was in holy Scripture.) Thus I continued above a year, and could not find the place, but at last, casting my eye into the Apocrypha-Books, I found it in Ecclesiasticus 2.10; this, at the first, did somewhat daunt me; but because by this time I had got more experience of the love and kindness of God, it troubled me the less; especially when I considered, that though it was not in those Texts that we call holy and Canonical, yet forasmuch as this sentence was the sum and substance of many of the promises, it was my duty to take the comfort of it, and I bless God for that word, for it was of God to me. (21–22)

The event illustrates passive reception giving way to active search of Scriptures, Bunyan's extraordinary diligence, his relative attention to the Apocrypha, and his secondary research in godly conversation. In fact, the Geneva Bible binds the apocryphal books between the Old and New Testaments. It would be wonderful to know how many times within the year he reread the whole Bible in quest of this single passage. In a lifetime of such athletic disciplined inquiry, he virtually memorized the Bible.

Bunyan's enormous output, and the numerous biblical references attached to even a brief passage, argue that his own fully stocked memory and his intense love of the Bible were his most important resources, but *Solomon's Temple Spiritualized* specifies "my Bible and Concordance [as] my only library in my writings" (Offor III:464). A contemporary bookseller's advertisement credits Bunyan with having created a concordance which has not survived. Its full title lists the desiderata of the genre: *A New and Useful CONCORDANCE to the Holy Bible, according to the last Translation, containing the most material Scriptures in the Line and Margent of the old and new Testament, together with the chief acceptations of special words, with notes to distinguish the promises, commands, and threatnings, being plainer, and much longer than any of this Volume yet extant.* Bunyan may also have had a hand in compiling a concordance published by Vavasour Powell (1670/1), a copy of the third edition of which (1673) survives with "John Bunyan/His Book" written on the title page.[12]

Several occasions from *Grace Abounding* dramatize Bunyan's progress in concordancing. In an early search for "a word of Promise, or any encouraging Sentence by which I might take relief," he first grasps Mark 3, but fuller consideration discovers Hebrews (45). A later opening leads him to resolution at one remove: "Now went I also home rejoycing, for the grace and love of God: So when I came home, I looked to see if I could find that Sentence, *Thy Righteousness is in Heaven*, but could not find such a Saying, wherefore my Heart began to sink again, onely that was brought to my rembrance, *He of God is made unto us Wisdom, Righteousness, Sanctification, and Redemption*; by this word I saw the other Sentence true, I Cor. I.30" (72). The culminating event of the first part of *Grace Abounding* moves from a surprise opening through disciplined textual exercise to joyful success and multiplying revelations:

> As I was sitting by the fire, I suddenly felt this word to sound in my heart, *I must go to Jesus*; . . . while I was on this sudden thus overtaken with surprize, Wife, said I, is there ever such a Scripture, *I must go to Jesus?* She said she could not tell; wherefore I sat musing still to see if I could remember such a place, I had not sat above two or three minutes but that came bolting in upon me, *And to an innumerable company of Angels*, and withal, *Hebrews* the twelfth, about the mount *Zion*, was set before mine eyes. *Heb.* 12.22, 23, 24. Then with joy I told my Wife, O now I know, I know! but that night was a good night to me, I never had but few better. . . . Thorow this blessed Sentence the Lord led me over and over, first to this word, and then to that, and shewed me wonderful glory in every one of them. (82)

The domestic scene charmingly backgrounds the process through which concordancing advances from "opening" as private psychic surprise to "opening" as disciplined Bible study with homiletic goals.

The collation of places proceeds by such general or random collections of related texts, but also by a more formal aligning of "parallels one beside another, that the meaning of them may more evidently appear" (Perkins 338). When the collating distinguishes between Old and New Testament analogues and uses that distinction for other kinds of argument, its name is, of course, typology. Bunyan often addresses both its theory and practice. *Solomon's Temple Spiritualized* inaugurates a definition in calling the details of Solomon's temple "but figures, patterns, and shadows of things in the heavens, and not the very image of the things," and in recognizing this Old Testament temple as "still more amplified, where it is written of the New Jerusalem, which is still the New Testament church on earth, and so the same in substance with what is now" (Offor III:464, 468). The prefatory epistle amplifies his typological procedures and intentions thus:

> Since those shadows of things in the heavens are already committed by God to sacred story; and since that sacred story is said to be able

to make the man of God perfect in all things—2 *Ti*. iii 15–17.—it is duty to us to leave off to lean to common understandings, and to inquire and search out by that very holy writ, and nought else, by what and how we should worship God. . . . And, although the old church-way of worship is laid aside as to us in New Testament times, yet since those very ordinances were figures of things and methods of worship now; we may, yea, we ought to search out the spiritual meaning of them, because they serve to confirm and illustrate matters to our understandings. Yea, they show us the more exactly how the New and Old Testament, as to the spiritualness of the worship, was as one and the same; only the old was clouded with shadows, but ours is with more open face. (Offor iii:464; see also *Questions About the Nature and Perpetuity of the Seventh-Day Sabbath* Offor ii:367–69, 379; *Ebal and Gerizzim* esp. ll. 584–613; *Paul's Departure and Crown* Offor i:742)

Bunyan's principles here endorse the traditional definition of typology as the transtemporal alignment of Old Testament types with New Testament fulfillments on the assumption that God has carefully foreshadowed in the Old Testament his ultimate or anagogical truths and intentions in the New.

This and a second Bunyan treatise align Old and New Testament parallels on a large scale. *Solomon's Temple Spiritualized* thoroughly "gospelizes" the Old Testament details of Ezekiel 43, while *The Holy City; or, The New Jerusalem*, with the same thoroughness, concords and "spiritualizes" the New Testament data of Revelation 21.10–22.4, a text Bunyan calls a "Mystery" and "so hard and knotty a Scripture" whose meanings he proposes to "unwrap" (iii:75, 70). Both sites provide lively speaking pictures of architectural details. Solomon's temple becomes "a light to guide us while searching into gospel truths" and is itself "only a type of that infinitely more glorious antitype, the Christian dispensation" (iii:460, 461). Solomon is a type of Christ as builder of the Church (465); Mount Moriah is "a type of the Son of God, the mountain of the Lord's house, the rock against which the gates of hell cannot prevail" (465); and, in smaller matters, "A golden censer is a gracious heart, heavenly fire is the Holy Ghost, and sweet incense the effectual fervent prayer of faith" (492). The second site, the Heavenly City of Revelation, completes the diptych. Its intention, like its scriptural location, is culminative, as Bunyan proceeds seriatim through a doctrinal exposition and concordancing discussion of each phrase of the twenty-one Bible verses. In Offor's words, Bunyan has here "richly developed the treasures of the Bible in reference to this solemn subject," a subject "of pure revelation" amplified "from the inexhaustible storehouse of God's Word" (Offor III:395–96).

The larger aim of these collation processes embodies the believer's and the minister's strictest duty, uses or applications. Intellectually, this third component of the sermon, according to Perkins, "is used for the information [i.e., formation] of the mind to a right judgment concerning things to be believed" or confuted; in practical terms, application encompasses instruction and correction with respect to life and behavior (343). Bunyan's *Vindication of Some Gospel Truths Opened* urges believers to "see that you are laborers after a more experimentall knowledge of our Lord Jesus Christ" (1:217). Applications are emphatically "experimentall" and "profitable," serving the several arenas of Puritan edification, self-examination and deepened faith, social godly discourse, and public exhortation. In a frequent metaphor, they are the harvest of a previously sown Word (see Mark 4.14ff.). In the authorizing text of 2 Timothy 3.15–17, the profitableness of Scripture divides according to doctrine, reproof, correction, and instruction in righteousness to make the man of God perfect and throughly furnished to every good work. When his audience are "so Sermon-smitten, and also so Sermon-sick by being smitten, that they knew not what to do" (*Holy War* 158), the preacher's applications dictate appropriate action.

Applications relate achieved and "reasoned" doctrine to future acts, and Bunyan regularly enumerates his advice under such headings as "helps" or counsels, or as a word of information, a word of direction, a word of examination, a word of caution, a word of encouragement, and a word of rebuke or reproof. At length *A Few Sighs From Hell* lists what it will draw out of Holy Writ as "both threatnings and promises, besides those heavenly counsels, loving reproofs, free invitations to all sorts of sinners," and it enumerates its five categories as counsel, instruction, forewarning, comfort, and grief to those that fall short (1:340, 341–42, and see 359). In enumerations, the general precedes the particular and advice precedes warnings. "Discoveries," "inquiries," "considerations" (i.e., points to be considered), and "topics for further study" remind us that applications may in part be summarized as invitations to meditation.[13]

As in these series, applications often distinguish between morally positive and morally negative audiences and outcomes and seek not just to make lessons operative but to reach their ingrained spiritual conditions.

Within this third phase of the Puritan sermon, Puritan psychology, rhetoric, and affective stylistics most come into play whether to terrify or to cajole. *The Holy City*, for example, explicitly addresses the range of its audience as four sorts of readers: "The Godly Reader," "the Learned Reader," "the Captious Reader," and "The Mother of Harlots &c." Typically, the initial stage of a sermon provides information; the second stage provides intellectual exercise and reinforcement with the beginnings too of such persuasive affect as may arise from points well argued. But with the final phase of applications, as Perry Miller describes the Puritan norm, "the preacher's intention was predominantly to move the emotions, to drive down the channel of the nerves to the heart, to the will and passions, those phantasms he had imprinted through the doctrine and the reasons upon the understanding" (*New England Mind* 344, 345–46, 346–47). Stylistically, while the doctrine should be delivered with moderation, the exhortation calls for fervor and vehemence as it calls upon the audience to believe and perform and be energized by the Holy Ghost (348). Characteristically, what is heightened in the latter reaches of Bunyan's sermon treatises is not art but sincerity and urgency.

Plainness of style is a or *the* Puritan ideal, along the lines Sacvan Bercovitch outlines in these terms: "To speak plainly was not primarily to speak simply, and not at all to speak artlessly. It meant speaking the Word—making language itself, or self-expression, an *imitatio Christi* because it conformed to scripture." Similarly, N. H. Keeble lists the key elements of Puritan plain style as "the need to communicate effectively and intelligibly . . . ; the obligation to avoid arrogant self-display which attracts attention to manner rather than matter . . . ; and the desirability of treating holy things with due awe and seriousness." The sermon's chief features are brevity, perspicuity, spirituality, concreteness and imagery drawn from daily life, immediacy and strength of effect, and "clarity, logical consistency, and general intelligibility to the thoughtful though not necessarily learned reader." The goal is to be eloquent not ostentatious, clear but not rude.[14] Puritan sermon manuals recommend a style wholly subordinate to the Bible, "nothing but a transparent glass through which the light of revelation might shine" (P. Miller, *New England Mind* 349). The delivery should suppress intrusive skill and distracting elements and persuade the audience that the spirit of God is speaking through the minister. The ideal style for Perkins is both to fit the people's understanding and "to express the majesty of the Spirit" (345).

What W. Fraser Mitchell offers as objections to Perkins's sermon advice

—its resulting "baldness and inelegancy of diction" and "the slightest possible amount of added comment" (101)—Bunyan follows as the loftiest principle. A prefatory epistle to *The Doctrine of the Law and Grace Unfolded* hopes that the reader will "finde this book empty of Fantastical expressions, and without light, vain, whimsical Scholar-like terms" and will find it filled with "a parcel of plain, yet sound, true, and home sayings" (II:16). Bunyan's "Address to the Learned Reader" of *The Holy City* similarly shows no wish "to beautif[y his] matter with acuteness of Language," preferring "pure and naked Truth" to "*high swelling words of vanity*" (III:71; Bunyan's italics).

Puritan stylistic severity was, however, qualified in one main particular. Ministers were encouraged to use similes, both to follow biblical precedent and to open up the linguistic and poetic riches of the Old and New Testaments. Thus David Leverenz can speak of "the flexibility of sermon imagery" that makes the otherwise obsessively rigid sermon form "capacious, supple, and vivid."[15] As with other Puritan elements, figural usage in the sermon is dictated and assessed by moral purpose. Thus, "if a simile or metaphor made truth more intelligible and rationally convincing it was good; if it simply tickled the senses and gave pleasure, or if it distracted the reader's attention from the doctrine, it was clearly bad."[16] Insofar as a figure is instructional and basically descriptive of God's world, it is to be applauded; insofar as it calls intrusive attention to the author's fancy it is, if not reprehensible, at least frivolous. The use of inherited similes does not have the effect we might expect, of promoting authorial individuality. Instead it makes a whole range of Puritan sermon imagery interchangeable and thus "synchroniz[es] author, reader, and scripture" (Bercovitch 31).

For three centuries Bunyan has been honored, and indeed loved, for his figurative skill, especially for the homely realistic details that conjure up the daily life of the seventeenth century. Beyond the striking sights and insights that occur occasionally, illustratively, almost accidentally, to some extent Bunyan's writing career may be measured by his developing skill and confidence in controlling large biblical metaphors to explore ideas and to structure whole works or large elements of them. At their fullest, such images control the allegories of *Pilgrim's Progress* and *The Holy War* but also such treatises as *The Barren Figtree, The Strait Gate,* and *The Heavenly Footman.* Because many late works lack even occasional illustrative metaphor, the development is not strictly chronological, but in general his Clarendon editor Graham Midgeley can trace in Bunyan's handling of metaphor a movement "from an incidental to a continuous use, . . . from a peripheral to a central position, from a mass of metaphors drawn from varied objects and actions to a body of metaphors all springing from one dominant metaphor, and in the use of the metaphor from an illustrative to an organizing and structural purpose" (v:xxxvii).

Bunyan uses metaphors to address professors not unbelievers, to combat backsliding rather than achieve the evangelical ends of conviction and conversion. In Midgeley's words, "Their aim is to awaken the awakened to their falling away, their hypocrisy and formalism, and to destroy the false belief that there is saving worth in a mere profession of faith and an observance of outward acts of piety" (v:xvi). Bunyan's treatises divide between two styles, one early, direct, simple, and controversial, aimed at peers seen to be struggling with Bunyan's own challenges of conversion and faith, and the other late, more decorated, more encouraging, and aimed at the obstinate, the backsliding, or women and children. Tindall describes these differences under the contrasting images of the sword and the fishhook: "On the evangelistic and controversial front he employed that straight and simple weapon the sword of the word, whose spiritual carnage conspicuously enlarged the province of the Lord; but for the capture and preparation of future theocrats, whose immaturity made the sword unchivalrous or inexpedient, he wisely preferred to angle with a bent and subtle instrument" (171–72). Such distinctions align with Bunyan's two roles of convert and minister and with his sermons' progress from texts of the law to those of grace.

The only surviving Bunyan sermon (as opposed to treatises evolved out of sermons) is his last, preached August 19, 1688, twelve days before his death.[17] It incorporates the traditional sermon elements we have been reviewing and also illustrates his late use of biblical metaphors. Brief by contrast with the published discourses generally—less than three pages in the Offor double-column folio format—it essentially follows their form in a highly polished fashion. The text, John 1.13—"Which were born, not of blood, nor of the will of the flesh, nor of the will of man, but of God"—transmutes into the subtitle *Shewing The Resemblance between a Natural and a Spiritual Birth: And How every Man and Woman may Try themselves, and know whether they are Born again or not.* Bunyan begins by contextualizing and then explaining the text; he "comes" as he says "to the doctrine," divides the reasons under two heads (or "similitudes"), subdividing the second under seven subheads (or "consequences"), before arriving at the applications. The first application calls upon the audience

"To make a strict inquiry." The second, his peroration—the last lines of the sermon, the last words we have from Bunyan—captures much of the teaching of his career in forceful expression: "Lastly, If you be the children of God, learn that lesson—Gird up the loins of your mind, as obedient children, not fashioning yourselves according to your former conversation; but be ye holy in all manner of conversation. Consider that the holy God is your Father, and let this oblige you to live like the children of God, that you may look your Father in the face, with comfort, another day" (Offor II:756–57, 758).

The body of the work develops a similitude between spiritual rebirth and the birth of a baby, supporting John 1.13 with the same metaphor from Ezekiel 16.8, 11, 13. It divides into a consideration of the baby's relation to its mother and then the child's relation to its father. The shift from baby to child, from one parent to the other, from one set of priorities to another, builds into this sermon a sequenced progress lacking in some of the treatises. This sermon analyzes and concords texts, seeks out illustrative examples, develops experiential anecdotes and realistic gestures to bring lessons home, and applies biblical analogues. It has no supporting (self-conscious) textual apparatus. Offor, perhaps for logistical reasons, suggests that in the absence of a holograph, what survives may represent the notes of the sermon by a member of the audience, but in form, style, content, and ambitions it is typical of Bunyan's treatise manner and matter generally. *Mr. John Bunyan's Last Sermon* reflects both the mellowing of doctrine and teaching purpose and some historical and biographical shifts remarked upon elsewhere. It also shows a confident and supple use of large metaphor for structural purposes, a well-integrated rather than appliquéd use of smaller decorative ones. Taken as a whole, it illustrates the practice of both Bunyan and Puritans generally.

II

THE TRADITIONAL Puritan sermon Evangelist delivers to Christian precisely follows the Perkins and Bunyan models described above to provide the most overtly embedded Puritan discourse within *Pilgrim's Progress* part I. Additional satellite sermon forms frame much of the content of the second half of the book. Just at the point of his escape from Worldly Wiseman and Mount Sinai, Christian encounters Evangelist for the second time. In a miniature sermon, Evangelist responds to Christian's confession by citing a biblical text, explicating the interaction of that text with the spiritual and biographical situations, then numbering his points, drawing a typological analogue, and finally calling for (and receiving) external supernatural confirmation of his discourse. In all this, Evangelist is proceeding through the generic sequence and intent of the Puritan sermon.[18] In its first phase the sermon's texts are Hebrews 12.25 and 10.38, the first invoking the Bible to embed a commentary upon the sermonic process and expectations within the discursive event itself: "See that ye refuse not him that speaketh; for if they escaped not who refused him that spake on Earth, much more shall not we escape, if we turn away from him that speaketh from Heaven. Now the just shall live by faith; but if any man draws back, my soul shall have no pleasure in him" (21). Evangelist focuses this second text upon Christian's travel in the Way in an explicit application: "Thou art the man that art running into this misery, thou hast began to reject the counsel of the most high, and to draw back thy foot from the way of peace, even almost to the hazarding of thy perdition" (21–22).

Evangelist introduces his texts with the formulaic: "Stand still a little, that I may shew thee the words of God" (21). His introduction presents doctrine, his second phase enumerates categories of exposition, and his final phase draws the applications to impel Christian toward the Wicket Gate and further travel upon the Way. The transition from doctrine to exposition occurs by way of *partitio:* "I will now shew thee who it was that deluded thee, and who 'twas also to whom he sent thee" (22). That distribution into causes is followed by a further division of the argument: "Now there are three things in this mans counsel that thou must utterly abhor" (22). As in the Puritan sermon, the items are first listed in outline and then discussed individually at length. The first point, "His turning thee out of the way," logically processes into a distinction between *his* turning and *Christian's* consenting to be turned. The second point, "His labouring to render the Cross odious to thee," is subjected to concordancing, and the margin lists five amplifying New Testament references. The third point invokes one of St. Paul's most developed typological contrasts in Galatians 4.21–27 (similarly Galatians 3.10), the contrast between Abraham's sons by the bondmaid and by the freewoman, "the Jerusalem which now is" and the "Jerusalem which is above [and] free, which is the mother of us all," or in Bunyan's phrasing the distinction between that which "now is" and that which "is in a mystery" (23). Appropriately for the immediate narrative purposes and Christian's conversional status,

Evangelist—like Paul before him—presents the law to be rejected with greater force and clarity than the distant promise. The applications briefly pursue the goals of 2 Timothy 3.15–17 in a lesson that has both negative and positive, both corrective and inspirational effects on Christian, who shows heightened awareness of past error and heightened eagerness for future amendment and salvation.

After Evangelist's thoroughly generic sermon, the second half of part I is free to dramatize variations on sermonic, meditative, and prophesying norms through a series of Christian's discourses with others and with himself. The first of Christian's peer socializings, with Faithful, comments upon both Christian's textual mastery and his development into the pastoral or mediating role. Christian responds to point after point of Faithful's personal history with a biblical text (2 Peter 2.22, Proverbs 22.14) or context (the Joseph type from Genesis 39.11–13), thus practicing both concordancing and typology. Tellingly, Christian identifies Adam the First as Moses (69, 71). Tellingly too, where Faithful assesses Talkative by way of Moses in Leviticus 11 and Deuteronomy 14, Christian proposes and propounds by way of 1 Corinthians 13.1–3 and 14.7: "*Paul calleth some men, yea, and those great Talkers too, sounding Brass, and Tinckling Cymbals;* that is, as he Expounds them in another place, *Things without life, giving sound.* Things without life, that is, without the true Faith and Grace of the Gospel; and consequently, things that shall never be placed in the Kingdom of Heaven among those that are the Children of Life: Though their *sound* by their *talk,* be as if it were the *Tongue,* or voice of an Angel" (80). Christian's discourse now frames sermonic procedures within fictional conversation. It evokes corroborating texts, pauses to define individual terms, develops the text as chains of words and recapitulations so that the narrative unit miniaturizes the Puritan sermon. Allegorically, these conversations between Christian and Faithful enact Faithful's developing textual capacity and thus deepen interconnections between the Word and faith[fulness] within the containing psyche of Christian.

The next stage of the narration advances sermonic procedure from doctrine to uses. After they assess Talkative's nature, Christian directs, and Faithful applies, a thorough sifting of his views. The testing intent and structures combine several Puritan discourses in an examination of contrasts between "Mouth-profession" (84) and the "Pure Religion and undefiled" (79) that manifests itself in full understanding and in action. Layered conversation sorts out as the questions and instruction through which a minister or church elders refine the testimony of belief presented by a would-be initiate to their congregation, or as the lively laymen's prophesying exchanges that might follow a sermon, or as the meditation through which a preacher might converse with himself to develop a future sermon. The goal of all these is what Faithful expresses as his aim: "I am only for seting things right" (81), that is, replacing empty words with a fully grasped, expounded, and applied text. The narrative appropriates questions and answers or objections and replies from treatises into character interaction and dialogue. Such interchanges refine expression, secure distinctions of thought, realign priorities to Godward (as Bunyan might say), and exploit biblical verses and types, their moral bifurcations giving way to enumerated arguments and applications—all components of the sermonic Word. Interestingly, the type Faithful cites to Talkative is Joseph from Genesis 39.15, recalling Christian's earlier instruction of himself (68, citing Genesis 39.11–13).

The early dialogue between Faithful and Talkative underscores these sermonic designs by attending to questions and preferences of style. Thus Faithful's edification replaces Talkative's emptiness with fullness of spiritual content and thereby honors the stylistic principles of plainness and perspicuity appropriate to an *imitatio Christi*. Faithful also speaks with mounting fervor and intensity of instruction and, like a preacher, takes fire from inspired perceptions of new truths in the texts he studies, expounds, and newly apprehends within the analogy of faith. Faithful's intensity shows especially in his glossing of nine biblical references for one set of propositions and seven for another (83). Faithful concludes by offering Talkative opportunities for objections and replies, that is for "prophesying" responses. After Talkative's departure, Faithful and Christian summarize the discourse as "plain dealing" and "faithful dealing" by contrast with the modern lapses they decry in "the Fellowship of the Godly" wherein professors "stumble the World, blemish Christianity, and grieve the Sincere" (85).

A number of small actions within *Pilgrim's Progress* part I glance at related typological proceedings. Christian's view of his travel as parallel with the Israelites crossing the Red Sea (44) foregrounds a typological possibility that often hovers behind the fictional pilgrimage as behind the Puritan sense of self and history in both England and America. The goal of Mount Sion and the Heavenly Jerusalem where the redeemed soul joins fellowship with Abraham, Isaac, Jacob, Enoch, Elijah, and Moses (159, 156, 161) is similarly generalized in both narrative and the Puritan sense of history. Other types and biblical spokespersons include: Tophet (10),

Sodom (110), Leviathan (132), David (62, 110, 130, 132, 133), Moses (132), Peter (105, 130, 131), Heman and Hezekiah (130), Hymenus and Philetus (120), John (110), and Job (131). When Demas (from Colossians 4.14 and 2 Timothy 4.10) claims to be the Son of Abraham, Christian places him more precisely with reference to 2 Kings 5.20 and Matthew 26.14–15 and 27.1–6, as having Gehazi for a great grandfather and Judas for a father (108). The shepherds concord and typologize by way of Esau, Judas, Alexander (1 Timothy 1.20, Acts 4.6), Ananias, and Saphira (122; see also *Fear of God* IX:14). Hopeful processes the opening provided by the text "Remember Lot's wife" along the lines recommended by the tradition of biblical meditation. After examining it from a series of angles, he aligns Lot's wife from Genesis 19.26 with Korah, Dathan, and Abiram from Numbers 26.9–10, as other signs and warning examples (109), and applies the meditation as richly as he can to his own immediate context and future. Christian's complementary processing of this text is cast in a sermonic rather than meditational mode, as advice to others rather than applications to the self.

The late encounter of Hopeful and Christian with Mr. Byends develops several satellite discourses. In a dialogue inset, Byends propounds a question that would allow a minister or tradesman to follow his calling for worldly gain. He and his schoolfellows analyze, define, divide, and enumerate their response into headings and subheadings in what becomes a miniature treatise. They enlist Abraham, Solomon, and Job in support of their profitable practice. Their procedure, like Talkative's speech, offers an empty parody of the structures Puritans would fill to their and others' edification, a parody of the ministerial role and the values of a prelatical or establishment Church as well. Pleased with their achievement, the Byends folk catch up with the proper pilgrims and propound the same questions to them. Christian's vigorously condemnatory answer proceeds, as theirs does, through sermonic formats, but differs in moral and argumentative rigor and in continuous biblical citation. As they referenced worldly values, Christian cites individual stories and divine assessments of conduct from Old and New Testament instances. He enlists and condemns "*Hamor* and *Shechem* [who] had a mind to the Daughter and Cattle of *Jacob*," hypocritical Pharisees, Judas, and Simon (105). Three of his five typological arguments explicitly recommend chapters and verses for further study. Christian's righteous confidence contrasts with the opponents' profitable flexibility, his openness to further inquiry contrasts with the opponents' comfortable complacency.

Christian's detailed recital of Littlefaith's history provides an opportunity for shared meditation upon the typal dimension of life history. Hopeful contrasts Littlefaith's not selling his jewels with Esau's selling of his birthright, assessing Esau in terms of Hebrews 12.16 as a profane person, a man who "fail[ed] of the grace of God" (12.15). Christian corrects his companion's typology and in so doing exercises proper typing and its benefits. That correction provides an expansive meditation or miniature sermon remarkable especially for its careful distinctions between spiritual and typological polarities:

> *Esau* did sell his Birth-right indeed, and so do many besides; and by so doing, exclude themselves from the chief blessing, as also that *Caytiff* did. But you must put a difference betwixt *Esau* and *Little-Faith*, and also betwixt their Estates. *Esau's* Birth-right was Typical, but *Little-Faith's* Jewels were not so. *Esau's* belly was his God, but *Little-Faith's* belly was not so. *Esau's* want lay in his fleshly appetite, *Little-Faith's* did not so. Besides, *Esau* could see no further then to the fulfilling of his lusts; *For I am at the point to dye,* said he, *and what good will this Birth-right do me?* But *Little-Faith,* though it was his lot to have but a *little faith,* was by his *little faith* kept from such extravagancies; and made to *see* and *prize* his Jewels more, then to sell them, as *Esau* did his Birth-right. You read not any where that *Esau* had *Faith,* no not so much as a *little:* Therefore no marvel, if where the flesh only bears sway (as it will in that man where *no* Faith is to resist) if he sells his *Birth-right,* and his Soul and all, and that to the Devil of Hell; for it is with such, as it is with the Ass, *Who in her occasions cannot be turned away.* When their minds are set upon their Lusts, they will have them what ever they cost. But *Little-Faith* was of another temper, his mind was on things Divine; his livelyhood was upon things that were Spiritual, and from above; Therefore to what end should he that is of such a temper sell his Jewels, (had there been any that would have bought them) to fill his mind with empty things? Will a man give a penny to fill his belly with Hay? or can you perswade the *Turtle-dove* to live upon Carrion, like the *Crow?* Though *faithless* ones can for carnal Lusts, pawn, or mortgage, or sell what they have, and themselves out right to boot; yet they that have *faith, saving faith,* though but a *little* of it, cannot do so. (128–29, and cf. Esau in *Grace Abounding*)

The sermonic mode here emphasizes individual words thoroughly expounded within the delivery; it uses anaphora, rhetorical questions, and iterations; and it registers homely analogues and proverbs for immediacy of effect and easy memory storage and retrieval. Even more important for our purposes than the precise and sequential moral polarizings, and thus the refinement of spiritual categories, are the tracing of the occasion to its Old Testament root and the amplifying of even that with a gesture toward Jeremiah's recital of the sins of Judah in the ass fable. As Faithful's interactions with Christian resulted in his developed capacity to call up apt biblical verses, so Hopeful's interactions include corrective instruction in the reasoning procedures proper for Puritan applications. The young Hopeful is brought to supplant his eagerness with "second thoughts" (129), to "consider the matter under debate. . . . [and] But consider again" (129).

Christian and Hopeful increasingly frame their discourse in numerical sequences as they assume instructional roles to other professors and to each other. A rightly instructed Hopeful can himself come to the enumerations that signal Puritan logic; with Ignorance, of course, the instructing Christian holds this high ground and skill. The topics Christian and Hopeful process late in their journey include attitudes toward the Word, faith, fear of the Lord, and backsliding. To show their achieved and rewarding fellowship when discussing the last of these, they cooperatively perfect applications, Hopeful presenting the reasons for backsliding, of which there are four, and Christian responding with the manners of backsliding, of which there are nine.

As these examples show, sizable blocks of evidence from *Pilgrim's Progress* part I compound structures normal to the sermon and meditation and embody them within the conversation of characters. Such appropriation answers narrative needs, of course, but shows as well what must have been normal to serious Puritans, what they called "godly conversation," "godly discourse," or in the words of *Pilgrim's Progress* "Saints fellowship" (137). The *conversion* of the first half has given way to the *conversation* of the second, and from its biblical uses *conversation* means not just speech but the practice of the Christian life after conversion or the ethics of living within the covenant (Hambrick-Stowe 200). Discussional compounds of sermon, meditation, and prophesying, including elements of catechism, look forward to deacons' dialogic examinations of new converts as they proffered, then polished, their conversion narratives for church membership, the subject of the following chapter.

CHAPTER FIVE

The Puritan Self as Narrative

> The true History of exemplary Lives, is a pleasant and profit-
> able recreation to young persons; and may secretly work
> them to a liking of Godliness and value of good men, which
> is the beginning of saving Grace.—Samuel Clarke, *Lives of*
> *Sundry Eminent Persons* (1683)

WE HAVE SEEN how the Reformation celebration of the Bible reached a late flowering in seventeenth-century bibliolatry; the corollary Reformation emphasis upon the individual reader led with similar inevitability to the Puritan fascination with life histories. For Puritans, the self was an example as well as a source of truth. Committed to the Way and a particular mode of the heroic, they eagerly studied, recorded, and reinterpreted the details of their spiritual lives, honoring Calvin's insistence upon a scrupulous examination of conscience for signs of salvation or damnation, such reviews of experience being conducted under the shadow of predestinate damnation and always with an eye on the heavenly goal. Absorbed in the mystery of their own identity and destiny, they were also keenly interested in the details of the lives of other "saints" alive and dead, especially achievements, falterings, and strengthenings in the arena of saving grace. They raised to both a necessity and an art the discursive method of reading how one's own individual life re-presented past scripts. By Bunyan's time, the precedents included the Bible and thus typology, Foxe's *Actes and Monuments* and thus English Protestant historical models of persecution, and rehearsals of conversion morphology ranging from a propagandistic ideal to the immediate realities in one's own neighborhood and one's own heart.

Seventeenth-century Puritans defined themselves as separatist, congregational, independent saints. Clearly set off from the more worldly society, they committed themselves to and required of each other fellowship, freely made religious commitment, and proven fitness for the holy life.[1] Honoring these principles was indeed time-consuming. Church membership required covenanting with other members, professing faith and thereby demonstrating an understanding of doctrines, good behavior, and submission to the discipline of the church. It meant participating in such public activities as sermons, prayers, prophesyings, Bible readings, disciplinings, alms, covenant-makings and renewals, and other ordinances. It meant also associating intimately and continuously in smaller social and family devotional exercises, in conferences, counsels, and godly conversations with peers, advisors, and potential or lapsed converts. At the private level, it also meant regularly practicing "closet" devotions, meditations, and diary-keeping. The sine qua non of "gathered" churches was the conversion narrations of entering members.[2] These professions are also the foundations of autobiography and biography, the discourses through which the present chapter examines the evidence of *Pilgrim's Progress*.

The contemporary fascination with life history is backgrounded in the propagandistic Protestant hagiography of Foxe's *Book of Martyrs*, with its particular vision of England's history and destiny, and in the growing commitment to empirical instruction and experiential proof. Other secular factors include fluctuations in the history of printing and censorship; greater education, mobility, and career choices; less insularity through military service and news of America; changing views of nature, science, travel, curiosity, knowledge, and opportunity; and the Puritan political ascendency coupled with the age's varied pressures for deliberate and active political and theological commitment; in summary, "a widely noticed upsurge of innovation and experiment in religion" and "the sense of living in a period of unusual activity by the Holy Spirit."[3]

Out of these dynamics, Puritanism evolved a series of interlocking genres embodying exemplary life history, self-examination, and progressive meditative reexamination, and part I of *Pilgrim's Progress*, with its various epitomizings of its author's Puritanism and times, uses such genres as one of its organizing principles. Christian repeatedly retells the story of his conversion and providences to those he meets; at House Beautiful he performs the entering ordinance of church membership by telling the narrative of his conversion to the doorkeeper and the assembled "family"; he later exchanges life histories with Faithful and Hopeful in an analogue of the Puritan experience meeting and practices godly conversation with a series of what prove to be false professors. In the first half, his

autobiography serves a credentialing function; in the second, the shared
contrasting biographies refine the definition of what a true pilgrim or true
professor is. Incremental spiritual histories structure part I as a series of
loops, a design importantly undergirded by Puritan principles of story-
telling, "gathering," and "separation"; and of course part II is regularly
referenced back to the life history of Christian as biographical, generic,
and theological precedent.

◄◙| I |◙►

PURITAN NARRATIVE EXERCISES, like virtually every detail of their lives,
use and are securely founded upon biblical texts, particularly one New
and one Old Testament injunction. The first epistle of Peter (3.15–16) lays
the groundwork for developing and using narratives of the self: "But sanctify the Lord God in your hearts: and be ready always to give an answer
to every man that asketh you a reason of the hope that is in you with
meekness and fear: Having a good conscience; that, whereas they speak
evil of you, as of evildoers, they may be ashamed that falsely accuse
your good conversation in Christ" (see *Some Gospel Truths Opened* 1:114).
Psalm 66.16 also divides attention between the narrator and the audience:
"Come and hear, all ye that fear God, and I will declare what he hath done
for my soul," a verse quoted on the title page of *Grace Abounding*. The biblical models for such narrations are the David of the Psalms and St. Paul in
Acts 22 describing his sinful past and sudden enlightenment and election
on the road to Damascus. A number of Puritan autobiographies, including Bunyan's, claim to be authored by "the chief of sinners," a distinction
echoing St. Paul in 1 Timothy 1.15 ("sinners; of whom I am chief") and
in Ephesians 3.8 ("less than the least of all Saints"). Such claims signify
an intensive but not really a comparative assessment (Watkins 232).

Puritans honored St. Paul's injunction "Let all things be done unto edifying" (1 Cor. 14.26). Expecting to enfold individual careers and erase
idiosyncrasies within codified schemes, they honored inherited character
models and codified procedures for studying and expressing their failures and successes and therefore their progress in the worthy conduct of
daily life. Formal meditation on the self guided individuals to examine
events from their experience, measure themselves against the exemplary
histories of the most visible of the visible saints, and progressively build
a unified rational whole out of their lives. Such self-examinations were
at once exhaustive and never-ending for, as with the study of the Word,

they looked for openings and expected progressive revelations of insight and pattern. They also drew upon interpreted histories and ideal patterns in conversation and in various formal and informal advisories of friends and enemies, such godly conversation being authorized by Ephesians 4.29: "Let no corrupt communication proceed out of your mouth, but that which is good to the use of edifying, that it may minister grace unto the hearers." Because these "visible saints" were so much given to godly conversation in all its forms, we might also call them "audible saints."

Besides treasuring personal experience for its evidences of election and its disclosures of the kind of rational whole their lives were elaborating, Puritans valued their life histories as texts inscribing divine doctrine and imperatives. They continuously sought to interread the Bible and the largest patterns and smallest details of their lives on the assumption that the Word and experience were reciprocally illuminating, and they understood their "interpreted" life experience to be a secondary scripture or *logos*, a de facto authority by contrast with the de jure authority of the biblical Word (Kaufmann, *Pilgrim's Progress* 205, 209, 203, 201). Bunyan speaks for the Puritan tradition more generally in claiming that a Christian "cannot, will not, dare not be contented untill he find his soul and Scripture together (with the thing contained therein) to embrace each other, and a sweet correspondency and agreement be between them" (*A Few Sighs From Hell* 1:358).

In a Puritan commonplace, experience is the proving ground of the Word. *Experience* here means both the accumulation of an individual's deeds and thoughts and also the public telling or record of such accumulations in either of two religious discourses. In the first *experience*, personal recitals of spiritual history provided the device by which separatist churches "gathered" their membership—a *professor* is, of course, one who "professes," that is tells or has told his or her conversion history. In the second exercise, the *experience* meeting (OED 4.b), church members shared with each other their continuing and additional graces and providences, their slips and backslidings, and most importantly their accumulating insights into the meaning and pattern of their lives. Set narrations opening up to dialogic sharing demonstrates a new epistemology in action, the growth and exercise of one's graces. The American Thomas Shepard defines such advances as "renewed conversions" by contrast with the original traumatic one.[4] They demonstrate increased understanding and articulateness in the individual and also a more cohesive social and spiritual community.

Bunyan participated actively in the various genres of self-writing, and

Grace Abounding's account of an experience meeting acknowledges the process and intentions underlying the related discourses. His conversion began when he overheard four poor Bedford women exchanging their stories and "talking about the things of God" with an understanding and vision that far exceeded his own, even though he was himself at this time "a brisk talker" on religious matters:

> Their talk was about a new birth, the work of God on their hearts, also how they were convinced of their miserable state by nature: they talked how God had visited their souls with his love in the Lord Jesus, and with what words and promises they had been re- freshed, comforted, and supported against the temptations of the Devil; moreover, they reasoned of the suggestions and temptations of Satan in particular, and told to each other by which they had been afflicted, and how they were borne up under his assaults: they also discoursed of their own wretchedness of heart, of their unbelief, and did contemn, slight, and abhor their own righteousness, as filthy, and insufficient to do them any good.
>
> And me thought they spake as if joy did make them speak: they spake with such pleasantness of Scripture language, and with such appearance of grace in all they said, that they were to me as if they had found a new world, as if they were people that dwelt alone, and were not to be reckoned among their Neighbours, Num. 23.9. (14–15)

Bunyan's responses are those that the practice was designed to encourage, stern contrasts with his own case and affective meditative recollection. The event prompts Bunyan to return frequently to Bedford to renew the encounter and, after working through the intense anxiety so foundational to Puritan piety, eventually to join their congregation.

Whether one's life story was written by others in the forms of funeral sermons or biographies, or written by oneself in the forms of conversion narratives, diaries, meditations on the self, or formal autobiographies, the pattern was basically a progress from sin to grace, the compound of precept and example translating life into *logos*, pious legend, edifying example. Categorizing these genres as "spiritual gossip," William Haller discovers their origins in the universal concern for salvation, a natural interest in the daily struggles and adventures of the inner life, a generally accepted psychological profile and standard of measurement, and thence opportunities for the most minute comparisons of one's own history with the paradigm and with other converts' inspiring successes and comforting failures.[5] At least once in their lives all converts were required to write their own spiritual histories, texts shaped against the texts of predecessors and fellow believers. To be a pilgrim was to travel in the "Way" of such texts within the Puritan culture as within *Pilgrim's Progress* parts I and II.

Conversion narratives targeted only the first exciting chapter of the model narrative, the particular psychological and vocational paradigm that elders predestined for salvation were presumed to have attained and that present pilgrims hoped to exemplify in their lives. Haller outlines the idealized Christian life:

> The story was characteristically supposed to begin with an account of the horrid sins or scarcely less deplorable dry indifference from which the soul destined to be saved was called and after terrific struggle converted, generally by the reading of some godly book or by the influence of some powerful preacher. Then followed the chronicle, which might be more or less extended according to the circumstances, of the saint's lifelong war against the temptation to despair and the other abominations of his heart, lightened by the encouragements vouchsafed to him by God in the form of good fortune and of worldly and spiritual success. The last scene was the deathbed, one last terrific bout with Satan and then triumph and glory forever after. (*Rise of Puritanism* 108)

The character model promotes sobriety, humility, godliness, righteousness, efficiency, religious scruple, meticulous reasoning, intense introspection, strong self-awareness, and energetic self-mastery and self-reform (Schucking 9). When one is locked into searching and tireless preoccupation with the self, such traits can go beyond excess to obsession, and as Alan Simpson remarks of the typical Puritan: "Taught to expect [sin] everywhere, and to magnify it where he found it, he easily fell into the habit of inventing it" (91).

Along with these dramatics of conversion, spiritual conflict, and grace, Puritan biography presented the lives of actual persons as edifying models, lives at once exemplary, commemorative, and hortative, lives of proven actions not merely theoretical advice and thus instruments for practical use, not just contemplation. Presumably, contemporary, known, even local models for imitation provide accessible, do-it-yourself guides for salvation. In such a scheme, autobiography and hagiography overlap, the most ordinary of Puritans being by definition also a "visible saint." The Puritan emphasis on ordinary people, individualized only by commonplace details, translates the particular into the typical experience of grace, reinforcing the notion that individual biography can be assembled out of interchangeable parts since the spiritual design is the same for all believers. Even though the humble lay life celebrated not miraculous works but private achievements of faith, it could claim as much spiritual dignity and interest as the exceptional life, and its literary genres show the same elevation of the ordinary or, if you will, the same leveling.[6]

Puritanism fostered a standardized rather than individualized personality model within what Keats called "the vale of soul-making" (quoted in Talon, *John Bunyan* 81), and it defined self-knowledge as "th[e] anxiety to determine whether one's every experience fits the proper pattern (or, more accurately speaking, th[e] zealous effort to make all experiences fit)" (Webber 137). Given the mutual interaction of doctrine and experience in the believer's life, each autobiographical act at once expresses both the Puritan tradition in general and also a personal response to it (Watkins 82). While theoretically at least Puritans considered rote recitations to be anathema, in practice they thought of "extraordinary" experiences, those that deviated from the orthodox pattern, as in danger of crossing the line into Ranterism, Quakerism, or other antinomian "notions." Autobiographical writing with no touches of individuality is, of course, rare, but contrary to modern norms, such deviations are accidental rather than prioritized, especially in conversion narratives where self-renunciation necessarily seeks out formulaic expression. Full-scale autobiographers normally have achieved sufficient distancing to recognize both patterns of alternation and progressive spiritual stages. All these models structure experience, obliterate differences and resistance, and intensify guilt even as they transmute the anxiety thus aroused into a kind of shared security.[7]

In *Israel's Hope Encouraged* Bunyan calls the study of past sins "a soul-humbling, a Christ-advancing, and a creature-emptying consideration" (Offor 1:617), and as Owen Watkins remarks, "A man was what he was through the process of being remade" (238). Between the rude beginnings in original sin and the ultimate goal of salvation lies an edifying present whose principal endeavor is living a godly life, that is, analyzing and applying gospel principles and texts to every part of existence and pursuing self-definition through the whole range of relationships to God, others, and one's own past and ideal selves. Self-study thus intertwines with progress, process, time, networks, and perfection, categories whose expression welcomes a narrative mode.

Puritan spiritual bookkeeping targeted the debts and credits of sin and forgiveness, conviction and consolation, past and future, and sorted itself along the lines of the Old and New Testament covenants of law and grace. Although its dramatic quality makes it loom large, in fact conversion constituted only a brief prelude to what would normally be an extended spiritual life. After the initial startled awakening, the convert was steadily alert to signs of saving grace and backsliding, always questioning the genuineness of the former and fearing false security. He or she went round and round in a regular rhythm of perplexity, quest for assurance, diligent self-examination, moral dissection, and remembering God's mercies and promises. Assurance, like joy, grief, or fatigue, generates its own other set of dangers such as pride, despair, or complacency. Each achievement can thus spark another cycle of guilt and self-testing.

Conversion narratives offer the shortest and the simplest Puritan genre for expressing self-study. Their status as at once a personal and public profession predetermines their content, form, audience, and purpose. These narrations align the *evidences* of an individual's life with the grids of conversion morphology and document the "experimental" proofs of God's providences and the particular works of grace in the soul. Sometimes also called *confessions* (i.e., of experience) and sometimes *professions* (i.e., of faith), such narratives were expected to demonstrate an understanding of Christian doctrine and to be reinforced by the living of a godly life. These "original" stories of inner turmoil and deliverance from sin are characteristically very brief, confessional, and introspective, but also short of specific time, place, and person references. They make much of biblical and sermonic Words as spiritual openings. They generally key legal fears and free grace, the conviction of sin and coming to Christ.[8] This initiation rite, or in Bunyan's phrase "Entering Ordinance," measures a newcomer's compatibility with the group both spiritually and socially.

Conversion narratives provided the evidence upon which a separatist congregation, exercising "the judgment of charity," voted to include or exclude candidates for membership. Hence, we find such formulations as Thomas Shepard's title *The Confessions of Diverse Propounded to Be Received & Were Entertained as Members* and John Rogers's advisory "Every one to be admitted, gives out some experimental evidences of the word of grace upon his soul (for the church to judge of) whereby he (or she) is convinced that he is regenerate, and received of God" (quoted in Nuttall,

Visible Saints 113). Collectively such narrations define a separatist church and reflect the spiritual conditions of all its members. This means, as Patricia Caldwell argues, that the unique communal nature of the congregational way depends upon the verbal skills of believers and upon complex linguistic and rhetorical interactions among community members: "The full-fledged relation made up a three-sided figure: for the speaker, it was meant to be not a set of doctrines intellectually assented to but a living experience of the heart, voluntarily told in his or her own words; for the audience, it was meant to be not just a passive absorption of information but a spiritual act—of hearing, of rendering the 'judgment of charity,' and of receiving (sometimes rejecting) a 'living stone' for the temple; and for the 'Militant-visible church,' it was the closest thing in this world to a guarantee of the purest possible membership" (108, 46–47).

The assumptions of everyman as storyteller and everyman as sympathetic and creative interpreter of others' stories fostered close observation of detail, developed speaking, listening, and interpreting skills, and encouraged a continuous consciousness of the intimate relation between human event and divine cause (Hunter 83). The audience's responsive understanding of such narrations, like the events and articulation of the stories themselves, signaled infusions of grace in all participants. Because all members had already given formal public accounts of their religious experiences and principles, they were well prepared to participate fully in the ongoing, "audible" life of the church and help each other grow in grace.[9] They considered it their duty to assist fellow saints along the narrow pathway to heaven by encouragements and warnings as well as by example, and their responsibilities included regular visits to prospective church members and to backsliders. Throughout even his years in jail, Bunyan often served on committees for such purposes and actively participated in the official correspondence of his church.

Within the shared intention of "gathering" membership, credentialing processes differed from one church to another, of course. Normally candidates came first before the minister and/or the elders "to declare [and be cross-examined on] the work of grace in their souls." Thereafter they came before the full congregation to profess or "propound" and be received into its fellowship. In practice, presentation was often made on behalf of female candidates (see 1 Timothy 2.11). Bunyan was himself received into the Bedford congregation with its carefully defined membership practices but toleration for a variety of views on, for example, baptism. From its earliest weekly records of 1656, the Bedford Church Book shows committees of brothers or sisters visiting, and until satisfied revisiting, prospective members, and speaks of candidates giving accounts of the work of grace in their souls, giving their experience, "professing" and "propounding." Normally they are received into full church fellowship about a month after their public professions.[10] *Grace Abounding* shows Bunyan proceeding through such steps, breaking his mind to church members, conferring with the minister, telling and retelling his condition, and finally "propound[ing] to the Church, that my desire was to walk in the Order and Ordinances of Christ with them, and was also admitted by them" (25, 26, 79). The formal occasion, the lay participation, the testifying, and the question and answer format of such proceedings recall the "prophesying" examined earlier.

A Confession of My Faith, and a Reason of My Practice (1672) outlines Bunyan's ministerial views on conversion narrative. For him, it is "a church relation" or "faithful relation," consisting of both profession of faith and confession of experience, and it, rather than baptism, constitutes "the initiating and entering ordinance" or "entering appointment" into church communion (Offor 11:605–7). Bunyan would receive into communion all but the openly profane, all who show themselves to be "visible saints by calling" through their faith and lives (Offor 11:616, 605–6). *The Holy City* bases membership upon "the appearance of Grace; as of Gospel-Repentance, of the Confession of Faith, and of a Conversation suitable to the same" (111:177). *A Confession of My Faith, Differences in Judgement About Water Baptism,* and *The Barren Figtree* all acknowledge the contractual claims of the receiving community as much as of the individual (Offor 11:605, 619, and v:15),[11] and the latter treatise also makes provision for duly processing errant professors out of the church (v:35–36).

Christian's visit to House Beautiful in part I fictionalizes contemporary conventicle membership practices. House Beautiful equates with the (or a) church; it is "a very stately Palace" for pilgrims' relief, security, and entertainment (45, 47). Its guardian lions reflect the "Timorous" and "Mistrustful" initiate's entering fears, but prove harmless when the "Watchful" church officer aids the pilgrim. The porter explains to Christian that according to "the Rules of the House" (later "the Law of the House") he can attain entry to "the rest of the family" if his account of himself answers the expectations of Discretion (46, 47). Christian propounds to her and then to Piety, Prudence, and Charity, and after further questions and answers is welcomed into the family community. His several retellings of his history—first to the equivalent of the minister and elders, then to the equivalent of the full membership—and their catechizing or "prophesying" responses help him progressively to reinterpret it. Questions from Piety, Prudence, and Charity elicit fuller information on both his "historical faith" and his "saving faith." A later interview at the Delectable Mountains (119) foregrounds the church's characterizing exclusiveness. When the shepherds inquire into his conversion—"Whence came you? and, How got you into the way? and, By what means have you so persevered therein?" (120)—the conventicle's, not the candidate's, values are primary. The Shining Ones in Beulah similarly query Christian and Hopeful's past and receive satisfying answers that close the inquiry into identity (156).

In the allegorical fiction as well as the Bedford church, believers recite their narratives over and over again. After joining a church, they expect to multiply their understanding of the evidence of God's workings in their lives and reformulate their stories accordingly. Bunyan's spiritual history covers some thirty-five years, and autobiographical references scattered throughout his career progressively retell his story in a number of genres. *Grace Abounding*, dating from 1666, describes the preceding dozen and more years, and its six expanded editions graphically demonstrate the continuous reinterpretation of his life (xxx–xxxi). Chronology is rather blurred, as in Puritan autobiographies generally, but probably he officially joined the Bedford church in 1653. His ministry evolved out of his contributions to prophesyings. On the basis of his demonstrated understanding of the Word and his expressional skills, his fellow saints encouraged him "to take in hand in one of the Meetings to speak a word of Exhortation unto them" (*Grace Abounding* 83). *The Church Book of the Bedford Meeting* summarizes his ministry: "Jn Bunyan began to preach some time in the year 1656: But was not ordained Pastor till 21st October—1671. He entered into the joy of his Lord 31st August—1688 So that he was a preacher of the gospel 32 years—& Pastor of this Church 17 years" (15).

Grace Abounding is sometimes taken to exemplify Puritan conversion narrative, but in fact it retells Bunyan's conversion history only after it had already been restudied for well over a decade. An autobiographical section of *The Doctrine of the Law and Grace Unfolded* (1659), much more than *Grace Abounding*, tells his story in a way that reflects the nature and limitations of the conversion narrative genre. The four-page account repeatedly identifies its genre through the key word *experience*: "I must needs speak a word from my own experience of the things of Christ" and

"Something of the Authors experience" (11:156, and gloss). It is sometimes highly formulaic and self-conscious about its own proceeding and
rhetorical purposes. Key phrases in the following echo the usual generic
formulas: "For the further conviction of the *Reader,* I shall tell him (with
David) some thing of what the Lord hath done for my soul: and indeed
a little of the experience of the things of Christ, is far more worth then
all the world" (11:156). Like *Grace Abounding,* this narration alternates
positive and negative spiritual workings upon and within him (11:158).
Each of four paragraphs interrelates experience and doctrine, as a claim
to notable sinfulness modulates into detailed assurances drawn from the
life and promise of Christ.

The opening two sentences of the major paragraph of this early spiritual history, though long in themselves, compress many pages of *Grace
Abounding.* In its own way this sample encapsulates the content, form,
and tone usual to the smaller genre, but with an unusual stylistic intensity and thus heightened sincerity and persuasiveness:

> Reader, when it pleased the Lord to begin to instruct my soul, he
> found me one of the black sinners of the world; he found me making
> a sport of oaths, and also of lies, and many a soul-poysoning meal
> did I make out of divers lusts, as drinking, dancing, playing, plea-
> sure with the wicked ones of the world. The Lord finding of me in
> this condition, did open the glass of his Law unto me, wherein he
> shewed me so clearly my sins, both the greatnesse of them, and
> also how abominable they were in his sight, that I thought the very
> clouds were charged with the wrath of God, and ready to let fall the
> very fire of his jealousie upon me: yet for all this I was so wedded
> to my sins, that thought I with my self, I will have them, though
> I lose my soul (O wicked wretch that I was); but God, the great,
> the rich, the infinite merciful God, did not take this advantage of
> my soul, to cast me away, and say, then take him devil, seeing he
> cares for me no more: no, but he followed me still, and won upon
> my heart, by giving of me some understanding, not onely into my
> miserable state which I was very sensible of; but also that there
> might be hopes of mercy, also taking away that love to lust, and
> placing in the room thereof a love to religion; and thus the Lord
> won over my heart to some desire after the means, to hear the word,
> and to grow a stranger to my old companions, and to accompany
> the people of God, together with giving of me many sweet encour-

agements, from several promises in the Scriptures: but after this, the Lord did wonderfully set my sins upon my conscience, those sins especially, that I had committed since the first convictions, temptations also followed me very hard, and especially such temptations as did tend to the making of me question the very way of salvation, *viz.* whether Jesus Christ was the Saviour or no: and whether I had best to venture my soul upon his blood for salvation, or take some other course. (II:156–57)

This conflict lasted for more than a year before the Lord "did set me down so blessedly in the truth of the Doctrine of Jesus Christ, that it made me marvail" (II:157–58). The long paragraph goes on to review the role of Christ in his comfortings, and thus fulfills the generic expectations by adding profession of principles to confession of experience. No biographical events are particularized, but it differs most from *Grace Abounding* and the genre in ignoring biblical verses and particularized sermons to package the spiritual history.

Vincent Newey has recently labeled *Grace Abounding* "the apogee of a tradition where the habit of self-scrutiny made the introspective conversion document, the presentation of one's life as a text, a requirement for church membership" (" 'With the eyes' " 190), and it is generally taken to illustrate Puritan autobiography at its best. It distributes its content, measured by numbered paragraphs, moving from Bunyan's sinful past (1–35) to the conversion drama (36–264), "A brief Account of the Author's Call to the Work of the Ministry" (265–317), "A brief Account of the Authors Imprisonment" (318–39), and a seven-paragraph conclusion. As the first two of these sections serve historical and memorial purposes, so the third and fourth translate private self-study into the exemplary ministerial life. Although nearly four-fifths of the book elaborates his conversion, the final sections secure the overall purposes as more largely autobiographical. Roger Sharrock finds it exceptional only in the "pathological intensity" of its self-examination, while Owen Watkins commends its unusually strong narrative line.[12]

Grace Abounding, far and away the most familiar example of Puritan life-writing, may be a conversion narrative insofar as it fulfills its promise to give "a taste of the sorrow and affliction . . . the guilt and terror" of Bunyan's soul, along with "a touch of [his] deliverance therefrom, and of the sweet and blessed comfort that [he] met with afterwards," but when it progresses into analysis, and when Bunyan offers his views of the causes of his temptations and of the advantages they became to his soul (74), it takes on the wider time frame and intellectual dimensionality of the progressively studied autobiography. In line with the conversion narrative, Bunyan can say "now I am speaking my Experience" (82), but the outwardly similar statement "I am here unfolding of my secret things" (53) in fact points to the more inquiring and open-ended procedures of the autobiographical genre. A new mode of inquiry governs his long study of one occasion from his past, after which he still must confess "I have not yet in twenty years time been able to make a Judgment of it" (53). Within this mode Bunyan interprets his life as a series of provisional structures as he seeks to balance experience and the Word, temptations and biblical models, existential and providential readings, particularized individuality and universal ideals (Nussbaum 28, 19; see similarly *A Few Sighs From Hell* 1:332–33). *Grace Abounding*'s fascination derives from the passionate intensity and sincerity of Bunyan's quest for balance and hope among such conflicting pressures. These qualities—usually in more moderate amounts—epitomize the genre.

Seventeenth-century Puritan spiritual autobiography covers all or most of the author's specifically spiritual life, not just conversion, and targets a larger occasion and audience than conventicle entrance. Its greater temporal distance from its events makes possible larger understandings, clearer patternings, greater order and unity (Ebner 19). It does not pretend to be a daily record or spiritual diary or account book of spiritual debits and credits. It seeks rather a perspective review of the past, a patterned sequence of events over time, a representation of the soul as gradually rather than suddenly transformed. In line with their temperamental allegiance to spiritual openings, memory, and repetition, the Puritan goal is not that such records should be hardened into closure but rather that they should be secured for subsequent progressive rereadings and enlightenment.

William C. Spengemann recognizes three distinct but overlapping modes of autobiography: historical self-recollection, philosophical self-exploration, and poetic self-expression. Building his model from St. Augustine's *Confessions*, Spengemann anatomizes his first category, the *confession* of historical self-recollection, into "at once a conceptual act (the arrangement of temporally scattered events into their one, true, eternal design), a penitential act (the painful recollection of old errors), and an act of thanksgiving to God" for guidance and deliverance. When it serves the purposes of philosophical self-exploration, however, *confes-*

sion becomes "no longer a revelation of the self to God, who already knows everything, but a revelation of the self to the self, an act of self-knowledge, a process of discovering the true meaning of one's life." The first mode treats conversion as an achievement of the past, but in the second, conversion marks only the beginning of a continuous process to be worked out through the medium of the autobiography itself.[13]

Where the conversion narration, including Bunyan's, rests securely in the first of these categories, *Grace Abounding* spans the first and second. The latter author is both the agitated protagonist and the enlightened narrator (Spengemann 4), both "the recreated self of the past (the protagonist) and the authorial self of the present (the narrator-teacher)" (Newey, "'With the eyes'" 195). Bunyan's shift from an account of experience to a mode of inquiry coincides with an adjustment of audience from a conventicle gathering with its "judgment of charity" to an interview with the self over time. Autobiography thus moves from putting forward a static model of truth to recording "the dynamic process of experience through which the truth becomes known" (Spengemann 6, 44). Indeed for Spengemann *Grace Abounding* serves as a "how-to-do-it" book for the writing of autobiography (48).

Thus decribed, the autobiographical act overlaps with one of the kinds of deliberative meditation, that is, meditation on the self, and with Richard Baxter's categories of cogitation and soliloquy, the latter including colloquy with the self and prayer. Meditation on the self combines preparatory "pre-meditation," description, intellect, and emotion. As analyzed by Barbara Lewalski, such meditation upon sins and evidences of election at regular intervals was generally prescribed by Protestants as a formal audit "to promote humiliation, repentance, and constant watchfulness over the deceitful heart" (*Protestant Poetics* 158–60). In Christian's words, it is a matter of vanquishing one's "inward and carnal cogitations" (50). In the structural model Louis L. Martz takes as paradigmatic, meditation processes experience through exercises of the memory, understanding, and will. The memory targets both God and the meditational subject; the understanding considers, inquires, searches out, ponders, and generally "forme[s] a true, proper, and entire conceipt of the thing that it meditateth"; and finally, the will translates the achieved insights into "sundry Affections, or vertuous Actes." The progress is from observed and related phenomena, through strongly personal perception and moral analysis, to acts of faith or devotion. It is a progress from outer to inner experience, and from fact to thanksgiving or prayer.[14]

While the conversion narration applies for membership in a particular congregation, autobiographies embrace a very different didactics, most often targeting an audience of the author's children or comparably conceptualized parishioners (Shea 111–12). If the possible purposes of autobiography are catharsis, devotion, and propaganda, *Grace Abounding* certainly also includes the last of these, self-advertisement as Margaret Bottrall describes it "creep[ing] in under the guise of humility" (84). *Grace Abounding* translates Bunyan's sinful beginnings into an exemplary ministerial life, into a memorial stimulus and guidebook. Like Puritan autobiography generally, it both expresses a personal retrospective and provides an instrument for others to use in their spiritual and memory exercises. *Grace Abounding* specifies this second intention as the hope "that, if God will, others may be put in remembrance of what he hath done for their Souls, by reading his work upon me" (2). For Bunyan as for Puritans generally, self-study projected exemplary personal history as what Kaufmann calls "parabolic drama," that is the elevation of individual history into public parable (*Pilgrim's Progress* 83). Such parables, like the Word, are to be interpreted, meditated upon, and thence integrated into one's moral and spiritual vision.

The Bunyan self-writings we have been examining progressively objectify the self, and an advance from conversion narrative through conversional autobiography to exemplary ministerial autobiography stands poised to make the move from autobiography to biography, from self to other. In *Good News For the Vilest of Men*, published in the year of his death (1688), Bunyan recapitulates the earliest conversional stage and genre preparatory to putting himself forward as salvational model. He begins by reviewing his past, or what he calls "an instance of poor I," and moves on to exploiting that past for homiletic persuasive ends:

> I speak by Experience; I was one of these lowzy ones, one of these great *sin-breeders*; I infected all the Youth of the Town where I was born, with all manner of youthful Vanities. The neighbours counted me so, my practise proved me so: Wherefore *Christ Jesus* took me first; and taking me first, the Contagion was much allayed all the Town over. When God made me sigh, they would harken, and enquiringly say, *What's the matter with* John? They also gave their various opinions of me: But as I said, Sin cooled, and failed, as to his full *carrier*. When I went out to seek the Bread of Life, some of them would follow, and the rest be put into a muse at home. Yea, almost

the Town, *at first*, at times, would go out to hear at the place where
I found good: Yea, young and old for a while had some reformation
on them; also some of them perceiving that God had mercy upon
me, came crying to him for mercy too. (XI:35–36)

As this proceeds, we are hardly surprised to find Bunyan examining himself through the eyes of his society and even casting himself in the third
person. The stance is quite in line with *Grace Abounding*'s acknowledgment that others' conversion narratives credited his ministry as God's
instrument in showing them the way to salvation (85).

The Heavenly Footman explains Bunyan's position on how to use other
people's life histories: "*Think much of them that are gone before. First,*
how really they got into the Kingdom. *Secondly,* how safe they are in the
Arms of *Jesus*" (V:168). Exemplary lives, he says, "will be as good as a
pair of *Spurs*, to prick on thy lumpish Heart in this rich Voyage" (166).
At one stage in his autobiography, however, he disdains the stories of
his contemporaries on the grounds that modern life-writings are removed
from direct experience and overly formulaic (40)—precisely the critique
to which conversion narrative is most vulnerable—and he longs "to see
some ancient Godly man's Experience, who had writ some hundred years
before I was born." Luther on Galatians precisely answers this need: "I
found my condition in his experience, so largely and profoundly handled,
as if his Book had been written out of my heart" (40–41). Transferring the
Pauline principle of the Holy Spirit writing biblical interpretation upon
readers' hearts to this secondary reading, Bunyan again transmutes the
experience of the text into the text of personal experience.

At a number of points in *Grace Abounding*, he comparably appropriates persons and stories from the Bible, reading himself not just into the
Bible's characters and events but even into its chronology. Of one such
experience he affirms "that when the Lord Jesus did speak these words,
he then did think of me, and that he knowing that the time would come
that I should be afflicted with fear, that there was no place left for me in
his bosome, did before speak this word, and leave it upon record, that I
might find help thereby against this vile temptation" (23). Biblical figures
sometimes become voices answering or conversing with him, and he resolves a spiritual crisis by aligning himself with David, Peter, Judas, and
the Chosen People (66). It is entirely fitting from Bunyan's point of view,
remarks Brainerd Stranahan, that Bunyan be consoled by the same words
as Paul: "His life has, as it were, repeated an incident already described

in Scripture, so that the same words can simply be used again" (334). On such occasions, Bunyan is able at once to personalize the Bible, to gospel-ize his situation, to articulate his sinfulness and his hope in the language of Canaan, and to mythicize his own psychology.

Puritans often unself-consciously projected their characters and his-tories as types or fulfillments of both patriarchal and New Testament analogues, and *Grace Abounding* interweaves the identities of author, narrator, and protagonist so that Bunyan's life takes on the status of an exemplum and becomes enfolded into the typological. Sacvan Bercovitch speaks of the Puritan tendency to read the Old Testament as a collection of exemplary lives and to trap the self between Old and New Testament exempla in the double processes of typology, "merg[ing] the saint's life with scripture history," and Christology, "equat[ing] the saint with the heroes of scripture."[15] In compounds of piety and hermeneutics, such transtemporal conflations and such assumptions of mutual participation in the vitalized Scriptures imply the universality (at least for those of a Protestant Christian persuasion) of the explicit and implicit action and reinforce the mythic dimensions of the narrative. The personal, histori-cal, and literary are all caught up in the curiously centripetal energies of the Puritan mind, and this typology, like the view of the self and the Word more generally, is at once expansive and contractive, simultaneously ele-vating, reductive, leveling, and universalizing (Luxon 452). It shows both a fascination with the self and a leaving of the self behind as it at once per-sonalizes the paradigms and universalizes the self. Generalizing his own repeated textual adventures and compounding them with the experiences of biblical characters elevates the believer (Bunyan in particular), affirms the codified norms of Puritan life history, and fuses the individual with the permanent experiences of the range of Christian culture.

◄◙| II |◙►

THE EVIDENCE OF NARRATIONS in *Pilgrim's Progress* part I enfolds these developments. In the opening half Christian repeatedly details his sin-ful past in a series of loops that serve for recapitulation and reflection. The second half shifts from credentialing narrations to comparative ones that develop sometimes subtle distinctions within the prevailing norms. Like the retrospections for evidences of election, this second activity also seeks to discern divine intention and unity operating in the individual life and to translate the Word into imperative applications (Kaufmann, *Pilgrim's Progress* 199–201, 205). As here practiced, exchanges of experience stories, cataloguings of providences, and godly discourse on points of theology or moral conduct include catechistical cross-examinations under numbered heads and eagerly sought and applied biblical texts in support of that *"Justifying righteousness"* and *"saving faith"* that Christian and Hopeful long for (148). Collectively, this evidence shows that Christian's true "progress" takes place in his mind and in the analytic discussions that externalize interpretation of experience by the light of Scripture.

From the outset, Christian's private self-examinations take shape as a church profession. At first Christian either suffers from inarticulateness or identifies himself only matter-of-factly. He says of himself, "I can better conceive of [things] with my Mind, then speak of them with my Tongue" (13), and similarly to Evangelist, *"Christian* knew not what to answer: wherefore, at present he stood speechless before him" (20). At their second meeting Christian confesses to Evangelist his (mis)adventures since their first meeting. Soon thereafter he loops his history to Good Will at the Gate and then to the Interpreter, as later he reviews his immediate past and then his whole past in conversation with the catechizing inhabitants of House Beautiful. Through these assisted examinations, Christian develops a progressively more integrated articulation of his history and begins to see the pattern within his past and for his future, the rhythms of repentance and hope. Each stage adds details and re-presents more and more earlier data in a widening circle of progressively interpreted and redesigned retelling. That narration becomes fully formed when Piety helps Christian select from his history his most significative providences or saving graces (48–49).

Small as well as large points in the early pages recycle narrative elements to develop the recapitulative structure that governs this work. Christian redeploys earlier details when retelling the same and differing parts of his story to each new character he meets. At the Slough, Help reconstitutes Evangelist. Evangelist's reappearance reinvokes not merely his previous appearance but also the intervening meeting with Worldly Wiseman: "What said that Gentleman to you? . . . And what said he then? . . . And what said he then?" (21). Worldly Wiseman had played himself against Evangelist as advisor, and although he chiefly serves to reconstitute the pressures of home and family and friends—he promises "much safety, friendship, and content" (19)—he also plays variations on the Old Testament values of experience and mere morality or legality or civility at the expense of grace and mystery. Mount Sinai reasserts the challenges of the Old Testament in the topographical mode, and Christian retracing his steps from Mount Sinai to the Way models a pattern taken up again at Hill Difficulty and Doubting Castle.

This sort of repetitive or circular design served Puritans as a pervasive organizing principle, even, according to Boyd Berry, underlying their military strategy. In progressively opening and reexamining their lives, they discovered those designs and ends that, though then not apparent, had existed from the beginning. H. R. MacCallum sees loops in Milton's retelling of biblical history in the final two books of *Paradise Lost*, a loop differing from a straightforward chronological order by presenting first a moment of triumph and then a review of the trials leading up to it. This device of placing the end before the beginning contrasts unredeemed linear human history with eternity and transcendence, chronos with kairos.[16] In the Ramistic logic that dominated Puritan educational and thinking processes, the end was first in the mind of the creator though last in execution, and end or final cause divided between the completion and the perfection of a thing, the examined life and the heavenly destiny.[17]

As we saw in Chapter 1, allegorical narratives normally begin with a miniature or epitome of what is to be the essential challenge and action; they develop as widening circles echo and expand that crisis. Red Cross Knight, to take one example, like Christian, must sometimes go backward, unwinding the evil or error before moving forward for good. Such looping patterns make a certain amount of narrative anticlimax inevitable because it is inevitable in this version of Christianity. When the most intense crisis, the highest alertness and blazing vision, occur with the initiation stage of one's spiritual history, it could hardly be otherwise. That event cannot be extended into the diachronic except by reworkings of it, each subsequent one necessarily entailing narrative loss. Throughout, faith is sought and demonstrated, but the pilgrim—Christian or a Puritan generally—damns himself if he lapses into assurance or confidence, and faith without confidence can degenerate into something of a quibble. The narrative problem is how to keep the hero impelled steadily forward when in important ways the defining goal has already been attained. Moreover, vigilance is not really a dramatizable category, since only lapses from it can be shown and since it hardly admits of intensification.

After his conversion narrative has fully credentialed Christian, *Pilgrim's Progress* plays variations on the generic norms of self-history. The encounter with Apollyon in the Valley of Humiliation enfolds multiple versions of Christian's story into his wrestlings with himself. Initially, he recounts his story to Apollyon as he has to others, but soon Apollyon tells his version of Christian's history back to Christian. Reflected narrative collapses into internal dialogue. As with Spenser's Despair, Apollyon's Old Testament emphasis upon sin and damnation provides the hero with an occasion to fully articulate affirmations of New Testament promise. When his personal history is used as a weapon against him—a frequent predicament of Red Cross Knight as well—Christian's salvific recourse is to biblical texts, here "realized" in weapons from the armory of House Beautiful, that is the church.

In a second variation of the genre, soon after and because of his success with Apollyon, Christian and his former neighbor Faithful exchange personal histories. Their conversation loops the previous narrative, setting up a prism on the same sites but differing people met. Faithful's new perspectives on the City of Destruction, Pliable, and such places as the Slough, Gate, and Hill at once glance backward to Christian's analogues and open up distinctions between Faithful's wrestling with the flesh and Christian's with the Word. Faithful easily traversed the Slough and the Valley of the Shadow of Death, but was seriously tried against Madam Wanton and Adam the First—both absent from Christian's history—and by the Valley of Humiliation. Faithful never pauses at House Beautiful. At the point of the Hill Difficulty where Christian slept, Faithful received several blows for his version of a failure of memory or purpose, for inclining after Adam the First. The striker here, and a second later figure who overcomes him, enact Faithful's version of the Old/New Testament conflict; Christian identifies the former as Moses, and Faithful recognizes the latter as Christ by the holes in his hands and side. Faithful's Valley of Humiliation is at first merely a matter of discontent and honor, but later a severe trial with the misnamed Shame, a bold shape-shifter subtly insinuating himself against his victim. He experiences the covert underside of humiliation as Christian had wrestled with the overt dragonized pride of Apollyon.

The later "brotherly covenant" (98) between Christian and Hopeful varies conversion narrative norms in different ways, especially when, in the dungeon of Despair's Doubting Castle, Hopeful repeats Christian's autobiography back to him: "My Brother, said he, remembrest thou not how valiant thou hast been heretofore; *Apollyon* could not crush thee, nor could all that thou didst hear, or see, or feel in the Valley of the shadow of Death; what hardship, terror, and amazement hast thou already gone through, and art thou now nothing but fear? . . . Remember how thou playedst the man at *Vanity–Fair*, and wast neither afraid of the Chain nor Cage; nor yet of bloody Death: wherefore let us . . . bear up with patience as well as we can" (116, 117). As Apollyon emphasized the damning elements in Christian's story, this displacement to Hopeful reflects the cumulative saving graces. The exchange dramatizes how to derive strength, confidence, and inspiration in times of trouble from one's own history. Like the Bible, each person's biographical text demands continuous exercises of memory and reinterpretation and provides openings and progressive revelations. Self-study awakens Christian to God's will as inscribed in his own history.

Only later is Hopeful's own spiritual history presented (137–44).[18] In form and content it encapsulates the genre, listing his sins, acknowledging his saving graces, celebrating his guides (Christian and Faithful), numerically itemizing his resistances to the work of the spirit and his spiritual promptings, and detailing his endeavors to mend his faults (or as he says "my Reformations" [139]), his interactions with biblical texts, his reasonings and instructions, especially in imputed righteousness, and his prayers and revelatory conversations with Christ. His guilty self-awareness is characteristically Puritan: "Another thing that hath troubled me, even since my late amendments, is, that if I look narrowly into the best of what I do now, I still see sin, new sin, mixing it self with the best of that I do. So that now I am forced to conclude, that notwithstanding my former fond conceits of my self and duties, I have committed sin enough in one duty to send me to Hell, though my former life had been faultless" (140). As in *Grace Abounding*, Hopeful's conversional text is 2 Corinthians 12.9, "My grace is sufficient for thee." His salvation and gratitude are also typical: "And now was my heart full of joy, mine eyes full of tears, and mine affections running over with love, to the Name, People, and Ways of Jesus Christ" (143).

Hopeful's history, the most distinct and fully developed conversion narrative of part I, loops, epitomizes, and culminates all the preceding analogues. As the last, it harvests their incrementations, especially by compounding several other Puritan discourses as well. Besides close parallels with *Grace Abounding*, it offers a miniature experience meeting, a variation on ministerial autobiography, the catechizing, prophesying, and profession of faith of church membership, and the analytical trappings and characteristic enumerations of the Puritan sermon. Like Puritan scriptural meditation, it handles the Scripture as homily and, through the application of the places of logic, proceeds as a kind of preaching to the self (Kaufmann, *Pilgrim's Progress* 120).

Telling, listening to, and exchanging personal histories confirm these worthy pilgrims in their individual and communal faith and practice as professors and as a gathered community of visible and audible saints, by contrast with the false professors that provide so much of the content of the latter portions of part I. Two rare Bunyan puns underwrite these characterizations. One contrasts *professors* of the truth with *possessors* of the same (*A Vindication of Some Gospel Truths Opened* 1:126), and a second complains of professors turning their *fictions* into *factions* (*Questions About the Nature and Perpetuity of the Seventh-Day Sabbath* Offor 11:385). As a rule the unworthy pilgrims, though identifying themselves as traveling to the Celestial City, hence as "professors," have entered the Way by some crossing road rather than the Wicket Gate. Just as one sign of the godlessness of Vanity Fair is the lack of interest in personal histories, so these figures take no interest in others' narratives or in revising their own histories. Despite a series of probing questions, Byends, for example, will reveal only his secular history, and that rather vaguely. He avoids even his own name.

Christian and Faithful, as a tiny community of believers, examine some bases of *profession* in their reflective interaction with the first of these false professors, Talkative, a conversation appropriately enough about talking and about learning—or not learning—by talking. Talkative is "the only good systematic theologian" in Bunyan's story, according to Gordon Campbell, and reflects the author's distrust of theoretical theology in favor of a theology of experience ("Theology" 258, 259). Bunyan's definition of Quakers in *Some Gospel Truths Opened* zeroes in exactly on some of Talkative's limitations: "those who thought it enough to be talkers of the Gospell, and Grace of God, without seeking and giving all diligence to make it sure unto themselves" (1:15). Talkative's mellifluous flow and copious multiplication of terms are antithetical to the preferred Puritan plainness, in both quantity and quality. His empty style dissipates awareness rather than refining faith. Despite a certain narrative and stylistic charm, his loquacity enforces the principle of 1 Corinthians 4.20 that "the kingdom of God is not in word, but in power." Faithful can reject Talkative insofar as his human activity seeks to supplant heavenly gifts (76), but it takes Christian's very differently heroic background and skillful application of the Word to discard Talkative's failure of works. As he says, "Hearing is but as the sowing of the Seed," and men are judged by fruits (79–80).

Hopeful and Christian later meet up with differently defined talkers in Byends, Ignorance, Vain-confidence, the Flatterer, Atheist, and Temporary. *The Strait Gate* (1676) grounds twelve classes of false professors that essentially array these encounters. All fall under the heading of Opinionists, that is, those "whose religion lieth in some circumstantials of religion" and who "think all out of the way that are not of their mode, when themselves may be out of the way in the midest of their zeal for their opinions" (v:125). According to this treatise, Britain is plagued with thousands of false professors; with Opinionists alone, Bunyan avers, "this kingdom swarms at this day" (v:125).[19] Some of the false professors in *Pilgrim's Progress* may represent not only other religious persuasions, against whom Bunyan entered the lists of controversy, but even some specifically nameable individuals. William York Tindall equates Byends from the town of Fair Speech, for example, with Bunyan's Latitudinarian opponent Edward Fowler (49–63). Byends is one who would attain salvation by ways other than imputed righteousness, the principle which Bunyan upheld more voluminously than any other throughout his writings. As with Talkative, Byends's depiction is again about talking and the gap between talk and right action.

Byends is a character of considerable wealth, family, and worldly success, who—as he says—"had alwayes the luck to jump in my Judgement with the present way of the times, whatever it was, and my chance was to get thereby" (100). He claims both Scripture and reason in support of his position (102). *The Strait Gate* comprehends Byends primarily under the heading of the temporizing Latitudinarian: "He is a man that hath no God but his belly, nor any religion but that by which his belly is worshiped, his religion is always like the times, turning this way and that way, like the cock on the steeple, neither hath he any conscience but a benumned or seared one, and is next door to a down right atheist" (v:125–26). His religion alters with his company. He is a self-serving and expedient conformist—who "can be for *any* thing, for *any* company"—in short, a Vicar of Bray. Like the Covetous Professor of *The Strait Gate*, such people make a gain of religion, and like the Wanton Professor "misplead Scripture, to maintain [their] pride" (v:124). Like Fowler to Bunyan, and like Opinionists generally, Byends and his friends find the pilgrims too rigid, too committed to their own views and too rejecting of others' views, in sum too "righteous over-much" (101).

Christian and Hopeful next see but do not speak with Turnaway from the town of Apostasy (125) whose nature is inscribed upon his back: "Wanton Professor, and damnable Apostate" (125). *The Strait Gate* defines

Wanton Professors as those who abuse Scripture in support of their gluttony and idolatry and are thereby "the snare and damnation of others" (v:125, 126). Turnaway is less important in himself than in reminding Christian of Littlefaith, whose exemplary spiritual biography parallels Christian's to illustrate the point that all salvation histories are essentially the same. In Carolynn Van Dyke's term, his embedded story "remetaphorizes" parts of *Pilgrim's Progress*.[20] Like Christian, who draws the parallel between them (129), he awakens from sleep, begins his pilgrimage, is beset by psychic projections, is threatened, beaten, and robbed, alternately forgets and remembers his talisman, alternately senses loss and comfort, and alternately stands up or is dismayed and submits. In line with the limitations of his name, his story shows a man stuck at one stage of the conversion sequence but nonetheless salvageable. He has "*saving faith*, though but a *little* of it" (129). In affirming the unwarranted grace he has received, his portrait counters the false profession of the Free-Willer in *The Strait Gate*.

Despite the shepherds' explicit warnings against him, Christian and Hopeful next fall victim to the Flatterer—"a false Apostle," a "fine-spoken man" (134), in sum a hypocrite—and then to Atheist. According to *The Strait Gate* the Flatterer is one "whose religion lieth only in your tongues . . . [and] who are little or nothing known from the rest of the rabble of the world, only you can talk better than they" (v:124). "A prating tongue," Bunyan warns, "will not unlock the gates of heaven, nor blinde the eyes of thy judge; look to it" (124). Atheist denies there is such a place as Mount Sion. Coming as he does within this series, he is to be defined not as a non- or anti-believer, but rather as a particular kind of errant professor. Although he is traveling in the Christian Way, he is headed backwards, away from the Celestial City and towards the City of Destruction. He is like the Formalist in *The Strait Gate*, "a man that hath *lost all* but the *shell* of religion" (v:125; Bunyan's italics).

The most important of these encounters is with Ignorance, who appears and disappears at several points, perhaps to show that the threat he enacts is ever-present (Keeble, *Literary Culture* 207–8). Upon their first meeting Christian assesses him as "wise in his own conceit" (Proverbs 26.12), and the gloss invokes Ecclesiastes 10.3 to underline the portrait: "When he that is a fool walketh by the way, his wisdom faileth him, and he saith to every one that he is a fool" (124). *The Strait Gate* defines the Wilfully Ignorant Professor as one who acts "as if it were unlawful for Christians to know more then hath been taught them at first conversion"; he is "for picking and chusing of truth, and loveth not to hazzard his all for that worthy name by which he would be called" (v:126). Ignorance professes falsely through complacency and self-indulgence. Besides his wilful ignorance, he embodies what *The Strait Gate* condemns as "the professor that would prove himself a Christian by comparing himself with others, instead of comparing himself with the word of God" (v:126). He is also a Free-Willer, one who denies the roles of Christ and the Holy Ghost in conversion, and a Libertine Professor, one who "pretendeth to be against forms, and duties, as things that gender to bondage, neglecting the order of God" (v:126–27, 125). Tindall finds in Ignorance as in Byends a portrait of Edward Fowler (61).

Ignorance is characterized by his lack of interest in Hopeful's narrative and indeed by his preference for solitude rather than their company. Since he has not been in the Way, he has no conversion narrative to tell, nor would he be able to progressively revise it if he did. Ignorance rests his claim to salvation on a confidence that he knows the Lord's will and that he has lived a good life; he trusts in the covenant of works and resists all humbling discipline of the Word and the good counsel (124) that is to be found within the church community by other means. Although he easily crosses the river with the help of a ferryman Vainhope, he is not received into blessedness for he has no certificate, he has not been "gathered" into a church community, he has not proceeded through the morphology sequence. In *Pilgrim's Progress*'s most remarkable anticlimax, Ignorance passes through a doorway to hell just next to the gates of heaven, a stern warning indeed! Although generally Ignorance is too lively and specific to be a mere abstraction, he is sometimes less a person than a state of being, specifically the blindness or refusal of vision that haunts Christian even very late in the story (Van Dyke 184).

Christian and Hopeful recognize the limitations of Ignorance's profession as widely shared; they lament his stifling of conviction of sin, his self-flattery, and his loss of the benefits that derive from right fear and reverence of God. They consider similarly the limitations of another "Opinionist," Temporary, a believer once "much awakened" and "towardly" (151 and gloss), but subject to backsliding. Unlike Ignorance, Temporary experienced initial conviction of sin, but did not progress through other stages of the morphology chain. Such folk are impelled forward only by fears and shame, and like Ignorance they refuse the benefits of progressive revelation. Temporary is an appropriate final figure for the series of false professors, especially in highlighting the opposite virtues of patience and perseverance in faith. Those postconversion virtues are essential for spiritual survival in what is here fictionalized as the soporific dangers of the Enchanted Ground, that possibly long and unremarkable spiritual plateau so psychologically subject to complacency or other lapses of full spiritual or salvific consciousness that follows conversion's exciting drama. Christian and Hopeful not only escape the dangers of sleeping here but their discussions, definitions, and refinements of faith and profession, their watchfulness, become a new mode of spiritual awakening.

The series of false professors shows the process, and the need, for continuous refinement of each believer's spiritual history, and in keeping with the juxtapositional, circular, and anticlimactic nature of this narrative, Ignorance reappears to reshuffle the story elements and narrative tensions once again. That reshuffling promotes the Puritan purposes noted earlier. The juxtapositions develop moral contrasts between individuals and clarify spiritual means and ends, and the anticlimax demonstrates that *Pilgrim's Progress* part I, like individual life histories and biblical texts, denies its readers comfortable closure on issues and requires them progressively and continuously to re-envision their procedures, assumptions, and goals.

By its very existence, part II similarly denies closure. Its dramatis personae, both those who travel and those who entertain pilgrims, gladly model themselves on the profitable histories of their predecessors from part I, but the uses to which they put life-writing differ in soteriology and tone. As part I variously exploits the conversion narrative model, part II acts out the more stable, more complacent discourse of recounting the growth of one's graces. Christiana is credentialed by naming her husband rather than by her own history, and is admitted to House Beautiful because of Greatheart, not because she has proven herself. A new preference for biography over autobiography builds in emotional and spiritual distancing. The narrative mode has progressed a long way toward the novel when Greatheart presents Fearing's biography as anecdotal counterpoint, the underside of heroic wayfaring viewed objectively from the outside and made instructional through his ministerial interpretations. We hear much of Fearing's "Behaviours" and his emotional reactions (glosses 249–53) rather than his spiritual crises, how he gestured and how he looked and how he allowed himself to be assisted toward salvation. In clear ministerial propaganda, Fearing is represented as a comfort or reassurance, not as a model and stimulus for imitation, as the willing but passive receiver of pastoral care. When Greatheart reviews the family's travels of part II, he focuses on his own success against giants rather than the family's spiritual occasions and graces (276); he develops the distanced heroic for admiration rather than the recapitulative for anxious reflection. Radical contrasts of this sort in narrative, values, tone, theme, and theology between parts I and II, and the patterns of historical and cultural difference that underwrite them, are the focus of the remaining chapters of this study. Safely distanced threats, responses, and discourses establish part II as a rich complement to part I, as mythic individuality disperses into fictional community, allegory into occasional similitude, the Word into works, and in general the theological into the chronological.

CHAPTER SIX

Christiana's Heroics

Here lyes,
A worthy Matron of unspotted life,
A loving Mother and obedient wife,
A friendly Neighbor, pitiful to poor,
Whom oft she fed, and clothed with her store;
To Servants wisely aweful, but yet kind,
And as they did, so they reward did find:
A true Instructer of her Family,
The which she ordered with dexterity.
The publick meetings ever did frequent,
And in her Closet constant hours she spent;
Religious in all her words and wayes,
Preparing still for death, till end of dayes:
Of all her Children, Children, liv'd to see,
Then dying, left a blessed memory.

—Anne Bradstreet, "An Epitaph On my dear and
ever honoured Mother Mrs. Dorothy Dudley, Who
deceased Decemb. 27.1643. and of her age, 61."

IN 1684, six years after publishing the very successful first part of *Pil-grim's Progress*, John Bunyan issued the sequel *Wherein*, according to the subtitle, *is Set Forth the Manner of the Setting out of Christian's Wife and Children*. This second "similitude" fulfills the possibility, proffered at the end of part I's concluding poem, that the author might at some future time be persuaded to "Dream again" (164). Despite several editions in Bunyan's lifetime, readers have not accorded the second part the welcome of the first, and, indeed, Bunyan criticism often equates *Pilgrim's Progress* exclusively with Christian's journey. The second part deserves more attention than it receives, for its very existence compels certain inferences about Bunyan's views of gender and his double enterprise. In brief, part II literalizes what Sagacity calls "second thoughts" (177), and it dramatizes Greatheart's proposition, "Relations are our second self" (292), with *self* now extending into new social and ecclesiological dimensions. The second part relates to the first not merely as an echo or as the completion of a diptych; they are more like the components of a stereopticon, the addition integrating dimensionality and thereby vitalizing the first and the whole.

Once Bunyan decided to reemploy the metaphor of pilgrimage and borrow his previous setting, he faced the challenge of executing the differences so as to create a worthy, equally edifying sequel and translating what had been a masculine narrative into a feminine and family mode. There must be likenesses in allegiance to the earlier success and to Puritan assumptions of a universal Way, but the variations testify to other intended and unintended principles as well. In summary, where Christian matches the paradigmatic hero of a thousand faces, Christiana is a heroine not a hero, and her context is comedic, social, and communal at base rather than desperate or individualistic. Part II is narratively diffuse rather than intense, centrifugal rather than centripetal, processional rather than traumatic. These differences attach to some telling Puritan traits, discourses, and expectations as well as to certain identifiable patterns of historical and theological change. Where Christian asked "What must I do to be saved?" part II proposes "Bowels becometh Pilgrims" (186), an unusual New Testament usage explicated by Bunyan's *Come, and Welcome, to Jesus Christ:* "the inclining of the will . . . which sets the mind a moving after, or towards [Christ], . . . the passions of my mind and affections" (VIII:255, and Colossians 3.12–14). The Lord of part II is said to be "one of very tender Bowels" (251), and the overall narration occurs within an atmosphere of family, general charity, specific mercies, and social bonding.

The given, indeed the sine qua non, of part II is its feminine cast, but female definition operates within several restrictions: acceptance of the status of "the weaker vessel" (1 Peter 3.7), Pauline injunctions to be chaste, silent, and obedient (1 Timothy 2.11, Titus 2.5), and the simultaneous innovation and invalidation of individuality. This last principle, implicit in the female version of conversion histories, deliberately reduces the rich particulars of daily life to formulaic abstraction and deliberately

submerges flesh-and-blood womanhood into the successful occupancy
of a series of discreet idealized marital and social positions. In Laurel
Thatcher Ulrich's crisp summation, "A good wife earned the dignity of
anonymity" (3). The epigraph of this chapter arrays the sanctioned roles
and qualities: The worthy matron was chaste, loving, obedient, friendly,
generous, wise, kind, just to servants, edifying to children, domestically
dextrous, and variously and always religious. Bunyan draws a similar list
of "what / Is proper to [women's] Sex and State, what not" in *The House
of God*:

> To be discreet, keepers at Home, and Chast;
> To love their Husbands, to be Good, shame-Fac'd;
> Children to bear, to Love them, and to *flye*
> *What to the Gospel would be Infamy.* (VI:291)

Such series echo the Bible's most expansive "Praise and Properties of a
Virtuous Woman" from Proverbs 31.10–31:

> Who can find a virtuous woman? for her price is far above rubies.
> The heart of her husband doth safely trust in her, so that he shall
> have no need of spoil. She will do him good and not evil all the days
> of her life. . . . She riseth also while it is yet night, and giveth meat
> to her household, and a portion to her maidens. . . . Her candle
> goeth not out by night. . . . Strength and honour are her clothing;
> and she shall rejoice in time to come. She openeth her mouth with
> wisdom; and in her tongue is the law of kindness. She looketh well
> to the ways of her household, and eateth not the bread of idleness.
> Her children arise up, and call her blessed; her husband also, and
> he praiseth her.

Ulrich attaches woman's options to three biblical models, with Bathsheba
focusing economic life, Eve sex and reproduction, and Jael the compound
of religion and aggression (5–6, 10).

Christian Behaviour records Bunyan's views on "The Duty of Wives."
Although she owes her husband respect and obedience (1 Corinthians
11.3, 1 Peter 3.1, Colossians 3.18, Ephesians 5.22), she is his "yoak-fellow"
not his slave. Her tasks are to guide the house, bring up the children, encourage and supervise domestic devotions, "be about [her] own husbands
business at home," and generally "rule all in his absence" (III:33, 34).
These last duties apply very particularly to the Bunyan household, for the
wife of an itinerant tinker and minister who spent twelve and a half years

of his married life in jail would be an active deputy indeed. Moreover, *A Relation of the Imprisonment of Mr. John Bunyan* records "from her own mouth" the second Mrs. Bunyan's industrious political and legal efforts to achieve her husband's release from jail (*Grace Abounding* 125).

Within *Pilgrim's Progress* part II, Gaius—the host of Romans 16.23 and the recipient and subject of the third Epistle of John—affirms the most positive features and precedents of women against a biblical background:

> I will now speak on the behalf of Women, to take away their Reproach. For as Death and the Curse came into the World by a Woman, so also did Life and Health; *God sent forth his Son, made of a Woman.* Yea, to shew how much those that came after did abhor the Act of their Mother, this Sex, in the old Testament, coveted Children if happily this or that Woman might be the Mother of the Saviour of the World. I will say again, that when the Saviour was come, Women rejoyced in him, before either Man or Angel. I read not that ever any man did give unto Christ so much as one *Groat*, but the Women followed him, and ministred to him of their Substance. 'Twas a Woman that washed his Feet with Tears, and a Woman that anointed his Body to the Burial. They were Women that wept when he was going to the Cross; And Women that followed him from the Cross, and that sat by his Sepulcher when he was buried. They were Women that was first with him at his Resurrection *morn*, and Women that brought Tidings first to his Disciples that he was risen from the Dead. Women therefore are highly favoured, and shew by these things that they are sharers with us in the Grace of Life. (261)

Gaius's "praise" inscribes contradictory biblical attitudes toward women and may also, as Roger Sharrock suggests, testify to the real contemporary importance of women in the gathered churches (*John Bunyan* [1968] 151). It is certainly true that women played crucial roles in Bunyan's own conversion, from his first wife's dowry of godly books to the Bedford women whose conversation initially brought him to church membership.

But women's roles were repeatedly contested and redefined during Bunyan's lifetime. The century saw radical changes in the parameters of women's lives as of class, economics, and politics generally, and Bunyan's Christiana reflects both the earlier norm and some later possibilities. She is both a dependent or an extension of her husband, as her name indicates, and also an autonomous being with a quite different spiritual history and a quite independent sphere and priorities. Contemporary law, science, and theology defined women as less strong, wise, active, and formative than men, less emotionally controlled and less fitted for heavy work or public life.[1] Antonia Fraser's composite biography of scores of seventeenth-century women under the title *The Weaker Vessel* copiously demonstrates the variety of female strengths that the middle decades of the century saw and in part created.[2] Despite this historical record, conservative commonplaces about woman's weakness were not to be eradicated in times either of revolution or of stability.

Both Bunyan's *Christian Behavior* and William Perkins's equivalent treatise, *Christian Oeconomy*, draw analogies between worshipping families and miniature churches and commonwealths. On the authority of Ephesians 5.22–33, "the holy estate of marriage," in Perkins's words, "is a lively type of Christ and his church; and . . . also a figure of the conjunction that is between him and the faithful."[3] Despite this conservative theory, the period also witnessed revaluations of the institution of marriage and role of the wife, particularly the emergence of what William Haller labels *amour bourgeois* by contrast with the *amour courtois* of the Middle Ages:

> Though the wife was bound to obey the husband, the husband was bound to love the wife, and each was to render without restraint or difference what was named "due benevolence" to the other. It was this relationship of love and obedience, reciprocal, inseparable, exclusive, and unique, which made marriage in truth the image, nothing less, of Christ's relation to his church. . . . The preachers seem to have felt less need for telling their hearers that men were superior to women in the order of nature than for insisting how nearly women might be expected through love and marriage to approach their husbands' level and how desirable it was that they should do so. ("'Hail'" 81, 83–84)

The conservative Thomas Gataker and the radical John Milton agree in emphasizing her companionable over her biological role. *Tetrachordon*, for example, defines marriage as "an individual and intimat conversation, and mutual benevolence" (*Prose* 2.609) and "a divine institution joyning man and woman in a love fitly dispos'd to the helps and comforts of domestic life" (612, and similarly *Doctrine and Discipline of Divorce*, *Prose* 2.246–47). In a similar spirit Milton's Adam asks God for a wife "fit to participate / All rational delight" (*PL* 8.390–91). Puritan marriage doctrine distinguished itself from Roman Catholic doctrine by its covenantal rather than sacramental nature and its emphasis on companionship rather than procreation. Puritans commonly employed analogies from friendship, government, business partnership, and especially the church to describe their biblically inspired model of marriage.[4]

⊷⊲| I |⊳⊶

RECENT KINDS OF LITERARY CRITICISM have taught us to look closely at textual junctures that are not smoothly seamed, and the opening proposition of part I, where Christian abandons a wife and children to pursue what we are supposed to admire as his heroic pilgrimage, presents just such a juncture. Ever since its first appearance in 1678, many readers have apparently agreed with Huckleberry Finn's summary assessment that *Pilgrim's Progress* is a book "about a man that left his family it didn't say why" (chapter 17). In fact, Bunyan does present very clearly, and more than once, his hero's rationale, but it is problematic to any but the most austere Christian believer and certainly at odds with the honor mid-seventeenth-century Puritans assigned to Christian marriage. Levin L. Schucking argues that since "it was of the very essence of [Bunyan's] particular creed to regard the bond between husband and wife not only as indissoluble but as a special aid to sanctification[,] . . . the very notion of that bond actually being severed, in the life of his model Christian must have struck him as a very grave moral flaw in his work" (117). Given the priorities of part I, Christian's choice is by no means a moral or theological flaw, but by the time of writing part II Bunyan may have perceived, or been persuaded to perceive, difficulties with it and thus attempted in part II to bring back to a position of honor the idea of marriage imperiled in part I.

The opening of part I foregrounds conflicting biblical injunctions. On the one hand, a Christian is required to leave behind the things and folk of this world in favor of the transcendent rewards of the next, but doing so risks severing the very faith he espouses from a future in which its goods would be multiplied, a future of harvesting what the subtitle of *Christian Behaviour* calls *the Fruits of True Christianity . . . in the Duty of Relations.* Christian's wife and children, seeing their husband and father running away from them and toward salvation, "began to cry after him to return: but the Man put his fingers in his Ears, and ran on crying,

Life, Life, Eternal Life: so he looked not behind him, but fled towards the middle of the Plain" (10). Bunyan's hero is literalizing Christ's words in Luke 14.26: "If any man come to me, and hate not his father, and mother, and wife, and children, and brethren, and sisters, yea, and his own life also, he cannot be my disciple" (similarly 14.33). *The Acceptable Sacrifice* depicts the domestic turmoil such new converts create: "Their sighs, their tears, their day and night groans, their cries and prayers, and solitary carriages, put all the carnal family out of order. Hence you have them brow-beaten by some, contemned by others, yea, and their company fled from and deserted by others" (Offor 1:689). When Worldly Wiseman questions him about his departure, Christian invokes 1 Corinthians 7.29—that "they that have wives be as though they had none"—to justify removing his burden over concern for his family. Commenting on this text in *The Desire of the Righteous Granted*, Bunyan says that such desire "breeds a divorce, a complete divorce, betwixt the soul and all inordinate love and affections to relations and worldly enjoyments. This desire makes a married man live as if he had no wife; a rich man lives as if he possessed not what he has. . . . This is a soul-sequestering desire. This desire makes a man willing rather to be absent from all enjoyments, that he may be present with the Lord" (Offor 1:758).

On the positive side, the Protestant family of the period constitutes the basic unit of social organization for the purposes of church and state, "the first and primary school for training in all aspects of a Christian life" (George and George 275). *Christian Behaviour* prescribes that the father care for both the spiritual and the outward conditions of his family. He must be "one that ruleth well his own house, having his children in subjection with all gravity" (1 Timothy 3.4) and "bring up his children in the nurture and admonition of the Lord" (Ephesians 6.4) on the assumption of Proverbs 22.6: "Train up a child in the way he should go; and when he is old, he will not depart from it." He is also to supply food and raiment, the wherewithal "*to maintain good Works for necessary uses, Tit. 3.14*" (25); to ensure that his children have a convenient livelihood; and to maintain Christian harmony in the household, formally through leadership in the Word and prayer, more generally through moderation (III:25). *A Holy Life* laments quarrels between husbands and wives and the unruliness of children under the headings of "house-iniquities" and "family-iniquities" (IX:319–20). The goal is to say with David, "I will walk within my house, with a perfect heart" (IX:319, Psalm 101.2).

Christian Behaviour also defines the father's role when his "Family is

ungodly and unruly touching all that is good" (III:23), a condition detailed in Emblem LXVI "Upon the Disobedient Child" (VI:264–65). The
allegory faults Christiana's fears of losing this world and the children's
foolish youthful delights (51), while this earlier treatise assigns responsibility to the head of a household to bring about the conversion of his
family members. The husband of an unbelieving wife must:

1. Labour seriously after a sence of her miserable state, that thy
bowels may yern towards her soul. 2. Beware that she take no occasion from any unseemly carriage of thine, to proceed in evil; and
here thou hast need to double thy diligence, for she lieth in thy
bosom, and therefore is capable of espying the least miscarriage in
thee. 3. If she behave herself unseemly and unruly, as she is subject
to do, being Christless & Graceless, then labour thou to overcome
her Evil with thy Goodness, her Frowardness with thy Patience and
Meekness: it is a shame for thee who hast another principle, to do
as she. 4. Take fit opportunities to convince her: observe her disposition, and when she is most likely to hear, then speak to her very
heart. 5. When thou speakest, speak to purpose; 'tis no matter for
many words, provided they be pertinent. *Job* in a few words answers
his wife, and takes her off from her foolish talking; *Thou speakest,*
saith he, *like one of the foolish women; shall we receive good at the
hands of God, and shall we not receive evil?* Job 2.10. 6. Let all be
done without rancor, or the least appearance of anger. (III:28)

The father of wayward children is "to rebuke their vice, and to shew them
the evil of their rebelling against the Lord . . . [to] labour to recover them
out of the snare of the Devil. . . . also to labour to draw them forth to God's
publick Worship, if peradventure God may convert their souls" (23). The
godly wife of an unbelieving husband receives similar but more carefully
strategized advice for bringing her husband "out of opposition to his own
salvation" (34–36).

At House Beautiful, Charity catechizes Christian on his conduct to his
family: "Have you a family? are you a married man? . . . And why did
you not bring them along with you? . . . But you should have talked to
them, and have endeavoured to have shewen them the danger of being
behind. . . . And did you pray to God that he would bless your counsel
to them? . . . But did you tell them of your own sorrow, and fear of destruction? . . . But did you not with your vain life, damp all that you by
words used by way of perswasion to bring them away with you?" (50–51).

When Christian's responses precisely reformulate the advisories of *Christian Behavior*, Charity clears him, saying: "If thy Wife and Children have been offended with thee for this, they thereby shew themselves to be implacable to good; and thou hast delivered thy soul from their blood" (52). She is supported by Ezekiel 3.19: "Yet if thou warn the wicked, and he turn not from his wickedness, nor from his wicked way, he shall die in his iniquity; but thou hast delivered thy soul." The addition of this conversation to the second edition of part I seems to show Bunyan responding to pressures to justify his hero's conduct on this key point.[5]

Bunyan goes beyond attaching "Charity" to the problematic departure six years later, when he launches the second part with two tamer versions of the domestic situation. In the opening paragraph the narrator explains: "I told you then also what I saw concerning his *Wife* and *Children*, and how unwilling they were to go with him on Pilgrimage: Insomuch that he was forced to go on his Progress without them, for he durst not run the danger of that destruction which he feared would come by staying with them, in the City of Destruction: Wherefore, as I then shewed you, he left them and departed" (174). Later the Dreamer asks Mr. Sagacity, "But, pray Sir, while it is fresh in my mind, do you hear any thing of his Wife and Children? poor hearts, I wonder in my mind what they do," and Mr. Sagacity responds: "Who! *Christiana*, and her Sons! They are like to do as well as did *Christian* himself, for though they all plaid the Fool at the first, and would by no means be perswaded by either the tears or intreaties of *Christian*, yet second thoughts have wrought wonderfully with them, so they have packt up and are also gone after him" (176–77). The second narrative fulfills his promise to provide his companion with "an account of the whole of the matter" (177).

Late in part II, two avatars of Christian reenact elements of the crisis of abandonment. Mr. Valiant-for-Truth denied his father and mother's efforts to dissuade him from going on pilgrimage (291–95), while Mr. Standfast on his deathbed asks Greatheart to conduct his wife and five small children in the future (310). The former had abandoned his family because he was inspired by Christian's history, while the latter begs Greatheart to awaken future generations by retelling Christian's and his own successful pilgrimages. Thus from the first page of part I to the next-to-last page of part II, Bunyan's allegory affirms the principle that a godly individual may expect to give up all family and familiar ties to pursue salvation, but his example in so doing invites their imitation.

Part II's tamer versions of the separation of Christian from his family may look like a compromised transition, but the nature of that compromise points to a crisis inherent within Christianity. N. H. Keeble exactly identifies the nexus: "Had Christian *not* abandoned his family in an apparently selfish desire to gain his own salvation, Christiana never would have set out. In other words, Christian has quite literally saved his family by abandoning it: in preferring Christ before the creature he has made possible the salvation of the creature" ("Christiana's Key" 10–11; Keeble's italics). When Mercy expresses anxieties similar to Christian's for having abandoned her carnal relations, Christiana responds in precisely these terms, now happily integrated into the dominant feminine and communal value scheme: "Thou dost for thy Friends, as my good *Christian* did for me when he left me; he mourned for that I would not heed nor regard him, but his Lord and ours did gather up his Tears and put them into his Bottle, and now both I, and thou, and these my sweet Babes, are reaping the Fruit and Benefit of them" (186). The sequel shows that what seems a personal and textual crisis illuminates God's mysterious ways and inclusive mercy. What we, and Christian, thought was an isolated and isolating action has in fact succeeded in multiplying God's providences for others. Christian's rejection of his family and Christiana's care for her children turn out to be complementary not contradictory commitments (Keeble, "Christiana's Key" 13).

Before part II allowed this larger resolution to emerge, part I left Bunyan with a hero apparently compromised by an absolute biblical injunction at odds with human norms, feelings, and indeed necessities for the survival of the race and multiplication of the faith. The intensity of the conflict reflects Bunyan's own spiritual calling at war with his deep family feeling and responsibilities. His biography demonstrates that Christian's abandonment of his family was no merely theoretical idea or ideal, for Bunyan himself spent the years 1660 to 1672 and the first six months of 1677 in jail. *Grace Abounding* both appeals to scriptural authority for taking the sternest measures in circumstances of spiritual trial and testifies to Bunyan's acute family feeling. Biographically, 2 Corinthians 1.9 taught him "that if ever I would suffer rightly, I must first pass a sentence of death upon everything that can properly be called a thing of this life, even to reckon my Self, my Wife, my Children, my health, my enjoyments, and all, as dead to me, and my self as dead to them" (97). This is confirmed for him by Matthew 10.37: "He that loveth father or mother . . . son or daughter more than me is not worthy of me," a proposition contextualized by verse 36 that "a man's foes shall be they of his own household." In

Pilgrim's Progress part I, wives and children are listed among the tempting vanities of Vanity Fair (88) along with Whores, Bauds, Preferments, Silver, and many other items.

Bunyan describes the separation from his own family in *Grace Abounding* in the most ardent and tender terms:

> The parting with my Wife and poor Children hath oft been to me in this place as the pulling the flesh from my bones; and that not onely because I am somewhat too fond of these great mercies, but also because I should have often brought to my mind the many hardships, miseries and wants that my poor family was like to meet with, should I be taken from them, especially my poor blind Child, who lay nearer my heart than all I had besides; O the thoughts of the hardship I thought my blind one might go under, would break my heart to pieces. . . . I cannot now endure the wind should blow upon thee: but yet recalling my self, thought I, I must venture you all with God, though it goeth to the quick to leave you: O I saw in this condition I was as a man who was pulling down his house upon the head of his Wife and children; yet thought I, I must do it, I must do it. (98)

When Bunyan went to jail in 1660, he left his second wife with four stepchildren, the most mature of whom was ten years old and blind. She was also pregnant with another child who soon died (128).[6] In this awful predicament he consoles himself with Scriptures that promise divine preservation of the widows and fatherless and that promise glory to the faithful while denouncing those who shrink from their profession of Christ. *A Holy Life* (1684) reflects that when Christians are "reproached for a vertuous life, God himself is concerned, will espouse our quarrel, and in his good time will shew our foes our righteousness, and put them to shame and silence" (IX:350), and *Come, and Welcome, to Jesus Christ* lists biblical precedents for what believers leave behind when they come to Christ, including Abraham leaving his country and kindred, Ruth leaving her parents and gods, and Paul leaving behind his own righteousness (VIII:380).

Seasonable Counsel, or Advice to Sufferers (1689) puts the crisis in larger perspective. On the authority of 1 Peter 4.19—"Wherefore let them that suffer according to the will of God, commit the keeping of their souls to him in well doing, as unto a faithful creator"—it argues that "Suffering comes not by chance, or by the will of man, but by the will and appointment of God"; it is "an extraordinary call" (Offor II:695, 723). It casts wives and children as "sore temptations" that would dissuade a Christian from accepting suffering, the wife perhaps like Job's arguing "Do not still remain in thine integrity" (733). Despite its review of sacrifices from the Old and New Testaments and from Foxe's *Book of Martyrs*, this treatise is entirely free of any reference to Bunyan's own years of persecution. In an additional extraordinary feat, it is also entirely free of any bitterness or regret or (on the other side) of any triumph or particular merit on his part. Given Bunyan's history, this work harvests years of biblical study focused precisely on this personal crisis.

A Holy Life affirms the governing principle that "A mans *house*, and his carriage *there* doth more bespeak the nature and temper of his mind, than all publick profession. If I were to judge of a man for my life, I would not judge of him by his open profession, but by his *Domestick* behaviours. . . . What a man is at home, that he is indeed" (IX:322; Bunyan's italics). Measured by this standard Bunyan himself fares well, and a contemporary biographer (1692) commends the strict discipline and godly service of Bunyan's family relations (*Grace Abounding* 172–73). *Christian Behaviour* extrapolates from his family experience the right relation of children to their parents. It casts in second-person address the advisory that children requite and honor their parents "For the pains they have taken with thee to bring thee up."

> Until thou hast Children of thy own, thou wilt not be sensible of the pains, watchings, fears, sorrow and affliction, that they have gone under to bring thee up; and when thou knowest it, thou wilt not easily yeeld, that thou hast recompenced them for their favour to thee: How often have they sustained thy hunger, cloathed thy nakedness? What care have they taken that thou mightest have wherewith to live and do well when they were dead and gone? they possibly have spared it from their own belly and back for thee, and have also impoverished themselves, that thou mightest live like a man. All these things ought duly, and like a man, to be considered by thee, and care ought to be taken on thy part to requite them; the Scripture saith so; Reason saith so; and there be none but dogs and beasts deny it. *It is the duty of Parents to lay up for their Children; and the duty of Children to requite their Parents.* (III:37–38)

Bunyan's domestic relations evidence the mid-seventeenth-century overlapping of Lawrence Stone's sociological categories of the restricted patriarchal nuclear family and affective individualism, especially the latter's "intensified affective bonding of the nuclear core at the expense of neighbours and kin; a strong sense of individual autonomy and the right to personal freedom in the pursuit of happiness." Such families are in the process of leaving behind the distance, deference, and patriarchy that characterized earlier eras in favor of the nuclear family, not just as a fact but also as a state of mind. Such a family structure, in Stone's words, reflects "perhaps the most far-reaching consequence of the Reformation in England."[7]

Bunyan died four years after the publication of part II, and its altered mood is sometimes said to reflect his achieved comforts. In the years between the two parts, the former prisoner was restored to the contentments of wife, children, grandchildren, and a loving Christian community within which he held a secure and respected place (Furlong 114, 124; Tindall 210; G. Harrison 171–72). No doubt counseling his Bedford parishioners also widened his sympathies and exercised his tenderer feelings, while preaching, sometimes as far afield as London, widened his social activity as well as his fame as a man of extraordinary spiritual and rhetorical gifts.

The late Bunyan is a man who has made peace with his own conscience and achieved at least a personal resolution of the dilemma troubling his allegorical hero. Christian at the beginning of part I, or a Christian convert more generally, must necessarily struggle to reconcile absolute biblical injunctions that press the two parts of his nature in irreconcilable directions—"pulling the flesh from my bones" as Bunyan puts it in *Grace Abounding*. When Bunyan is able to transmute the departure trauma of part I into the broadened family and community of part II where communal pilgrimage is regularly sparked and fueled by reminders of Christian's precedent journey and heroic sacrifices, Bunyan has come to terms with the spiritual and personal challenge and found a way to translate into narrative art his own development from Bedford martyr to Bedford minister and father, from jail to pulpit and family hearth.

◄◊| II |◊►

ON THE FACE OF IT, the second part of *Pilgrim's Progress* offers the female analogue of the masculine first part. It has been dubbed more a walking tour or travelogue than a spiritual pilgrimage, "a delightful ramble through a country from which most of the dangers have been removed."

It is said to "breathe the charm of settled domestic life" and to gradually unfold "a more humdrum world, but a gracious and good-humoured one," a domain dominated by charity and Christian fellowship, not the "crisis theology" of part I. With its usual group scenes, part II is less retrospective, less occupied with doctrinal discussion and distinctions, less critical of sin and other signs of human weakness. It is pastoral rather than heroic, comedic rather than tragic, social rather than egocentric.[8] In a suggestive schema, Monica Furlong counts seventy-three bad and seventeen good characters active or referred to in part I, but twenty-seven bad and twenty-nine good characters in part II (106, 117). Such distinctions have generally been adduced to disparage Bunyan's sequel, but when we describe the female pilgrim's progress in alternative vocabularies its positive features and thereby the compound design emerge more clearly.

Some of those vocabularies are distinctly secular. Even though everything Bunyan wrote was to a large extent theologically propagandistic or, as Puritans would prefer, "edifying," at the same time the two parts of *Pilgrim's Progress* are nested in dichotomous secular patterns that have immemorially explained and contained human (or Western) understandings of the nature of life and conduct. This subchapter considers the domestic equipment, attitudes, and relationships, the material and social culture, sociological history, and even cultural anthropology or ethnography inscribing the feminine in part II, and thus the inventive and expressive means through which Bunyan signified its gender ideology within a more general social, religious, and cultural context. Ellen Messer-Davidow formulates the philosophical base of such a feminist literary approach in these terms: "In a gendered culture, people express sex/gender ideas in *bricolage*. With elaboration and justification these ideas become a system, an ideology that organizes social existence by specifying the behaviors, duties, powers, and relations of the sexes; their opportunities for education, labor, and pleasure; and their possession of material goods. The object of feminist criticisms is to reveal, not additionally create, the sex/gender ideologies expressed in cultural *bricolage*." The variety of disciplines upon which such an approach necessarily draws practices an eclecticism characteristic of feminist criticisms, because, as Messer-Davidow explains, gender representations imply, indeed create, resonating differences also between public and private, work and leisure, economic and domestic, political and aesthetic spheres.[9] As it advances, the present study will move us, in Clifford Geertz's terms, from description to thick description to "specification," from data to contemporary meaning to what is signaled about the society more largely and to later interpretation (27). The basic data invite "specification" with regard to contrasting literary and social discourses and also ultimately to contrasting ritual bases and psychic structures.

A journey ordinarily offers the hero an unusual opportunity to develop courage, independence, and growth in unfamiliar surroundings, and part I gives mythic form to such travel. Because for the most part Christiana's journey is as much a protected environment as her home, the heroic within her narrative must be pursued differently. The seventeenth century defined a woman's character and world by her relation to her husband, to her home, to her children, and to the larger community. Puritan motherhood assumed fruitfulness and demanded tenderness and self-denial. Extensive rather than intensive, it reached beyond offspring to servants and extended family and offered affection within the several essentially authoritarian systems it overlapped. Ulrich traces the normal maternal progression "from an intense nurturing of infants through the haphazard but pious watchfulness of growing children to an old age characterized by economic dependency, religious resignation, and an absorbing concern with the next generation" (157, 154, 162). Although she resembles a widow on pilgrimage and is denied husband and household as arenas of self-definition, Christiana essentially enacts the stages of this progression over the course of her narrative.

If part I is "the epic of the itinerant" (Hill, *World Turned* 406), part II is a varied affirmation of domesticity. It emphasizes the texture and quality of life, and it builds its narrative out of references that never receive even brief mention in part I. It regularly takes into account diet, clothing, sleeping arrangements, health and sickness, childcare, dirt and house-cleaning, menus and table-settings, herbs, letters, gossip, and—surprisingly—coach travel (239). The pilgrims' gear in part II includes or comes to include an earthen pot, an anchor, pills, a mirror, a map or book, a lamp and/or lanthorn, and a tinderbox. We also read of a frying pan, smelling salts, crutches, hose, coats, other garments, silk and velvet fabrics, numerous items of jewelry, purses, and money. The most frequently mentioned piece of furniture is a bed, but we also read of tables, benches, a settle, and a couch. Three stopping places have separate dining rooms as well as numerous chambers. Interestingly, the history of furniture supports the prioritized importance of the bed at this time, and according to architectural history the seventeenth century witnessed an increasing assignment of rooms to specific domestic functions. Dozens of references to musical instruments, dances, and songs define the atmosphere. As the evidence accumulates of architecture, furniture and chattels, housekeeping, nurturance, comfort, and adornment, hardly an accoutrement customarily associated with women's lives goes unnoticed. This new evidence, so radically different from the data of part I, reflects the seventeenth century's increasing appreciation of comfort, and perhaps too the biographical suggestions that Bunyan associated women with refinement (Furlong 117) and that Bunyan loved good food (Talon, *John Bunyan* 192).

Where Christian was a stranger and pilgrim upon the earth (Hebrews 11.13), Christiana is quite at home. Despite its ostensible pilgrimage, most of part II takes place within safe houses rather than on the road and affirms the material structures and gestures of everyday life. The predominating houses, rooms, indoor activities, even an enclosed garden and a summer parlor, are always positively valued. Outdoors the family are threatened by dogs and weather more than by the allegorical embodiments of evil so prominent in part I. They may enjoy an occasional picnic or make music and dance on the road (283), but they sleep only indoors. Typically we read, "*Christiana* then wished for an Inn for her self and her Children, because they were weary" (258). Normatively when the party arrives at stopping points, immediate attention focuses on travel relief, room assignments, meal preparation, and hospitality generally. After stops of a month or more at House Beautiful, Gaius's inn, and Mnason's house, their departures are attended by varied gifts and provisions. It is a nice touch that this party's journey is sometimes cheered along by birds (235–36). Part I is dominated by what James Turner calls a "vocational" use of space and part II by a "recreational" use. It is the difference between "a single furrow" and "a variety of 'places' in casual arrangement," between constriction and expansion of landscape, and between "painful exclusion and privileged expatiation."[10]

Gaius's welcome articulates the principles of hospitality: "Be of good Chear, you are welcome to me, and to my House; and what thou hast a mind to, call for freely; and what thou would'st have my Servants do for thee, they will do it with a ready Mind" (269), and Mnason speaks similarly: "Whatever you want, do but say, and we will do what we can to get it for you" (273). By contrast, the worst travel moments of part II occur amidst darkness and mist, "Dirt and Slabbiness," bushes and sore feet, and where there is "not so much as one *Inn*, or *Victualling House*, therein to refresh the feebler sort," and the yelling children have lost their shoes (296, 299). As the story draws to a close, the dominant values take idealized form in the refreshment, music, gardens, and wonderfully smelling cleanliness of the Land of Beulah. By contrast, Christian is "refreshed" chiefly by reading along the way. Indeed, so antithetical is sleep to his quest that the gloss at Hill Difficulty reads "He that sleeps is a loser" (42).

Even the overall goal of the second pilgrimage is couched in terms of domesticity and hospitality, specifically as *"the House prepared for us"* (243, and similarly 235). The Lord offers Christiana "promise of entertainment" (182) and invites her to his table where he will "feed [her] with the Fat of his House" (179). Christ is described as the master of a country house and as something of an innkeeper in providing for pilgrims (238–39). He nurtures them "with un-asked kindness" (197), supplying smelling salts (190) or wine, corn, pomegranates, figs, and raisins (234), whereas in part I he was an absent referent, "the Governour of that Countrey" (i.e., heaven) (14), the lawgiver, and the warrior who had fought with and slain powerful enemies with great danger to himself and great loss of blood (52).

The accumulation of this kind of evidence shows that although Christiana leaves behind her household in the City of Destruction, she creates and carries domesticity with her. A recent popular study of the history of the idea of the home by Witold Rybczynski backgrounds this issue. Rybczynski traces to the seventeenth century the distinction between "house" and "home," the latter emerging as not merely a place but more importantly a state of being or of mind. *Home*, he argues, "brought together the meanings of house and of household, of dwelling and of refuge, of ownership and of affection. 'Home' meant the house, but also everything that was in it and around it, as well as the people, and the sense of satisfaction and contentment that all these conveyed." The seventeenth-century home became more intimate, more female governed, more clean, orderly, and domestic. Calling it "one of the principal achievements of the Bourgeois Age," Rybczynski defines domesticity as relating to family, intimacy, felt emotions, and loyalty to the home and the objects in it, now endowed with emotional and imaginative projections from its inhabitants. Intermeshed with the intensified Puritan sense of family in the seventeenth century, this heightened domestic consciousness focuses new attention not just on family life, locale, and privacy but also on architecture, furniture, room decoration, and the emerging awareness of and desire for comfort.[11] Adjusted to Bunyan's class, status, geographical position, and fictional pilgrimage, this domestic and distinctly feminine ideology underwrites the radically altered data and atmosphere of part II.

What Rybczynski describes in secular terms is susceptible to a specifically Puritan overlay, and for American colonists at least, Amanda Porterfield has linked contemporary women's creation and maintenance of the home to their capacity to sacralize space. This "domestic consciousness" translates what might have seemed household imprisonment into expansive spirituality, stretching to commitments to the human family at large and to artistic recognitions of the human soul as a household in itself. Domesticity thus conceptualized aligns with female receptivity to authorities and allegiance to God's beauty versus male competition for authority and allegiance to God's power and stern truth (10, 9, 49).

Besides this material culture, part II also privileges social texture, inclusiveness, companionship, and intercession rather than moral discriminations, and this results in its variously diffuse or less intense narration. "Relations [as] our second self" significantly alters the meaning of "self," now resonating outward rather than plumbing inward depths. Christiana's social sphere is numerous, diverse, and regularly increasing. She sets off accompanied by her four sons—her Flesh and Bones, the Fruit of her Body (182, 183)—and a younger companion and helper, Mercy. From the Interpreter's house on, Greatheart joins them. The party swells with the additions of the old and weak figures of Honest, Feeblemind, Ready-to-Halt, and Despondency, and the strong ones of Standfast and Valiant-for-Truth, as well as wives for the now-adult sons, and thence grandchildren for Christiana. The sense of congregation widens when messengers warn of robbers and report a pilgrim, Mr. Notright, struck dead by lightning (269), and when Mr. Mnason's many friends come to visit at Vanity Fair. By the time they arrive at Beulah, the entourage has become very numerous indeed. Within this expanding society, Christiana is characteristically concerned with matters of betrothal, marriage, pregnancy, and childrearing, even at one point catering to the apparently irrational whim of a pregnant woman (287).

Where the material evidence argues a particular historical locus, the social evidence for the most part transcends history in favor of essentialist gender and genre distinctions as popularly understood. Thus the masculinity dominating part I is characteristically concerned with physical courage, assertiveness, authority, independence, and ownership, with power, law, and hierarchical structures, with escaping oblivion and the flux of experience. In one formulation: "The masculine principle is linear, temporal, and transcendent, for it aims to construct something in the world and within time that will enable the individual to transcend nature (which is cyclic), time, and mortality" (French 21–22). Above all, the masculine principle exalts the unique individual Self, and the masculine hero tends to be one who "explains and justifies himself, he finds fault with himself, he insists on himself, he struggles to be true to himself" (Bamber 6). Bunyan's Christian fits this character paradigm. He is notable for his courage and endurance; he struggles to tame and to fulfill himself within a progressive, legalistic, linear structure; his goal is to trade participation in nature, time, and mortality for transcendence. His is a problematic self, and his history is radically based in self-consciousness, self-discovery, self-judgment, and self-definition and redefinition.

The analogous feminine gender principle describes the actions and values of part II as fundamentally benevolent, nutritive, compassionate, merciful, regenerating, and supportive. Its allegiance is chiefly to nature rather than supernature, to time rather than eternity, to continuity rather than transcendence, to quality of life rather than power, to the body rather than the mind or soul, to "impulses toward acceptance of simple continuation, of present pleasure, of surrender to mortality" (French 22). Clearly, just such a principle interweaves Christiana's history with material culture, social networks, and transformed goals.

An expansive time frame and narrative structure accompany part II's increasingly inclusive social circle. Christiana's children start out as very young, but by Mnason's house all four are fully grown and have married "fruitful" wives. By Gaius's inn Christiana, a youthful widow at the outset, has become an "aged matron." By contrast with the urgency, impatience, and strenuousness of Christian's quest, we find leisure and endurance in hers. Christian pauses for essential physical rest only reluctantly, while the party of part II take time to proceed in an orderly, gracious, and well-provisioned manner (207, 223, 282). They defuse sites and challenges by anticipation and arrive at hostelries as expected visitors. Where Christian has to gird up his loins (28, 37) to run swiftly the race where the immortal garland is to be run for not without dust and heat, the pilgrimage of part II with its emphasis on leisure, patience, future-provisioning, and generation(s) is an anti-urgent tour, a patterned progress to old age covering years and culminating in a series of peaceful deaths.

The widening society and chronology of the second or comedic part support what Linda Bamber calls "decentralized form" (28), a form that results because part II, like comedy, celebrates flexibility and delights in plurality and multiple possibility.[12] The very essence of the comic mode consists of an alterable self, social priorities, a preference for flexibility,

survival, and growth over the absolute and transcendent. Part I super-
imposes a series of retrospective narrative loops upon a distinctly linear
model. Part II is marked by progressively widening or "decentralized"
circles, not the retrospective revisionary exercises in progressive revelation favored by Puritan meditation. The incremental layered community
that builds around the female protagonist of part II may be likened to
"bits of mosaic slowly accumulating around a central image or idea," or
to "concentric haloes around a sun," or to "an endless stream in which
we are participants but not the whole story" (French 37, 38; Snyder 41).
In generic models, women's narratives organized as increasingly expansive elaborations of themes contrast with constrictive or disintegrative, as
well as linear, male and tragic norms (French 38). While part I celebrates
the unique, part II encodes the normative. In keeping with the comic—
and feminine—modes, part II presents not transcendence but survival,
not escape from but affirmation of the continuities of life. In the Puritan
context this is a matter of family reproduction and thus also of multiplying the faith through enlisting and sustaining church membership.

The evidence of social relationships, structures, and attitudes in part II
invites interpretation with an eye toward several kinds of modern research. The sociological categories of Lawrence Stone glimpsed earlier
reinforce the social evidence as does the thick description and specification of material culture. The conflict between part I's "personal" hero
and an "impersonal" role for women in part II supports the formulations of the popular psychotherapist Jean Baker Miller that men are the
doers and women the givers, that women's sense of self is organized
around making and maintaining affiliations with others rather than self-
enhancement, and, following Freud, that women have less developed egos
and superegos than men and therefore more permeable ego structures or
less rigid ego boundaries. Christiana's place in her world is illuminated
by Baker's sense that women consistently privilege emotional relatedness
over events, manifest a "greater recognition of the essential cooperative
nature of human existence," and found their lives upon serving others.[13]

Other feminist commentaries distinguishing male personal abstraction, autonomy, and competitiveness from female immediacy, empathy,
and contextuality provide supplementary vocabularies for distinguishing
the governing modes of the two parts. Thus Nancy Chodorow develops
the psychoanalytic case for female self-definition through relations to
others and the outer world, and in these terms "girls grow up with more
ongoing preoccupations with both internalized object-relationships and

with external relationships as well": "Girls come to experience themselves as less differentiated than boys, as more continuous with and related to the external object-world and as differently oriented to their inner object-world." Moreover, male self-definition proceeds in negative terms, female self-defintion in accepting and affirming ones (93, 167–69, 182). Similarly, Carol Gilligan has determined that women not only define themselves through relationships but also judge themselves on the basis of their ability to care. Through sensitivity to others and acceptance of responsibility for others, women characteristically attend to voices other than their own and make judgments that include others' points of view. Hence Gilligan images the male view of relationships as a hierarchy, the female as a web (17, 16, 62).

Two bodies of evidence—one from the opening, one from the closing of each narrative—reaffirm these principles and designs. "The Author's Apology" for part I describes Bunyan writing allegory not for an audience but "mine own self to gratifie" (1) and tentatively sharing the manuscript with a doubtful and divided audience. Part I's expressed goal is participatory: "This Book will make a Traveller of thee" (6), while the "Apology" chiefly outlines Bunyan's edifying intent and method and biblical precedents. In it a series of scattered brief metaphors align teaching and reading with farming, fishing, fowling, jewelry, carpentry, and of course traveling.

Part II links the reading experience with hospitality. The new "pilgrim"—Christiana or her book—is to call as a visitor at various doors, expecting to be invited to enter. Readers are presumed to be "friends, not foes" (171), "Courteous Companions" for the now pleasant journey ahead. Readers and dramatis personae will experience not just hardship but also "dainty things"; their deity is a loving provider of "goodly Mansions" (167–68). Conscious of his fame and responsibilities to his public, the author's new stance is a propitiation rather than an assault. It packages some of its content within an objection and answer format reminiscent of the Puritan sermon. Bunyan now confidently deals in "dark similitude[s]" or riddles because of their greater appeal to and retention by the fancy, heart, and head (171, 170), whereas part I addressed the threat "Metaphors make us blind" (4). In summary, he casts the relation of the two parts in these terms:

> Besides, what my first *Pilgrim* left conceal'd,
> Thou my brave *Second Pilgrim* hast reveal'd;
> What *Christian* left lock't up and went his way,
> Sweet *Christiana* opens with her Key. (171)

Christiana's leisurely departure contrasts the memorable opening emblem of Christian as a ragged, tormented reader whose diffuse traumatic disorientation gave way to Evangelist's guidance. Detail after detail carries the motifs we have been considering, as social and familial faults not moral ones motivate Christiana, and her pardon is prevenient rather than laboriously achieved. She embarks upon pilgrimage not from terror of destruction, nor ardor for the celestial, but rather because "second thoughts" "beg[i]n to work in her mind" (177). These include the loss of her husband and marriage, "heavy Cogitation," tearful remembrance, guilt and a clogged conscience, recrimination, and fear of her children's future. Her conversional stage is specifically "Convictions seconded with fresh Tidings of Gods readiness to Pardon" (179). Through a perfumed letter written in gold, a "Secret" emissary of the heavenly realm invites her to enjoy God's food and table (179) and "to dwell in his Presence with Joy, forever" (180). Where Christian questions (e.g., "What must I do to be saved?"), Christiana exclaims (e.g., "Oh, Wo worth the day" [178]). Where her husband's male ego was projected in Obstinate and Pliable, Christiana's "fleshly reasonings" (gloss 183) become embodied in Mrs. Timorous and Mercy, the former fearfulness being left behind and the latter, like Good Deeds in *Everyman*, cleaving to her.

Come, and Welcome, to Jesus Christ, published in the same year as part I (1678), puts these inaugurating events in perspective. On the text of John 6.37—"All that the Father giveth me, shall come to me; and him that cometh to me, I will in no wise cast out"—it divides "the Coming of the *minde* unto him, even the moving of the heart towards him" into two modes. The first echoes evidence of part I, specifying that some come to Christ as flying from the wrath to come, as leaving all family behind as recommended in Luke 14.26–27, as crying out "Life, Life" and "What shall I do to be saved?" and as escaping their neighbors' assumptions and suggestions (VIII:255, 258–64, 382, 336–37). Isaiah 27.13, quoted on the title page, underscores these motives: "And they shall come which were ready to Perish." *Come, and Welcome* also makes provision for saving those who, like Christiana, require comfort. Matthew 11.28 reinforces this position: "Come unto me, all ye that labour and are heavy laden, and I will give you rest." This kind of salvation comes not "according to the firceness of outward motion," but "rather by those secret groanings, and complaints which thy soul makes to God against that sloth that attends thee in duties." It welcomes even those whose infirmities make them come along slowly. Its inclusive dispensation absolutely and unconditionally communicates the good things of grace. Its logic is circular: "*None comes, but those to whom it is given of the Father:* But thou comest, therefore it is given to thee of the Father" (VIII:266–68, 275–76, 270).

The distinction between Christians who inherit the promises through faith (like Christian) and those who inherit through patience (like Christiana) governs the death scenes as well as the departures (Hebrews 6.12. and *The Strait Gate* V:84). When the jailed Bunyan of *Grace Abounding* faced the prospect of his own imminent death, like Christian in the River of Death, he was beset by doubts and terrors, but able to make the spiritually heroic leap of faith, asserting "I am for going on, and venturing my eternal state with Christ, whether I have comfort here or no; if God doth not come in, thought I, I will leap off the Ladder even blindfold into Eternitie, sink or swim, come heaven, come hell; Lord Jesus, if thou wilt catch me, do; if not, I will venture for thy Name" (101). 2 Timothy 4.6–8, the text of *Paul's Departure and Crown*, puts this mode of death in perspective: "For I am now ready to be offered, and the time of my departure is at hand. I have fought a good fight, I have finished my course, I have kept the faith: Henceforth there is laid up for me a crown of righteousness, which the Lord, the righteous judge, shall give me at that day; and not to me only, but unto all them also that love his appearing" (Offor 1:722, and see also *One Thing Is Needful* VI:71, 87).

The patient pilgrims of part II, however, await "the good hour" when the Messenger of Death will call upon them (304 and gloss). *Christ, A Complete Saviour* images an agent of death visiting passive receivers much like them: "Death is God's sergeant, God's bailiff, and he arrests in God's name when he comes, but seldom gives warning before he clappeth us on the shoulder; and when he arrests us, though he may stay a little while, and give us leave to pant, and tumble, and toss ourselves for a while upon a bed of languishing, yet at last he will prick our bladder, and let out our life, and then our soul will be poured upon the ground, yea, into hell, if we are not ready and prepared for the life everlasting" (Offor 1:221). Dying in both the treatise and the second part of the allegory is something that happens to awaiting people, especially after their full lives have been lived.

The serial deaths in *The Life and Death of Mr. Badman* (1680) model the Puritan ideal in such matters. Mrs. Badman dies a thoroughly Christian death, her heart broken by her husband's wastrel, rebelliously wicked ways: "She dyed bravely; full of comfort of the faith of her Interest in Christ, and by him, of the world to come: she had many brave Expressions in her sickness, and gave to those that came to visit her many signs of her salvation; the thoughts of the Grave, but specially of her Rising again, were sweet thoughts to her. She would long for Death, because she knew it would be her Friend. She behaved her self like to some that were making of them ready to go meet their Bridegroom." She envisions death as membership in a celestial conventicle: "I am going," she says, "to the great Meeting, to the general Assembly, and Church of the first-born which are written in Heaven" (227–28). A few pages later, "a godly old Puritan" dies accompanied by blessed and ravishing music, an anecdote repeated in *Paul's Departure and Crown* (Offor 1:742).

Mr. Badman also narrates contrasting deaths, the devil snatching one sinner away and tearing another to pieces for persisting in their wickedness, and one of Mr. Badman's brothers dies a suicide, another in despair. Badman himself dies relatively young from overindulgence in his cups and his "Queans" (240), within what is from the Puritan point of view that most lamentable spiritual condition, security, thoroughly without knowledge of his sin and without repentance. Although a quiet death by no means assures salvation, and although the godly will continue insecure up to the very moment of their passing, their community can readily gauge their eternal destiny from the daily choices and acts of their lifetimes (255, 266, but cf. Offor 1:742).

The culminating events, like the inaugurating ones, offer especially clearcut contrasts between the two modes. In what Sharrock calls "consciously arranged and harmonised set piece[s]" (*John Bunyan* [1966] 53), the deaths of both principal characters build upon closely woven pastiches of biblical passages and bring earlier designs and motifs to the lofty resolutions anticipated in preceding narratives. At a basic level, part I tarries in Beulah only to highlight the transcendence of the other side of the river, while Part II welcomes residence in Beulah and only glimpses that bourne. Part II looks at the process and rituals of dying as witnessed by others, whereas Christian's river-crossing enacts the internal experience of dying, with its increase of darkness, loss of sensory perception, and the like (157–58). On the other side he is transfigured before moving onto streets of gold and attains the heroic victory which has guided his destiny at least since the Valiant Man tableau at the Interpreter's house, while awaiting chariots spare Christiana even the rigors of Christian's climb up the hill.

Where the pilgrims of part I rush eagerly into death (as heroes traditionally do), those of part II are reactive rather than active, passive rather than ardent. They make an extended stop in Beulah, now a bus-

tling town, before being sequentially and formulaically summoned across
the river according to their ages and frailties. With only slight variations,
each death is recounted in the stages of an invitation, a message confirmed through an emblematic token, bequests to friends, and last words.
Except for Christiana's death token—"an Arrow with a Point, sharpned
with Love, let easily into her Heart" (305)—the deaths distribute the data
of Ecclesiastes 12.5–7.[14] As Standfast remarks, those who die in their sleep
"beg[i]n their journey with Desire and Pleasure"; they "acquiesce" (300).
Biblically derived spices perfume the chambers and anoint the bodies for
crossing the river. Eight listed spices from the Song of Solomon 4.13–14
(and see also Proverbs 7.17) reinforce the bridal and sensuous atmosphere, and two of them—myrrh and aloe—are also among the spices
Nicodemus contributed to the embalming of Christ's body (John 19.39–
40), reinforcing the funereal dimension.

Part I's representation emphasizes the continuous challenge and transcendent rewards of the heroic spiritual individual, while the multiple
and socially ritualized death scenes of part II emphasize not the idea of
death but the process of dying, the community context, and the culminative nature of the event. The former is a private, soul-defining experience,
while the latter is public, ceremonial, and witnessed. Funeral arrangements are imaged, indeed celebrated, as preparations for a journey. The
now-privileged causes of death, deathbed bequests and pronouncements,
dispositions of the body, and other funeral arrangements highlight the
mourning community, responsible for the physical and material remains
and closure of another's life. Where Christian's legacy consisted of encoded markers of his pilgrimage, Christiana and her companions leave
behind specific bequests that encapsulate their life achievements not in
resonating narratives but in things. Part II pays little attention to transcendence, not even to invoke the indescribability topos.

The contrasting deaths of parts I and II reflect differences between
theological theory and cultural practice, differences David Stannard's *The
Puritan Way of Death* distinguishes as death and dying. Such differences
align also with Clifford Geertz's distinction between *culture* and *social
structure*. Part I dramatizes Geertz's *culture*, that is "the framework of beliefs, expressive symbols, and values in terms of which individuals define
their world, express their feelings, and make their judgments," while
part II enacts Geertz's *social structure*, that is, "the ongoing process of
interactive behavior." The former provides a fabric of meaning to guide
and interpret actions, and the latter the forms of action and the social
networks (144–45).

Elsewhere Geertz develops a helpful distinction between *worldview* and *ethos*. *Worldview* is a people's "picture of the way things in sheer actuality are, their concept of nature, of self, of society . . . their most comprehensive ideas of order," while a people's *ethos* refers to "the tone, character, and quality of their life, its moral and aesthetic style and mood." It is a difference between a culture's cognitive, existential values and its general order of existence (126–27). The latter evolves out of the former, as part II out of part I, and as a prescribed "way" of dying evolves out of a developed concept of death. As Geertz develops the distinction: "Religious belief and ritual confront and mutually confirm one another; the ethos is made intellectually reasonable by being shown to represent a way of life implied by the actual state of affairs which the world-view describes, and the world-view is made emotionally acceptable by being presented as an image of an actual state of affairs of which such a way of life is an authentic expression" (127). Despite their dissonances, the culminating events of both parts of *Pilgrim's Progress* are "authentic expressions." That of part I, though emotionally intense, is intellectually based in its Puritan religious context and concepts, while that of part II is both more simply grounded in cultural practice and more emotionally diffuse.

What cultural anthropology describes in one way, Puritan theology and ecclesiology describe in another. While variously pressured to highlight the moment of death, Puritans were caught in a cultural dissonance between a terror of death and damnation and the expectation that they would make the sort of "good" death authorized by Revelation 14.13: "Blessed are the dead which die in the Lord from henceforth: Yea, saith the Spirit, that they may rest from their labours; and their works do follow them" (Stannard 91). A "good" death is a peaceful one and in Bunyan's recurring image a musically accompanied one. Bunyan's paired allegories set forth not so much conflicting belief systems as gendered dissonance, realizing two contrasting modes of experience, action, and thought within masculine and feminine narrative representations. By adding the sequel to his original masculine narrative, Bunyan was able to achieve a credible reconciliation of conflicting claims within a family distribution and thereby not only resolve the design but also evolve a whole greater than the sum of its two parts.

In line with Geertz's semiotic approach to culture (24) and Messer-Davidow's feminist eclecticism (90), these collections of mostly secular evidence recognize contrasting systems or codes within parts I and II of *Pilgrim's Progress*. Contrasts modulate into continuities or, appropriately for these works, into "progress." What begins as a simple sequel to include women within a hugely popular and resonating male myth becomes an enterprise differently vitalized by its feminine subject matters and intents. What begins with the exclusive individual broadens toward the inclusive communal church. What begins as an echo comes to sound forth its own special musical tones. When rituals of dying in part II replace the trauma of death of part I, earlier differences of gender, material culture, social integration, genre, and ethnography may be seen in their fullest specification as encoding changes in the author's life and, as later chapters show, changing patterns of social, cultural, and church history as well.

◄◙│ III │◙►

THESE DIFFERENCES sustain a radically altered view of the heroic. Summaries list Christian's trials as "Wearisomness, Painfulness, Hunger, Perils, Nakedness, Sword, Lions, Dragons, Darkness; and in a word, death, and what not" (18), and "Molestations, Troubles, Wars, Captivities, Cries, Groans, Frights and Fears" (175). In a rare literary gesture Bunyan even likens him to Hercules (292). Christian makes sometimes highly consequential mistakes: he several times steps off the Way, he enacts the self-description "an undeserving Rebel" (25), and he literalizes "trespass" by walking upon Despair's lands. The Interpreter places his and masculine journeys generally in perspective in observing that "the more healthy the lusty man is, the more prone he is unto Evil" (203). On the positive side, Christian escapes enemies, kills at least one fiend or monster (56), and perseveres victoriously against large, subtle, varied, and frequent challenges.

By contrast, companionship among the weak and intercession by the strong govern the society of part II. Sir Walter Scott calls attention to both woman's "weakness" and what he calls her "inspired heroism": "Christian . . . a man, and a bold one, is represented as enduring his fatigues, trials, and combats, by his own stout courage, under the blessing of heaven: but to express that species of inspired heroism by which women are supported in the path of duty, notwithstanding the natural feebleness and timidity of their nature, Christiana and Mercy obtain from the interpreter their guide, called Great-heart, by whose strength and valour their lack of both is supplied, and the dangers and distresses of the way repelled and overcome" (61). Although domestically capable, traveling women are presented as weak, fearful, and in need of protection. Early in the story, Christiana and Mercy are endangered by dogs and assault, and when he comes to their rescue the Reliever admonishes them thus: "I marvelled much when you was entertained at the Gate above, being ye knew that ye were but weak Women, that you petitioned not the Lord there for a Conductor: Then might you have avoided these Troubles, and Dangers: For he would have granted you one" (196). From Interpreter's house on, they are led and protected by Greatheart, whose public service includes leaving the path to destroy three giants (267, 276, 282).

Christiana herself never strays from a road made safe by her husband's precedence. No mountains threaten her party, and they cross the Slough of Despond easily even though it has been marred rather than mended since Christian's travel. The spring at Hill Difficulty is now muddied, but they purify it. She meets with no Worldly Wiseman, or Apollyon, or Vainconfidence, or Doubt, or Despair, or Hill Lucre, or Diffidence, just as Christian does not stop at Gaius's inn or the Plain of Ease. Where Christian is in danger from arrows from Beelzebub's Castle (25), the eldest son now steals fruit from Beelzebub's orchard. Christiana has no burden to be dropped at the sepulcher, but does temporarily mislay her bottle of spirits where Christian had traumatically lost his scroll. Her son easily retrieves it for her while Greatheart encapsulates the simplified lesson, "Pilgrims should watch and remember" (217). They are warned against rather than confronted by robbers (258), and there is never any real danger that they will step out of the Way.

Theirs is a muted and humdrum rather than dangerous Way. Weather more than animate obstacles externalizes internal states, states now more emotional than spiritual. Hill Difficulty is for them "a breathing Hill" and puts them in "a pelting heat" (215, 216). As Honest remarks: "It happens to us, as it happeneth to Way-fairing men; sometimes our way is clean, sometimes foul; sometimes up-hill, sometimes down-hill; We are seldom at a Certainty. The Wind is not alwayes on our Backs, nor is every one a Friend that we meet with in the Way. We have met with some notable Rubs already; and what are yet behind we know not, but for the most part we find it true, that has been talked of of old, *A good Man must suffer Trouble*" (275). The pilgrims in both parts encounter darkness, noises, snares, and demons in the Valley of the Shadow of Death, but the party of part II cross "this doleful place" (241) by daylight under Greatheart's valorous and experienced protection. Where Christian prevailed by mobilizing Scriptures, in part II the strong shepherd the weak, and the community generally cheer and alert each other. All but one of their major trials—a demon, a lion, a gaping pit—recede of their own volition, but in an exhausting battle Greatheart defeats Giant Maul, a figure equated in Bunyan's *Jerusalem Sinner Saved* with Satan's "master argument" and "master-piece," the sinner's temptation to think himself the most sinful, unworthy, hypocritical, and profane of strangers to Christ (Offor 1:96).

The Way of part II is largely overdetermined, its events dominated by the meanings inherited from part I. Because of Christian's precedence, his wife's travel is essentially reactive rather than active, as heroic achievement as well as errors elude her. Christian fought Apollyon because of previous "slips," but as Greatheart asserts, "here is nothing to hurt us, unless we procure it to our selves" (236), or again "a *Christian* can never be overcome unless he shall yield of himself" (247). For Christiana, the Valley of Humiliation is a place of contemplation and a foretaste of the Land of Promise—"as fruitful a place, as any the Crow flies over" (236)— while her husband's battle here against Apollyon (i.e., Pride) was a searing crisis of selfhood. The shepherds' service divides into a warning for the unruly (Christian) and a support of the weak (Christiana) (285), and Mr. Holyman's division of pilgrims' needs into courage and an unspotted life (276) similarly dominates the values of the separate parts.

Part II's female protagonist is interwoven with a social group, social surfaces, and external reality by contrast with the male's interiority. As is usual in female narratives, she serves as a centrifugal center shaping not so much an individual life as an encompassing social design. The woman ministers, as Linda Bamber puts it, "to our sense of community, to friendships and marriages, to whatever is voluntary and pleasurable in the bonds between its citizens" (28). Bunyan attends less to Christiana as a distinct personality than to the larger community which her energies serve, and she is characteristically encumbered rather than autonomous. Christian must function within a doctrinally rigid and threatening Way, while Christiana operates under the dispensation of "Benevolent natural law[,] the only one comedy holds sacred" (Snyder 48). This privileging of the suprapersonal can mean that even the principal female character will be incidental, inessential (Simone de Beauvoir's words), and referenced to or an echo of a male character or system.

Just as male narratives, tragedies, and part I celebrate the unique self and its life-and-death identity issues, female narratives, comedies, and part II prioritize the Other, the typical, the ordinary (Bamber 39–40). The woman's active "self-denial" means that in the absence of ethical

judgment and autonomy, she will always be a static character by contrast with males who are mobile, dynamic, and judged according to their
moral excellence and fallibility. Western literature, according to Marilyn
French, allows only male characters to function as "the image of the
human, the standard, in the moral, political, or philosophical dimension"
and allows only such stories to be interesting and significant (26–27). It
has been usual to find that women's stories participate less than men's in
ethical or "human" categories, but women's stories show not quantitative
but qualitative difference, redefining the human as communal, outward
reaching, and adjusted to mortality rather than merely theoretical and
self-referential.

Bunyan usually endorses gender principles along these lines, but he
is quite capable of circumventing their simplifications in the service of
larger purposes, including both Puritan edification and the comprehensive unity of his own double narrative. As Christian's abandonment of
his family transmogrifies into their salvation, so Mercy, part II's secondary female protagonist, not only fulfills the expected feminine role but
also echoes, subsumes, and elevates elements of Christian's heroism from
part I en route to herself becoming a full realization of the practice of
Christian charity inscribed in her name. This evidence brings the duplex
narrative and its theology full circle, affirming a Puritan "progress" from
the Word to deeds.

Margaret Thickstun describes a layer of part II in which Christiana
becomes absorbed into the familiar male heroism of Mr. Standfast, a
character first met just before Beulah, kneeling in prayer in an emblem
of Christian from part I and the Christian believer generally. Through
prayer he has triumphed over the enticing purse and person of Madam
Bubble, "the Mistriss of the World" (301). "Standing fast" is, of course, the
essential act heroically achieved in Milton's *Paradise Regained* IV.561 and
enjoined by the completed armature of Ephesians 6. Standfast is the last
of eight pilgrims to be summoned to death, and in Thickstun's reading,
Bunyan appropriates for his deathbed the distinctly feminine language
belonging previously to Christiana, casting him in the role of the Bride of
Christ, his male perfection elevating him as "the type of a higher chas-
tity." This Thickstun calls "the displacement of the female implicit in the
controlling [that is, for her the sexual] metaphor of the second part."[15]

The argument for such "subsumption" can have only limited force in
that Standfast does not even enter the story until a dozen pages from
the end, and his language evidence is minimal. But at least two other

heroic males in part II can be said to subsume the feminine, if by *subsume* we mean displace by inclusion. Mr. Valiant-for-Truth also emblematizes Christian and displaces Christiana. He enters the Way just at the point where Littlefaith figured in part I and fulfills his name by succeeding where Littlefaith had been overwhelmed. Reflecting part II's shift of values, where Littlefaith suffered at the hands of Faint-heart, Mistrust, and Guilt (125), Valiant-for-Truth overcomes Wild-head, Inconsiderate, and Pragmatick (290). Littlefaith was the only sympathetic figure in part I to share weaknesses of body or spirit with the late recruits of part II, while Valiant-for-Truth is chiefly characterized by the military trappings and actions in which he is first encountered, especially by his "right *Jerusalem* blade" (290) and by his fighting "till my Sword did cleave to my Hand" (291). His salvation history was inspired by and recapitulates Christian's. On her deathbed Christiana asks him to watch over and comfort her children. In his first role, the displacement of Littlefaith, Valiant-for-Truth transmutes weakness into strength, and in the second, by echoing Christian and part I so fully within the family framework of part II, he takes on the paternal role and draws both parts of the book to full resolution by encompassing the feminine and family mode within his masculine heroism. The entourage is complete when Valiant-for-Truth, the "guard" traveling in the rear, complements Greatheart, the "guide" in the lead (296).

Even more than Standfast or Valiant-for-Truth, Greatheart "subsumes" the feminine. As the experienced conductor of parties of pilgrims, he joins Christiana and her family at Interpreter's house, absorbs the family duties Christian had abandoned in the City of Destruction, and fulfills pastoral and patriarchal roles in the extended family of pilgrims, as knowledgeable guide, wise counsellor, and militant protector of his "congregation" (from *grex* 'flock'). As is often remarked, Greatheart acts out Bunyan's biographical history as Bedford minister (1672–88).

Besides these strong male figures, Christian's four sons grow from childhood to full maturity over the course of the story, joining in battles against giants and marrying "fruitful" wives before they reach the Delectable Mountains. Like their father, they variously multiply the faith. An additional series of males in part II are subject to the bodily and spiritual weaknesses usually associated with females. After the Valley of the Shadow of Death, the multiplying pilgrim family are progressively joined by "the old, the infirm, those plagued by scruples and haunted by despondency, timidity, and fear" (Keeble, "Christiana's Key" 14). Feeblemind speaks for these recruits—Honest, Ready-to-Halt, Despondency, Much-

Afraid—and captures many of the dominant values when he avers, "I am a man of no strength at all, of Body, nor yet of Mind, but would, if I could, tho I can but *craul*, spend my Life in the Pilgrims Way" (267).

Aged and infirm males cross over the usual boundaries between strong male and weak female roles, and complementarily, and more surprisingly, Christiana's companion Mercy goes well beyond what is usually defined as the female role. By modifying Christian's spiritual history, she provides crossovers not just between male and female roles but also between parts I and II. Through the threshold or initiation phase of Interpreter's house, she echoes the conversion morphology and thus the narrative of part I, but emphasizes not doubt and despair so much as acceptance, assurance, and final glorification. Mercy is notably a "doer," and as we were told in part I, "The Soul of Religion is the practick part" (79). In the overall narrative, she epitomizes and translates into spiritual terms the principles of nurturance that dominate part II. By the end she has translated the theoretical theology of part I into a full program of works and thereby subsumed the mode of masculine achievement within a fully realized, empowered, comprehensive, and multiplying feminine heroism.

In *Psyche as Hero: Female Heroism and Fictional Form*, Lee R. Edwards distinguishes between the terms "heroine" and "female hero." Christiana fully instances the former. She loves, nurtures, comforts, solaces, and endeavors to please; she is innately selfless, weak, and passive, by nature a submitter to, not a subverter of, the structures of her patriarchal society. As Edwards puts it, "the heroine obeys, falls into line, takes second place." Although the male hero functions as a subject, she is always an adjunct. By contrast, the "female hero" finds ways to endow with value her impulses to love, nurture, solace, and please, and thus redeems the "human" so as to include women. Like Campbell's paradigmatic male hero, Edwards's female hero assumes a mythic role, like Psyche defying and robbing the gods, facing their love and enmity, suffering isolation and even a trip to the underworld, achieving impossible tasks and extraordinary awareness, and finally triumphing.[16]

Mercy does not extend female heroism to mythic proportions, but she does represent Bunyan's version of the female heroic. Like Christian, and unlike Christiana, Mercy makes some real progress in the course of the narrative, developing, as John R. Knott describes it, "from fearfulness to joy, and from illustrating the comprehensiveness of divine mercy to exemplifying mercy herself." Her spiritual adventures are more developmental and exciting and endow her with a narrative and character interest never attached to Christiana (Knott, "Bunyan" 212–14; Kaufmann, *Pilgrim's Progress* 95–97). In part I, following scriptural admonition, for example Matthew 10.39, Christian loses himself in order to find himself, but Mercy enacts the disappearance of self more entirely. Where Christ may be seen *in* Christian or the *visible* Puritan saint, Christ is seen *through* Mercy— and not merely seen but energized and multiplied.

In keeping with the communal values of part II, Mercy is sparked to pilgrimage by friendship for Christiana; they share a godly fellowship. Mercy is a hired companion, not precisely a servant so much as a family member, a status resting upon contemporary Puritan thinking that distinctions between masters and servants were fundamentally unchristian (Schucking 117; *Christian Behaviour* III:30–32, 40–43). Mercy is the young active virgin, "always busying her self in doing" (226–27), making and bestowing needments, a combination of New Testament virgin and Old Testament handmaiden (Thickstun 92). Although her suitor, the worldly Mr. Brisk, commends her as "a good Huswife" who is "never idle" (227), he rejects her because he cannot "like her conditions," that is her in-eradicable generosity to the poor. Through marriage to Matthew, Mercy becomes a full member of the "Christian" family.

Mercy requires the kind of theological interpretation that dominates part I as Christiana does not. Especially in its early stages, her pilgrimage reenacts the Puritan conversion struggle. Like Christian she feels a low level of self-worth and a high level of anxiety. Although she has "fall[en] in love with her own Salvation" (186), she anticipates failure and danger. She travels without an invitation or proof of promise. When the others gain easy entry at the Wicket Gate, Mercy is left outside, "much dejected in her mind, for that she comes, as she thinks, without sending for" (189, and see Kaufmann, *Pilgrim's Progress* 96). Impatiently, like Christian she knocks vigorously on her own behalf, and the gloss reads: "The delays make the hungring Soul the fervener" (189). Entry for her, as for Christian, is felt as the difference between life and death: "I also thought that I must either knock again or dye" (191, glossed to Christian's history at 24–25). Knocking at the gate equates in Puritan parlance with fervent prayer.[17]

The most telling links between Mercy and Christian occur in their relations to biblical texts. Mercy is motivated to pilgrimage because her heart burns within her, and, like Christian, she leaves her father, her mother, and the land of her nativity (206, as enjoined by Luke 14.26 and 33). Like Christian too she has come to see the City of Destruction as no

longer habitable, motives the Interpreter translates into typological heroism by analogy with Ruth's relation to Naomi (206–7). Like Christian,
Mercy repeatedly interprets her experience through the biblical medium,
citing Matthew (twice), Psalms (thrice), the Song of Solomon, and Hosea
(191, 216, 218, 239). Expansively she describes her service to the poor in
the words of 1 Timothy 6.17–19 (227). Christiana's relations to the biblical
Word are in a quite different mode. Where Christian and Mercy enfold
their beings and circumstances within the scriptural locus, the passive
Christiana merely applies biblical labels (see Chapter 8). In interpreting
an early dream, where Christiana draws a practical lesson on provisioning, Mercy draws religious conclusions about human imperfections and
God's providential kindness (197).

Her threshold experience, however, differs in emphasis from Christian's. Mercy is included within a general or communal call to salvation
rather than the object of a special call. Thus she represents, as does part II
more largely, not so much the individual believer as the church or conventicle as a whole. The gatekeeper is no longer Good Will (as in part I)
but now Christ himself, and entry derives not from self-centered conversion morphology but from Christ-centered justification by imputed
righteousness. Mercy is so conscious of her weakness and doubtful of her
welcome at the Wicket Gate that she faints and is *led* over the threshold,
not pushed from behind. Mercy thus benefits from salvational inclusiveness and receives divine mercy rather than enacting it herself. Similarly,
when Christiana intercedes on her friend's behalf, it is Christiana who
manifests the quality in question.

Mercy's dream at the Interpreter's house attaches her journey to the
conversion morphology scheme, but soon moves beyond it to issues more
important for part II:

> I was a Dreamed that I sat all alone in a Solitary place, and was be-
> moaning of the hardness of my Heart. Now I had not sat there long,
> but methought many were gathered about me to see me, and to hear
> what it was that I said. So they harkened, and I went on bemoan-
> ing the hardness of my Heart. At this, some of them laughed at me,
> some called me Fool, and some began to thrust me about. With that,
> methought I looked up, and saw one coming with Wings towards
> me. So he came directly to me, and said *Mercy*, what aileth thee?
> Now when he had heard me make my complaint; he said, *Peace be
> to thee:* he also wiped mine Eyes with his Handkerchief, and *clad*

me in *Silver* and *Gold*; he put a Chain about my Neck, and Ear-rings
in mine Ears, and a beautiful Crown upon my Head. Then he took
me by my Hand, and said, *Mercy,* come after me. So he went up, and
I followed, till we came at a Golden Gate. Then he knocked, and
when they within had opened, the man went in and I followed him
up to a Throne, upon which one sat, and he said to me, *welcome
Daughter.* The place looked bright, and twinkling like the Stars, or
rather like the *Sun,* and I thought that I saw your Husband there, so
I awoke from my Dream. (222–23)

Mercy's account of her solitariness and hardness of the heart gives way
to reciting the sort of personal narrative required for membership in a
gathered church. This in turn gives way to a personalized, all-powerful,
nonjudgmental savior and celestial welcome as Mercy's anxiety transmutes fully to assurance.

Mercy's name is importantly multivalenced, and *An Exposition . . . of
Genesis* reminds us, "names of old were ofttimes given according to the
nature and destiny of the persons concerned" (Offor II:495). That the God
governing part II is "one that delighteth in *Mercie*" (185, Micah 7.18) contextualizes several ranges of her action and meaning. The names of her
sister, Bountiful, also remarkable for showing kindness to the poor (228),
and of her sisters-in-law, Grace, Phebe (i.e., shining), and Martha (see
especially John II.27), amplify her portrait. Mr. Honest extends her name
into her nature thus: "*Mercie,* is thy Name? by *Mercie* shalt thou be sustained, and carried thorough all those Difficulties that shall assault thee
in thy way; till thou come thither where thou shalt look the Fountain
of Mercie in the Face with Comfort" (248). In part like Honest, Mercy
bears the name of the virtue she hopes to attain—a virtue not of her very
substance but in pursuit of which she is exemplary.[18] *Mercy,* however, is
a substantive not an adjectival designation. She pursues not so much the
quality but the occasions within which that quality can be made operative. Like her mirror, to which we shall return in a moment, she reflects
not her self but her Christic service. Matthew 25.40 provides an authorizing text: "Verily I say unto you, Inasmuch as ye have done it unto one of
the least of these my brethren, ye have done it unto me," and James 2.13
adds, "mercy rejoiceth against judgment."

A number of Bunyan's lesser works illuminate the nature of Mercy.
One Bunyan title registers a key point: *Good News For the Vilest of Men,
Or, A Help for Despairing Souls. . . . Shewing That Jesus Christ would*

have *Mercy in the First Place offered to the Biggest Sinners* (1688). This
work images Mercy as "the only Antidote against Sin.'Tis of a thawing
nature: 'twill loose the Heart that is frozen up in Sin: yea, 'twill make
the Unwilling willing to come to Jesus Christ for Life" (xi:34). *Israel's
Hope Encouraged*—on the text of Psalm 130.7: "For with the Lord there
is mercy"—distinguishes *Mercy* from the sometimes synonymous terms
Grace and *Love*. Grace shows royal bounty, and Love complacency and
delight, but Mercy manifests "that goodness that is in God's heart towards
us," the desperateness of human need and God's compassion and pity
(Offor 1:594, 599; similarly Offor 1:644; and see 1:679). This work exhaustively lists biblical references to *mercy* under the headings tender,
great, rich, manifold, abounding, compassing us round about, following
us, doing every good turn, and everlasting (Offor 1:593–604). It recognizes converting mercy, preserving mercy, and glorifying mercy, mercies
that diminish and mercies that multiply by the using, and it celebrates
"A multitude of common mercies; of every day's mercies, of every night's
mercies, of mercies in relations, of mercies in food and raiment, and of
mercies in want of these things there is; and who can number them?"
(1:597). *Reprobation Asserted* sees mercy as enormous, unfailingly sympathetic, and inexhaustible and distinguishes between "eternal Mercy" and
"present Mercy" (Offor II:357–58). *The Resurrection of the Dead* (III:236–
37) appropriates the parable of the talents—"Well done thou good and
faithful servant . . . enter thou into the joy of thy lord" (Matthew 25.21
and 23)—to commend the good works through which mercy shows itself.
But Bunyan, like Puritanism generally, is insistent that good works be
products of faith not substitutes for it.

Honest's description of Mercy's destiny as "look[ing] the Fountain of
Mercie in the Face with Comfort" anticipates the emblematic mirror she
receives from the shepherds at the Delectable Mountains. In part I, the
shepherds shared an analogous visual machine with Christian and Hopeful in the form of a "Perspective Glass" on Hill Clear for glimpsing the
gates of the Celestial City (122–23). Mercy's differing allegorical nature
requires a target, a reflection, in order to fulfill itself. As the s(Word) of
Ephesians provides the dominant biblical emblem of part I, so Mercy's
mirror extends the analogous text and reading skills of part II: "Now the
Glass was one of a thousand. It would present a man, one way, with his
own Feature exactly, and turn it but an other way, and it would shew
one the very Face and Similitude of the Prince of Pilgrims himself. . . .
Yea such an excellency is there in that Glass, that it will shew him to one

where they have a mind to see him; whether living or dead, whether in Earth or Heaven, whether in a State of Humiliation, or in his Exaltation, whether coming to Suffer, or coming to Reign" (287). Marginal glosses identify the mirror as "the Word of God" and point to the Epistle of James which blesses those "doer[s] of the work" who, looking into a mirror, see not their natural faces but rather "the perfect law of liberty" (1.25); to 1 Corinthians which distinguishes between seeing through a glass darkly and seeing (and being seen) face to face (13.12); and especially to 2 Corinthians 3.18. The unstrained quality of mercy is a capacity to see the variously layered spiritual potentiality behind the data of homely experience, in the words of St. Paul to take away the veil: "But we all, with open face beholding as in a glass the glory of the Lord, are changed into the same image from glory to glory, even as by the Spirit of the Lord" (2 Corinthians 3.16, 18).

In his study of Puritanism and the self, Sacvan Bercovitch cites a characteristic Puritan understanding of the mirror that exactly evaluates Mercy's mirror. Whereas Renaissance humanists understood a mirror as reflecting the unique self of modern individualism, Puritans sought not their own reflection but the divine image: "They sought Christ, 'the mirror of election,' and 'Prospective-Glass for Saints'—or rather mirror, prospective glass, and image all in one: communion meant '*a putting on of Christ*,' transforming oneself completely into his Image. . . . The Puritans felt that the less one saw of oneself in that mirror, the better; and best of all was to cast no reflection at all, to disappear." [19] In Bunyan's character Mercy, self-reflection disappears in favor of a continuous, copious, and sympathetic ministering to the basic human needs of others, contextualized by part II's depiction of Christ as a nurturing and domestic presence rather than a lordly or military one. Mercy's characteristic activity of clothing the naked, of "making of Hose and Garments for others, and bestow[ing] them upon them that had need" (227), becomes enfolded into service to Christ (Matthew 25.36, 38) and ultimately into the saviorial role itself.

Mercy multiplies in another way as well. Where Christiana is subsumed within her familial roles and within the strengths of other members of her party, Mercy emerges from that "family" compound to define and bear feminine redemptive energies. Although at the outset Mercy reenacts Christian's self-absorption—simultaneously an overriding concern for salvation—after she has crossed the threshold into assurance, Mercy can advance into full selflessness. The shepherds' gift of the mirror to a pregnant Mercy seals her achieved identity as now "a young, and a breeding Woman" (287). As the story advances, Mercy becomes a mother —and can say with Christiana, "Now I am risen a Mother in *Israel*" (219, Judges 5.6–7)—and her new family offers Christian continuity beyond the serial deaths of the aged and infirm with which part II concludes. Besides multiplying works, Mercy carries forward into the future a combination and integration of Christian's and Christiana's modes of achievement, both regeneration and generation.

CHAPTER SEVEN

The Church

All human societies implicitly or explicitly refer to two contrasting social models. One . . . is of society as a structure
of jural, political, and economic positions, offices, statuses,
and roles, in which the individual is only ambiguously
grasped behind the social persona. The other is of society as
a communitas of concrete idiosyncratic individuals, who,
though differing in physical and mental endowment, are
nevertheless regarded as equal in terms of shared humanity.
The first model is of a differentiated, culturally structured,
segmented, and often hierarchical system of institutionalized positions. The second presents society as an undiffer-
entiated, homogeneous whole, in which individuals confront one another integrally, and not as 'segmentalized' into
statuses and roles.—Victor W. Turner, *The Ritual Process:
Structure and Anti-Structure*

VICTOR TURNER'S contrasting social models underscore the differing religious emphases of the two parts of *Pilgrim's Progress.* Part I enacts the individualism, structuralism, and positioning of the first of these, as part II
enacts *communitas* with its shared humanity and homogeneous wholeness. Unstructured and unsegmentalized, the latter's "boundaries [as]
ideally coterminous with those of the human species" admit the greater
social inclusiveness of Bunyan's sequel. Although it begins in immediacy
and spontaneity, even such a *communitas* tends to develop into a normative structured social system "under the influence of time, the need
to mobilize and organize resources, and the necessity for social control
among the members of the group in pursuance of these goals." In a helpful
illustration, Turner notes that within a century after St. Francis's death,

the Franciscan Order had divided into the "spirituals," who practiced an even stricter observance than the founder, and the "conventuals," whose practice relaxed the rigor of the founder's ideal.[1] *Spiritual* captures much of part I of *Pilgrim's Progress* and, as we shall see in this chapter, *conventual* similarly encapsulates part II. Moreover, the progress from the first to the second also records the individual Puritan's salvational or conversion ideal transmuting into wider systematic and distributed mobilization, organization, and control.

While the secular discourses of the previous chapter illustrate what Coleridge called "the Bunyan of Parnassus," this chapter deals with his "Bunyan of the Conventicle" (*Coleridge* 475), with the ways that the church and church rites and practices are fictionally represented in part II, with church membership and leadership, and with the discipline and sacraments that distinguish Bunyan's religion. Puritanism was a family phenomenon, and in context *family* is both a real and a metaphoric designation. Bunyan often endorses the Calvinist commonplace of worshipping families as "little churches," an analogy authorized by Philemon 2 and 1 Corinthians 16.19. Private family devotions provided daily domestic equivalents of such public Sunday church ordinances as the sermon, bible-reading, prayer, psalm-singing, and thanksgiving, what *The Life and Death of Mr. Badman* lists as "this *praying*, this *reading of Scriptures*, and *hearing*, and *repeating* of Sermons" (98). The home as much as the church provided an arena for what Levin L. Schucking calls "family theocracy," a system wherein family dynamics could bring pressures for self-reform and religious integration to bear from all sides all the time (56). As the family is a church so is the church a family, when for example identifying its members as sons and daughters of a father God (2 Corinthians 6.18) or as brothers and sisters, a usual New Testament practice. Early in his career too Bunyan felt the influence of the principle in Arthur Dent's *The Plaine Mans Path-Way to Heaven*, that "he that hath not the Church for his mother, cannot have God for his father."[2]

While part I dramatizes an allegory of the soul and the struggles of the separatist professor, its lonely heroism glossing the autobiographical trauma of *Grace Abounding*, part II embraces church matters in more institutionalized form, the meditative growth of a holy community with its diversities and solicitudes. As the first "disturb[s] the comfortable," the second "comfort[s] the disturbed." The second part, as its commentators regularly observe, "presents a cheerful, teeming picture of the life of a seventeenth-century godly family and of the small separatist community made up of a few such families" or re-creates "the Christian life as it was lived by ordinary people going about their ordinary everyday concerns." Bunyan translates Sharrock's general observation—"Calvinism begins with an extraordinary interest in the self and ends with a perhaps excessive attention to the affairs of other people" (*John Bunyan* [1968] 138)—into radically altered representations of religious, spiritual, and biographical priorities in parts I and II and into two distinct literary encodings of historical change. We may recall also the Augustinian formulation that "piety begins with fear and is perfected in love."[3]

Viewed historically, part I enfolds the crisis of persecution in the 1660s that defined Bunyan's conversion history and his Bedford church, while the second part reflects "the atmosphere of the world which is being made safe for Puritanism" (Sharrock, *John Bunyan* [1968] 152). As S. J. Newman summarizes it: "The novelty of [Christian's] pilgrimage is rescinded to orthodoxy amidst the communion of saints."[4] *Pilgrim's Progress* is not a history of the church in the sense that Book I of *The Faerie Queene* represents the macrocosmic within a microcosmic narrative line. The second part offers not Christian history in its beginnings and vicissitudes so much as the record of sectarian life in the England of the 1680s, not corporate history but a compounding set of individuals whose differences are heightened, not lost, within the larger pattern.

What matters in part II is the church as *communitas*, as institution, as participating in time and ideality, and as a particular earthly fellowship of believers gathered together in freedom and in accord with the practice of primitive churches to live a life of holiness. Even at the simplest definitional level, *church* means many things, including the ideal of Hebrews 12.22–23: "But ye are come unto mount Sion, and unto the city of the living God, the heavenly Jerusalem, and to an innumerable company of angels, To the general assembly and church of the firstborn, which are written in heaven, and to God the Judge of all, and to the spirits of just men made perfect." Bunyan speaks of the church as "the place of God's presence" and "the place of God's desire on earth" and, compounding Genesis 2.8 and Song of Solomon 4.12, as "a garden enclosed" (Offor II:451; Offor I:758; Offor II:425). At the practical level, the word *church* refers: (1) to a building, real or metaphoric, or a public institution more generally; (2) to a religious society, community, or sect, or all official and unofficial believers throughout history, the collective body of Christians, especially as the Church Triumphant or Church Militant; and (3) to a service of worship, the clerical profession, an organization of ecclesiastical power or government, or even the whole conceptual framework and practices of such a community. The following discussion covers these headings in this order, with the proviso that Bunyan's representations fade into and out of categories because typological and metaphoric usages answer to the biblical sources they reference and reverence.

Bunyan devotes at least four works to the nature and operation of the church, to what Christopher Hill calls its mystery and its history (*Tinker* 330): *The Holy City* (1665), *Solomon's Temple Spiritualized* (1688), *Of the House of the Forest of Lebanon* (post.), and *A Discourse of the Building, Nature, Excellency, and Government of the House of God* (1688). The last of these is in verse, the others prose. The early *Holy City* addresses the millennial ideal, the Church Triumphant; the other interlocking ones from the 1680s concern the Church Militant or the visible church within history, flawed, persecuted, but moving toward a post-Antichrist reconstitution of a perfected and empowered spiritual community. These three, along with *Of Antichrist and His Ruin* (post.), show that the later Bunyan had developed an historical sense not found in or necessary to the youthful convert. Transitionally, *Peaceable Principles and True* of 1677 dismisses the idea of an invisible universal church in favor of the Church Militant, the visible particular mobilized congregation of his own experience (Offor II:650, and similarly *A Confession of My Faith* [1672; Offor II:606]).

The Holy City, a commentary upon Revelation 21–22, outlines three distinct epochs in the history of the church as it considers the New Jerusalem's displacement of the Old. The first consists of Jerusalem in its original and pure state, in the eras of Solomon and of Christ and the apostles; the second is Jerusalem in its declined or captive state when the Jews were carried into Babylon and in the days of Antichrist; and the third refers to its recovered and restored state, the New Jerusalem of Revelation. Interpretively viewed, the first he specifies as "*Jerusalem* in the Letter" and the last—and therefore the compound of the three—as "our *Gospel-Jerusalem* . . . our New-Testament-Church" (III:78–79). Separate Bunyan treatises record his views on each of these eras, with *Solomon's Temple Spiritualized* considering and typologizing the first, *Of the House of the Forest of Lebanon* taking up the second, and *Of Antichrist and His Ruin* and *The Holy City* incorporating Bunyan's vision of the nearly attained ideal of the gospel church of his own time (III:117).

Bunyan's sense of historical patterning derives from the second book, besides the Bible, to which he was deeply devoted, Foxe's *Actes and Monu-*

ments, which recognizes a similar series of stages: "First there was 'the suffering time of the Church, which continued from the Apostles age about 300 yeares. Secondly . . . the flourishyng tyme of the churche, which lasted another 300 yeares.' Then came a long period during which the church was continually 'declinyng or backeslidying.' Now finally has come the 'reformation and purging of the Church of God.'" Ancient Rome, not recent England, was guilty of innovation, and the Reformation returns to an earlier perfection. Such an authoritative multistage sequence allows Bunyan to conflate synchronic design (providence) with diachronic experience (history), kairos with chronos, to develop his own optimistic amalgam of the historical patterns the seventeenth century allowed: history as decay, history as cycles, and history as progress, with providential history as a possible overlay for any of these three. As Achsah Guibbory observes, typology combines a cyclical reading of history with a linear, eschatological view by denying that historical repetition is directionless, an adjustment especially important in relation to Puritan typologizings of the self and of immediate cultural forces.[5]

All four of Bunyan's works on the church equate it with a woman and image it through architectural models. Even if he had wished to, Bunyan could not have escaped the representation of the love between Christ and his bride the church from the Song of Solomon, but *The Holy City* enfolds the metaphor of church as woman into architectural types to trace the church's history. The authorizing text is Revelation 21.1–2's vision of "the holy city, new Jerusalem, coming down from God out of heaven, prepared as a bride adorned for her husband" (see also 19.7 and 22.17). Bunyan's Emblem LVIII, "Of the Spouse of Christ," traces the sequence, as Christ's bride, "his Joynt-Heir . . . Of all that shall be, or at present is" (VI:258), progresses from outcast and beggar to queen. Comforted and supported by her bridegroom Christ, she emerges from the wilderness where she was naked, defiled, and assaulted by the dragon, and when she is restored to dignity and home, she becomes the cleansed and ornamented "Heiress of the best Kingdom" (258) in her perfected beauty. Future pride, linked with Roman Catholicism, threatens reversion to her original state. Elsewhere this poem invokes Revelation 12.1 and 13, Ezekiel 16, and Song of Solomon 3.6, 5.10, 16 to describe the lady and to outline the historical changes.

To sort out equations of the church with city and/or woman chronologically is also to sort out relations between the Song of Solomon and Revelation, and thus between Old and New Testaments. *Solomon's Temple*

Spiritualized typologizes the beauties of the church from the Song of Solomon, such as her neck, eyes, nose, hair, and smell (Offor III:463).[6] *The House of the Forest of Lebanon* figures the church as a comely and delicate woman, vulnerable, isolated in the wilderness, and subject to being ravished and defiled by the godless. The god-fearing are differently overcome: The lady now "in her weeds of widowhood, is become the desire of the eyes of the nations . . . that whoso sees but the utmost glimpse of her, is easily ravished with her beauties" (Offor III:523; see also *The Faerie Queene* I.iii and vi). A third projection, closer to this treatise's argument, compares the church "to the condition of a woman in travail, struggling with her pains . . . to show her fruitfulness to God-ward in her most afflicted condition" (Offor III:514). *Of Antichrist and His Ruin*, drawing heavily from Revelation, represents the church of Antichrist, of course, as the whore (Offor II:57). *The Holy City* explains "Why the Church at this day is called by the name of a City, rather than a Woman, Temple, House, or the like" (gloss III:80) and attributes the reassignment of images to the Spirit of God (the Bible). At the conclusion of the present era, this treatise suggests, the image of woman, now adorned, will become reabsorbed within a revitalized city to show how numerous, enriched, and empowered the church has become (III:80–81).

Within this historical patterning, *The Holy City* develops out of Revelation 21–22 a full definition of the Church Triumphant at once visionary and prescriptive. It reconciles biblical prophecies about the millennial community, explicates the city's structure, decoration, and workmanship in terms of doctrinal perfection, "of pure and undefiled understandings of God's Word and not by fleshly delights," and adumbrates "the church on Earth" and also the individual soul (III:xli, 178, 77). As in *The House of God*, God is the builder. Again and again the city's elements equate with Christ, including its temple ("the body of Christ" [156]); its walls ("salvation of God through Christ" and "the Lord Jesus Christ Himself in his precious Merits, Benefits and Offices" [131, 132]); its entrance ("Communion with the God and Saviour of this City" and "Communion with the Inhabitants and Priviledges of this City" [101]); and the great and high Mountain on which the city is set ("the *Lord Christ*, on which the Soul must be placed" [77]).

By contrast with such millennial hopes, the later *Solomon's Temple Spiritualized*, like the poetic *House of God*, seems almost practical in its content. Under some seventy headings, this work, like the former one, proceeds through individual items of the construction, material, furnishings, disposition, and worship of the House of Israel, this time from Ezekiel 43ff. It divides the history of the church between the two cities "Sion and Jerusalem . . . the true and the false, and their seed Isaac and Ishmael" (Offor III:463). Although it methodically visualizes a historical temple, Bunyan's real interest is in the church of his own era: For him the New Jerusalem, the New Testament church on earth, and "what is now" are all the same (468). He goes beyond traditional typology to recognize antitypes from his own era, though always, as he says, "comparing spiritual things with spiritual" (464). Mount Moriah is "a type of the Son of God, the mountain of the Lord's house, the rock against which the gates of hell cannot prevail" (465) as well as a type of our gospel church (467); the workmen are "types of our gospel ministers" (466); and, more minutely, "the gifts and graces of the true church were set forth by the spices, nuts, grapes, pomegranates, that the land of Canaan brought forth" (463). Like the previous work, *Solomon's Temple* enfolds into its architectural model the personification of 2 Corinthians 6.16: "Ye are the temple of the living God." In this mode, "Christ Jesus, the builder of his own house, WHOSE HOUSE ARE WE, doth build his holy habitation for him to dwell in" (Offor III:466).

Of the House of the Forest of Lebanon again practices innovative typologizing to extend the churches of the Old and New Testament into "our Gospel Church in the wilderness" (Offor III:515), his own persecuted, embattled separatist church, more largely the Church Militant. Though plain and ungarnished, this house shares the same foundations, support, and steadfastness of the earlier temple at Jerusalem, differing from it in circumstantial but not substantial points (Offor III:516–17, 520). The construction and furnishings of this house, also built by Solomon and larger than his earlier temple, itemize details from 1 Kings 7. Where the temple relates to Canaan's practice of religion, the house figures forth the assaulted, persecuted, defensive church "scattered among the nations" (513–15, 528). Architecturally, the church is now "a castle, or Stronghold . . . a tower built for an armoury" and "a place of fortification and defense," but a site for offense as well as defense (516, 514, 526). This wilderness church suffers from divisions within as well as external enemies and is thus "the church in her low estate," "in affliction," "in a bewildered state," "in her sackcloth state," reflecting "the deplorable state of a professing people" (525, 515, 523, 513, 536). It was built "to show us how we should be while standing before the face of the dragon, and while shifting for ourselves in the wilderness" (525).

As a coda to these interlocking treatises, *Of Antichrist and His Ruin* looks to the end of the wilderness era and provides Bunyan's most pointed commentary upon the church and the politics of his own lifetime. Under the guise of commenting on King Artaxerxes' personal and financial generosity to Ezra and his Jewish brethren, Bunyan speaks of the persecutions of sixteenth- and seventeenth-century English history and warns his contemporaries against blaming kings and magistrates for the troubles of the church of God. He calls himself "one of the old-fashion professors" because of his agreement to honor the king as well as fear God[7] and urges his contemporaries to "labour to see the true cause of trouble, which is sin; and to attain to a fitness to be delivered out thence, and that is by repentance, and amendment of life" (Offor 11:45, 74). This posthumously published treatise makes explicit the spiritual deterioration Bunyan attributes to the preceding twenty years:

> Let us mend our pace in the way of reformation, that is the way to hasten the downfall of Antichrist, ministers need reforming, particular congregations need reforming, there are but few church-members but need reforming. This twenty years we have been degenerating, both as to principles, and as to practice; and have grown at last into an amazing likeness to the world, both as to religion and civil demeanour: Yea, I may say, so remiss have churches been in instructing those that they have *received* into fellowship with them; and so careless have the *received* been, of considering the grounds of their coming into churches, that most members, in some places, seem now to be at a loss; yea, and those churches stand with their fingers in their mouths, and are as if they would not, durst not, or could not help it. (45)

He claims even such decline or "need for reformation" as a sign of hope and imminent victory on the basis of Revelation 11.7–12, where the death and resurrection of those bearing witness for God in the world, like the success of the Antichrist, are forerunners of more general deliverance and ascent to heaven (64–65, 60). As they await the fulfillment "in God's time," here as in *The House of the Forest of Lebanon*, Bunyan urges the practice of patience and hope in God (Offor 11:53, 73, and 111:516, 528). Like *The Holy City*, *Of Antichrist* echoes Revelation in anticipating a perfected faith and Church Triumphant.

The full title of *The House of God*, Bunyan's last and most ambitious poem in scale, complexity, thought, and technique (v1:lix), outlines the inclusive intention: *A Discourse of the Building, Nature, Excellency and Government of the House of God. With Counsels and Directions To the Inhabitants thereof.* This fourth Bunyan work on the church aligns more closely with the data of *Pilgrim's Progress* than do the theological and historical treatises just considered. Part I is governed by the millennial ideal church of *The Holy City*, the Church Triumphant, architecturally projected in the supratemporal Celestial City, an ultimate goal envisioned as early as Christian's departure from the City of Destruction, and reenvisioned as the still distant glories which receive Christian and Hopeful at the end. Part II, however, visits communal sites serving as architectural and metaphoric analogues of the Church Militant, sometimes typological, sometimes persecuted, but regularly progressing through time toward higher spiritual attainment. The serial sites of part II represent the institutional practices of a contained and supportive religious community. Part II is preoccupied with "the separateness of God's people, the faith and holiness that testify to their distinctiveness, the suffering that their different way entails, the joy arising from their fellowship, their sense of being nurtured by God"; in John R. Knott's summary phrase, it "distill[s] the essence of the life of this [separatist] community" ("Bunyan" 225).

The authorizing text of *The House of God* is Psalm 26.8: "Lord, I have loved the Habitation of thy House, the place where thine Honour dwelleth." Its eleven sections chart the emphasis:

I By whom this HOUSE is built (1–30)
II Of the Beauty of the Church (31–57)
III Of the Conveniencies of this House (58–97)
IV Of the Strength and Defence of this House (98–128)
V The Delicateness of the Situation of this House (130–72)
VI The way of Receiving those that would here Inhabit (174–246)
VII Of the Governours of this House (247–597)
VIII The Order and manner of the Government here (598–1015)
IX The way of reducing what's amiss, into Order here (1017–1311)
X The present Condition of those thus dealt with (1313–27)
XI An Expostulation with such to return (1329–1450)

The later sections incorporate applications to lapsed members, as the earlier ones fulfill a definitional, descriptive, indeed prescriptive intention. Bunyan's purposes are here modern, procedural, and instructive contrasting with the visionary, typological, and apocalyptic modes of the treatises on church eras. It is a point of some interest that Bunyan's prose is more mystical, while his poetry, as here, is more down-to-earth.

Bunyan's *House of God* begins with a series of practical architectural similitudes.

> The *Builder's* God, *Materials* his Elect;
> His *Son's* the *Rock*, on which it is Erect;
> The *Scripture* is his rule, Plummet or Line,
> Which gives proportion to this *House divine*. (vi:274)

It reinvokes some earlier categories—"Call this a *Temple* or a House of *Prayer*, / A Pallace, *Oracle*, or *Spouse* most fair" (ll. 17–18)—and projects the church as a cottage, beggar's hall, almshouse, a palace with cellars and a banqueting house, a castle with battlements, groundworks, and gates, a horticultural paradise of gardens, streams, orchards, fields, and mountains, an inn called "*Mercies Arms*," and a hospital or refuge for debtors, convicts, and runaways (vi:275, 277–80). "The House of God" as *Mercies Inn*, echoing Gaius's inn, encapsulates part II's data of hospitality, comfort, and need. That in part II the shepherds at Delectable Mountains now operate out of a palace rather than tents glances at both the architectural motif and the greater stability and security of the new mode. Wayside representation epitomizes the action of both poem and allegory:

> The road to *Paradice* lies by her *Gate*,
> Here *Pilgrims* do themselves *accommodate*
> With *Bed* and *Board*, and do such *Stories tell*
> As do for Truth and Profit, all excell.
> Nor doth the *Porter* here say any nay,
> That hither would turn in, that here would stay. (279)

The verses list the "Conveniencies" for both as clerical abundance, opportunities for sacrifice, divine judgment and instruction, pleasure, solace, recreation and soul's health, and prospect and retirement (276–77).

Part II's variations on *edifice* embody the Puritan category of *edification*, "the end [i.e., purpose] of the gospel, or the reason of instituted worship" according to *Differences in Judgement About Water Baptism* (Offor II:635). Individually, its houses intertwine the sacramental with the idealized diurnal by dramatizing communal meals, music, instruction, a sense of Christian community, and the communal life of the church past and present. Their sequence incorporates the church's mysteries, teaching, and fellowship. The guidelines for the first building apply to the others as well: The Interpreter's house is "for the relief of Pilgrims" (197) and is "a priviledged place for those that are become Pilgrims"

(198). Each site highlights particular practices, with Interpreter's house enacting ritual baptism and House Beautiful representing the Lord's Supper through a ritual meal as well as the curative *ex Carne & Sanguine Christi* (229). Mnason's house emphasizes the communal separateness of gathered believers, and in Beulah, now a bustling, stable, sensuously rewarding, earthly epitome of a godly community, the chief rituals are funereal. We find such non-liturgical church practices as catechism at House Beautiful, Sunday school at the Delectable Mountains, and analogues of prayer meetings here and there (e.g., 188, 221, 262). A formal kiss welcomes the entrants to Interpreter's house, and the shepherds "call in by Name" all members of the party (284).

Such fictionalized data show how much church practice was absorbed within the norms of everyday living, and the two devotional works that made up Bunyan's first wife's dowry include models for devotional imitation along just such lines (Hambrick-Stowe passim, esp. 145–49). The activities make up godly relations as Bunyan describes them: "we have had many meetings together, both to pray to God, and to exhort one another, and that we had the sweet comforting presence of the Lord among us for our encouragement" (*Grace Abounding* 118). The houses in part II also preserve and vivify the continuing tradition of believers and link modern communities with the communion of saints in the Church of all past ages (R. Frye 158 and similarly 160). The Christian fellowship at the houses of Gaius and Mnason—as these names suggest—is modeled upon the apostolic or primitive church, "communities of the faithful planted in a hostile environment" such as St. Paul visited in Acts (Knott, "Bunyan" 221–20). Gaius enfolds his company within the historic and universal church of believers from the early martyrs through the recent history of Foxe's *Actes and Monuments* and projects the church future through Christiana's sons (260). At Beulah "a Record [is] kept of the Names of them that had been Pilgrims of old, and a History of all the famous Acts that they had done" (304). When part I glanced at historical Christianity, its emphasis was always upon the monumental and exemplary quality of individual believers, upon what in their histories was transcendent over or outside of time. In part II, however, it is the temporal quality itself and temporal continuity that are of greatest importance.

◄◙ I ◙►

PURITANS BELIEVED that God's Spirit had elected to work upon human hearts through two specific means: the Word and the ordinances.[8] *Pilgrim's Progress* part I predominantly honors the first of these; it surprisingly minimizes sacraments while maximizing the entering professions of faith and experience. Part II's emphasis upon the institutionalized church rather than the priesthood of the individual believer appropriately attends to representations of the ordinances of baptism and holy communion, despite the qualification of *A Defense of the Doctrine of Justification* that either sacrament is "a thing of so indifferent a nature, a thing not good in itself, but with respect to certain circumstances" (Offor II:285). Emblem XIV of Bunyan's *A Book For Boys and Girls* speaks of

> Baptism and the Supper of the Lord:
> Both Mysteries divine, which do to me,
> By God's appointment, benefit afford.
> (VI:212, and see *A Confession of My Faith* Offor II:604)

Correctly viewed, religious ceremonies are edifying emblems of Christ, imaged in Emblem LXIII as eyeglasses because they allow us to see heavenly things which would otherwise be hidden from our earthly natures (VI:263).

Although baptismal differences often defined contemporary sects, Bunyan repeatedly downplays its importance because it has sparked so much controversy. For him, baptism is "an initiating and entering ordinance" (605) or, in *A Holy Life*, a "significative ordinance" of secondary spiritual value but not essential to church membership (IX:258–59). Both it and communion are merely "shadowish, or figurative ordinances . . . of excellent use to the church in this World," but "not the fundamentals of our Christianity, nor grounds of rule to communion with saints." Although the Scriptures describe baptismal practice, they do not require it, and Bunyan refuses to "ascribe unto them more than they were ordered to have in their first and primitive institution" (Offor II:604). He echoes Puritan and Restoration discourse generally in saying little about the Lord's Supper, except that its societal nature displaces the individualism of baptism (Greaves, *John Bunyan* 144). A gloss of 1659 summarizes his thinking on the subject and his sharing of Puritan anxieties about the dangers of idolatry generally: "I do honour [ordinances] in their places: yet would not that any of them should be idolized, or done in the wrong spirit" (II:74, and similarly VI:213). The sacraments are by definition mysteries, the minister tendering outward signs while the Holy Spirit mediates deeper meaning, and Calvin equated their office with the Word of God, but only when they are received by faith (R. Frye 153). Geoffrey Nuttall projects these dangers upon a larger screen when he recognizes Puritanism's repudiation of papistry and the sacerdotal system, first because it preferred the believer's direct and immediate communion with God and rejected outward and "creaturely" aids, and second because Catholic sacraments concentrated power in the hands of priests (*Holy Spirit* 91–92).

Four Bunyan works are devoted primarily to baptism. The earliest three are part of a serial controversy; the fourth, *The Water of Life* (1688), attends a more open and mystical range of meanings. *A Confession of My Faith and Reason of My Practice* (1672) begins a chain of action-reaction controversial commentaries, followed by *Differences in Judgement About Water Baptism* (1673) and *Peaceable Principles and True* (1674). It is difficult to overestimate the importance of this controversy according to its close student William York Tindall.[9] Twice in his life, and at the beginning of the two distinct phases of his career, Bunyan participated in serial controversies against opposing theological positions. The earlier one, to which Bunyan contributed *Some Gospel Truths Opened* (1656) and *A Vindication of Some Gospel Truths Opened* (1657), targeted Quaker opponents and Quaker prioritizing of "the inner light" over the disciplining Word and these, as Bunyan's first two published works, established his status and, in some ways, his style. The second baptism controversy attaches to his new status as pastor of the Bedford Meeting upon his release from jail in 1672. Against opponents within his own denomination, the issue is not the largest foundations of faith and salvation but correct specific in-house practices. Whether arguing against Quakerism or for "openness" of baptism, or on the issues raised in *Questions About the Nature and Perpetuity of the Seventh-Day Sabbath* (1685), or against separate women's prayer meetings, the subject of *The Case of Conscience Resolved* (1683), Bunyan grounds his polemical as his edificatory theology upon what is and is not explicitly required within the biblical Word, and since the Bible does not record the spiritual exclusion of the unbaptized, Bunyan refuses to do so as well. When his opponents claim support from the practices of primitive Christianity, Bunyan argues for church inclusiveness on the grounds of love and labels their insistence upon water baptism "heart-breaking" and "church-rending" (Offor II:653, 656).

Pilgrim's Progress part II depicts both baptism and communion through separate cumulative sequences that, like the representations of experience stories in part I, "progress" as they accumulate. In the case of baptism, the movement is toward a more natural, more open, more generous and generalized occasion. Even the early Bath Sanctification does not dictate a particular church ritual. Although Gordon Campbell wishes to withhold judgment on this matter because "the allegorical depiction of ordinances that are in themselves shadowish and figurative is not conducive to precise interpretation,"[10] in fact a larger reading presents itself. In the allegory as in the tracts, Bunyan privileges the spirit behind the practice, in effect deritualizing the church rites he represents or desymbolizing their data and action. Simultaneously, the narrative spiritually empowers the objects and processes of everyday life developing not so much metaphors as variations on normal human behavior (Van Dyke 191). When backgrounded in Bunyan's *The Water of Life*, baptismal practice in *Pilgrim's Progress* so much blends into communion practice as to leave behind any reliance upon the dangerous "creaturely aids" that worried Puritan theorists.

On their second day at Interpreter's house, Christiana and Mercy experience a baptism by immersion through which they are made "clean from the soil which they have gathered by travelling": "Then *Innocent* the Damsel took them and had them into the Garden, and brought them to the *Bath*, so she told them that there they must wash and be clean, for so her Master would have the Women to do that called at his House as they were going on *Pilgrimage*. Then they went in and washed, yea they and the Boys and all, and they came out of that *Bath* not only sweet, and clean; but also much enlivened and strengthened in their Joynts: So when they came in, they looked fairer a deal, then when they went out to the washing" (207). Insofar as the bath is specified for women, it includes the Jewish practice of mikvah, or postmenstrual cleansing, and perhaps also postchildbirth purification (Leviticus 12). Thus prepared, the Interpreter pronounces them *"fair as the Moon"* and inaugurates a further initiatory ritual: "Then he called for the *Seal* wherewith they used to be *Sealed* that were washed in his *Bath*. So the *Seal* was brought, and he set his Mark upon them, that they might be known in the Places whither they were yet to go: Now the seal was the contents and sum of the Passover which the Children of *Israel* did eat when they came out from the Land of *Egypt*: and the mark was set between their Eyes. This seal greatly added to their Beauty, for it was an Ornament to their Faces. It also added to their gravity, and made their Countenances more like them of Angels" (207–8). This baptism, like that in *The Desire of the Righteous Granted*, is accompanied by the "comfortable influence" of the Holy Ghost (Offor 1:757). Initiation progresses from ritual bath to ritual meal and is outwardly confirmed by new clothing of fine white linen, an external enhancement rather than the radical exchange of rags for glory that Christian experienced in part I. Some commentators read Bath Sanctification as an explicit representation of adult baptism by immersion and even as an echo of the apocryphal Susanna and the biblical Bathsheba.[11] But the surer and more interesting interpretation is that the bath is designed both to suggest and to elude baptismal representation, to escape the dangers of idolatry while translating the most religious of church practices into the pattern of everyday living.

Two later analogues of baptism transform equivalents from part I while advancing this spiritual inscription of diurnal data. The first, at Gaius's inn, focuses upon church history, and the second at the Delectable Mountains institutionalizes instruction of the young. In both, the travelers are refreshed at natural water sites along the Way. Christian's brief stop at a spring before climbing Hill Difficulty is authorized by Isaiah 49.10: "They shall not hunger nor thirst; neither shall the heat nor sun smite them: for he that hath mercy on them shall lead them, even by the springs of water shall he guide them." When Christiana and her party arrive at the same site, Greatheart distinguishes between the clear and good water Christian found and what these pilgrims find: " 'tis Dirty with the feet of some that are not desirous that Pilgrims here should quench their Thirst." The gloss editorializes: " 'Tis difficult getting of good Doctrine in erroneous Times" (214). The part II version of this event thus positions itself in relation to Christian's history but also, as other evidence has led us to expect, to Christian history generally.

The Water of Life, the fourth Bunyan work on baptism, is far removed from the controversy examined earlier and from Bunyan's sectarian and ministerial self-definitions of the early 1670s,[12] and it clarifies both the clear and the dirtied water from the allegory. *The Water of Life* defines its title phrase as "the Spirit of grace, or the Spirit and grace of God" (Offor III:540) while *The Saints' Privilege and Profit* similarly calls it "a reviving cordial" (Offor 1:652). Like Bunyan's other discourse on Revelation 21–22, *The Holy City* (1665), *The Water of Life* (1688) participates in the oracular prophetic envisioning inseparable from its apocalyptic text. Both read the dirtying of the water in terms of the sequential church history noted above. The earlier work looks toward the time "when Grace runs clear without the dirt and mud of the Traditions of men commixed therewith" and affirms that "at the day of the New *Jerusalem* the Doctrine of Grace shall be cleansed from all those dirty and muddy inventions, that sin, Satan, and the wisdom of this world hath thrown into this River, and into its goodly Crystal Streams" (III:184, 180). The later work accuses "Romish beasts" of muddying John of Patmos's clear water "with their own dirt and filthiness," with "the false glosses and sluttish opinions of erroneous judgments, . . . the very stain of tradition and superstition," and with "the human inventions and muddy conceptions of unsanctified and uninstructed judgments" (Offor III:555–56). Against such deterioration within the fiction, Greatheart recommends returning to primitive Christianity by allowing the dirt to settle to clear the water (214–15), housekeeping advice that collapses the Reformation into a telling metaphor.

A second, later site develops the baptismal opportunity in differing terms. Between the Pillar of Lot's wife and Bypath Meadow, Christian and Hopeful pause for several days of restoration at "a pleasant River, which *David the King* called the *River of God; but, John, The River of the water of life*" (110). The waters are "pleasant and enlivening to their weary Spirits," and fruit and leaves from nearby trees are delightful, medicinable, and preventive of surfeits. Bunyan's works, like the Bible, gloss the occasion, including not just *The Water of Life* and *The Holy City* but also *A Book For Boys and Girls* (VI:206), *The House of God* (VI:278), and *Solomon's Temple Spiritualized*. The latter work, like *Pilgrim's Progress*, combines these waters with the tree of life as "a type of the word and Spirit of God" (Offor III:504; and see *The Holy City* III:178–91).

In part II the site continues to be safe, refreshing, perennially green, and medicinable against surfeits. Here are "delicate *Waters*, pleasant *Medows*, dainty *Flowers*, variety of *Trees*, and such as bear *wholsom Fruit* . . . Fruit that procureth Health where there is none, and that continueth and increaseth it where it is" (280). What was formerly medicinal to travelers is now institutionalized as "an Hospital to young Children, and *Orphans*" (281). The sheepcote of the shepherds of Delectable Mountains serves as "an House built for the *nourishing* and bringing up of those Lambs, the Babes of those Women that go on Pilgrimage" (280) and biblicizes and compounds part II's priorities of ecclesiology, edifices, the feminine, and family development.

> Also there was here one that was intrusted with them, who could have compassion, and that could gather these Lambs with his Arm, and carry them in his Bosom, and that could gently lead those that

were with young. Now to the Care of *this Man, Christiana* admon-
ished her four Daughters to commit their little ones; that by these
Waters they might be housed, harbored, suckered and nourished,
and that none of them might *be lacking in time to come*. This man,
if any of them go astray, or be lost, he will bring them again, he will
also bind up that which was broken, and will strengthen them that
are sick. Here they will never want Meat, and Drink and Cloathing,
here they will be kept from Thieves and Robbers, for this man will
dye before one of those committed to his Trust, shall be lost. Besides, here they shall be sure to have good *Nurture* and Admonition,
and shall be taught to walk in right Paths, and that you know is a
Favour of no small account. (280)

Pastoral place collapses into the person of Christ, a welcoming, nurturing, even maternal physician of souls, and like so much else, what was
a matter of internalized spiritual trial and triumph in part I dissolves
into the ecclesiological sociability of part II. The visit includes a formal,
perhaps sacramental feast (285).

Unlike his attitude toward the optional church ordinance, baptism,
Bunyan viewed the Lord's Supper as fully authorized and required by
the Word: "Church Communion is scripture communion" he enunciates
in *Peaceable Principles and True* (Offor II:656). *Differences in Judgement*
defines the Lord's Supper as "a part of that worship which Christ hath
instituted for his church, to be conversant in as a church; presenting them
as such, with their communion with their Head, and with one another
as members of him" (Offor II:620–21). Further, such breaking of bread is
"a duty incumbent on the church, as a church; and on every member of
that body as such" (621); it is to be often reiterated, "it being an ordinance so full of blessedness, as lively to present union and communion
with Christ to all the members that worthily eat thereof" (639). Indeed,
in keeping with the emphases we have noted between the two parts of
the allegory, this treatise assigns primacy to the sacrament of the Lord's
Supper for the church as church, but primacy to the entering ordinances
for the individual convert (Offor II:639).

The authorizing texts include Paul's exhortation to "flee from idolatry" in 1 Corinthians 10.16–17: "The cup of blessing which we bless, is it
not the communion of the blood of Christ? The bread which we break,
is it not the communion of the body of Christ? For we being many are
one bread, and one body: for we are all partakers of that one bread." (See

Isaiah 25.6 and 2 Corinthians 13.14.) Other texts break down barriers between exceptional sacramental moment and normative if idealized daily social behavior. Jude 12 speaks of "feasts of charity, when they feast with you, feeding themselves without fear," and Acts 2.42 of newly baptized converts "continu[ing] stedfastly in the apostles' doctrine and fellowship, and in breaking of bread, and in prayer." Bunyan's usage blurs differences between *communion* as fellowship and *communion* as Eucharist (see, e.g., Offor I:757, Offor II:602, and Offor III:553). In keeping with the hospitality mode of part II, all such festivities are enfolded within what Gaius describes as "ministring Doctrines *to* thee in this Life, [to] beget *in* thee a greater desire to sit at the Supper of the great King in his Kingdom . . . the feast that our Lord will make for us when we come to his House" (262; Bunyan's italics).

Perhaps because communion is even more tightly linked with Roman Catholic and Anglican worship than baptism, it receives less attention than baptism in Bunyan's Puritan pilgimage narrative. Where present, it is yet peculiarly encoded. After his battle with Apollyon, Christian takes communion as a restorative. He is healed by leaves from the Tree of Life and consumes bread and drink provided by the Interpreter. What is unusual about this as a version of communion is that he partakes of it in solitude (60–61), a privacy in itself denying the sense of *communion* as church fellowship.

Representations of communion in part II are sometimes distinctly sacramental and sometimes more generalized. Sometimes they signal "the Church in communion with God," but when the communal meals feature something other than bread and wine, they signal the church "in community with itself under God" and express the mutuality of the Christian life within the most familiar of human activities (R. Frye 157–58). The Interpreter's house develops an analogue with Passover. House Beautiful offers two versions, the first a sacramental meal of "Lamb with the accustomed Sauce belonging thereto," combining Old Testament hospitality with New Testament marriage feasts (Sadler 59), the second a medicinal purge *"ex carne et sanguine Christi"* that moves away from Old Testament purgation and toward New Testament repentance and redemptive grace. This most explicit communion occasion in part II reaches architecturally beyond God as nurturer and the house of God as palace, manor house, and inn to the church as hospital and Christ as physician. It develops Richard Sibbes's description of the church as "a common hospital, wherein all are in some measure sick,"[13] and of course *salve* is buried within *salvation*

(R. Frye 156). Many Bunyan minor works elaborate this traditional metaphor (see, e.g., *Justification By an Imputed Righteousness* [Offor 1:327];
The House of God [vi:282, 283]; Emblem LXII, "Of Physick" [vi:262–63];
and *The Water of Life* [Offor iii:540]).

Part II fully works out the medical metaphor at House Beautiful when
a sickness in son Matthew's bowels is cured "*ex Carne & Sanguine Christi*"
(229; "The Lattine I borrow" [gloss]). Contracted by eating fruit from
Beelzebub's orchard (229), the malady so pains Matthew "that he was
with it, at times, pulled as 'twere both ends together" (228). The ancient
and approved physician Mr. Skill diagnoses and cures him. When medicines from the Old Testament prove too weak, he applies New Testament
pills, to be taken with fasting and tears of repentance, and authorized by
John 6.53–57, Mark 9.49, and Hebrews 9.14. Mr. Skill credits "*The Master
of the Colledge* of Physicians" with this "Universal Remedy" (gloss 230),
preventive as well as restorative, indeed conducing to eternal life (229–
30; similarly *Seasonable Counsel* [Offor ii:693 and *The Water of Life* Offor
iii:558]). Later in the Valley of the Shadow of Death son James takes some
of Skill's pills when sick with fear (241).

Matthew's cure combines the particularized physiological with the explicitly eucharistic, in borrowed Latin no less, and a contemporary audience would also have read a pharmaceutical message no longer likely to
register, since "Matthew's Pills" was a well-known patent medicine of
the time.[14] *The Water of Life* similarly collapses pharmacy, commerce, and
edification to present itself as a contemporary advertisement for patent
medicine, describing the dosage, usage, cost (free), and previously cured
patients (Offor iii:539–40; and similarly the applications 557–58). This
compound, like Bunyan's handling of baptism and communion practices,
breaks down barriers between the spiritual and the realistic and thus
elevates—he might say redeems—the ordinary data of daily life.

◄◙| II |◙►

THE CHURCH OF part II consists primarily of the support provided by
Christian community and the leadership that impels its action and articulates its principles. Reflecting Bunyan's doctrinal tolerance on questions
of baptism and communion, this church welcomes those of especially
tender conscience or strict scruples. It contrasts with the strenuous and
monolithic conversion morphology of part I and with the theological and

liturgical prescriptions of opposing sectarian leaders. Where the sense of part I is neatly captured in "A Man may have Company when he sets out for Heaven, & yet go thither alone" (26 gloss), part II acknowledges that "all the Kings Subjects are not his Champions" (130) and its corollary that "Christs Bosome is for all Pilgrims" (222 gloss). In sum, we now find that the Puritan God calls differently to different Christians: "Some are strong, some are weak, some have *great* faith, some have *little*" (130). In a contemporary formulation, a church is "a company or congregatione of the faythfull called and gathered out of the worlde by the preachinge of the Gospell, who followinge and embraceinge true religione, do in one unitie of Spirite strengthen and comforte one another, daylie growinge and increasinge in true faythe, framinge their lyves, governmente, orders and ceremonies according to the worde of God."[15]

For a number of historical reasons, the Puritan familial religious community was defined by clear boundaries. Where early in the era a *Puritan* differed from a *separatist* in wishing to cleanse the church from within, by Bunyan's time the former includes the latter and both stand outside the established church (Nuttall, *Holy Spirit* 8–9). *Nonconformist* is a positioning against the Book of Common Prayer, while *dissenting* and *sectarian* contrast against parochial and institutionalized worship more generally. The often-cited scriptural authority is 2 Corinthians 6.14–18:

> Be ye not equally yoked together with unbelievers: for what fellowship hath righteousness with unrighteousness? and what communion hath light with darkness? And what concord hath Christ with Belial? or what part hath he that believeth with an infidel? And what agreement hath the temple of God with idols? for ye are the temple of the living God; as God hath said, I will dwell in them, and walk in them; and I will be their God, and they shall be my people. Wherefore come out from among them, and be ye separate, saith the Lord, and touch not the unclean thing; and I will receive you. And will be a Father unto you, and ye shall be my sons and daughters, saith the Lord Almighty.

These verses emphasize *separateness*, along with the family analogy and architectural imagery glimpsed earlier. Bunyan's is also a *gathered* church or *conventicle*, whose "setting apart" and "coming together" contrast with the world and the worldly. Christiana acknowledges the atmosphere of threat and envy in commenting to Mercy: "For can it be imagined, that the people that design to attain such excellent Glories *as we do*, and that are so envied that Happiness *as we are;* but that we shall meet with what Fears and Scares, with what Troubles and Afflictions they can possibly assault us with, that hate us?" (188; Bunyan's italics).[16] Matching persecutions from without, the sense of themselves as *chosen people* and as *visible saints* established boundaries from within based upon moral rectitude (Sir Toby Belch would say self-righteousness).

Such terms highlight the sense of excluding or being excluded and of purification upon which the category of *Puritan* generally rests. The more than three decades of Bunyan's writings target both self-selected converts rejecting the world around them and the persecuted and embattled church community "in the wilderness," especially when, as we have seen, both "churches" provide synecdoches for his own history. Bunyan prefers the term *professor* (those who have made a profession) to describe individuals and types within his separatist community (e.g., II:61), but for the most part when he wishes to refer to the collective body rather than individuals, he uses the term *saints,* as in the two posthumous titles *The Saints' Knowledge of Christ's Love* and *The Saints' Privilege and Profit.* Synonymous phrasings include "fellowship in the things of the kingdom of Christ . . . church communion, the communion of saints," and "a chosen generation, a royal priesthood, an holy nation, a peculiar people" (Offor II:602, 603).

A church communion is made up of "visible Saints by calling and Profession" (III:174; similarly Offor II:602), and *A Confession of My Faith* enumerates seven bases for church membership:

1. The called of Christ Jesus. (Romans 1.6)
2. Men that have drank into the Spirit of Jesus Christ. (1 Corinthians 12.13)
3. Persons in whom was God the Father. (Ephesians 4.6)
4. They were all made partakers of the joy of the gospel. (Philemon 1.7)
5. Persons that were circumcised inwardly. (Colossians 2.11)
6. Persons that turned from idols to serve the living and true God. (1 Thessalonians 1.9)
7. Those that were the body of Christ, and members in particular, that is, those that were visibly such; because they made profession of faith, of holiness, of repentance, of love to Christ, and of self-denial, at their receiving into fellowship. (Offor II:603)

Going beyond such candidacies, the province of part I of *Pilgrim's Progress,* *A Case of Conscience Resolved* distinguishes three populations of church membership and leadership: (1) "mixed assemblies . . . made up of saints and sinners"; (2) the church distinct from the world meeting with themselves; and (3) "assemblies . . . made up of the elders, and principal brethren of the church, none of the rest of the congregation being present" (Offor II:662).

If part I is structured around the one who makes a profession of faith and experience, part II treats the audience who receive and respond to such professions in a combination of community and communion. Militarily, as Christian was discovering his weapons and capacities, part II presents either seasoned veterans and proven campaigners or else raw recruits, "sincere believers who are so tormented by difficulties and scruples that they cannot enter conscientiously into the full life of the church without very careful handling" (Sharrock, *John Bunyan* [1968] 149). *The House of the Forest of Lebanon* expresses the revised attitude as "those cordial and large affections which the church in the wilderness has to all, and for all them that love the truth, and that suffer and are afflicted for the sincere profession thereof" (Offor III:534). The change is from a prioritized self to prioritized others, and is thus variously away from unity and private integrity (integer-ness, one-ness) and toward multiplicity, variety, difference, from an exclusive Christianity toward an inclusive one. Imputed righteousness is the way to heaven in part I, and moral righteousness is the way in part II, and thus in terms of the Christian virtues, faith and hope give way in part II to charity.[17] Where Christian achieved fellowship with Faith(ful) and that faith modulated into Hope(ful) just where the narrative and theological emphasis shifted securely from the past and this world to the future and the next, Christiana is appropriately companioned by Mercy (Charity in action). Technically, the move is from a particular to a general calling to salvation. In terms of covenantal theology, or what Perry Miller calls Puritan sociology, the shift is from a covenant of grace (displacing the covenant of works) to a church covenant, the former operating between God and a saved individual, while the latter holds between God and a group of (presumably) saved individuals.[18]

Where only those who have been tested and fully and progressively edified achieve the desired goal in part I, part II widens the dispensation to allow the strong to share their surplus achievement with the needy. It distinguishes between church membership and church leadership, with the strongest assuming the ministerial role to the deficient and frail on the authority of Romans 15.1–2: "We then that are strong ought to bear the infirmities of the weak, and not to please ourselves. Let every one of us please his neighbour for his good to edification." (This passage is discussed in *Differences in Judgement*, Offor 11:627.) *The Saints' Privilege and Profit* recommends that "the infirm member [be] most cared for, most pitied, most watched over to be kept from harms, and most consulted for" (Offor 1:674; similarly *The Greatness of the Soul* ix:238), but *Of the House of the Forest of Lebanon* argues as well that "the most feeble of his flock, when Christ shall stand by and strengthen them, are able to do and bear what the strong have underwent" (Offor iii:534).

Bunyan's lesser works image character variety through catalogues of household utensils (*The Barren Figtree* v:18), of schoolchildren (*The House of God* vi:292–93), of Moses' clean and unclean beasts from Deuteronomy 14 (*Grace Abounding* 23–24), of flowers (*Christian Behaviour* iii:54), and of birds (Emblem XLIII vi:246). *Pilgrim's Progress* part II similarly arrays believers as musical instruments and flowers. Mr. Honest appropriates the practice to describe the various travelers and ways and results of traveling he has seen upon the road.

> I have seen some that have set out as if they would drive all the World afore them, who yet have in few days, dyed as they in the Wilderness, and so never gat sight of the promised Land. I have seen some that have promised nothing at first setting out to be Pilgrims, and that one would a thought could not have lived a day, that have yet proved very good Pilgrims. I have seen some that have run hastily forward, that again have after a little time, run just as fast back again. I have seen some who have spoke very well of a Pilgrims Life at first, that after a while, have spoken as much against it. I have heard some, when they first set out for Paradice, say positively, there is such a place, who when they have been almost there, have come back again, and said there is none. I have heard some vaunt what they would do in case they should be opposed, that have even at a false Alarm fled Faith, the Pilgrims way, and all. (257–58)

Insofar as this listing seems to sift and reject false professors it may remind us of Talkative, Byends, Ignorance, and the like in part I. But the difference is important. Honest is just passively describing history; he is tolerant rather than judgmental and thereby expresses the more inclusive theology that undergirds part II. Calls to salvation accommodate these differences in the Interpreter's image of a mother hen's "fourfold Method towards [her] Chickens" (201, and see *Come, and Welcome* viii:355, 356).

In keeping with this wider vision and broadened sympathy, part II prioritizes shared experience and intention over radical self-redefinition and overscrupulous and judgmental inquiry into differences. Now claims of the self must bend before community needs. In his welcome to Mr. Feeble-mind Greatheart outlines the lengths to which the party must be willing to go to accommodate differences: "You must needs to along with us; we will wait for you, we will lend you our help, we will deny our selves of some things, both *Opinionative* and *Practical*, for your sake; we will not enter into doubtful Disputations before you, we will be made all things to you, rather then you shall be left behind" (270–71). Greatheart speaks for a varied community willing to adjust to increase unity and fellowship with each other. The same higher priorities of love, harmony, and peace, of inclusion and nurturance, guide the ministerial office and Bunyan's practice of it. Faith alone is no longer the exclusive end; the goal is rather to create an atmosphere within which spiritual life can proceed without interference.

Sharrock generalizes that "the quality of vision in the Second Part represents not a surrender to humanism but an assured theology of charity which naturally looks at the points of contact between divine and human love for the growing places of the knowledge of God" (*John Bunyan* [1966] 47). The social arena as "growing place" contains two populations and two expressions of growth, church membership and church leadership. Church membership requires love, humility, forgiveness, watchfulness and prayer, being one's brother's keeper, sincerity, meekness, temper-ance, patience, and entertainment to others (*The House of God* VI:295–304, 308–9). This population must avoid self-righteousness, vainglory, a forward spirit, and backsliding. But Bunyan is even more interested in defining church leadership, translating the retrospective 2 Timothy 4.6–8 into prospective advisories: "For I am now ready to be offered, and the time of my departure is at hand. I have fought a good fight, I have fin-ished my course, I have kept the faith: Henceforth there is laid up for me a crown of righteousness, which the Lord, the righteous judge, shall give me at that day; and not to me only, but unto all them also that love his appearing." *Paul's Departure and Crown* develops this text into a detailed review of "enabling" conduct for such an office.

"A Brief Account of the Author's Call to the Work of the Ministry" (*Grace Abounding* 82) describes Bunyan's transition from church member to church leader and implies some governing general principles for the ministerial role. After he had been "awakened" to Christ for five or six years and proved able in understanding the Word and in utterance, some leaders of the Bedford Meeting ask him "to speak a word of Exhortation unto them" (83). After "discover[ing] [his] Gift amongst them," he goes on to "sometimes speak a word of Admonition" (83), as later an effectual Word (86) and an awakening Word (87). After due and solemn prayers and after experiencing "a secret pricking forward thereto," Bunyan comes to more formal and public preaching. Despite self-doubt, many "count [him] Gods Instrument that shewed to them the Way of Salvation" (85). After two years of "preach[ing] what I felt, what I smartingly did feel" (85), carrying and applying the fire of his own stricken conscience (85), he achieves an altered preaching mode of peace, comfort, and the grace and mystery of Christ (86). In procedural terms, he "labour[s] so to speak the Word, as that thereby (if it were possible) the sin and the person guilty might be particularized by it" (86), and he feels during his delivery "as if an Angel of God had stood by at my back to encourage me" (87). He exults in the role: "My heart hath been so wrapt up in the glory of this excellent work, that I counted myself more blessed and honoured of God by this, than if he had made me the Emperour of the Christian World" (88). By the time of writing *Pilgrim's Progress* part II, Bunyan had long been established as the very successful minister to a flourishing church in an era of diminished persecution, and his spiritual message is necessarily inclusive, tolerant, and sympathetic. If he has lost some of the fervor of the recent convert, he has also lost the self-absorption and the sometimes debilitating traumas of terror and despair. He becomes less insistent, but also more benevolent.

The House of God recognizes a hierarchy of "Governours of this House" all guided by the principles of serving

> with *Love and Care;*
> Not *Swerving* from the *Rule*, nor yet intrud[ing]
> Upon *each others* Work, nor are they *rude*
> In managing *their own:* But to their trust
> They labour to be *Honest, Faithful, Just.* (vi:282)

The first and chief governor is Christ himself, the second the Holy Ghost. The earthly or "under-Officers"—ministers, rulers, deacons, and widows —*inspect* conversations and *direct* employments (vi:289). *A Case of Conscience Resolved* images church elders as "watchmen, overseers, guides, teachers, rulers, and the like" (Offor ii:665). Its proposal, that "our elders and watchmen covet . . . that our worship be performed by the most able" (666), constructs a continuum of spiritual success and value and a realizable ideal to which others aspire.

The minister represents the epitome of such service, and forward progress is dangerous or even impossible without his superior wisdom and example (vi:285–89). His tasks are "to counsel, comfort, exhort, and teach
the people" and "to instruct, and counsel people to forsake their sins, and
close in with Christ, lest they did miserably perish" (*A Relation of My Imprisonment* 107). *Solomon's Temple Spiritualized* speaks in similar terms:
"Let the churches love their pastors, hear their pastors, be ruled by their
pastors, and suffer themselves to be watched over, and to be exhorted,
counselled, and if need be, reproved, and rebuked by their pastors" (Offor
III:478). *The House of God* domesticates these tasks within such metaphors as a watchman upon the tower for warning and defense, steward of
the Word, overseer of the house, cook and sub-physician supplying nourishment and medicines, prophet, and guide. The minister's role exactly
glosses Greatheart in imagery appropriate to pilgrimage:

> This Officer is also call'd a Guide,
> Nor should the People but keep by his side;
> Or tread his Steps in all the paths they walk,
> By his Example they should Do and Talk.
> He is to be to them instead of Eyes,
> He must before them go in any wise;
> And he must lead them by the Water-side,
> *This is the work of this our Faithful Guide.* (vi:288–89)

The ultimate model, Christ, is "a priest to save, a prophet to teach, and
a king to rule his church" (*Of the House of the Forest of Lebanon* Offor
III:519, and see Isaiah 33.22), but Noah presents an Old Testament exemplar—being "perfect in his generations," that is "in his carriage, doctrines and life, before both God and man" (Offor II:463), as does Aaron in
Solomon's Temple Spiritualized.[19] St. Augustine's *De Doctrina Christiana*,
IV.iv, sees the minister as "the interpreter and teacher of Holy Scripture,
the defender of the true faith, and the opponent of error, both to teach
what is right and to refute what is wrong, and in the performance of this
task to conciliate the hostile, to rouse the careless, and to tell the ignorant both what is occurring at present and what is probable in the future."
As the audience requires, his sermons sometimes teach, explicate, clear
away doubts, closely reason, and exhibit proofs; they also rouse to action,
diligence, and true feeling through heightened emotional appeals (quoted
in Mitchell 93); they divide, in other words, between curbing the unruly
and encouraging the weak and needy. The title *minister* defines his role.

The Protestant, demystified version of the pastor assumes responsibility for the welfare of his flock while pursuing ideal conduct for himself. His success depends upon his personal abilities and initiatives and the power of his exemplary life, thus contrasting with the automatic functioning of the Roman Catholic priest's office (George and George 327–28).

Grace Abounding endorses precisely such an epitome of Reformation principles: "He hath also cause to walk humbly with God, and be little in his own Eyes, and to remember withall, that his Gifts are not his own, but the Churches; and that by them he is made a Servant to the Church, and that he must give at last an account of his Stewardship unto the Lord Jesus; and to give a good account, will be a blessed thing!" (92). In embodying the ideal within the conduct of his life, the good minister may show a variety of special strengths: "'To one is given by the Spirit the word of wisdom, to another the word of knowledge;' to one the gift of healing, to another faith; to this man to work miracles, to that a spirit of prophecy; to another the discerning of spirits, to another divers kinds of tongues" (*Solomon's Temple Spiritualized* Offor III:481). Even the best of ministers will succeed better in some activities than others. Utmost care is required to choose worthy guides, and *The Greatness of the Soul* lists the dangerous and the only safe options:

1. There are Idol Shepherds.
2. There are foolish Shepherds.
3. There are Shepherds that feed themselves and not their Flock.
4. There are hard hearted and pitiless Shepherds.
5. There are Shepherds that instead of healing, smite, push and wound the diseased.
6. There are Shepherds that cause their flocks to go astray.
7. And there are Shepherds that feed their flock. (IX:227–28, and see also Offor II:323–26)

The unworthy are recognizable by bad action, deception, hypocrisy, delay, or boasting, and especially by failure to take proper heed to the care of their own souls (IX:229–30).

Both parts of *Pilgrim's Progress* promote exemplary ministry through theological guides who provide inspiration and guidance, defend against enemies, elicit confessions, inaugurate self-correctional procedures, apply apt biblical texts to a variety of occasions, admonish or sternly comfort, and generally lead pilgrims through life and dying. Part I's most explicit minister, Evangelist, mediates the Word to individuals, awakens potential converts, and instructs them in the independent Bible reading, analysis, and application that are the root of Reformation salvation. In part II son Matthew outlines the ministerial duties in these theoretical terms: "Ministers should fetch their Doctrine from God . . . [and] should give out what they know of God to the World" (231).

Part II's ministerial figures do not so much celebrate the Word they carry as depict the person and handling of their office. They interact with a multiple audience, foster religious socialization and consensus theology, and perform social service more than textual mediation. Greatheart is a much-traveled guide, a "Conductor of Pilgrims" (220 and 236), "a Friend," and well-armed and experienced defender (220) who "lend[s] a hand at need" (216); he has "it in Commission, to comfort the *feeble-minded*, and to support the weak" (270). He leads series of travelers to their destination either on assignment or by request. He defines his roles as: "I am a Servant of the God of Heaven, my business is to perswade sinners to Repentance, I am commanded to do my endeavour to turn Men, Women and Children, from darkness to light, and from the power of Satan to God" (244), later adding "It is my duty . . . to distrust mine own ability, that I may have reliance on him that is stronger then all" (246). "I have a Commandment," he summarizes, "to resist Sin, to overcome Evil, to fight the good Fight of Faith" (281), but it is on others' behalf not his own. Part II, like part I, projects the ministerial role onto several figures who now answer to the maturing needs of the pilgrims, including Secret, the Reliever, Valiant-for-Truth, and Standfast, whereas in part I, the ministerial figures who help Christian—and Mr. Help is one of them—intersect the narrative only briefly and disappear without explanation.

Specifically and most largely throughout part II, Greatheart serves the Interpreter as "one of the King of the Celestial Countries Conductors of Pilgrims to the Place" (282). As the portable result of Christiana's visit to Interpreter's house (208), he fulfills the church needs of pilgrims after they have been initiated into the Word and interpretive process. He does the knocking at the porter's door (219) on their behalf, for example, and the shepherds need not provide the warnings of part I to these travelers because of his presence (288). Greatheart is capable of delivering a brief sermon with appropriate Bible verses as in the Valley of Humiliation (237), or briefly dividing a biblical text as at Gaius's inn (266), but his usual expository role targets the Word as applications rather than as doctrines, as practical directives rather than openings.

Commentators regularly credit Greatheart rather than Christiana as the proper heroic successor to Christian. Henri Talon, for example, calls Greatheart "Christian under another name and at another stage of his growth" and commends his adjustment of Christian's spiritual urgency to the pace of travel appropriate to women, children, and the frail and elderly.[20] Sharrock makes the related point that whereas "the puzzled, searching Christian" is a character to be identified with, Greatheart is held up for a more distanced admiration; he is a man of ringing authority, admirable discipline, and cheerful wayfaring and warfaring (*John Bunyan* [1966] 48). Where Bunyan wishes his readers to see Christian as the typal actor succeeding where they themselves might fail—and thence to identify sympathetically with him—he also wishes the audience to show their admiration of the more distant Greatheart by following his leadership rather than enacting his example.

While Christian in part I dramatizes the achievement of the ministerial role, Greatheart in II represents the perfection of the role in service to others. Where Christian needed a map from the shepherds, Greatheart carries his own map in his pocket and consults it in timely fashion by the lantern he also carries (297). Where Christian was sometimes errant and passive, Greatheart is fully sufficient and both aggressively and compassionately more active. Bunyan plays with the names of both characters to attach *grace* to Christian and *heart* to Greatheart, a radical shift in the foundation of salvific energies for the two parts. As Christian develops from Graceless to Greatgrace (46, 126), Greatheart answers Littlefaith's need for "a great[er] heart" (twice 129) and helps Fearing "get some Heart" (251). Where Christian fights the enemy with an undefined weapon "*All-prayer*" (54, 63), Greatheart pauses to strengthen himself through prayer for fighting giants as a public service (245).

Part II also twice critiques the ministerial role. At the Slough of Despond, Mercy and Christiana encounter the effects of flawed and misleading ministers, a particular danger for the church in the wilderness. Appropriate to the governing travel metaphor, ministers are here envisioned as "the Kings Labourers," that is his road crew (187). Recent pretenders to this service role "say they are for mending the Kings Highway . . . [but they] bring *Dirt* and *Dung* instead of Stones, and so marr, instead of mending" (187). They enact the several errors of false shepherds listed earlier from *The Greatness of the Soul* (IX:227–30).

A second and more complex ministerial critique arises tangentially from the weak women's need for spiritual aid, and underscores Bunyan's representation of the ministerial role as self-descriptive and propagandistic at least in the arena of sexual politics. Christiana's earnest and repeated knockings at the Interpreter's door are at first unsuccessful because of the terrifying barking of a great mastiff. Two glosses specify "The Dog [as] the Devil, an Enemy to Prayer" and "*Christiana* and her companions perplexed about Prayer" (188). Renewed knocking does, however, achieve success, and Christiana is able to speak with the gatekeeper with "low obeysance" (188). This initiative differs from the norm of part II, where a watchful Christiana seeks help when she needs it from the power and resources of Greatheart. The narrator commends both her and him for such transactions: "Yea, for ought I could perceive, they continually gave so good heed to the Advice of their Guide, and he did so faithfully tell them of *Dangers*, and of the *Nature* of Dangers when they were at them, that usually when they were nearest to them, they did most pluck up their Spirits, and hearten one another to deny the Flesh" (297).

Both here and later at House Beautiful, Christiana's need for strong protective male guidance is insisted upon. Indeed she is twice chided for having attempted to travel without such a guide (see also Heedless 244). In the Reliever's words, "I marvelled much when you was entertained at the Gate above, being ye knew that ye were but weak Women, that you petitioned not the Lord there for a Conductor: Then might you have avoided these Troubles, and Dangers: For he would have granted you one." Christiana responds reasonably enough: "Who could have thought that so near the Kings Palace there should have lurked such naughty ones? indeed it had been well for us had we asked our Lord for one; but since our Lord knew 'twould be for our profit, I wonder he sent not one along with us."[21] But later to Mercy, Christiana blames herself: "My fault is so much the greater, for that I saw this danger before I came out of the Doors, and yet did not provide for it where provision might a been had. I am therefore much to be blamed" (196–97). Later Greatheart dismisses pleas from Christiana, Mercy, and son James to accompany them beyond House Beautiful, saying: "Here you failed at first; for when he bid me come thus far with you, then you should have begged me of him to have gon quite thorough with you, and he would have granted your request. However, at present I must withdraw" (220). Christiana is twice blamed for failures of foresight which she could not have averted!

Such dramatized chiding and power relations, and such narrative backtracking, signal another of those textual fissures which requires attention. Since *Pilgrim's Progress* part II was published one year after *A Case of Conscience Resolved* (1683), it is difficult not to read in the allegory an encoded version of the controversy that arose in the Bedford Meeting when church women, with the encouragement of a Mr. K, sought to justify their practice of separate women's prayer meetings.[22] *A Case*, documenting Bunyan's response to this congregational feminist movement, speaks of women's place in the church, and thus in society more generally, and claims "not to degrade them" but "to keep them in their place" and "to set [them] right" (Offor 11:674). Called upon to examine the biblical precedents and authority for separate women's prayer meetings, Bunyan interprets the issue as whether or not particular biblical injunctions state that women *should* or *must* meet separately and without male leadership. Although he addresses Mr. K's Scriptures, as he says, to "pick the bones of their carcasses" (666), Bunyan cannot deny a series of Old and New Testament occasions of women's praying, but he finds no evidence that women are anywhere assigned the *duty* to meet separately. According to Bunyan, "The Holy Ghost doth particularly insist upon the inability of women, as to their well managing of the worship *now* under consideration, and therefore it ought not to be presumed upon by them" (664).

From such quibbles, his argument reverts to the negative instance of Eve who "was baffled, and befooled . . . [and] utterly failed in the performance" when she stept out of her place to worship alone and thereby "overthrew, not only, as to that, the reputation of women for ever, but her soul, her husband, and the whole world besides" (664). His conclusion contextualizes Eve and her punishment:

> Methinks, holy and beloved sisters, you should be content to wear this power, or badge of your inferiority, since the cause thereof arose at first from yourselves. It was the woman that at first the serpent made use of, and by whom he then overthrew the world: wherefore the woman, to the world's end, must wear tokens of her underlingship in all matters of worship. To say nothing of that which she cannot shake off, to wit, her pains and sorrows in child-bearing, which God has rivetted to her nature, there is her silence, and shame, and a covering for her face, in token of it, which she ought to be exercised with, whenever the church comes together to worship. (673)

In the furthest stretch of his case, Bunyan likens women to angels as the ornament of the church, and reasons that since "angels are inferior to the great man Christ, who is in heaven . . . the woman is inferior to the man, that truly worships God in the church on earth" (672–73). He dismisses such texts as Galatians 3.28, favoring women's equality, as referring to the church as a "true mystical body" and not to a "particular congregation of professing Christians" (671). He does promise, however, that women's inferiority will end with the New Jerusalem (672).

Although we can read here a less confident and authoritative Bunyan than elsewhere, we cannot now tell the outcome of this controversy. Sharrock sees Bunyan's arguments as apparently successful in defeating the uprising (*John Bunyan* [1966] 45–46), but such assertions rest upon an absence of evidence and assume the usual outcome in gendered power encounters. In the course of amassing the very large collection of Bunyan works for his nineteenth-century edition, George Offor discovered *A Case* to be a rare, never reprinted, never collected Bunyan work, conditions that may bespeak a continuing sense of the dangerous or threatening nature of its issues (II:658).

One product of the controversy does take tangible form of interest to our inquiry. Late in *A Case of Conscience Resolved*, Bunyan promises to remedy women's despair and redefine their position in the church, and William York Tindall, I think correctly, supposes that part II of *Pilgrim's Progress* generally fulfills that promise, "consol[ing] the women . . . with the promise that at a future time he would say something else about them" (57). Specifically, Tindall speaks of Bunyan's "gentle lesson" of placating and correcting the women of his church through "a eulogy of women and a statement of their proper servility" put into the mouth of Gaius (66). Closely examined, this formal speech supposedly in praise of biblical women contains its own oddly political tensions and fissures:

I will now speak on the behalf of Women, to take away their Reproach. For as Death and the Curse came into the World by a Woman, so also did Life and Health; *God sent forth his Son, made of a Woman*. Yea, to shew how much those that came after did abhor the Act of their Mother, this Sex, in the old Testament, coveted Children, if happily this or that Women might be the Mother of the Saviour of the World. I will say again, that when the Saviour was come, Women rejoyced in him, before either Man or Angel. I read not that ever any man did give unto Christ so much as one *Groat*, but the Women followed him, and minstred to him of their Substance.'Twas a Woman that washed his Feet with Tears, and a Woman that anointed his Body to the Burial. They were Women that wept when he was going to the Cross; And Women that followed him from the Cross, and that sat by his Sepulcher when he

was buried. They were Women that was first with him at the Resurrection *morn*, and Women that brought Tidings first to his Disciples that he was risen from the Dead. Women therefore are highly
favoured, and shew by these things that they are sharers with us in
the Grace of Life. (261)

The Epistle Dedicatory of *A Case of Conscience Resolved* (659) closely
parallels this speech.

Gaius may be merely restating the culture's ingrained view of Eve's
heirs, but the speech raises a question upon which another similarly fis-
sured Bunyan work sheds some light. *An Exposition . . . of Genesis* necessarily reviews Eve's Edenic folly and error, but it also addresses at least
briefly some of the more profeminine Scriptures. Commenting on Genesis 5.2, he states: "For the Holy Ghost . . . counteth not by male and
female, but 'ye are all one in Christ Jesus.' Ga. iii.28. Wherefore, women
are not to be excluded out of the means of salvation; nay, they have, if
they believe, a special right to all the promises of grace that God hath
made to his saints in all ages" (Offor 11:455). And in another rare gesture, Bunyan admits the tiny possibility of female capability in extraordinary circumstances: "Although the scripture doth lay a great blot upon
women, and cautioneth man to beware of these fantastical and unstable
spirits, yet it limiteth man in his censure: She is only then to be rejected
and rebuked, when she doth things unworthy her place and calling. Such
a thing may happen, as that the woman, not the man, may be in the right,
(I mean, when both are godly,) but ordinarily it is otherwise" (Offor
11:439).

For the most part, the condemnation of Eve is pursued with such gusto
and at such length as to suggest that Bunyan may be using the occasion
of a work only posthumously published to register second thoughts or get
in the last word in a feminist controversy still rankling in his memory.

This therefore I reckon a great fault in the woman [Eve], an usurpa-
tion, to undertake so mighty an adversary [the Serpent], when she
was not the principal that was concerned therein; nay, when her
husband who was more able than she, was at hand, to whom also
the law was given as chief. But for this act, I think it is, that they
are now commanded silence, and also commanded to learn of their
husbands: 1 Co. xiv.34, 35. A command that is necessary enough for
that simple and weak sex: Though they see it was by them that sin
came into the world, yet how hardly are some of them to this day

dissuaded from attempting unwarrantably to meddle with potent enemies, about the great and weighty matters that concern eternity. (428–29)

He compounds Genesis 3.16 with 1 Timothy 2.11–14 to insist that "whenever [women] would perk it and lord it over their husbands, [they] ought to remember, that both by creation and transgression they are made to be in subjection to their husbands." The clinching argument for Bunyan is that this is St. Paul's conclusion too (438). Characteristically, these examples stretch well beyond scriptural exposition to register pointed applications to Bunyan's own immediate social and ecclesiological world.

Not surprisingly, a detailed consideration of part II of *Pilgrim's Progress* leads in various ways into history, into even some minor skirmishes to which the Church Militant is subject in the wilderness. Where early chapters showed Christian operating within and out of a realm of myth, and where the previous chapter examined some of Christiana's ties to the temporal, this chapter's consideration of church history and practice in their larger and smaller forms locates the narrative securely within time's patterns. The Conclusion of this study outlines some of the most telling continuities and contradictions of this descent into history, but before that argument can be made, Chapter 8 brings forward patterns within part II's epistemology and artistic expression that supply appropriate vehicles for the encompassing design.

CHAPTER EIGHT

Meditational Discourse

Solidity, indeed becomes the Pen
Of him that writeth things Divine to men:
But must I needs want solidness, because
By Metaphors I speak; was not Gods Laws,
His Gospel-laws in older time held forth
By Types, Shadows and Metaphors? Yet loth
Will any sober man be to find fault
With them, lest he be found for to assault
The highest Wisdom. No, he rather stoops,
And seeks to find out what by pins and loops,
By Calves, and Sheep; by Heifers, and by Rams;
By Birds and Herbs, and by the blood of Lambs;
God speaketh to him: And happy is he
That finds the light, and grace that in them be.

—John Bunyan, "Apology,"
Pilgrim's Progress (1678)

THREE SEPARATE CHAPTERS proved necessary to explicate the constellation of issues attaching to the biblical Word and the characteristically Puritan discourses of the sermon and the personal narrative in the first part of Pilgrim's Progress. The comparable evidence of part II collapses those categories within some unifying principles of Puritan epistemology and Bunyan's style. Instead of meditations on the Scriptures and the self, here we find occasional meditations that theologically interpret the kind of daily and domestic data considered in Chapter 6. In line with the principle in The Advocateship of Jesus Christ, that often "Christians . . . talk

too much at *rovers,* or in *generals:* They should be more at the Mark"
(XI:212), occasional meditation foregrounds the precise, vivid, invigorating, and deeply engaging detail that characterizes Bunyan's style. Greatheart repeatedly insists that his interlocuters move from generals to particulars (244, 256), and in part II the content and procedures implicit in
occasional meditation take fictional form as emblems, riddles, catechism,
similitudes, and a revised mode of typology. Part II's adjusted attitudes
toward biblical texts and the self reflect some historical changes in matters of gender and church history between the 1660s and 1680s noticed
earlier and developed fully in the concluding chapter.

❧ I ❧

FOR WILLIAM PERKINS, theology, or "the science of living blessedly forever," depends upon the knowledge of God and of ourselves, of God and of
His works—in an echoing commonplace, the book of God's Word and the
book of God's works (177). *Instruction For the Ignorant* endorses the Puritan view that true knowledge occurs where experience and the Scriptures
coincide (VIII:20). Although awareness of the creatures provides only
secondary knowledge, works provide a nonetheless invaluable medium
of divine revelation and human edification. The Bible validates experience and experience validates the Bible in an ongoing process of circular
proof that Carolynn Van Dyke finds "magnificently vital" when part I
continuously interchanges the allegorical and the empirical, but less successful when part II substitutes internalized metaphor, reductive realism,
and fabricated interpretation for Word-empowered experience. The second mode empties Scripture of its mystery, domesticates it, demotes its
reference to the life of the senses.[1]

As part I celebrated God, God's Word, and instruction in God and the
Word, so part II credits God's works as medium of instruction and arena
for living and community. Responding to a world of *creatures* as *preachers,* the disciplined individual meditatively processes the material and
events of daily life. Meditation upon the "creatures" emphasizes the target of attention (creature = creation, the thing[s] created by the Creator),
while meditation upon "occasions" recognizes that a particular target or
perceptual transaction has been at least briefly infused with heightened
spiritual significance along lines similar to the scriptural openings exam-

ined in Chapter 3. Both biblical doctrine and applications to the self, now differently weighted and arranged, affect that transaction. Fear of the Lord and personal anxiety give way to other, now catechistical purposes, to glorify God and enjoy Him forever.

According to Joseph Hall's *Art of Divine Meditation* (1606), all forms of meditation are "a bending of the mind upon some spiritual object, through divers forms of discourse, until our thoughts come to an issue." As practiced in the seventeenth century, the "issue" was likely to be a brief, even very brief, essay, generally one item in an extended series of considerations of disparate topics. Meditations upon occasions or creatures differ from meditations upon doctrines and upon the self in being "extemporall" rather than "deliberate" and in treating the beauty and wisdom of the Creator rather than God's providence or terrors and hopes. These meditations are "occasioned" by outward circumstances and arise from immediate, sensuous provocation of the memory, not from topics formally chosen and methodically developed in a time set apart for disciplined thought.[2] Insofar as the model continues to be the Puritan sermon, the "text" is drawn not from the Bible but from the data of daily life. The Bible enters the process only at a late stage to crystallize the insight and application.

Hall defines the process of extemporal meditation as generally rule-free, but the act itself as essential to a thoughtful and spiritual life:

> Forasmuch as our conceits herein vary according to the infinite multitude of objects and their divers manner of proffering themselves to the mind, as also for the suddenness of this act. Man is placed in this stage of the world to view the several natures and actions of the creatures; to view them, not idly, without his use, as they do him. God made all these for man and man for His own sake; both these purposes were lost if man should let the creatures pass carelessly by him, only seen, not thought upon. He only can make benefit of what he sees, which, if he do not, it is all one as if he were blind or brute. . . . The thoughts of this nature are not only lawful but so behooveful that we cannot omit them without neglect of God, his creatures, ourselves. The creatures are half lost if we only employ them, not learn something from them. God is wronged if His creatures be unregarded; ourselves most of all if we read this great volume of the creatures and take out no lesson for our instruction. (73–74)

Occasional meditation assumes that all details of daily life, as of Scripture, are fraught with meaning and that the godly draw spiritual edification from everything. Successful meditation is threatened by superstition, farfetchedness, overfamiliarity, and repetition (Hall 74).

Baxter's *Saints' Everlasting Rest* similarly recommends that believers

> make an advantage of every object thou seest, and of every passage
> of Divine Providence, and of everything that befalls in thy labour
> and calling, to mind thy soul of its approaching Rest. As all provi-
> dences and creatures are means to our Rest, so do they point us to
> that as their end. Every creature hath the name of God, and of our
> final rest written upon it, which a considerate believer may as truly
> discern, as he can read upon a post or hand in a cross-way, the name
> of the town or city which it points to. This spiritual use of creatures
> and providences is God's great end in bestowing them on man; and
> he that overlooks this end must needs rob God of his chiefest praise,
> and deny them the greatest part of his thanks.

Baxter speaks of meditations upon creatures as *ejaculations*, "when in the midst of our business we have some good thoughts of God in our minds . . . when some unusual occasion doth put us upon it at a season extraordinary." [3] For him, occasional meditation compares the objects of sense with the objects of faith, and thereby enacts theological accommodation by elevating believers' minds toward heaven as a consequence of divine condescension to the limits of earthly capacity. "What a deal of the majesty of the great Creator doth shine in the face of this fabric of the World!" he exclaims (168–69). Baxter particularly directs his audience to awareness of the overall purpose (for him "Rest") as well as of the role of the senses. Both his intention and a process are captured in the encouragement to "make our senses here serviceable to us" (168).

Translating theory into practice, Hall's second volume, *Occasional Meditations* (1630), underscores the "occasionalness" of the practice, the accidental, opportunistic, fragmented nature of such stimuli and proceeding. His son Robert, who edited the collection, describes the contents as his bishop father's "voluntary and sudden thoughts . . . to improve those short ends of time which are stolen from his more important avocations" and as the "recreations" which "have unsought offered themselves unto him" (121, 122). Hall himself invites his readers "to learn how to read God's great book by [reading] mine" (123).

Puritans generally understood the capacity to *spiritualize* any circumstance, no matter how trivial, as demonstrating election and a sanctified heart (Kaufmann, *Pilgrim's Progress* 183, 185), and Perry Miller captures both their theory and practice in commenting:

> Everything in experience [for the Puritan] was specifically and con-
> tinuously ordered by God; the rising of the sun, the blowing of the
> wind, the very breathing of the lungs, were all, like the decay of
> the rose, immediate acts of God, ordained for good and sufficient
> reasons. Events might conform to 'laws' of nature, but only because
> those were God's 'usual' methods of acting. To the Puritan, phenom-
> ena had significance because they were intentional. In causing this
> particular rose to be blasted on precisely such and such an evening,
> God had a purpose. The duty of man was to observe the event and
> to find out the purpose; most decidedly, it was not to give way to an
> emotion, whether of admiration or terror, excited by the appearance
> of things.

Anne Bradstreet's "Meditations Diuine and morall" proclaims the principle: "There is no obiect that we see. no action that we doe, no good
that we inioy, no evill that we feele, or fear, but we may make some spiri-
tull aduantage of all and he that makes such improvment is wise as well
as pious."[4]

What is most striking about Puritan examples of the practice is the
lengths to which meditators go in seeking out the most apparently unlikely or unpromising objects for transmutation into edification. Some of
Hall's early examples feature the very familiar—"The Barking of a Dog,"
"Lying down to Rest," "The Putting on of his Clothes"—but others show
how the unusual may arise from them:

Upon the Frame of a Globe Casually Broken.
Upon the Sight of a Grave Digged Up.
Upon Occasion of a Redbreast Coming into his Chamber.
Upon the Sight of a Crow Pulling off Wool from the Back of a
    Sheep.
Upon the Flies Gathering to a Galled Horse.
Upon the Hearing of a Swallow in the Chimney.
Upon the Sight of a Piece of Money under the Water.
Upon the First Rumor of the Earthquake at Lyme, Wherein a
    Wood was Swallowed up with the Fall of Two Hills.
Upon the Sight of a Great Library.

Mary Rich records some "providences" of her life under the headings "Upon walking in autumn among dead leaves," "Upon seeing a silk worm spin," "Upon seeing a hog lie under an acorn tree, and eat the acorns, but never look up from the ground to the tree from which they fell," "Upon a Hen of my Lady Essex Rich" (quoted in Fraser 49). While the ideal may have been to translate the meditational process into a constant mental discipline, in fact the results were a series of aperçus. Of course, their numerousness, partially countering their randomness of subject, provides its own kind of discontinuous continuity.

Puritans read the book of the creatures with the same high seriousness and intertextuality of the world, the self, and God as they read the Scriptures (Kaufmann, *Pilgrim's Progress* 179). It is a matter of considerable importance that data are not sought out but rather *present themselves* to a willing if passive reader. For Hall, things *proffer themselves*, as for Baxter they have the name of God written upon them waiting to be read. It is a small but transforming step from interpretations mediated by the Word and imposed upon the experiential world to interpretations generated by the visibilia and then tagged or translated into a spiritual— or sometimes just moral—vocabulary. Such tagging expresses a closured truth very different from the expectations of meditational inquiry. G. S. Starr remarks: "Since mere trifles can have the gravest consequences if allowed to pass unheeded, it follows that nothing is beneath the notice of an alert Christian. The prudent man draws warning or encouragement from seeing trifles, and the account of them in his autobiography may warn or encourage others, if the implication of each detail is made clear. Indeed, the more mundane the circumstances narrated, the more challenging the task of interpreting them spiritually" (19–20). Theoretically at least, the meditator does not create the spiritual significances or vestiges of God within the data but rather discovers them. In keeping with Ramistic logical proceedings, any "argument" (i.e., thing, idea, etc.) contains within itself all its causes, adjuncts, comparisons, and the like. As these are revealed to or "discovered" by the reasoner, the objects may be said to *show* or *speak* their meanings, along the lines of Psalm 19.1: "The heavens *declare* the glory of God" (my italics). Only the unfallen Adam was endowed with a perfected and instinctive knowledge of all the meanings contained within such objects as the animals he names in Genesis 2.19– 20.[5] For fallen beings, the understanding makes its way from within the object to the perceiver through a process more like discourse than what *Paradise Lost* describes as Adam's divinely endowed "sudden apprehension" (VIII.354). In *Pilgrim's Progress*, Kaufmann uses the terms "inner debate" and "oratory" to describe the methodology of Puritan meditation generally (24), but in fact occasional meditation proceeds rather in a dialogue. For the Puritan the creatures, like the Bible itself, were presumed to be the conduit through which the voice of God spoke.

Such dialogues and unleashed invention would seem to license a problematic multiplicity of meanings unless we understand that the goal is not to establish a once-and-for-all equation between an object and an edifying meaning. As Bunyan's emblems show, the same object may (and should) stimulate even contradictory meanings at different times. The overriding principles are active participation in a process and divine guidance "opening" meaning within the interpreter-object transaction. Though the target is now secular data rather than the Word, the practice fulfills the Reformation ideal of the priesthood of all believers, encouraging subjectivism in reading nature and art on the assumption that God as the creator of both things and illumination is responsible for whatever "discoveries" or "inventions" occur.

Such meditation encourages both sensuousness and the imagination in a Puritan consciousness generally insistent upon the strictly rational grounds of its proceedings. Conveniently for our purposes, *The Greatness of the Soul* (1682) sets forth Bunyan's version of faculty psychology. Not surprisingly, it privileges biblical grounding and deplores "notions." Bunyan calls the soul, among other things, God's breath of life, God's own image, the intelligent and inventive energy, the psychic element that treats invisibles as well as "every excellent thing of this life" (IX:158–59, 164–65). It consists of eight powers or members: understanding, conscience, judgment, fancy or imagination, mind (to which the fancy presents its data for review), memory, affections, and will (146–48). The memory is "the Register of the Soul" (147). The imagination, suspiciously linked with the senses, "presenteth to the man the *idea, form* or *figure* of that, or any of those things wherewith a man is either frighted or taken, pleased or displeased" (147). On the authority of Genesis 8.21— "For the imagination of man's heart is evil from his youth" (and Jeremiah passim)—he aligns it with sin. Its inflammatory motion stimulates desire and "from this desire the Soul proceedeth to a purpose of enjoying, and from a purpose of enjoying to *inventing* how, or by what means it had best to attempt the accomplishing of it" (196). *Invention* here moves beyond discovery, or even creativity, into dangerous self-indulgence. As hearing dominates part I, so seeing is the key faculty for part II, often supported by the other senses. Bunyan's psychology projects the soul's five spiritual senses analogous to the five bodily senses, influenced by either good or evil invisibles and impassioned for either good or evil ends depending upon the principle from whence they flow and the object upon which they are pitched (149, 151).

Bunyan's *Exposition* of the arrayed data of Genesis 1 reflects both his sense of meditational objects and these psychological principles. The biblical creation consists of visible things "in their own simple essence by themselves" arising out of chaos and taking on matter, substance, form, place, time, and order (Offor II:417). Each is quite literally an individual product of the *Word* of God: "Neither did God make them, because he saw they would attract a goodness to themselves; but he made them in such kind, as to bring forth that goodness he before determined they should" (418, 424). Each does not *attract* but *reflects*, a matter less of *inspiration* (breathing in) than of *expression* (pressing out). Creation's goodness is both essential and transactional: "In this his wonderful work, neither his will or understanding did here terminate, or make a stop; but being infinite in wisdom, he made [heaven and earth], that both as to matter and manner, they might present unto us, as in a mystery, some higher and more excellent thing; in this wisdom he made them all. . . . There is also besides many excellent things in the manner and order of the creation of the world, held forth to those that have understanding" (418). In a related argument, *The Water of Life* acknowledges that "the best of the things that are of this world are some way hurtful," and that "All things indeed are pure, that is, all creatures in themselves are good and serviceable to man, but they are not so good as grace" (Offor III:554), and, of course, it is grace that allows understanding to penetrate the "mystery."

The Resurrection of the Dead opens "the Mystery of the Creatures" in these terms:

> For the whole Creation, that is before thee, are not onely made to shew the power of God in themselves; but also to teach thee, and to preach unto thee, both much of God and thy self; as also Righteousness, and Justice of God against sin. . . . The Creation then of the World, namely, of the *Heavens, Earth, Sun, Moon, Stars*, with all other Creatures of God: they preach aloud to all men, the Eternal Power and God-head of their Creator. *Psal.* 8.3. *In Wisdom he hath made them all:* to be teachable, and carrying instruction in them: and he that is wise, and will understand these things, *even he shall*

*understand the loving kindness of the Lord; for the Works of the Lord
are great, and sought out of all them that have pleasure therein.* Psal.
104.24. Psal. 107. Psal. 111.2. (111:255)

This work references the practice of "carrying instruction" to the biblical authorities and precedents and recognizes that Christ, the prophets, and the apostles draw their similitudes, proverbs, and parables from the created world the more easily to instruct uninformed and recalcitrant audiences with the aid of the Holy Spirit (258–59). The creatures teach obedience to God and to superiors, fruitfulness ("a fruitful life to Godward" [256]), wisdom, industriousness, fear of the wrath to come, dependence on God, love, and pity, lessons aligning animal activities with collections of biblical texts (256–57).

Occasional meditation formalizes what the Scriptures also invite. Two texts, in particular, authorize proper objects of attention and proper procedures: the Old Testament Solomon's advisory, "Go to the ant, thou sluggard; consider her ways and be wise" (Proverbs 6.6), and the New Testament directive, "Consider the lilies of the field, how they grow" (Matthew 6.28; Luke 12.27). The opening verses of Proverbs outline the "Uses" that bridge the gap between experience and the largest understanding of it: "To know wisdom and instruction; to perceive the words of understanding; To receive the instruction of wisdom, justice, and judgment, and equity; To give subtilty to the simple, to the young man knowledge and discretion. A wise man will hear, and will increase learning; and a man of understanding shall attain unto wise counsels: To understand a proverb, and the interpretation; the words of the wise, and their dark sayings" (1.2–6). Proverbs 2.10–11 registers a similar point: "When wisdom entereth into thine heart, and knowledge is pleasant unto thy soul; Discretion shall preserve thee, understanding shall keep thee." Romans 1.19–20 explains the theory for "considering" the ant or "considering" lilies of the field: "That which may be known of God is manifest in them. . . . For the invisible things of him from the creation of the world are clearly seen, being understood by the things that are made, even his eternal power and Godhead," a text *Instruction For the Ignorant* compounds with Psalm 19.1–2: "The Heavens declare the Glory of God, and the Firmament sheweth his handy-work" (VIII:10).

Bunyan's preferred descriptor is "the Book of the Creatures" or "the Book of the Creation." Like Hall he understands the "occasional" nature of the edifying surprises offered and the desire "to teach weak minds how to improve their thoughts" (Hall 123). When processed with judgment, even *inconsiderable* and unlikely *things* will be found to be "warning words of God to your Souls" (*The Resurrection of the Dead* III:258). Like Baxter, he exclaims in wonder: "This Book of the Creatures, it is so excellent, and so full, so easie, and so suiting the capacity of all, that there is not one man in the World, but is catched, convicted, and cast by it. This is the Book, that he who knows no letters, may read in: yea, and that he who neither saw New Testament, nor Old, may know both much of God, and himself by" (III:258–59).

The Holy War allegorizes Bunyan's views through a character called Mr. Meditation, a citizen under Mansoul's second redemption. Formerly "an honest poor man . . . of no great account in the days of Apostasie, but now of repute with the best of the Town" (243), Mr. Meditation receives the sequestered wealth of Mr. Letgoodslip when Mansoul is redeemed and is to pass it on to his son Mr. Thinkwell in due course. Mr. Meditation's marriage to Mrs. Piety, the daughter of Mr. Recorder, miniaturizes both the religious intent and the memorial structure that underlie the genre. Under the earlier administration of Mansoul, Lord Understanding functioned analogously, indeed along the lines of the different epistemology that governs part I of *Pilgrim's Progress*. He lived in a tower of defense near Eyegate with instructions to "read in the *Revelation* of Mysteries all the days of his life, that he might know how to perform his Office aright" (118). This character's more dedicated doctrine and uses contrast with the more generalized and more public and financialized "goodness" of Mr. Meditation, and thus express key differences of tone, values, and perception behind the differing dispensations and eras of parts I and II.

As a Puritan artist, Bunyan wrestles frequently with biblical precedents and authority. The "Apology" to part I (see chapter headnote) commends the way the "solidity" of specific objects encourages believers to seek out the light and grace divinely inscribed in them. *Solomon's Temple Spiritualized* finds a wise God "speak[ing] to us ofttimes by trees, gold, silver, stones, beasts, fowls, fishes, spiders, ants, frogs, flies, lice, dust, etc." and asks "how should we by them understand his voice, if we count there is no meaning in them?" (Offor III:500). *The Advocateship of Jesus Christ* similarly asks: "Shall he be called a *King*, a *Priest*, a *Prophet*, a *Sacrifice*, an *Altar*, a *Captain*, a *Head*, a *Husband*, a *Father*, a *Fountain*, a *Door*, a *Rock*, a *Lyon*, a *Saviour*, &c. and shall we not consider these things?" (XI:195).

The assumption that "God has made nothing in vain" comprehends numerous small instances of occasional meditation in Bunyan's works within the literary forms of similitudes, proverbs, and parables (*Resurrection of the Dead* III:259) and as "words," proverbs, signs, and similitudes in *Pilgrim's Progress* (223). Elsewhere emblems and riddles label closely proximate discourses, and it is not unusual to find Bunyan using the terms *similitude* and *metaphor* interchangeably (XI:190). In his hands, all such small kinds compound the visual with edifying meaning and also with mimetic intensity.[6]

Because Bunyan was more inclusive than precise with the vocabulary, we need not strictly separate such categories, except for an instructive distinction between occasional meditation and multimedial emblem that focuses a present transition from privileged process to foregrounded product. Commentators often invoke *emblem* to encapsulate the most memorable features of Bunyan's art in *Pilgrim's Progress*, what Henri Talon calls its "clear-cut outlines" and "lapidary formula." Emblems may be defined as "symbolic pictures with explanatory mottos and poems," often collapsing their lessons into the stasis of a simple picture or diptych. Such expressions, no matter how brief, are notably self-contained. Their allegiance is to their own matter and instruction, and indeed in *Pilgrim's Progress* they seem often separable from the narrative whose progress they retard. In presenting datum plus lesson, or picture plus verse, the emblem is grounded in principles of equation and substitution rather than the richer processes of analysis or synthesis (Talon, *John Bunyan* 181; Sadler 112; Freeman 216).

Emblems are by definition witty in drawing connections between disparate realms, and as Rosemary Freeman's study of the English tradition of emblem books explains: "It is the wit, the apparent lack of any relation between two ideas and the subsequent establishment of an intellectually convincing link between them, that pleases; it does not matter how forced and arbitrary the link may seem to common-sense or to feeling" (3). Where this secular definition acknowledges a gap, Bunyan, and the Puritan tradition he speaks for, recognize an opportunity to achieve some unifications within the fragmented world. Such "opportunism" occurs frequently in part II of *Pilgrim's Progress*, whose implicit reconciliation with the things of this world differs radically from part I where "carnal sense" and "things present" are in damning opposition to "things to come" (32).

Whether in the allegorical prose of *Pilgrim's Progress* or the verse of *A Book For Boys and Girls*, Bunyan's emblems are characteristically rooted in the Puritan ideals of utility and profit, and they picture comparisons that are lively, direct, effective, and multileveled, but never labored or tediously lengthy. Like other late emblems, Bunyan's are individualistic and elastic in form and content and allow notable freedom of interpretation and handling.[7] Typically, his *Book For Boys and Girls* intends to show children (of all ages) that "their Souls [are] entangle[d]" by the things of this world, each toy, "each *Fingle-fangle,* / On which they doting are," and to teach them rather to leave behind Sin and Vanity and "them entice, / To mount their Thoughts . . . To Heav'n" (VI:191). Most of these poems divide into a vividly descriptive or realistic word picture followed by a separate "comparison" forcefully registering the "moral."[8] While acknowledging "the Inconsiderableness / Of things, by which I do my mind express," Bunyan's governing principle is that: "Great Things, by little ones, are made to shine" (VI:192). Written in a variety of verse forms, his emblems recall the subject matters and process of occasional meditation, as for example, "Upon the Lark and the Fowler," "Of the Mole in the Ground," "Of the Fly at the Candle," "Upon a Penny Loaf," "On the Kackling of a Hen," "Upon a Sheet of White Paper," "Of Moses and his wife," "Upon the barren Fig-tree in God's Vineyard."

One striking example, "The Sinner and the Spider," enacts emblem theory within verse, as the spider literally voices its own varied purpose:

> My Webs becoming snares and traps for Flies,
> Do set the wiles of Hell before thine eyes.
> Their tangling nature is to let thee see,
> Thy sins (too) of a tangling nature be. . . .
> The Fly lies buzzing in my Web to tell
> Thee, how the Sinners roar and howl in Hell. (VI:217)

By such means, "*Spiders* may teach men the way to Heaven," and by the end the instructed Sinner acknowledges:

> Thou art my Monitor, I am a Fool;
> They learn may, that to Spiders go to School. (220–21)

The Resurrection of the Dead, now in prose for adults, also copiously arrays experiential items along with their edifying "comparisons." It regularly employs the verb *preach* to designate the emblematic transaction (III:255–58).

Emblems miniaturize the practice and content of meditation. In particular, the Protestant tradition of occasional meditation distinguished between two subject matters or two modes of "occasion," the sacramental and the emblematic. The sacramental—the governing mode of part I as we have seen—sees selected objects as divinely invested with religious significances. This kind of inscription occurs as arbitrary rather than natural meaning or, in literary terms, as symbol rather than image. The second mode, of present concern, views objects as morally instructive and exemplary and assumes the meditator's willingness to derive and apply the meaning (Lewalski, *Protestant Poetics* 162). Where the sacramental requires scripturally endowed significations, the emblematic may or may not gesture toward the Bible in presenting and educing lessons in moral conduct rather than revelation. It prioritizes not divine imposition of meaning but rather the interpreter's unpacking of the message.

Sacramental occasions exercise the trope of synecdoche with an eye toward Reformation theology, whereas emblematic ones operate within the simpler order of similitude. In part I such sacramental objects as Christian's book and burden, the wicket gate, the scroll, and the key of promise are divinely invested with soteriological significances. Taking hold of such an object allows the meditator access to the highest patterns of grace and law, good and evil, salvation and damnation. A very different transaction occurs, however, in part II in a map glossed as "Gods Book" and a lantern as "the light of the Word" (297, 299); or when Christiana pays for hospitality with her mite (234–35, i.e., the widow's mite) or the cost is borne by the Good Samaritan (270). These may require the reader's familiarity with the biblical source, but the items align realistic and theologically significative analogues in simple ways, the two spheres being handled as equals in quantity though not in quality. Emblematic transactions like these are theologically retrofitted rather than promisory. When Christian wields the s(Word) "All-prayer" against Apollyon, the narrative, Reformation theology, and Ephesians 6 collapse into that weapon to epitomize the entire artistic and thematic construct of part I, but when Valiant-for-Truth's sword is identified as "*a right* Jerusalem *Blade*" (290), a merely convenient label attaches for incidental emphasis to a piece of narrative equipment.

Part II provides lucid explanations as a matter of course for the kind of interpretation Christian struggled with experience and memory to achieve at desperate moments in part I. When metaphoric narrative data occur simultaneously with their interpretational guidelines, part II establishes a very different realm of narration, expression, and understanding. The Way and travel on it become overdetermined—clearly, and devitalizingly, dominated by their meanings. In Michel Foucault's terms, things and actions here translate into mere discourses or mental occurrences; metamorphosis descends into commentary and recollected anecdote; metaphors call attention to themselves as inventions not as truth; the allegorical becomes subservient to the realistic it used to transcend; and supernatural forces and psychic effects descend into playful imaginative creations, even harden into rule-dominated games.[9]

❧ II ☙

PART II PLAYS VARIOUSLY with objects of meditation as similitudes based in natural phenomena, artifacts, or human activities. Two small instances will clarify the practice. In one, a gloss labels the boys' fear of the lions at House Beautiful as "An emblem of those that go on bravely, when there is no danger; but shrink when troubles come" (218), and in another, the youngest boy translates his experience with Hill Difficulty into emblem or memorial: "And I remember now what my Mother has told me, namely, That the way to Heaven is as up a Ladder, and the way to Hell is as down a Hill. But I had rather go up the Ladder to Life, then down the Hill to Death" (216). Characteristically, emblematic objects in part II occur in series rather than individually and enfold simple moral lessons and sometimes biblical applications into narrative integrations of the real and spiritual realms.

Chapter 3 showed the Interpreter guiding Christian's advanced exercises in reading doctrine and applying it to his salvational history and prospects. At his house, sacramental imagery, luminously exemplary characters, and paradigmatic soteriological actions reinforced and inspired Christian's nature and destiny. The Interpreter's lessons, imagery, and instructional methods and goals for Christiana, however, are very different: his method now emblematic; his data homely, popular, familiar; and his tone simplistic and condescending. Romans 15.4 authorizes the proceedings in part II: "For whatsoever things were written aforetime were written for our learning, that we through patience and comfort of the scriptures might have hope." Romans 5.3–4 glosses the passage: "Tribulation worketh patience: And patience, experience; and experience, hope." *An Exposition . . . of Genesis* invokes these verses to describe Noah as an interpretive model and reads his olive leaf as "a sign . . . and a good experience of the continued love of God to his servant," a sign "not

written for [Noah's] sake only, but for us also that believe in God, that
we might now exercise patience, as Noah; and obtain the tokens of God's
goodness, as he." Bunyan privileges the interpretive process: "Prove these
stories; look if they be not dead and lifeless fancies; see if you can find
that they were plucked off from the tree that is green" (Offor 11:479–80).

The Interpreter's scenes in part II divide into two phases, "signs" and
"good experience." Soon after their arrival, the Interpreter takes the
family into what are now labeled "his *Significant* Rooms" (Bunyan's italics) to review the tableaux from part I in a quick and random order:
"Here therefore they saw the *Man* in the *Cage*, the man and his Dream,
the man that cut his way thorough his Enemies, and the Picture of the
biggest of them all: together with the rest of those things that were then
so profitable to *Christian*" (199). Part II thus comprehends what went before, with Christiana specifically *digesting* them (199). "A Woman quick
of apprehension" (200), she easily grasps, and is taught to grasp, the first
of her own lessons, but the Interpreter soon pays little attention to involving her in the learning process. Like the later instructors Prudence and
Gaius, he infuses information directly into his pupils, commending their
passive receptivity to instruction rather than providing them with a process for independent inquiry, in marked contrast with the insistence upon
Christian's autonomy and primary salvational responsibility in part I.

Eight new emblems in part II realistically mirror the data of rural
domestic life. Where Christian's tableaux recapitulated and prolepsized
his pilgrimage, Christiana's remain distant and impersonal, familiar yet
generalized. Where his scenes figured active characters and stimulated
him to action of his own, hers project passive figures and responses. In
the first, a downward-looking man rakes straws, sticks, and dust while
an emblematic figure standing over his head offers to exchange a celestial crown for the muckrake. In keeping with the gloss, "The man with
the Muck-rake expounded" (199), Christiana labels him a man of this
world, and the Interpreter links his rake with a carnal mind. The scene
does not—as would have been the case in part I—show the man in the
act of choosing between earthly and celestial claims, but the Interpreter
"reads" his insistently downward glance as an indication that such a
choice has already been made. The transaction is of static and enclosured
emblems, not sacramental dramatizations and symbolic self-projections.
A passive Christiana "applies" the scene to her life with the prayer, "O deliver me from this Muck-rake." This opening emblem typically targets
circumstances from everyday nature and artifice proffering themselves

for interpretation. Typically too, as Kaufmann notes, "the elements [have been] selected beforehand to yield the desired scheme of significances" (*Pilgrim's Progress* 192). The preselection condescends to its audience; it assumes a pedagogical transfer of information, but only a narrow supply of information. This and the other emblems of part II may redeem the occasions of immediate experience by reducing things and events to mere statement, but they also create a more manageable but decidedly less numinous world.

Christiana's second scene figures the process as well as product of meditational instruction. Set in "the very best Room in the house, (a very brave Room it was)" (200), it turns occasional meditation into a game. Christiana and Mercy are to "see if they could find any thing profitable" in a room that contains nothing "but a very great Spider on the Wall." At first Mercy says she sees nothing in the room and Christiana keeps silent. When queried, Mercy acknowledges "an *ugly Spider*, who hangs by her Hands upon the Wall." When challenged again, Christiana admits to perceiving numerous destructively venomous spiders. The Interpreter's repeated questions implicitly recommend that meditators persist in their inquiry. Mercy learns to look more closely at the reality before her, but the silent and more perceptive Christiana enacts a larger lesson grounded in Proverbs 30.28, "The Spider taketh hold with her hands . . . and is in Kings Pallaces" (201), as a base for his "reading": "to shew you, that how full of the Venome of Sin soever you be, yet you may by the hand of Faith lay hold of, and dwell in the best Room that belongs to the Kings House above" (201). Christiana first reads herself and Mercy as ugly and venomous creatures in fine rooms of which they are unworthy, but she cheerfully abandons this negative interpretation of the spider in favor of the Interpreter's lesson in "*how to act Faith*" (201; Bunyan's italics). In so doing, she leaves behind the harsh Calvinism of part I in favor of the more humane and inclusive dispensation of part II. The Interpreter augments her tropological reading with his anagogical one, her negative with his positive one. Her reading is not so much rejected as made more inclusive. The Interpreter seems to commend the passivity of Christiana's responses, her "holding her peace" in the first phase, the quiet tears that are all that is allowed to signal her "quick[ness] of apprehension" (200) in the second stage, and her self-deprecation and again tears in the third phase.

A series of emblems represent maternal and paternal authority figures and hierarchically lower and more numerous subjects to them. A hen and chickens encourage Mercy and Christiana to learn from close observation of phenomena. In its first phase, a chicken lifting up its eyes to heaven when it drinks acknowledges the mercies that come therefrom, while its second shows a mother hen in fourfold communication with her chicks. When the Interpreter explicates her four calls as analogues of God's speech to his obedient followers, he is assigning coded labels to the preselected phenomena before them. In other brief scenes, an about-to-be butchered sheep teaches patience and long-suffering (202); variegated flowers embody lessons in accepting one's place without quarreling; grain harvesting teaches industriousness; and, finally, a robin with a spider in its mouth warns against insincere professors (robins) and the harms they can bring to innocent victims (spiders). Here as in the second tableau—and against obvious visual expectation—the Interpreter attaches a positive reading to the spider and condemns the more attractive and sociable robin.[10] After a series of proverbs to which we will turn in a moment, the Interpreter troops the visitors to the garden to examine a tree whose fair outside and rotten inside again are made a comment upon false professors. In general, although Christiana and Mercy are encouraged to participate in interpreting the first two of their scenes, they take only a passive part in the final five, scenes chiefly themselves directed to teach passivity, obedience, and patient continuance in the faith despite bad examples. When Greatheart looks back upon this instruction from the vantage of the sepulcher, he encapsulates the essence of the meditational activity in saying, "All that you have, my Daughters, you have by a peculiar impression made by a Divine contemplating upon what I have spoken to you" (213). Presumably the party have been meditating on this emblem during the intervening travel.

As this peripatetic instruction cum house-tour draws to a close, in response to Christiana's request that he "*show* or *tell* [them] of other things that are Profitable" (203; Bunyan's italics), the Interpreter "tells" a series of secular and sometimes "gospelized" aphorisms and paradoxes against the superficial and hypocritical, against social rather than spiritual dangers. These random aperçus, based in the natural and artificial worlds and in human actions and interactions, align with other more obviously meditational and emblematic series in part II. The topics or "occasions" include a sow, an ox, women's neatness, sleeplessness, trading ships, an ungrateful friend, cockle and barley, and sitting down to a meal, each carefully moralized for edification and memorability (203–4). The disparate units draw upon women's domestic sphere and conduct within a social and busy world rather than guiding the intense, single-minded

individual toward salvation. They vacillate between prescribed and pro-
scriptive aphoristic lessons and formal rhetorical questions to constrict
further inquiry. A textual gloss targets both process and reward: "Pray,
and you will get at that which yet lies unrevealed" (203).

Christiana's visit to the Interpreter's house concludes with a song that
echoes Proverbs 1.7 and formally registers each emblem as an "Argument
of weight,"

> To move me for to watch and pray,
> To strive to be sincere,
> To take my Cross up day by day,
> And serve the Lord with fear. (209)

The biblical precedent for series of proverbs is of course the Book of
Proverbs, a work which presents "sundry observations of virtues, and
their contrary vices" (KJV argument chapter 10). Behind its serial listings lie the principles outlined in Proverbs 1.7 and repeated throughout:
"The fear of the Lord is the beginning of knowledge: but fools despise wisdom and instruction." *The Desire of the Righteous Granted*, a treatise on
Proverbs 11.23 and 10.24, lays down Bunyan's views of both the content
and form of proverbs:

> This book of Proverbs is so called because it is such as containeth
> hard, dark, and pithy sentences of wisdom, by which is taught unto
> young men knowledge and discretion. i-vi. Wherefore this book is
> not such as discloseth truths by words antecedent or subsequent
> to the text, so as other scriptures generally do, but has its texts or
> sentences more independent; for usually each verse standeth upon
> its own bottom, and presenteth by itself some singular thing to the
> consideration of the reader; so that I shall not need to bid my reader
> go back to what went before, nor yet to that which follows, for the
> better opening of the text; and shall therefore come immediately
> to the words, and search into them for what hidden treasures are
> contained therein. (Offor 1:744)

Like the occasional meditation and emblem genres, proverbs "disclose"
to "consideration" the "hidden treasures" they "contain"; they are "sin-
gular," "independent," and self-contained ("standeth upon its own bottom"), precisely the format and process seen in earlier blocks of text.

Like her husband's visit to Interpreter's house, Christiana's confirms
her narrative's dominant imagery, value scheme, and theological cate-

gories, and here that means attaching spiritual and convential meanings to the data of everyday life. Where the sacramental part I employs the sort of arbitrary meaning usually called symbol, the emblematic part II deals in images, that is data with nonarbitrary meanings which when found prove entirely native and natural, an outpouring from the thing itself if the reader will "open" to it. To achieve understanding in part I requires the mediating Holy Spirit's guidance into biblical texts, while in part II understanding presents itself through nature and reason. The former is anticipatory or promisory, while the latter reflects the accumulated wisdom of the past. Christiana pursues general principles not biblical texts as enacted into the myth of her own personal history. As Kaufmann argues for part I, Bunyan was "concerned that Christian learn from his experiences, but in the last analysis he does not trust the adequacy of event as a vehicle of edifying meaning" (*Pilgrim's Progress* 19). For the purposes of part II, however, we may say Bunyan *does* trust in phenomenal adequacy!

In another rich insight, Kaufmann observes that where Christian learns through action, Christiana primarily learns through reflection and meditation (*Pilgrim's Progress* 188). Reflection is made explicit when, "according as our Custom is to do with Pilgrims," the ladies of House Beautiful present the party with a series of items "on which thou mayest meditate when thou art upon the way" (232–33): Eve's apple, Jacob's ladder, a golden anchor, and Abraham offering up Isaac. This list packages biblical verses within portable memorial utensils. When asked her thoughts on the apple, Christiana is uncertain whether " 'Tis Food, or Poyson" but when they "opened the matter to her" she was filled with wonder. "A sight of Sin is amazing" says the gloss (233). In viewing angels ascending Jacob's ladder, the family "stood feeding their Eyes with this *so pleasant a Prospect*," and the gloss now instructs: "A sight of Christ is taking" (233). They respond with wonder too to the sight of Abraham's sacrifice. The golden anchor is glossed to Hebrews 6.19, a verse whose encouragement to enter within the veil registers as an advisory on meditation. These exemplary visual occasions dictate attitudes of wonder and amazement while leaving the interpretive process otherwise undefined. The party carry an anchor forward on their pilgrimage, but this baggage is an incidental attachment rather than a luminously symbolic epitome of the soul's essential relation to salvation along the lines of Christian's scroll or key of promise in part I. Prudence encapsulates into song the items of this series for future memorial use:

> *Eve*'s Apple we have shewed you,
> Of that be you aware:
> You have seen *Jacobs* ladder too,
> Upon which angels are.
> An Anchor you received have;
> But let not these suffice,
> Until with *Abra'm* you have gave,
> Your best, a Sacrifice. (234)

Similarly, her sister Piety presents "a *Scheme* of all those things that thou hast seen at our House: Upon which thou mayest look when thou findest thy self forgetful, and call those things again to remembrance for thy Edification, and comfort" (236). Where Christian's experiences along the way variously fortified him for salvational action, his family's anticipate future reflection.

The same purposes govern the presentation of "Rarities" at the Delectable Mountains. Here "new places" are again added to the series from part I. They offer not so much emblems as tableaux vivants, with significances added by authoritative instructors. Mount Marvel embodies lessons in faith overcoming travel difficulties; Mount Innocent embeds its moral advisory in unsoiled garments; Mount Charity enacts clothing the naked; and an unnamed site expounds hypocrisy. Christian's sites, Hill Error, Mount Caution, and Hill Clear, were named for the perspectives they allowed; Christiana's are tagged for the ethics they intend to transfer to the audience. Part II advises how to live in the world and community, not how to escape this world for the next. The final event, a Byway to Hell, contrasts a distanced spectacle of self-damnation in part II against a typological, textually mediated lesson on specified hypocrites in part I (122).

For Christian, carnal sense and things to come are in radical opposition (32), a generally dominant principle of part I vigorously dramatized in Vanity Fair, and enacted too in Bunyan's own life where such "wandering thoughts" as "the form of a Bush, a Bull, a Besom, or the like" turn to naught his "labour[s] to compose [his] mind and fix it upon God" (*Grace Abounding* 34). The Interpreter cites 2 Corinthians 4.18 to Christian to define the distinction: "*For the things that are seen, are* Temporal; *but the things that are not seen, are* Eternal" (32), a challenge brought home to the jailed Bunyan of *Grace Abounding* who sought "to live upon God that is invisible" (97). St. Paul's review of his own preaching in 1 Corinthians 2.11–14 draws the contrast and evaluation: "The things of God knoweth no man, but the Spirit of God. Now we have received, not the spirit of the world, but the spirit which is of God; that we might know the things that are freely given to us of God. Which things also we speak, not in the words which man's wisdom teacheth, but which the Holy Ghost teacheth; comparing spiritual things with spiritual. But the natural man receiveth not the things of the Spirit of God: for they are foolishness unto him: neither can he know them, because they are spiritually discerned." *Reprobation Asserted* comments on this passage that, "nature being below the discerning of things truly, spiritually, and savingly good, it must needs fall short of receiving, loving and delighting in them," and on natural man at best as "not only corrupted and infected, but depraved, bewitched and dead; swallowed up of unbelief, ignorance, confusion, hardness of heart, hatred of God, and the like" (Offor 11:349–50, and see *Justification By Faith*, Offor 11:282, 310). Part II leaves behind natural man as reprehensible and nature as the dark goddess to whom Edmund pays allegiance in *King Lear* and moves toward the "Unerring nature, still divinely bright, / One clear, unchanged, and universal light" by whose "just standard" Pope's *Essay on Criticism* advises us to frame our judgments (ll. 68–71).

A contrasting and recurrent Pauline principle underwrites part II: "For the invisible things of him from the creation of the world are clearly seen, being understood by the things that are made, even his eternal power and Godhead" (Romans 1.20), or again "that which may be known of God is manifest," and deliberately so, for "God shewed it unto them" (Romans 1.19). John 3.12 poses the threatening question in the words of Christ himself: "If I have told you earthly things, and ye believe not, how shall ye believe, if I tell you of heavenly things?" Part II depends upon a deity manifest in the data of this world and hinges faith upon an acceptance, not a rejection, of earthly things. The world, or the visual world, as it impinges on Christian, is a matter of profit, power, ambition, and the like external and potentially damning "gains" and distractions, but the support systems and experiential texts of Christiana's world provide vehicles of edifying meaning, now available not merely through the ear and hearing but through vision and the other senses. By contrast with the aural action of part I, in part II even the Valley of Humiliation is beautiful and fruitful, especially for one who "delighted himself in the sight of his Eyes" and who seeks what is "profitable" (237). Early in the seventeenth century Francis Bacon called for "the commerce of the mind with things," and by the 1680s both *things* and an interaction well characterized as *commerce* have come fully into their own (Hill, *Century* 79). For part II, "carnal sense" and "things to come" belong to the same beneficent and progressive continuum.

◄§| III |§►

MOST OF THE ACTIVITY grounded in occasional meditation in part II seeks to instruct not Christiana but her four sons and thus stretches to family and church practices. These edifying "readings" proceed under the advisory: "Pray, and you will get at that which yet lies unrevealed" (gloss 203). The colloquy between Prudence and Mathew amplifies the principle:

> Pru. *What do you think of the Bible?*
> Mat. It is the Holy Word of God.
> Pru. *Is there nothing Written therein, but what you understand?*
> Mat. Yes, a great deal.
> Pru. *What do you do when you meet with such places therein, that you do not understand?*
> Mat. I think God is wiser then I. I pray also that he will please to let me know all therein that he knows will be for my good. (226)

Elsewhere Greatheart recommends the metaphors of Revelation for "the ripening of the Wits of young Readers" (253), but before "dark Similitudes" can take effect, readers must be willing to participate and to submit to an authoritative intermediary.

Prudence's edifying dialogue at House Beautiful initiates Christiana's sons into processing the trope of similitude. Her pious but nonscriptural instruction rests upon the questions: What does a thing mean? and Why does a thing act or exist in this way? Prudence's answers are always that the thing exists in order to *shew* or teach. By *to teach*, however, she does not mean "to provide new information or awareness," but rather "to reinforce and secure what is already known." Echoing an earlier proposition that "God has made nothing in vain" (201), Prudence advises the boys to "observe also and that with carefulness, what the Heavens and the Earth do teach you" (226), a learning medium to be reinforced by their mother, godly conversations, and meditations on the Bible. Her dialogic instruction presumes a relatively simplified transfer of spiritual information (or propaganda) through straightforward acknowledgment of units of famil-

iar reality. The format recalls the discontinuous series of proverbs at the
Interpreter's house, but where the Interpreter fused data and significations, this evidence distributes them into a question-and-answer-format.
Dividing questions and answers between learner and teacher gives structural form to the triggers and products of occasional meditation. Prudence
invites the boys to ask her questions that might prove profitable (230), and
the recuperating Mathew begins by inquiring about his illness. Prudence
translates each element into moral precepts as in these samples:

> Mathew. *Why does Physick, if it does good, Purge, and cause that
> we Vomit?*
> Prudence. To shew that the Word when it works effectually,
> cleanseth the Heart and Mind. For look what the one doth to the
> Body, the other doth to the Soul.
> Mathew. *What should we learn by seeing the Flame of our Fire go
> upwards? and by seeing the Beams, and sweet influences of the Sun
> strike downwards?*
> Prudence. By the going up of the Fire, we are taught to ascend to
> Heaven, by fervent and hot desires. And by the Sun his sending his
> Heat, Beams, and sweet Influences downwards; we are taught, that
> the Saviour of the World, tho' high, reaches down with his Grace
> and Love to us below. . . .
> Mat. *Why doth the Fire fasten upon the Candle-wick?*
> Pru. To shew that unless Grace doth kindle upon the Heart, there
> will be no true Light of Life in us.
> Mathew. *Why is the Wick and Tallow and all, spent to maintain
> the light of the Candle?*
> Prudence. To shew that Body and Soul and all, should be at the
> Service of, and spend themselves to maintain in good Condition that
> Grace of God that is in us. (231–32)

Their thirteen exchanges—strikingly free of specific biblical reference—
enunciate guides to godly conduct in what Kaufmann identifies as a terse
catalogue of the clichés of traditional occasional meditation (*Pilgrim's
Progress* 177, 176).

What is remarkable in most of the exchanges is the arbitrariness of
the "reading" and connectives. An algebraic logic posits a meaning for X
and then adjusts later elements to that meaning. In the first example
cited, if X equals Word, then Prudence's conclusion may follow. But, of

course, X or Physick may very well equate with other accoutrements of Christ the physician. Elsewhere, candle is pressed into service as "Heart," a consequence of fire's equation with grace, but fire could just as well equate with hell. The procedure recalls the spider at Interpreter's house, open to either a positive or negative signification. So long as the intention is pious and the lesson edifying, such freedom of interpretation is allowable. In epistemology as in dramatis personae, where part I presses toward a monolithic psychology out of which individual differences have been carefully refined, part II tolerates, even celebrates, variety, at least within safe limits.

House Beautiful instructs the sons through two question-and-answer formats, two models of Puritan discourse practiced in other Bunyan works. The exchange just reviewed compounds the genres in *A Book For Boys and Girls*, that is, emblem and occasional meditation, with alphabet, primer, and doctrinal guide (Tindall 204). The second format echoes *Instruction For the Ignorant*, Bunyan's catechism for adult as well as youthful learners. It is a small step from compounds of "creatures," meditation, and emblematics into the secondary discourse of catechism where the question-and-answer format differs from emblematic and proverbial lessoning in discarding the creatures in favor of biblical texts.

By definition, a catechism dictates indoctrinational exercises through which an authority—a parent, a minister, a teacher—repeats a set series of progressively more complex theological questions in order to elicit from pupils concise memorized formulations of basic matters of faith and dogma. Successful performance of the exercises proves the pupil's rote achievement to the questioning authority. Since the learner memorizes and may supply questions as well as answers, the exercise can proceed without an external authority as well. As its title perhaps suggests, Bunyan's *Instruction For the Ignorant* radically recasts the roles of questioner and respondent so that the uninformed pose the questions and the theological authority the responses.[11]

Some answers divide a question into multiple parts, but usually the answers consist of one or more biblical authorizations carefully channeling further inquiry. A typical sample focuses upon the book of creatures:

Q. *Is this God, being a Spirit, to be known?*
A. Yes, and that by his Works of Creation, by his Providences, by the Judgments that he executeth, and by his Word.

Q. *Do you understand him by the Works of Creation?*

A. The Heavens declare the Glory of God, and the Firmament sheweth his handy-work: so that the invisible things of him from the Creation of the World, are clearly seen, being understood by the things that are made, even his Eternal Power and Godhead, *Psal.* 19.1, 2. *Rom.* 1.20.

Q. *Doth his Works of Providence also declare him?*

A. They must needs do it, since through his Providence the whole Creation is kept in such harmony as it is, and that in despite of Sin and Devils: also if you consider that from an Angel to a Sparrow, nothing falls to the ground without the Providence of our Heavenly Father, *Mat.* 10.29. (VIII:10)

At several late points the questioner merely asks for biblical texts.

A contemporary (false) etymology of *catechism* derives from the Greek for *echo* (Fish, *Living Temple* 17–18), and this term well describes the genre's duplex format and Bunyan's practice in *Instruction For the Ignorant* and at House Beautiful in part II. With Christiana's permission to "see how [she] had brought up her Children" (224), Prudence assumes the instructor's role. She begins with *echoes*, that is, chains of set questions with predetermined memorized answers. When asked who made him, the youngest son James answers, "God the Father, God the Son, and God the Holy Ghost." When asked who saves him, his answer is the same. When asked seriatim, How the Father saves him, how the Son, and how the Holy Ghost, he answers: (1) by his grace; (2) by his righteousness, death, blood, and life; and (3) by his illumination, renovation, and preservation (224). Later questions to Joseph on man's salvation, to Samuel on heaven and hell, and finally to Mathew on God's nature and the Bible gradually become less formulaic and less echoic and allow somewhat more open inquiry. Prudence makes explicit the assumption underlying catechism generally, that later answers imply full understanding of earlier ones.

If, as one commentator suggests, the monthlong stay at House Beautiful in part II is "a house party" (Furlong 117), the stop at Gaius's inn is even more socially festive. This site's discourses vary the "occasional" model, now compounding less random serial secular data with biblical referents. In its first phase, the host and instructor Gaius attaches theological significances to the details of his hospitality and grounds each emblematic item in biblical precedents. In the largest intention of this

evidence, divine nurture is superimposed upon domestic nurture to diur-
nalize the spiritual, and the data of Gaius's metaphoric meal bring into
focus both the feminine interests examined in Chapter 6 and the church
practices examined in Chapter 7.

Part II foregrounds its own pedagogy when Mathew observes that the
laying out of the tablecloth, trenchers, salt, and bread whet his appetite,
and Gaius "gathers" (gloss 262) its significances: "So let all ministring
Doctrines *to* thee in this Life, beget *in* thee a greater desire to sit at the
Supper of the great King in his Kingdom; for all Preaching, Books, and
Ordinances here, are but as the laying of the Trenshers, and as setting of
Salt upon the Board, when compared with the Feast that our Lord will
make for us when we come to his House" (262). The author's emphases
on *to* and *in* encapsulate an earlier distinction between things "proffering" themselves and the recipient "reading" out the edification. The first
course of meats "shew[s] that they must begin their *Meal* with Prayer and
Praise to God" (262), and Gaius links "the *Heave-shoulder*" and "*Wave-
breast*" he serves with David and Leviticus 7 and 10. When a bottle of
wine arrives, Gaius encourages them to "Drink freely, this is the juice
of the true Vine, that makes glad the Heart of God and Man" (262) in
a formulation that recalls but goes beyond the biblical Lord's Supper,
compounding Matthew 26.27 with John 15.1 and 5. After "a Dish of Milk
well crumbed" for the children, the party partake of "a Dish of *Butter*
and *Hony*," with Gaius's encouragement, "Eat freely of *this*. . . . this was
our Lords Dish when he was a Child" (262), another compounding that
enfolds the Eucharist both into further biblical texts and into daily life.

Part II not only foregrounds but seeks to make delightful its edifying
designs. For the final courses of apples and nuts, Gaius casts his interpretation into versified game structures whose intensified speech deconstructs
their meditational objects. We may suppose that the family have in fact
been "meditating" upon Eve's apple as advised at their departure from
House Beautiful (233). When Mathew questions the Edenic precedent for
apples, Gaius concordances *apples* in order to reject what is historical
from Genesis in favor of what is metaphorical from the Song of Solomon:

> Apples were they *with* which we were beguil'd,
> Yet *Sin*, not Apples hath our souls defil'd.
> Apples forbid, if eat, corrupts the Blood:
> To eat such, when commanded, does us good.

> Drink of his Flagons then, thou, Church, his Dove,
> And eat *his* Apples, who art sick of Love. (262)

His preference for the promisory elements in these Old Testament citations affirms the more inclusive dispensation that governs part II generally. The second set of verses treats dinner items not as emblem but as
riddle and in so doing sets forth the theory that underlies not merely this
series but earlier compounds of data plus meanings as well.

> Hard *Texts* are *Nuts* (I will not call them *Cheaters,*)
> Whose *Shells* do keep their *Kirnels* from the *Eaters.*
> Ope then the Shells, and you shall have the Meat,
> They here are brought, for you to crack and eat. (263)

The advisory again attaches typological, tropological, and anagogical
meanings to the data of everyday life while confirming the habit of seeking
out such significances.

A later after-dinner moment explicitly identifies such discourse as
riddle. Where emblems are visual, riddles are cryptically verbal, featur-
ing terseness, paradox, and surprise (see Emblem XIII VI:211 and Offor
III:751). A riddle functions, in Sharrock's phrase, as "a poor relation of
the emblem," and as the antithesis of a pun (*John Bunyan* [1968] 151).
Where the pun plays multiple meanings against each other, the riddle,
at least such Puritan riddles, assumes a single true meaning obscured by
familiar associations and syntax. Nick Davis's description of unlocking
or "opening" a riddle goes to the core of Puritan ways of knowing: "The
vanquisher of a riddle gives the impression of having released a truth previously hidden from common awareness, and of having reaffirmed the
power of language to deal directly with what is enigmatic in human experience" (195–96).

Riddles divide into something like question-and-answer exchanges. In
the first example, Honest poses:

> A man there was, tho some did count him mad,
> The more he cast away, the more he had.

According to the gloss, "Gaius opens it" thus:

> He that bestows his Goods upon the Poor,
> Shall have as much again, and ten times more. (263)

In Greatheart's second, and this time a double, riddle, the paradox normal to the genre does not collapse into the interpretation:

> He that will kill, must first be overcome:
> Who live abroad would, first must die at home.

Honest "opens" it:

> He first by Grace must conquer'd be,
> That Sin would mortifie.
> And who, that lives, would convince me,
> Unto himself must die. (264)

The first example unties a knot of paradoxical, implosive speech in which the posed paradox collapses into profitable edification. While glancing at the rich young ruler whom Christ required to abandon all worldly goods, it celebrates the multiplication of "goods" in the language of a commercial transaction. "Nothing teaches like Experience" (263) in the first of the riddles, while in the second "good Doctrine" displaces edifying experience in a generalized affirmation of grace (265) and reaffirmation of earlier transcendent and self-transcendent values.

Other after-dinner activities advance from formal riddles to "a Story, worth the hearing" and "A Question worth the minding" (gloss 265)—the question of whether the young pilgrim or the old shows greater virtues. After a reading of Isaiah 53, the assembly propounds its verses into further formal questions that Greatheart explicates. This process deconstructs the Bible into a series of occasions for practicing the sort of algebraic, or "if . . . then," interpretation we saw operating upon earlier data. The festive sequence generally models godly conversation. From first to last it enfolds its events into the written and spoken Word. Experience presents riddles, or "Hard Nuts" of text, which the Bible explicates, and the Bible presents riddles which the Bible and experience "open," in a process affirming what is so basic to Puritan epistemology, the transmutation of the a posteriori into the a priori.

Like Gaius's dinner party, *The Holy War* includes riddles in banquet festivities celebrating Mansoul's deliverance from Diabolus, but the riddles now equate directly with what the gloss identifies as "The Holy Scriptures," allegorically King Shaddai's "Riddles . . . upon *Emanuel* his Son, and upon his wars and doings with *Mansoul*." Emanuel's exposition of riddles casts his procedures in the theoretical vocabulary before us:

"opened," "evidently *see*," "gathered," "read," and "lightned," "rarities . . . couched in so few and such ordinary words," and "Yea, they did gather that the things themselves were a kind of a *Pourtraicture*, and that of *Emanuel* himself" (116). By definition, riddles align likes with likes, read natural experiential data as divine portraiture or schemes, release previously hidden truths, and capture rare insights in few and ordinary words. To read the Word and the world, Scriptures and experience and the self, is a continuing exercise in solving riddles, in decoding divine inscription.

•❧| I V |❧•

DIVINE SPEECH is essentially figurative, and it is not surprising that Bunyan's *Greatness of the Soul* should call the Bible "the Book of signs" (IX:232). Within that general expectation, Bunyan uses interchangeably a number of terms that modern readers and even his contemporaries sorted out with care: emblem, figure, and riddle we have seen (also II:94); similitudes, proverbs, and parables (III:259 and I:246–47); types, figures, and similitudes (Offor III:462); and even similitudes, metaphors, and "a *momento*" (XI:190 and Offor I:647).[12] For convenience, the following discussion includes these varied categories under the heading *similitude*. The secular standards by which Thomas Hobbes measured similitude in 1650 were aptness, comeliness, and instruction, similitudes themselves being produced by breadth of knowledge. They exploit language appropriate to one domain as a way of envisioning a second in a transaction at once cognitive and emotionally charged. With their three components of substitution, comparison, and interaction, they not merely interact with each other as trope and frame, or tenor and vehicle, but they also set in motion the reader's creative participation in the transaction.[13]

Theologically considered, tropic categories operate as kinds of incarnation, verbally fusing worldly and divine realities. According to *The Barren Figtree*, similitude sorts out into "*First*, The *Metaphors* made use of. *Secondly*, The Doctrine, or *Mysteries* couched under such *Metaphors*" (V:12). Metaphors and mysteries provide the vehicle or invitational carriage of the data and also the tenor or freight borne and produced by an active acceptance of the invitation extended. Metaphor attaches too to the Old Testament, law, and works and mystery to a new dispensation of faith, grace, and creative transcendence of experiential data. In Bunyan's incarnational poetic, the ur-metaphor and the ur-mystery are always and essentially Christ, for through him is fulfilled the pattern within the principle, since Christ's earthly nature allows for accommodated visibility, while his godhead transcends vision (see further in Offor II:234, 283, 422–23, and IX:159). Bunyan extends an image from typography to emphasize the point: Christ "sheweth forth expressly, in capital characters, by all his works and doings in the world, the beauty and glory of the Father" (Offor II:423).

Bunyan's miscellaneous works express a poetics of similitude out of which his allegories operate, following the principle enunciated by William Tyndale that "Similitudes have more virtue and power with them than bare words, and lead a man's wits farther into the pith and marrow and spiritual understanding of the thing than all the words that can be imagined" (quoted in Madsen 78). In ordinary usage, similitude seeks out contingent even opportunistic links between images and themes, and in Bunyan's hands it draws always upon godly awareness generally, if not explicitly upon the Bible. Similitudes both limit expression and unlock very rich expressional possibilities not otherwise to be come by (VI:125, XI:190, Offor II:343, and Offor III:464, IX:170). A visible image gives access to the higher order which it mediates and by which it is transcended. "An image, or the likeness of any thing," Bunyan theorizes, "is not the thing of which it is a figure" and "is doubtless inferior to that of which it is a figure" (Offor II:422–23). Bunyan practices similitudes "because the Scripture seems to smile upon such a way of Discourse" and because "Similitudes, if fitly spoke and applyed, do much set off, and out, any point"; they "illustrate, as well as affirm" (XI:148, III:95–96). God invented such expressional means to *tie up*, *butt*, and *bound* his expression, and "to be an help to the weakness of his people of old" (Offor III:462, 463).

In part I of *Pilgrim's Progress*, Bunyan is self-conscious about his soteriological fiction, and his "Apology" lays claim to the same authority and emulative stylistics as the Bible:

> I find that holy Writ in many places,
> Hath semblance with this method, where the cases
> Doth call for one thing to set forth another:
> Use it I may then, and yet nothing smother
> Truths golden Beams; Nay, by this method may
> Make it cast forth its rayes as light as day. (6)

Like the Bible, part I's "dark and cloudy words" are thus authorized to hold "the Truth" as "Cabinets inclose the Gold" (4). His narrative truth, like Christ's, is *mantled* (4); his parables, like Paul's, contain gold, pearls, and precious stones worth digging for (5).

Where part I worries about fictional similitudes as spiritual temptations for author and readers, part II worries about the needs and limitations of an audience faced with a riddling text. The new goal is

> to stir the mind
> To a search after what it fain would find,
> Things that seem to be hid in words obscure,
> Do but the Godly mind the more alure. (171)

Here Bunyan now embraces "similes" and "dark Similitude[s]" because they more impress the fancy and remain better in the memory than nontropic speech (171). Faculty psychology, social interaction, and moral conduct now govern, not the salvific and authorizing Word, and indeed the "Preface" memorably translates the overall proceedings into what is distinctly a game:

> Besides, what my first *Pilgrim* left conceal'd,
> Thou my brave *Second Pilgrim* hast reveal'd;
> What *Christian* left lock't up and went his way,
> Sweet *Christiana* opens with her Key. (171)

Bunyan projects even the relation between parts I and II of his allegory as the components of a riddle!

It is a small step for Bunyan from "Bible reading" to "reading," that is to "*all* reading," and he appropriates from the Bible the precedent of marginal commentaries that strikingly visualize differences between metaphors and mysteries. Glossed biblical references are notably more frequent and more important in part I than part II (348 to 158). Instead glosses in part II tend to reference part I analogues, or to offer general moral advisories or emphatics ("Mark this"), or even call attention to their own embedded discourses (e.g., 183, 254, 264–66). They multiply in part II but also move this text away from biblical authority and toward mere fiction (Cunningham 236). Part I's glosses "open" particular, theologically expansive awareness, the visual separation of gloss from text itself encouraging layered interpretation. Part II's glosses, however, enjoy a relation of equality rather than of lessers or greaters. They quickly reward and then quickly check any move toward interpretation. They reaffirm general knowledge or consensus wisdom, not the heroic action of the individual mind in quest of its own unique destiny. They represent an emblematic not a sacramental device, imagery not symbol, similitude not synecdoche.

Like allegory, typology is both a system of signs and a process of decoding, and in the context of part II what was once traditional typology metamorphoses into a new mode of epistemology and expression. Traditional typology—that is, the Bible's transtemporal, transdispensational, and transpositional expression—accommodates human limitations through parabolic speech. It imposes chronology upon figural interpretation connecting one event or person that signifies both itself and a second event or person, the second encompassing or fulfilling the first. It aligns two terms within the stream of real historical life in such a way that their transhistorical understanding is a distinctly spiritual act. Traditional typology reads exemplary persons and paradigmatic actions, such as crossing the Red Sea, by way of Pauline practice and such Scriptures as Hebrews 1.1–2: "God, who at sundry times and in divers manners spoke in time past unto the fathers by the prophets, hath in these last days spoken unto us by his son." It devalues temporal sequence while registering that biblical patterns are continuously repeating themselves and thereby makes scriptural narrative constantly relevant and immediate (Auerbach, *Scenes* 54, 53; Roberton 301). Bunyan's *Light For Them That Sit in Darkness* (1675) distinguishes three Old Testament expressions of this sort of types (prophetical, providential, and typical promises) and three typal forms (men, beasts, and insensible creatures) (VIII:60). Christically referenced, all such types, "being virtually of the force of the Promise, . . . are written to beget Faith in the same Lord Jesus Christ" (VIII:63; see also *Genesis* Offor II:423).

The early Bunyan and part I consistently follow such guidelines, while the later Bunyan and part II break free from the strict Old/New Testament parallels to include contemporary applications within transtemporal figuration—in other words, he comes to generate his own types. He was writing just when biblical narrative was losing its privileged status and being subjected to new standards of realism, literalism, and verisimilitude, and when the application of biblical categories to interpret the world we live in was giving way to an application of the world we live in to interpreting the biblical categories (Damrosch 176). Hans W. Frei's overview of the relation of the Bible to history backgrounds this radical change in the nature of understanding and proof. In Bunyan's era biblical commentators saw the true historical reference of a biblical story as concomitant with its making literal sense, while in the following century they assumed that because a passage made literal sense, it proved itself to be a reliable historical report. The former view admits extensions of the literal into the typological, but the latter discredits it both as literary and logical device and as historical argument. In the new mode, the literal and figural senses become opposites not allies. Thus, the seventeenth-century pressure to focus contemporary events typologically reflects, as Frei argues, the breakdown not the cohesion of literal bible stories and historic events (2, 6–7, 4). Among other things what was lost were the analogical sense and the Eucharistic knowledge of history. Instead of Christ as the Word made flesh, Christ becomes the Word *illustrated* by the flesh. Instead of discovering analogical and typological relationships in being itself, the new search is for correlates *in* objects *for* subjects. As Malcolm M. Ross summarizes the change: "Typological symbolism which assumes a fulfillment in the historical but not in the sacramental Christ loses analogical validity and is reduced to the status of metaphorical adornment" (106, 85, 102). In embracing the new figuration, Bunyan may have thought he was more fully empowering the Word that he carried, certainly not that he was draining it of its numinousness.

Samuel Mather's *Figures or Types of the Old Testament*, published one year before part II, both treats typology according to the old rules and theorizes the emerging Puritan variant. The older types are God's metaphorical expression shadowing forth future good things, "an instituted resemblance of Gospel-Truths and Mysteries," recognizable through: (1) express scriptural statement; (2) permutations of names between type and antitype (e.g., David = Christ); and (3) "when by comparing several Scriptures together, there doth appear *an evident and manifest* Analogy *and parallel between Things under the Law, and things under the Gospel.*" Like Bunyan, Mather takes literally the view of Hebrews 1.1, that God spoke to his Elect "at sundry times" as well as "in divers manners." For Mather, traditional typology, "legal Types and Shadows," is just one of seven diverse manners of divine speech.

Mather also presents systematically what occurs in scattered form throughout Bunyan's late works. He authorizes an expanded, innovative typology through a distinction between type and similitude, while widening the new dispensation beyond the person of Christ to include his benefits and thence "all Gospel Truths and Mysteries." From the logical principle that similitudes include both resemblance and disparity, Mather distinguishes between "Types total" and "Types partial" and thence between "fixed Types" and "arbitrary Types." For him, similitudes are partial and arbitrary, but require at least some implicit scriptural grounds; they are not to be merely fanciful indulgence. A compound example attaches a series of "real Types" to Noah's experience with the ark, but also recognizes a number of more arbitrary ones: the ship equals the Church; its pump is repentance; its sails are affections; the wind is the Spirit; the rudder is the Word; the ark's three stories are the visible Church, the mystical Church Militant, and the Church Triumphant. In what is perhaps Mather's chief point, similitudes are used only "occasionally" whereas types are "institutional," *institutional* reflecting a divine author and multivalenced truth, *occasional* moving far toward desacramentalized adornment. As *Figures or Types of the Old Testament* also demonstrates, "institutional" and "occasional" can hardly avoid collapsing into each other when the divine author has transmuted into a human author claiming inspiration from the Holy Spirit operating within.[14]

The new typology claimed the inspired expression of the Judeo-Christian inheritance for its arbitrary, partial, modern descriptors in what Paul Korshin terms "correlative typology" and "abstracted typology." As we saw earlier, Puritans tended to read national history as they read their own individual histories through an Old Testament vocabulary. But by the late century, instead of subsuming temporality within scriptural analogy, they were absorbing Scripture into their own, now-prioritized history. The politico-historical Absalom and Achitophel, for example, displace the mythic Adam and Eve. As J. Paul Hunter has argued, this broadened typology violated the aims of traditional typology while retaining its methods. It "relieved biblical history of primary interpretive attention and instead made this history the ultimate symbolic (. . . 'emblematic') referent of contemporary events"; it collapsed the present into the meaningful past of biblical times to make similitudes out of historical events not just creational objects, out of time as well as space.[15] Appropriating a patterned understanding of the past and divine purpose gave to the chaos of immediate events a mythic dimension, a stability that was also instinct with hope. It promised divine control over the movement of earthly history toward its fulfillment along with the opportunity to participate in such anagogy. Given this chronological readjustment, it is not surprising that Bunyan's late works, like so much else in the age, attach great importance to the Apocalypse. Paradoxically, however, analogical means overwhelmed the anagogical end.

The late Bunyan embraces Mather's typological expansiveness and similarly collapses the traditional theological *type* into the more generalized, secular, and innovative *similitude*. He eagerly draws analogues not just between Old and New Testament eras but with regard to the "gospel times" of his own religious history as well. His late and posthumous works use the word *type* very loosely to mean something like analogue or general spiritual comparison. He sometimes equates type and similitude, but increasingly with the years allows type to cover both the biblically derived analogues and also those he himself piously generates.

This happens with particular frequency in *An Exposition . . . of Genesis*, a work that goes well beyond the book of creation to translate Genesis into a systematic commentary on such other "creatures" as the salvation of a modern soul and the history of the faith. This text is not, or not yet, cast as a sermon or treatise, and although a didactic intention is never far from Bunyan's mind, the expository mode here admits at least some glances behind that manipulative intent. It was left on several hundred numbered scraps of paper at the time of Bunyan's death (Offor II:414), and its remarkably uneven focus and emphases allow us to come closer than polished works would to Bunyan's thought processes.

Any commentary on Genesis 1 will necessarily wrestle with the sequenced data of the created universe, but Bunyan overlays such reference with additional schematized meanings that make very clear his typological base: "Hence it is that other things are also called a creation: As, 1. The essential conversion of a sinner. 2 Co. v.17. 2. The recovery of the church from a degenerate state. *Re.* xxi.5. And therefore, as Moses begins with the creation of the world, so John begins with the gospel of salvation. *Ge.* i.1. *Jn.* i.1" (418). Whatever beings are "without a New Testament impression upon them . . . are void of the sovereign grace of God" (418), and hence without salvational meaning. "There is wrapped up a blessed gospel-mystery" in the Old Testament data (420), and the truth emerges from juxtaposing, even the physical act of juxtaposing, Old and New Testaments.

Bunyan expands creation to the re-creations of the sinner and the degenerate church against a recognition of the Old Testament as material cause and the New Testament as formal cause. The Old Testament power of God gives being to the world and man, while the New Testament Word gives man "form and beauty" and later "framing and glory" (418). A similar relation of ontological matter plus teleological form underwrites metaphor plus mystery, image plus theme, creational world plus Christ. Thus when darkness is upon the face of the deep in Genesis 1.2, the deep is "a type of the heart of man before conversion" (418), and, similarly, a man is without form and void, "until by the spirit of the Lord he is transformed into the image of Jesus Christ" (418). "Let there be light" translates into the Holy Ghost touching human understanding with spiritual illumination in an alignment that recognizes 2 Corinthians 4.6–7 as an overlay of Genesis 1.3. Bunyan goes on to equate the separation of land and waters with a separation of the church from the world with the help of Ezra, Zechariah, and Isaiah (420–21), sea creatures align with men of the world by way of Zechariah and Isaiah, and whales with devils by way of Job in typological transmutations that allow Bunyan to focus upon his sectarian context while giving reign to his unique envisioning of the theological "treasures" within the "earthen vessels" so real to his experience.

When the exposition takes up Noah—and especially the waters and mountains of his flood—Bunyan tags data as "types" in the later, more loose or expansive mode of typology. The waters are thus:

- a type of the way that shall be made for the justice of God upon ungodly men, when Christ hath laid aside his mediatorship; for he indeed is the sluice that stoppeth this justice of God from its dealing according to its infinite power and severity with men. (471)
- also a type of the bottomless pit, that mouth and gulf of hell, which at the day of judgment shall gape upon the world of ungodly men, to swallow them up from the face of the earth, and to carry them away from the face and presence of God. (471)
- a type of the wrath of God that in the day of judgment shall fall upon ungodly men. . . . a type of those affections and persecutions that attend the church. (473)
- a type of persecutors and persecution. (475)

The typology explodes in contrasting directions when Bunyan reads the two mountains of Noah's flood, the first on which the remnant of his contemporaries stood before drowning and the second the emergent and promisory Mount Ararat. The first negative extreme offers "types of the hope of the hypocrite, upon which they clamber till their heads do touch the clouds, thinking thereby to escape the judgment of God" (474), while Ararat is a type of Christ, and "the resting of the ark on the mountain, was a figure of our trusting on Christ . . . a figure to the church of some visible ground of deliverance from the flood" (477). The discussion allows Bunyan to glance at his own procedures in an algebraic reasoning that targets his own place in history and ecclesiological history.

Although *An Exposition . . . of Genesis* does not entirely avoid traditional typology, the first small step from typal characters to covenantal types soon licenses proliferations into contemporary time, persons, and practices. Thus on the fourth day of creation, the sun is a type of Christ ("Sun of righteousness"); "the moon a type of the church, in her uncertain condition in this world; and the stars are types of the several saints and officers in this church" (421). In a further extension, "The heaven is a type of the church, the moon a type of her uncertain state in this world; the stars are types of her immovable converts; and their glory, of the differing degrees of theirs, both here, and in the other world. Much more might be said, but I pass this" (422). In a particularly stretched typological extension, Bunyan describes Eve's genesis in 2.21–22 as "a blessed figure of a further mystery": "Adam's wife was a type of the church of Christ; for that she was taken out of his side, it signifies we are flesh of Christ's flesh, and bone of Christ's bone. *Ep.* v.30. And in that she was taken thence while Adam slept, it signifies, the church is Christ's, by virtue of his death and blood" (427).

Self-conscious glances at his own interpretational procedures manifest a radically altered attitude toward the Scriptures from what we saw in Chapter 3. At a simple level, in identifying Noah's rainbow as a type, he explains: "I find then by the scriptures, where this Bow is mystically spoken of, that the Lord Jesus Christ himself is encompassed with the bow." A more complex example moves from "mystical speech" to "bring in more": "I told you before, That [Noah's] ark was a type of Christ, and also of the works of the faith of the godly. And now he seems to bring in more, and to make it a type of the church of Christ. . . . Now as the ark was a type of the church, so according to the description of this verse [Genesis 6.16] she hath three most excellent things attending her. 1. Light. 2. A Door. 3. Stories of a lower and higher rank" (465). The flood too is called a type of three things: "A type of the enemies of the church," "A type of the water baptism under the New Testament," and "A type of the last and general overthrow of the world by fire and brimstone" (466). Acknowledging the divergences of meanings, Bunyan himself prefers the third. When considering Genesis's specified timing of Noah's flood, he comments: "As to the month, and the day of the month I have but little to say: though doubtless, had not there been something worthy of knowing therein, it would not so punctually have been left upon record; for I dare not say this scribe wrote this in vain, or that it was needless thus to punctilio it; a mystery is in it, but my darkness sees it not; I must speak according to the proportion of faith" (471). The Bible still holds his respect but when a certain impatience tempers his awe, he catches himself up and retreats, as here, to the analogy of faith.

Bunyan no longer anchors his being upon the secured Word. He is now sometimes tentative, as in discussing the mist that arose out of the earth in Genesis 2.6: "But again, *I have sometimes thought* by this mist, *might be held forth . . .*" or again "*I have also sometimes thought, that by this mist might be typified. . . .* but *whatever this mist did signify (in other men's judgment) certain it is,* it was for present necessity" (425, and similarly 456; my italics). Bunyan is also sometimes openly speculative as when commenting on Genesis 4.10 he proposes, "And let me here take leave to propound my private thoughts," a passage glossed in the margin with "Bear with this conjecture" (447–48). He opens and keeps open optional readings as in the discussions of Genesis 3.8 and 4.25: "If you take the trees in a mystical sense as sometimes they may be taken; *Eze.* xxxi.8–11. then take them here to signify, or to be a type of the saints of God, and then the gospel of it is, That carnal men, when they are indeed awakened, and roused out of their foolish fig-leaf righteousness; they then would be glad of some shelter with them that are saved and justified freely by grace" (433) and "Take Adam for a type of Christ, and his wife for a type of the church, and then this observation followeth; namely, That so long as Christ and the church hath to do with one another, it is in vain for Cain to think of suppressing religion" (453). An algebraic formula structures both arguments: "If you take . . . in a mystical sense, then take them here to signify, or to be a type of . . . then the gospel of it is . . ." At other points, Bunyan is clearly impatient at the interpretational process itself, saying in connection with Genesis 4.15, for example: "But my business here is brevity, therefore I shall not launch into that deep" (450). It is hard not to see in interpretations no longer securely authorized by an absolute Word and truth that Bunyan comes to practice just such a compounding of logic and invention as he earlier had labeled "notions" and condemned in the most outraged terms as the idle product of errant fancy. What perhaps saves it as a procedure is that Bunyan is always guided by pedagogical practicality, by sincere devotion to what will edify his flock.

•⦿| V |⦿•

EDIFICATION GOVERNS part II of *Pilgrim's Progress* as it did part I, but the typology, like so much else, is in the process of coming to terms with the needs and benefits of deliberate artistry and the forward flow of history. Bunyan no longer relies upon the sincere projection of himself, and himself as Christian, as exclusive model for imitation. The typological figures of part I are regularly admonitory and inspirational along similar lines; they collapse into absorptive typological models to enact the Christic ideal toward which types point. In the markedly contrasting types of part II, however, energy and affirmation flow toward, not away from, the earthly self, toward future exigency not past perfection, and now radical sincerity gives way to artful manipulation. The new types, shorn of numinousness, serve chiefly as confirmatory or descriptive labels and decoration.

An early interview between Christiana and the Interpreter features the new typology and new scriptural attitudes more generally.

> *Christ.* I am that Woman that was so hard-hearted as to slight my Husbands Troubles, and that left him to go on in his Journey alone, and these are his four Children; but now I also am come, for I am convinced that no way is right but this.
>
> *Inter. Then is fulfilled that which also is written of the Man that said to his Son, go work to day in my Vineyard, and he said to his Father, I will not; but afterwards repented and went.*
>
> *Christ.* Then said *Christiana,* So be it, *Amen,* God make it a true saying upon me, and grant that I may be found at the last, of him in peace without spot and blameless.
>
> *Inter. But why standest thou thus at the Door, come in thou Daughter of* Abraham, *we was talking of thee but now: For tidings have come to us before, how thou art become a Pilgrim.* (198–99)

Christiana describes herself realistically; the Interpreter comprehends her status within the parable of the two sons from Matthew 21.28–29; Christiana then closes the issue; and the Interpreter tags her with a residual typological gesture as "Thou Daughter of *Abraham.*" The first effort to absorb Christiana within a parable layers one edifying fiction within a second, Christically authored fiction. Typologically, "Then is *fulfilled*" (my italics) captures the altered chronology and a new complacency. Christiana as modern typal fulfillment is distinctly noninspirational by contrast with traditional typology wherein, on principle, Christ is always the radically inspirational antitype.[16]

Some other occasions of nontraditional typology are strictly gendered, as in the Interpreter's alignment of Mercy with Ruth: "Thy setting out is good, for thou hast given credit to the truth, Thou art a *Ruth*, who did for the love that she bore to *Naomi*, and to the Lord her God, leave Father and Mother, and the land of her Nativity to come out, and go with a People that she knew not heretofore. *The Lord recompence thy work, and a full reward be given thee of the Lord God of* Israel, *under whose Wings thou art come to trust*" (206–7). The quotation is from Ruth 2.12, immediately following Boaz's commendation of the widowed Ruth's chosen exile from family and country in loyal and loving service to her mother-in-law, a concatenation of events touching Mercy's pilgrimage at many points. In a second example, Christiana typologically identifies herself to Giant Grim and so far generalizes the type as to suppress the name of the biblical figure (Deborah) entirely: "Then said *Christiana*, Tho' the Highways have been unoccupied heretofore, and tho' the Travellers have been made in time past, to walk thorough by-Paths, it must not be so now I am risen, *Now I am Risen a Mother in Israel*" (219). The gloss identifies the scriptural reference to Judges 5.6–7, a text ending with "I Deborah arose . . . I arose a mother in Israel." Here Christiana's biblical borrowing describes her present situation; she does not, as her husband did, transfer herself out of present circumstances into the text itself. These two gendered differences coincide with larger typological and epistemological alignments.

Elsewhere part II similarly manifests a typology shorn of numinous resonance and flattened or domesticated to match the mundane feminine and ecclesiological priorities of part II. A voice at the Slough of Despond proclaims "*Blessed is she that believeth, for there shall be a performance of the things that have been told her from the Lord*" (187) in an echo of Luke 1.45 that chiefly celebrates Christiana's maternal role, the salutation to a pregnant Mary (mother of Jesus) of a pregnant Elizabeth (mother of John the Baptist); Mary then replies "My soul doth magnify the Lord, and my spirit hath rejoiced in God my Saviour" (1.46–47). A similarly naturalized Word credentials Mercy and Christiana after the Bath Sanctification as "Children of *Israel*" (207–8), glossed to Exodus 13.8–10: "And thou shalt shew thy son in that day, saying, This is done because of that which the Lord did unto me when I came forth out of Egypt. And it shall be for a sign unto thee upon thine hand, and for a memorial between thine eyes, that the Lord's law may be in thy mouth: for with a strong hand hath the Lord brought thee out of Egypt. Thou shalt therefore keep this ordinance in his season from year to year." The full reference privileges what is variously characteristic of the undertaking of part II, a religious practice, a church rite, a sign or memorial for the guidance of future religious rite, a ritual meal, in short, the domestic and ecclesiological motifs noticed in earlier chapters. The present gloss offers not so much a precise parallel, translated into biblical numbers, as an expansive interpretational understanding that aligns the present with Old Testament history to affirm chronological continuity and redeem the modern analogue.

Several key names in part II—for examples, Mercy and Honest—derive from a base similar to the norms of part I with some key differences to which we shall return. The handling of names generally in part II, however, follows the lines of the new typology. They attach biblically borrowed labels not resonant types. In this way, Gaius invokes Christian's progenitors from the New Testament and Foxe's *Actes and Monuments:* Stephen, James, Paul, Peter, Ignatius, Romanus, Policarp, and (by allusion) Marcus of Arethusa (260, 349n.), and backgrounds Christiana with a series of Old and especially New Testament women. He mentions none by name (261) even when those names are available in the Bible. These two lists of labels carry the cataloguing or generalizing intent that makes part II so different a social and stylistic document from part I.

Most of the "family" characters in part II bear biblical names. Gaius, one of Paul's companions in travel (Acts 19.29), is "mine host" from Romans 16.23 and the recipient of the third Epistle of John, "the well beloved" one who walks in the truth (3 John 1). Mnason, from Acts 21.16, is "an old disciple, with whom we should lodge." Similarly, Gaius's daughter Phebe, who marries son James, is the carrier of Paul's letter to the Romans described as "our sister" in Romans 16.1. Son Joseph marries Mnason's daughter Martha, the biblical sister of Mary and Lazarus, who is "cumbered about much serving" and is "careful and troubled about many things" in Luke 10.40–41. Honest makes the goal of such biblical tags explicit: "And then said he unto them, *Mathew,* be thou like *Mathew* the Publican, not in vice, but Virtue. *Samuel,* said he, be thou like *Samuel* the Prophet, a Man of Faith and Prayer. *Joseph,* said he, be thou like *Joseph* in *Potiphar's* House, Chast, and one that flies from Temptation. And, *James,* be thou like *James* the *Just,* and like *James* the brother of our Lord" (248). In a telling miniature of part II's reductive theology, Grace is merely an incidental character who passively and offstage marries Christiana's son Samuel (274, 277).

Honest, Mercy, and Greatheart are named according to Bunyan's principles that "names of old were oftimes given according to the nature and destiny of the persons concerned" and that "names are to distinguish

by . . . especially when by the *name*, the *nature* of the thing is signified
and expressed; and so it was in their original, for then *names* exprest
the nature of the thing so named" (*Genesis* Offor 11:495; *The Fear of God*
ix:11). Biblically derived naming, however, intends to ease the transtemporal biblical participation so dear to the Puritan heart, to inscribe
typology upon modern character in hopeful imitation, even incantation,
of the primitive Christianity they sought to "reform." The names are thus
memorial and telic.

Additional, sometimes surprising typological uses, also characteristic
of part II, reflect a weakening of scriptural authority variously symp-
tomatic of the waning Puritan culture for which Bunyan spoke in the
late decades of the seventeenth century. Mr. Valiant-for-Truth invokes
Psalm 27.3 in what becomes a post-Restoration condemnation of militancy: "*Though an Host should encamp against me, said one, My Heart
shall not fear. Tho War should rise against me, in this will I be Confident,*
etc. Besides, said he, I have read in some Records, that one man has
fought an Army; and how many did Sampson slay with the Jaw Bone of an
Ass?" (290). His use of "etc." bespeaks a now casual relation to the Bible.
Greatheart reductively enfolds a series of typological antitheses into the
description of Madam Bubble: " 'Twas she that set *Absalom* against his
Father, and *Jeroboam* against his Master. 'Twas she that perswaded *Judas*
to sell his Lord, and that prevailed with *Demas* to forsake the godly Pilgrims Life" (302). In a distinctly countertypological catalogue, Selfwill
appropriates Scripture to justify his presumptuous self-indulgence.

> He said, to have to do with other mens Wives, had been practised
> by *David*, Gods Beloved, and therefore he could do it. He said, to
> have more Women then one, was a thing that *Solomon* practised,
> and therefore he could do it. He said, that *Sarah* and the godly Mid-
> wives of *Egypt* lyed, and so did saved *Rahab*, and therefore he could
> do it. He said, that the Disciples went at the bidding of their Mas-
> ter, and took away the Owners *Ass*, and therefore he could do so
> too. He said, that *Jacob* got the Inheritance of his Father in a way
> of Guile and Dissimulation, and therefore he could do so too. (256)

Both lists disregard strict alignments in representing the dark underside
of typal expectation. It perhaps goes too far to see in these evidences a
critique of traditional typology, but clearly a radically altered reading of
biblical exemplars has displaced the awe and imitative thrust of part I.

◄◙| VI |◙►

CHARACTERISTICALLY, THE HERO of *Grace Abounding* wrestled with as-saultive texts to attain the comprehensively illuminated and counseling Word of Puritan expectations. Through heroic agons, the Scriptures struc-tured for him both experience and character developments. Christiana's, however, is a fully secured Word, and she and Mercy sprinkle their con-versation with biblical texts as a matter of course. They are much less interested in doctrine than in the human response to experience and find they need only patiently meditate to arrive at the point where biblical texts enclose an experiential occasion. In Patricia Caldwell's image, such meditations serve "as a midwife to the deliverance" of awareness (Baird 92; Caldwell 31); in Foucault's, they translate experience into discourse. In an extreme case like Mathew's illness, a medicinally applied Word can be applied to cleanse the heart and mind (231), but for the most part char-acters just quietly tag experiences with appropriate scriptural labels to set them apart as providences and memorials; they extrapolate authori-tative analogues of ordinary temporal events. The Song of Solomon, for example, lends its lilies of the valley (2.1) to describe the Valley of Hu-miliation (237). On one of their military excursions, the party's men so well keep in the road that, invoking Isaiah 11.6, "*A little Child might lead them,*" a biblical glance more adventitious than comprehensive, for the biblical little child leads a set of unlikely animals into harmony. Proverbs 14.10 crystallizes Christiana's new understanding of her husband's prece-dent in the Valley of the Shadow of Death: "The heart knows its own bitterness, and a stranger intermeddleth not with its Joy" (242).

Christiana invokes Proverbs 13.15 ("the way of transgressors is hard") and Proverbs 15.19 ("the way of the slothful man is an hedge of thorns: but the way of the righteous is made plain") to describe other travel occa-sions (215). In so doing she is turning outward to the Bible, not, as her husband characteristically does, turning the Bible inward. Proverbs, as noted earlier, is a variously apt Old Testament book for the purposes of part II, but between Christiana's two citations Greatheart repeats much of Jeremiah 44.16–17 to assess Formality and Hypocrisy in what proves to be a differently telling biblical reference: "As for the Word that thou hast spoken unto us in the name of the King, we will not hearken unto thee; but we will certainly do whatsoever thing goeth out of our own Mouths, &c." (215). His dismissive "&c." again expresses a casual attitude toward the sacred Word; it also allows him to omit what is inappropriate in the verses. Thus verse 17 continues: "out of our own mouth, to burn incense unto the queen of heaven, and to pour out drink offerings unto her as we have done, we, and our fathers, our kings, and our princes, in the cities of Judah, and in the streets of Jerusalem: For then had we plenty of victuals, and were well, and saw no evil." The KJV argument to Jeremiah 44 describes such idolatry as the "inflexible obstinacy" of the remnant of Judah. A related example inserts a Bunyan analogue into parenthesis within an otherwise biblical quotation: "This Valley is that from whence also the King will give to his their Vineyards, and they that go through it, shall sing, (as *Christian* did, for all he met *Apollyon*)" (239). A full quotation of Hosea 2.15 would conclude, "and she shall sing there, as in the days of her youth, and as in the day when she came up out of the land of Egypt." The texts that arrived to Christian had a way of absolutely crystallizing the whole narrative and psychic action, but here "&c." and textual displacements camouflage analogues that are both stretched for and also only partially apt, reflecting a notably less intense narrative and scriptural allegiance. Curiously, Jeremiah 44.17 is similarly cut short in *The Fear of God* IX:20.

Where part I enacts Sword/*All-prayer* within the narrative, part II merely labels Valiant-for-Truth's sword "*A right* Jerusalem *Blade*" (290) and generalizes: "Let a man have one of *these Blades*, with a Hand to wield it, and skill to use it, and he may venture upon an Angel with it. He need not fear its holding, if he can but tell how to lay on. Its Edges will never blunt. It will cut *Flesh*, and *Bones*, and *Soul*, and *Spirit*, and all" (291). The text seems almost to go out of its way to avoid pointing directly to the Ephesians 6.12–17 and Hebrews 4.12 of its glosses. Additional later description functions similarly: "I fought till my Sword did cleave to my Hand, and when they were joyned together, as if a Sword grew out of my Arm, and when the Blood run thorow my Fingers, then I fought with most Courage" (291). Glosses to the passage cite 2 Samuel 23.10 and then list: "The Word. The Faith. Blood." 2 Samuel 23.10 reads: "He [David] arose, and smote the Philistines until his hand was weary, and his hand clave unto the sword: and the Lord wrought a great victory that day; and the people returned after him only to spoil." A partially applicable verse, one in part also distinctly unapt, contrasts Christian's absorption within the Bible, while Valiant-for-Truth is merely attaching Bible bits to himself.

In general, distancing rather than immediacy characterizes the biblical usages of part II. When Mr. Feeblemind appropriates the self-defense of Job 12.5 to describe his isolation—"He that is ready to slip with his Feet, is as a Lamp despised, in the thought of him that is at ease" (270)— he absorbs the Bible into his own syntax while speaking of himself in the third person. The effect is a labeling and reductive characterization. More complexly, the keeper of the gate relieves Mercy's swoon by the mediating "midwifery" of Jonah 2.7: "O Sir, said she, I am faint, there is scarce Life left in me. But he answered, That one once said, *When my Soul fainted within me, I remembered the Lord, and my prayer came in unto thee, into thy Holy Temple.* Fear not, but stand upon thy Feet, and tell me where-fore thou art come" (190). The loose citation, "That one once said," raises the question whether the name of Jonah is being deliberately or negli-gently suppressed, perhaps forgotten. The keeper imposes the appropriate biblical speech upon Mercy to mediate her experience of deliverance. By translating what she has said into Old Testament speech, elevating her action into patriarchal heroism, and recasting the Interpreter's house as "the Holy Temple," he is also practicing the new typology through tem-poral as well as verbal tagging.

It is sometimes hard to filter out what is and is not directly scriptural in the speech of Greatheart—or the keeper here or the Interpreter in an earlier example—so imbued are they with the book of their allegiance. Greatheart's conversation often not so much alludes to the Bible as shows his thorough absorption of its words and precedents. He tends to enfold similitude within a transtextual amalgamated language (Keeble, *Literary Culture* 251–52). In the Valley of the Shadow of Death, for example, he comments: "This is like doing business in great Waters, or like going down into the deep; this is like being in the heart of the Sea, and like going down to the Bottoms of the Mountains: Now it seems as if the Earth with its bars were about us for ever. *But let them that walk in darkness and have no light, trust in the name of the Lord, and stay upon their God*" (242– 43). This insistently translates experience into similitude, and similitude itself into labels of the typological present. Besides the explicit and itali-cized biblical reference to Isaiah 50.10, Greatheart feels free, as speakers in part I did not, to transform syntax and content: "Who is among you that feareth the Lord, that obeyeth the voice of his servant, that walketh in darkness, and hath no light? let him trust in the name of the Lord, and stay upon his God." What Isaiah presents as interrogative and as dis-tinguishing believers from nonbelievers, Greatheart presents as settled, labeled affirmation. Implicitly Jonah references this passage as the earlier instance, and especially 2.6: "I went down to the bottoms of the mountains; the earth with her bars was about me for ever." In the background also lies Psalm 107.23–24: "They that go down to the sea in ships, that do business in great waters; These see the works of the Lord, and his wonders in the deep."

Members of the family are less free than Greatheart to voice biblical texts, and not surprisingly, Mercy does so more frequently than Christiana. She identifies herself to Mr. Brisk through 1 Timothy 6.18–19: "I do these things, said she, *That I may be Rich in good Works, laying up in store a good Foundation against the time to come, that I may lay hold on Eternal Life*" (227). Later she draws from the Song of Solomon 7.4, Psalm 84.6 (glossed as 84.5–7), and Hosea 2.15 to phrase her response to the Valley of Humiliation (239). When the family refresh themselves at an arbor, Mercy exclaims: "How sweet is rest to them that Labour" (216). She here appropriates only a part of Christ's words from Matthew 11.28: "Come unto me, all ye that labour and are heavy laden, and I will give you rest," and feels free to incorporate that borrowing casually within her own syntax as an exclamatory assessing label. In a similar mode, she invokes Psalm 120.3–4 to judge the memorials of Timorous and Mistrust: "This is much like to the saying of the beloved, *What shall be given unto thee? or what shall be done unto thee thou false Tongue? sharp Arrows of the mighty, with coals of* Juniper" (218). David had used the lines to pray against the calumnies of Doeg that had driven him among strangers in one of a series of Psalms identified as "A Song of Degrees." Mercy's phrasing, "Much like to the saying of," paves the way for likeness rather than quotation, and there is here only a gesture of contextual similarity at best. For her as for others in part II, the Bible serves as a secondary decorative resource, more than as an absolute injunction that, if honored, will lead to salvation and, if ignored, to damnation.

Reading in part I is a priori, while reading in part II is definitively a posteriori. At the sepulcher where Christian was inwardly and outwardly transformed (38), Christiana merely pauses to prompt Greatheart's discourse upon pardon by Word and Deed (209ff.), a theological point raised initially by the Interpreter (190), and thus a matter upon which presumably the party have been meditating since their departure from his house. That discourse, unlike the sermonic norms of part I, does not proceed via doctrines, reasons, and uses, or numbered heads, or even reliance upon biblical citations. It includes a scant three references to Romans and one to Galatians in three pages, and even these are tangential rather than integral to the argument. Narrative setting and travel disappear completely in favor of bare instruction. Christiana offers two brief inquiries and one request for greater clarity, but for the most part her role (and the others' as well) is to be passive, receptive, and memorial as summarized in her responding: "This is brave. Now I see that there was something to be learnt by our being pardoned by *word* and *deed*. Good *Mercie*, let us labour to keep this in mind, and my Children do you remember it also" (211–12).

For a variety of reasons, the two parts of *Pilgrim's Progress* rest upon differing assumptions about reading the Bible. Conveniently for the purposes of this argument, these sets of assumptions are expressed in two Bunyan commentaries on Revelation 22.1, one a part of *The Holy City* (1665), and the other, the whole of *The Water of Life* (1688), one three pages, the other nineteen and one-half in the Offor folio edition. Revelation 22.1 reads: "And he shewed me a pure river of water of life, clear as crystal, proceeding out of the Throne of God, and of the Lamb." *The Holy City* proceeds in a mechanized enumerating fashion to examine individual words of the passage, and long ago G. B. Harrison pointed out that *The Holy City* prepared Bunyan to write *Pilgrim's Progress* by exercising him in the reverse process of decoding—now we would say "deconstructing"—that most knotty of allegorical texts, the Book of Revelation (93). *The Holy City* practices traditional Typology, acknowledges Scripture's "diverse ways" of reading, but itself follows Pauline precedent in interpreting the sun of Revelation 21.23 as "the good and pure Word of the Gospel of Christ, unfolded, opened, and explained by the Servants of Christ; which sun is the same that before you find to be darkened by the *Antichristian Fog and Mist*, which was darkened, I say, even *to a third part of it*" (III:159; Bunyan's italics). In what we saw much of in Chapter 3, Bunyan acknowledges his present interpretation as subject to later progressive illumination and his era as advanced beyond sixteenth-century Reformers and subject to supercession by later insights (III:158, 70). Such phrases as "he [John of Patmos] tells us here" or "he now comes to shew us" (III:178, 182) reflect the textual allegiance of a Bunyan in direct dialogic interaction with the Bible.

In general content and edifying purpose, the two commentaries are very much in harmony, including several direct parallels and echoes, but the later version proceeds through the nature, quantity, and quality of the Water of Life, not through the sequence of the scriptural verse (557). It proceeds also with greater leisure and more rhetoric, reflecting an author no longer totally absorbed within the Word but now aware of audience appeals and of his own positioning in culture and history. It begins by referencing arrays of biblical rivers "for our better understanding" and proceeds, as he says, to "draw some inferences therefrom" (Offor III:541, 543). Realistic features of water are now more important than the sacred Word, though by way of similitude religious meanings lurk just behind "riverness": River water is common and spreads, descends, and causes fruitfulness; it arises from the confluence of many smaller streams and is constantly replenished with fresh new waters; it makes its own circuitous way through a countryside to the sea; every creature desires it; and it cleanses as well as quenches thirst. Realistically too, by contrast, individuals are like ponds, pools, and cisterns that hold little water and that, from foulness and stasis, require emptying and refilling with fresh waters (544). Although biblical analogues are regularly cited, the organizing principle is now not the accidents of biblical analysis or openings, but a reasoned examination of "a creature" in the mode of occasional meditation. Biblical passages are attached as casual tagging or decoration rather than compelling authority. The proceeding is a posteriori not a priori, a reflection upon, an accretion, not an ardent quest for ontology, authority, and wholeness. Furthermore, the healing qualities of the water gesture toward contemporary patent medicines and also the spas at Bath, Tunbridge Wells, and Epsom (543, 558). Its prefatory epistle and first application exploit the vocabulary of contemporary advertising ("bills of conviction"), and indeed self-consciously acknowledge such imagery: "If you ask why I thus allegorize, I answer, the text doth lead me to it" (539, 558).

Of special interest, of course, are what we can glean of the two works' changing attitudes not just toward Bunyan's audience, text, and purpose, but also toward the nature of figurative language itself. *The Holy City* claims the simpler biblical example articulated in the verse "Apology" to *Pilgrim's Progress* part I and elsewhere: "For both the word *Water*, and that of *Life*, they are but metaphorical sayings, under which is held forth some better and more excellent thing. And indeed it is frequent with God in Scripture to speak of his Grace and Mercy under the notion of Waters, of a Fountain, a Sea, and the like" (178). Elsewhere in this early treatise, Bunyan describes the processes through which John of Patmos offers and he himself accepts the offer of attached meaning:

> In that he saith, he *saw* this River, he giveth us in a Mystery also to understand how openly and plainly this River shall in all its Crystal Streams and Currents be apprehended and seen by the Children of

this City; for in this Vision he doth as it were represent in his Person
the Children of New *Jerusalem;* as God said to *Ezekiel* in another
case, *Thou shalt be their sign, and they shall do as thou hast done.*
So here, I SAW, saith John, *a pure River of Water of Life.* I am in this
a signe to the House of the *Israel* of God, and to the Inhabitants of
this City; they shall do as I have done, and shall also see as I have
seen. (180)

The Bible supplies vision as well as a set of representational signs through
which readers apprehend "a Mystery."

Twenty-three years later, *The Water of Life* proposes: "These words,
water of life, are metaphorical, or words by which a thing most excellent is presented to and amplified before our faces" (Offor III:540). A key
difference between closely parallel definitions of the nature of metaphor
encapsulates the differences between the two eras of Bunyan's career and
the Puritan and English history it stands for. The earlier phrasing signals the sacramental, hierarchical, self-transcending trope we have seen
as foundational to part I generally, while in the second, metaphor as
mere "presentation" and "amplification" is fully in line with the emblematic, descriptive, algebraic kind of similitude operating foundationally
throughout part II.

The Holy City presents the earlier, biblically derived similitude when
it amplifies "the Water of Life" with reference to the "Living Waters"
from Ezekiel 47.3–5. The description of Ezekiel unfolding a mystery to
us introduces a paraphrase not an interpretive reading of the prophet's
distinction between waters reaching to the ankles, the knees, then the
loins, and over the head. These stages Bunyan reads as the childhood,
youth, maturity, and eternal life of Christians (III:182). He cites Ezekiel
47.3–4 in the later *Water of Life* to affirm patterns of historical change:
"But what is ancle-deep to that which followeth after? It is said also to
come out from Jerusalem, where, I perceive, were no great rivers, to intimate, that as long as the first priesthood, first temple, and type, were in
their splendour, only the shadow of heavenly things were in use, and that
then grace ran but slowly, nor would run much faster, because Jesus was
not yet glorified" (Offor III:546). What vast distances Bunyan has trav-
eled to reach the point of applying geographical hydrology to critique the
Bible! He now practices the independent interpretation of data and new
typology featured in *An Exposition . . . of Genesis.* By sea in Ezekiel 47.8
"is meant the world, and by fish the people, and thither shall run this

river of water of life" (543). God's chosen are fish, Bunyan reasons, in that water is the element in which they live and in that they die if removed from it (544). Continuing the metaphor, false professors thus may be frogs or otters for whom water is not the exclusive element, and hardened sinners drown (544). What operates behind this is what I have called "algebraic" reasoning. Thus if X (sea = world), then Y (fish = people) follows. When *The Holy City* recognizes the relationship between water and fish, it is to equate fishers and gospel ministers, an equation explicitly authorized by Christ himself in Matthew 4.19 and Mark 1.17, while the later treatise's typology stretches to contemporary church history.

The Water of Life, appropriate to its publication date in the last year of Bunyan's life, provides a summary of the points that have been raised throughout this chapter. It extends the range of typological possibility, integrates Bunyan's views of the Bible from Genesis to Revelation, glances at faculty psychology and occasional meditation, and finally registers its point in the homely imagery for which Bunyan is justly famous.

> Now when this living water is received, it takes up its seat in the heart, whence it spreads itself to the awakening of all the powers of the soul. For, as in the first creation, the Spirit of God moved upon the face of the waters, in order to putting of that creature into that excellent fashion and harmony which now we behold with our eyes; even so the new creation, to wit, the making of us new to God, is done by the overspreading of the same Spirit also. For the Spirit, as I may so say, sitteth and broodeth upon the powers of the soul as the hen doth on cold eggs, till they wax warm and receive life. And this drinking in of the Spirit is rather as the ground drinks in rain, than as a rational soul does through sense of the want thereof. (Offor III:552)

Its Bath and Jerusalem references demonstrate that Bunyan has discovered geography to go along with the discovery of history noted earlier, and the new historical awareness anticipates radical positive change: "The river, then, is nothing else but the fulfilling of promises; the *faithful* fulfilling of promises" (545):

> True, it runs not so high now as in former days, because of the curse of God upon Antichrist, by whose means the land of God's people is full of briers and thorns. *Is.* xxxii.13–17. But when the tide is at the lowest, then it is nearest the rising; and this river will rise, and

in little time be no more so low as but ancle-deep; it will be up to the knees, to the loins, and be a broad river to swim in. *Eze.* xlvii. For 'there the glorious Lord *will be* unto us a place of broad rivers *and* streams.' *Is.* xxxiii.21. 'And there shall be no more curse' in the church, 'but the throne of God and of the Lamb shall be in it, and his servants shall serve him' without molestation. *Re.* xxii.3–6. (550)

The imminent apocalyptic progress enfolds sectarian freedom and triumph in an answerable style. Where the early Bunyan had set forth simple, clear statements grounded in the seeker's impassioned sincerity and scriptural allegiance, now the late Bunyan practices rhetorical strategies and soars in the confident mastery of achieved prophecy.

Conclusion

> The increasing emphasis laid by the Renaissance humanists
> upon the moral life, the relevance of good works to sal-
> vation, and their increasing preoccupation with the active
> life rather than the contemplative, with ethics rather than
> metaphysics, is a development complementary and parallel
> to the gradually increasing priority of reason and nature
> over faith and revelation in religion. This reestimate of
> man's true good is for many individual thinkers and writers
> a change in emphasis, not an altering of the goal. Salva-
> tion in a Christian heaven remains the ultimate destination,
> but the moral life of virtuous activity supplants (at least
> in the interest indicated by the number of pages devoted
> to it) the intellectual contemplation of God or truth, as
> the most urgently recommended exercise leading to that
> destination.—Hiram Hadyn, *The Counter-Renaissance*

Despite a chronological proximity and the variety of information he commanded, no one would designate John Bunyan a Renaissance man, but
he is in a number of ways very much a Reformation man carried to a
late and attenuated extreme. To be, as the late Bunyan is, also a Restoration man is to participate in some trends that Hiram Hadyn labels
"Counter-Renaissance." Theologically, such figures emphasize ethics over
revelation, the living of a moral life over conversion. In various cultural,
technological, psychological, and religious arenas, they advocate sim-
plification along with decentralized particular experience. The Counter-
Renaissance man resembles not such a synthesizing quester as Sir Philip
Sidney with all his graces or Sir Francis Bacon with all knowledge for his
province, but rather the specialist concentrating in one arena of knowl-

edge or experience and proceeding upon the grounds Hadyn captures in this series of contrasts: "Practice and fact, not theory; the particular, not the universal; the intuitive or instinctive or pragmatic, not the speculative or abstract or logical"; in a later formulation, "the intuitive or volitional or empirical, not the speculative or intellectual or logical" (Hadyn 51, xv–xvi, 85).

The seventeenth century witnessed a progressive, widely encompassing secularization. As Malcolm M. Ross remarks, "In the history of culture the Christian rhythm is always away from the sanctification of the profane to the profanation of that which is no longer sacred because no longer expedient." Ross elsewhere calls the seventeenth century "an age of disintegration" as well as of revolution. Varied deconstructions of preceding synthesis emerge in religion, politics, culture, epistemology, and expressional modes. The inherited traditional Christian "uni-verse" disperses into deliberately distinct realms and disjunct priorities. If the components are no longer dramatically clashing, it is because they are moving in such differing directions.[1]

Bunyan is a departmentalized specialist, finding in religious reading and instruction the key to all thought and action and, with the passing of the decades, increasingly targeting himself upon the practical, the particular, and the pragmatic. Bunyan's Puritan progress—and specifically the patterned differences between parts I and II of *Pilgrim's Progress*—is in various ways a shift of emphasis from the theological and the eternal to the chronological, the temporal, and the mundane, from faith to practice, from individual soteriology to communal ethics, from the sacred Word to the artful similitude. This concluding chapter addresses some of the larger progresses that background Bunyan's place in history and his encoded narratives. The family of pilgrims in part II have achieved control over both the external world and their understanding and expression of it. They are not threatened by supernatural forces, indeed are not even surprised by the world around them. Part I's vital spiritual and psychic testing and synecdochic transactions descend into reductive similitude and the control over data and meaning implied in that new, more commonsensical mode. The externalized threats of part I collapse into the ideas and discourses of part II.

Bunyan's century began with at least some shared sense of an ordered and divinely guided world, a coherence lamented as displaced by doubt as early as Donne's *First Anniversary* (1611). After decades of extreme religio-political factionalism, a new science begetting a new epistemology, and a cornucopia of new utensils and social systems, the century settled into stable but very different relationships among things, people, and God. The shared all-encompassing natural resonances of Elizabethan order gave way to proliferating mechanical and analytical awareness in the latter decades of the century and ever since. In one of its larger sweeps, such changing usages reflect differences between the veneration of ancient authorities, as for example Aristotle as student of natural history or natural philosophy, and such adjustments for human fallibility and the cooperative collections of projects embodied in the Royal Society (founded 1662). At its most optimistic, it is a difference between worship of the past and hope for future progress. At its most threatening, it is a breakdown of absolute allegiance to a written Word when that Word is contradicted by phenomenological observation and empirical reasoning.[2]

The two parts of Bunyan's most popular narrative provide a unique nexus of both the empirical observation that helped disrupt that earlier world and also the passionate allegiance to the Bible that believed it could solder the fragments. Part I acts out certain principles of Reformation theology, and thereby clings to some of the older, even medieval assurances. By the time of part II, however, the implications of Baconian thought have begun to catch up with the Christian family (or the family of Christian), and Bunyan's sequel enacts several retreats into conservatism, an inevitable emotional recoil from the forced abandonment of old and safe assumptions and a fear of a dangerous present and an uncertain future. Christiana's world of the 1680s has moved beyond a secure micro-macrocosmic order and hierarchical symmetry into various philosophical disintegrations and political experiences of defeat and of compromised victory.

Bunyan writes not out of the shared understanding of basic principles of order, hierarchy, and analogy that writers as different as E. M. W. Tillyard and Michel Foucault have claimed for the late sixteenth century. He inhabits instead what Christopher Hill calls *The World Turned Upside Down* and *The Experience of Defeat*. Like the larger Puritan culture of his time, he passionately insisted upon a strict biblical Word. So long as that Word was supported by victorious public righteousness under Cromwell's leadership or by the heroics of persecution, martyrdom, and lesser separatist ardor immediately thereafter, the Puritan movement could sustain its vitality, if with less and less public favor and more and more both desperation and relaxation. With the exhaustion of Puritan political hopes in England, and with the easing of Acts of Indulgence and Toleration,

Puritanism collapsed into itself in a surprisingly short time, with only the capacity for some residual shaping of the Whig and Chapel movements of later history. With his death in 1688 Bunyan escaped some later developments, but a number of his posthumously published miscellaneous works, as we have seen, evidence the kinds of adjustments he found it necessary and possible to make toward such a future.

Michael Walzer has called the chain of being "a pre-Protestant view of the Cosmos" (153), and it is certainly true that in its later reaches the theological Reformation entailed a re-formation of consciousness that inevitably left behind this conveniently imaged, ontological static model. The chain located the units of creation on the basis of their material and formal causes rather than their behaviors. It assumed a definable creation not subject to change. For Shakespeare, indeed even for the belated humanist Milton, the hierarchical and analogical structures of the older worldview still held, and multiple, simultaneously functioning planes of natural, cosmic, moral, social, and spiritual reality and experience could be wrestled into poetry by protean art. For our period generally, however, such stasis has given way to the motions of modernity or what we might include under the heading "progress." Walzer crisply weds the image to the argument in saying: "Puritan writers, employing many of the old images but enlarging upon the idea of sin, produced descriptions of chaos which sounded very much like Hobbes' view of nature. And if chaos were natural, there was no great chain" (159).

Foucault explicates the century's epistemological revolution as differences in ways of perceiving and expressing the human relationship to the external world. What are left behind, he argues, are hierarchical analogies, a world governed by resemblances and requiring interpretation. What lies ahead are analysis, a world governed by difference and insistent upon order. The transition is away from a tertiary reading of the world and toward a binary perception where what has been lost is the shared "conjuncture" or basis of similitude. Earlier comparison was at once unified and tripartite, its elements consisting of "that which was marked, that which did the marking, and that which made it possible to see in the first the mark of the second"—in other words the significant, the signified, and the conjuncture. Foucault calls this third element "resemblance," the name also for the composite process. As the seventeenth-century advances, Renaissance resemblance is replaced by the merely binary, hence the reductive comparative mode of the classical age: "The relation of the sign to the signified now resides in a space in which there is no longer any intermediary figure to connect them: what connects them is a bond established, inside knowledge, between the *idea of one thing* and the *idea of another."* What is lost is the profound kinship between language and the world. Post-Renaissance signs are "set free from that teeming world throughout which the Renaissance had distributed them" and henceforth lodged "in the interstices of ideas, in that narrow space in which they interact with themselves in a perpetual state of decomposition and re-composition." Similitude is no longer the shared comprehensive grounds of ordered perception, but occasional expression; it is casual not causal. Similitude is now "a spent force, outside the realm of knowledge . . . empiricism in its most unrefined form" (51–52, 55, 57, 64, 63, 67).

Foucault's earlier mode describes what we have seen governing Bun-yan's practice in part I, the superimposition of hermeneutics and semi-ology, of the learning and skills that, on the one hand, discover the mean-ing of signs and, on the other, enable one to define what constitutes them as signs and to know how and by what laws they are linked (29). This philosophically described difference also explains what we have seen in the similitudes and new typology of Bunyan's later thinking. Ross's cate-gory of the *desacramentalized* captures the essence of the change, for what drops out of Bunyan's late practice—though he would be horrified to hear it said of him—is the authority of the Word, the participation of the interpreting Holy Spirit in the processes of seeing and understand-ing. The end of conversion becomes less epistemological discovery and more psychological benefit (Caldwell 24). In Foucault's secular vocabu-lary, as the key to the earlier *episteme* is interpreting, so the key to the later one is the order within reality itself in which the proper function of knowledge is seeing and demonstrating (40). It is the difference too be-tween ordinary language and what Foucault later calls "literature," that is self-conscious style.

J. Paul Hunter, looking back upon Puritanism's "attraction to the doomed world view" and the "rather desperate commitment to pictorial-ness" that was threatened by the breakup of the system of correspon-dences, recognizes their brave substitution of the equally pictorial mode of emblem (95–96). For him, the seventeenth-century transition from analogy to emblem is simultaneously a transition from *logical* argument to *apparent* similitude, in Ross's phrasing from *true* analogy to *mere* meta-phor (182). When, for example, the earlier organic image of the body politic gives way to the politicized Puritan equivalent of the ship of state, the views of history, humanity, power relations, and similitude have radically altered indeed! It is also a transition between a likeness being "manifest" and a likeness being "put" or created by an author (Walzer 176, 179). At its furthest reach Roger Sharrock can describe Bunyan's age as one wherein "the idea of the universe as a book of the creatures to be read in terms of complex similitudes was giving way after Hobbes to a preference for restricted *trompe-l'oeil* effects and one-to-one likeness" ("'When at the first'" 72). By the late century, organic expression, what Christopher Hill in *Some Intellectual Consequences of the English Revolution* calls "the animism of the old cozy magical universe" (66), gives way to abstract mechanism and "cosmic equality" among the elements of the creation: "The mechanical philosophy replaced the universe of correspondences and analogies, poetic because integrated, animistic, magical. In its place rose the abstract, empty, unfriendly mathematical universe of the Newtonians" (83). After the change, poets often felt themselves alienated from society, even to the point of madness.

In a number of ways, the displacement of Calvinism by Latitudinarianism encapsulates the argument of this book. It shows up in miniature in chronologically grounded changes in Bunyan's style. The preface to *Grace Abounding* distinguishes two expressional modes, the one "plain and simple, and lay[ing] down the thing as it was," the other "higher," more "adorned," and more playful (3–4). For his autobiography, as indeed for part I of *Pilgrim's Progress*, Bunyan knowingly opts for the first of these, but by 1682 he describes *The Holy War*'s style in quite different terms:

> It came from mine own heart, so to my head,
> And thence into my fingers trickled;
> Then to my Pen, from whence immediately
> On Paper I did dribble it daintily.
> Manner and matter too was all mine own,
> Nor was it unto any mortal known,
> 'Till I had done it. (251)

Roger Pooley labels the earlier of these styles "Biblical" and the later one (post-1678) "Colloquial." The former is marked by "austere fierceness," the latter by confidence, control, and imaginative expansion, but also by "Cavalier abandon." These styles align with religious "progress" from "the essentially metaphoric doctrines of the Reformation" to exercises in virtue and obedience.[3]

In figuration as well as in verbal expression, Bunyan leaves behind manifest comparisons in favor of manufactured similitudes, the old for the new typology. Where Shakespeare can generate a Ulysses speech on order or Richard II's projection of self in terms of sun, divine agency, national territory, or whatever, the late Bunyan is locked into generating analogies with Scripture, now no longer the time-honored types of St. Paul and the church fathers, but what Bunyan also called "types," virtually any parallels he could come up with between biblical categories and the church or accoutrements of faith in his own time and experience. This new typology allows him to interpret the observable world according to his understanding of history. If the new science was blurring the divine significance of contemporary events, Bunyan and other Puritans countered by collapsing the present into the meaningful past of biblical times and by modern projections of ultimate spiritual and conceptual realities (Hunter 99, 102). The late ministerial Bunyan, as we have seen, shows an insistent faith in the theological emblematics he is himself creating.

This epistemological transition necessarily heightens a writer's self-consciousness about his inherited and new expressional means, and deprived of one-to-one analogy and consensus "conjuncture," late-century authors sought alternative discourses for comprehending and expressing relations between the physical and the metaphysical. It is not surprising that a provincial conservative like Bunyan would cling tenaciously to certain forms and processes salvaged from a disintegrated world. Moreover, when occasional meditation licensed "readings" of experience according to the accidents of memory and psychic openings, it encouraged accidental, individualized, even contradictory views of the same phenomena, the spider, for example, as the archenemy or as the most ennobling exemplar of virtue. It leaves behind Ramistic procedures for breaking down an occasion into its constituent parts in order to "invent" full comprehension and spiritual insight, and instead practices a mere substitution of one level of theological meaning for another and more concrete one. The earlier analysis presupposed universal integral coherence susceptible to logic, while the later factitious and temporary transaction merely shores fragments against a perceived ruin.

Late seventeenth-century Puritans found themselves caught between assumptions of a self-contained comprehensive world order and an impending mechanistic hegemony. No longer able to participate in the analogical discovery of meaning in being itself, they were forced to seek out in the world of objects appropriate correlatives for their deepest subject matters in what approaches a Cartesian dualism of subject-object and value-fact (Ross 85). In a surprising development, when others lay claim to what had been their province, Puritans found themselves relinquishing reason in favor of a transcendence more elusive than ever. Pooley contextualizes the issue by explaining *plainness* as a contested term between Puritans and Anglicans in the Restoration period, meaning for Puritans "a forthright, unmistakable laying out of the options," and meaning for Anglicans stylistic refinement and restraint, a lack of mystery in discussing spiritual matters. The contestation is thus between class, doctrine, politics, and spirituality, but also between historical epochs (97).

Caught in the dissolutions of spirit from flesh, Ross's *desacramentalization*, caught between metaphorical and mathematical models, Bunyan's Puritan contemporaries generated an at least temporarily workable stylistic synthesis. Although they believed in the plainest of styles, simple and transparent words to convey truth directly, they were also well aware of the opacity of language and the impossibility of bridging the gulf between language and the ultimate realities they sought to express (Damrosch 5). To ease the difficulty, they embraced various means, notably imposing patterns of time and motion, hence "progress," upon inherited schemes. The resulting style could be in N. H. Keeble's phrasing "vital, animistic and significant, a revelation of its divine creator and providential sustainer." To effect the transition or to reempower their version of the older synthesis, late-century Nonconformists developed what Keeble calls a "Providential" style that was allusive, expansive, and all-encompassing. Rooted in Puritan confidence that all things exemplify eternal verities, this style reaches from the present and immediate to all time and space, from the individual to the total range of human experience. It counters the newly fashionable "plain" style and simplistic rationality of the Royal Society by insisting upon the complexity of human nature, the mystical and revelatory power of nature, and divine immanence. It deals, Keeble concludes, "in ultimate realities" (*Literary Culture* 257, 252–53).

Because such a gulf can be bridged only temporarily, however, the goal of expressing such encompassing realities soon enough becomes a mere adjustment in attitudes toward the particular and the general, and, as we know, in expression as in understanding of character and "nature," the general was destined to triumph in the dominant eighteenth-century voices. The waning of consensus systems of correspondence and the post-Copernican loss of the internal aesthetic coherence are matched by the waxing of a new view of "nature," now meaning what is expected and normative in both human nature and natural phenomena. The growing rationalism—or self-consciousness about reasoning—leaves behind the supernatural and the fancy in favor of common sense and judgment, privileging demonstrable and shared truth over personal vision, inspiration, enthusiasm, novelty, singularity. The seventeenth-century fascination with individual self gives way to Pope's "proper study of Mankind [as] Man" (Sutherland, *Preface* chap. 1). Bunyan shows himself touched by such philosophical currents when his 1685 *Discourse Upon the Pharisee and the Publicane* sorts out "a two-fold proof of Experiments" into a distinction between results based on faith and results based on practice, and similarly distinctions among "Scripture, Reason, and Nature of things as they ought to be" (x:216, 214). Because the motion away from the concrete and specific is also away from the Christian and toward the secular (Ross 18), the century's end finds fully in place Locke's philosophical version of "secularized, respectable Puritanism."[4]

◄§| I |§►

PART I OF *Pilgrim's Progress* has always been recognized as pressing to an extreme the extension of biblical doctrine into fictional particularity. By whatever accidents of artistry and history, it presses with equal success toward inclusiveness, universality, the mythic as we saw in Chapter 2. By the time Bunyan wrote part II, the moment for that unique balance between radically conflicting claims had passed, and hence his sequel "progresses" away from an amalgam of allegory and myth and into fiction, away from a concern with a uniquely universalized self and toward representative human nature. As precursive of the novel, part I is often associated with the epic and part II with the novel of manners, alternatively with the novel of character or action versus the novel of manners (Baird 58; Talon, *John Bunyan* 219–20). Part I's internalization of travel gives way—in literary, cultural, and psychic history—to such extremities of external travel as *Robinson Crusoe* (a variant of the personal and conversion narrative) and *Gulliver's Travels*. By the time of *Tom Jones* the interconnections between external and internal travel and travel metaphor have resolved themselves into the normative settings of the great tradition of the English novel. Part II anticipates the novel through its secure grounding in time, place, and human community and continuity. Christiana and her family move less into the transcendence that welcomed their husband and father and, instead—like Adam and Eve at the end of *Paradise Lost*—with wandering steps and slow and with Providence their guide, they make their way into history. Secular activity becomes meaningful not just as an inscription of divine intention but as an end in itself.

Questions of theology and history in *Pilgrim's Progress* reshape questions of artistry, and—to cite just one commentary—Beatrice Batson can commend the unifying literary structure and power and the extraordinary felicity of language in part I even when Bunyan's tools are sometimes crude, while acknowledging part II as a narrative advance at the expense of less realized allegory. As she sees it, part II's rapidly moving and progressive scenes and humanized characters and relationships externalize the inner life into conversations with a consequent loss in allegorical intensity[5] and, I may add, with the real loss of the reader's creative investment in the theological enterprise. For Bunyan and his readers, the comfortable familiarity of part II displaces part I's fascination with ultimates, an exchange backgrounded in distinctions between the metaphysical, where the values are spiritual and intellectual, and the Augustan, where the values are merely social (Walton 14).

Part II's secular artistic base contrasts with part I's securely theological groundwork and aspiration, and when the standards of measurement are artistic, differences between the two parts are more than just chronological. Thus, following Erich Auerbach's *Mimesis*, the two parts of *Pilgrim's Progress* enact two distinctive literary representations of reality in Western culture, part I following the Old Testament style and part II the Homeric (chap. 1). The former attaches the narrative and stylistic features of part I to the spiritual tradition of which it is a late flowering. This Old Testament narrative mode is deliberately selective, mysterious, pieced together, and abrupt; it chooses details for their ethical not their realistic or fictionalistic significance and provides only information essential to a present crisis. The illustrative example of Abraham's journey to sacrifice Isaac may remind us of Bunyan's similar lack of attention to travel detail: "The journey is like a silent progress through the indeterminate and the contingent, a holding of the breath, a process which has no present, which is inserted, like a blank duration, between what has passed and what lies ahead" (Auerbach 7). In this mode, speech does not so much externalize thought as point toward motives and purposes that remain unexpressed (8). Heavy silences and fragmentary speech emphasize only the decisive points of the narrative in a context of suspense and teleological priorities.

This narrative mode accommodates becoming rather than being, the sublime, the tragic, and problematic. It is fraught with "background," that is, the referential depths of multilayered and conflicted personal history and spiritual struggle as well as legend, interpretive theology, and complex social and political interrelations. Stories so essentially concerned with moral, religious, and psychological phenomena are necessarily vertical rather than horizontal. They claim to transcend reality and to present universal history, but these very claims force them to constantly reinterpret their own content (13), enacting the very essence of the mythic mode. As with Abraham's story, it is impossible to put the narrative to the use for which it was intended without active belief, and the stories and the religious doctrine they embody thus practice a kind of tyranny over their readers (12). Secondary and concealed meanings progressively generate new illuminations within a framework that is both open-ended and external to the story.

Bunyan's part I is well described by such art and expectations, for its narrative mode is deliberately selective, and its mysterious omissions frustrate the now usual fictional expectation. Its antiprogressive structure and fragmented, highlighted texture create "openings" which require the reader to bring to bear additional outside materials, in this case a felt knowledge of Reformation Christian, and specifically Puritan, doctrine and belief. The obligatory reader participation, as well as much of its content, imagery, and diction, operate under the authority of a thorough biblical "background." It is written not to convert but to nourish the already converted; it is, in A. Richard Dutton's words, "the product of a mind given to self-justification rather than constructive dialogue with alternative points of view" (443).

Auerbach's alternative, the Homeric representation of reality, attaches to Bunyan's second part, its greater simplicity correlating more clearly with the norms of the novel. Where part I presents demanding narrative gaps and doubles back upon itself in Fish's "anti-progress," Bunyan's sequel offers continuities, completeness, progressivity, and foregrounding. Auerbach's illustrative example here is Odysseus's scar, endorsing Schiller's view that Homer presents "simply the quiet existence and operation of things in accordance with their natures" (3). The entirely different way of developing conflicts in this mode carefully externalizes and uniformly illuminates story elements in smoothly transitioned, leisurely narrative. Clarity, coherence, completeness, differentiation are its governing principles. The author fully expresses a foregrounded world, "a uniformly illuminated, uniformly objective present" (5) whose goal is not truth but realism, not psychic but physical existence. It builds up an externalized world of fixed spatial and temporal relations (4) and, of course, proceeds without suspense.

This mode's narrative continuities, leisure, domestic and societal realism, and its local and temporal foregrounding capture precisely what we have seen in the domesticated, ecclesiological, and differently metaphored world of *Pilgrim's Progress* part II. Part II's characters are more fully developed, its scenes more dramatized and sharply focused than part I's. Charles Baird lists its advanced narrative techniques as "a reduction in the proportion of undramatized narrative and expository material, an enlargement and refinement in the development of separate scenes, a closer integration of successive scenes, and a fuller exploitation of three mimetic capabilities of dialogue. These potentialities are the power of Bunyan's dialogue to suggest immediacy and spontaneity, to externalize inner conflicts effectively, and to convey a vivid, precise impression of the character of both major and minor speakers primarily by *what* they say" (58, and similarly 133). By contrast with part I's rapid narrative, part II "presents many memorable scenes with a sharp focus, sustained tension, a climactic order of events, 'natural' dialogue, and an effectively varied tempo" (75). We may appropriate a Leopold Damrosch formulation to say that part I is "an allegory that keeps turning into a novel in spite of itself," while part II is "a novel that intermittently tries to revert into allegory."[6]

These differing narrative modes attach to some Puritan principles and paradoxes miniaturized in Damrosch's recent title, with Christian in part I acting out "God's Plot," and the family community of part II "Man's Stories." Puritanism's characteristic quest for the epiphanic moment and characteristic admiration of the grace that rescues each separate instant from the void align with Auerbach's Old Testament representational mode, while their awareness of temporal sequence and their tendency to interread daily life and historical events favor Auerbach's alternative and anticipate the novel. Further complications include balancing the particular against the general, transcendent universal explanatory patterns against empirical particularity (Damrosch 68, 61). Much of part I occurs as epiphanic moments and the rescuing grace, while much of part II moves instead and perhaps anticlimactically to trace temporal sequence within narrative data and reconstitutions of typological church history. While the first fictional mode may be, as Damrosch suggests, a retreat to the ahistorical in reaction to the public chaos of the midcentury (61), the corollary of greater stability during the 1680s naturally shapes itself within a more continuous and even narrative line and, of course, allows history itself to assume a more coherent shape. Bunyan's sequel may thus reflect a revulsion against the chaos of contemporary history by projecting a tamed narrative that also sometimes rises above realistic history toward ahistorical typological history. These narrative changes, like the stylistic adjustments noted earlier—from the old to the new typology, from sacramental images to merely decorative similitude—now show themselves as "generated and controlled by the suddenly urgent struggle of a religious myth that was losing its ontological certainty" (Damrosch 15).

In a corollary paradox, Puritan psychology exaggerated the obligations of both self-analysis and self-abnegation and of both predestinate damnation and self-reliantly earned escape. Part I dramatizes the process and results of self-analysis conducted under the threat of predestinate damnation, while part II prefers the abnegations of self in Christiana's motherhood and Mercy's works and offers such actions and motives as means for meriting salvation, acted out within an arena of human frailties and variations of character. What began as Puritanism's emphasis upon a radical self tensely driven to sustained defiance of this world in favor of the next turns out to encourage a recognition of this world as the theater within which God's people are commanded to work out their salvation for themselves in a temporal process that is necessarily more relaxed and flexible.

Damrosch is deeply right in recognizing that, while the Puritans saw themselves psychologically and as individuals, their enemies saw them sociologically and as rigid conformists. Part I presents a full-scale and psychologically articulated enactment of the Puritan vision of the spiritual individualist, while part II describes a sociological reality whose broadened parameters and categories feature closely defined worlds, activities, and social, familial, and power relationships: "What looked from the inside like individualism looked from the outside like rigid conformism, albeit conformism to a rebelliously eccentric pattern." Paradoxically, Puritanism generated a collection of profoundly isolated individuals, even as it insisted upon the most tightly knit of sectarian groups, each keenly intent upon the principles and continuities of its own "separateness." Such groups range from the individual family to the large, newly modeled

Parliamentary army. In its impetus and through much of the seventeenth century, Puritan ideology must be seen as "inwardly, a radical analysis of the self, and outwardly, a radical critique of the social order" (Damrosch 21). By the 1680s, however, that critique had largely faded into settled comforts and conformities.

•◖| II |◗•

PURITANISM IS ESSENTIALLY a religious movement, but as with Protestantism more generally, with the passage of time it bred a coincidental and secondary social theory. In their comprehensive review, Charles H. and Katherine George recognize the paradox that while Christianity exists to bring about an individualized personal relationship between God and the human soul, it also and contradictorily seeks to embrace all humanity within an ethic of brotherly love. It tries to balance the needs and claims of the individual and the group, "the force which presses toward the individual's intimate, immediate, and unique contact with deity, and that which presses toward externalizing, regularizing, and institutionalizing such contacts" (75, 307).

When Bunyan adds the second to the first part of *Pilgrim's Progress*, his compound text incorporates new theological priorities as well as new experiential modes and epistemological assumptions, a change dramatized in transformed attitudes toward the word *works*. The theological contestation takes shape as how to reconcile law with spirit, grace with works, justification with sanctification; how to get from spiritual openings to applied morality, from inspiration to contextualized conduct, from a breaking down of words to a building up of works; how to adjust personal belief and the claims of individuality to public morality and the standards of the community; how—in a scheme of individual election like Puritanism's—to integrate the unique individual working out a unique salvation within the comprehensive social order and thereby make possible temporal and generational continuity; in the sermonic vocabulary, how to make the transition from doctrine to uses. Whether it is the individual or the consensus that is prioritized, how can one go about establishing and maintaining continuity while also allowing for the incorporation of inevitable change?

Chapter 2 examined differences between the first and second covenants as background for Christian's encounters with the threats of the law and the temptations of works, as embodied in Mount Sinai and Mr. Worldly Wiseman, and Christian's later participations in the second covenant of grace, a covenant that makes man responsible for fulfilling faith not the strict obedience of the first. Bunyan discusses the covenants expansively in his early treatise *The Doctrine of the Law and Grace Unfolded*. The present chapter considers two chronological adjustments of the covenantal design, the first a contestation between sequential valuations of works, the second an inevitable declension when early converts' faith accommodates familial salvation, when regeneration comes to terms with generation(s).

Covenantal theology is the cornerstone of Puritanism,[7] and for much of the seventeenth century, Puritanism was able to strike a successful balance between the conflicting claims of the two covenants, between the Puritan commitment, on the one hand, to human depravity and the divine grace that deprives works of value and, on the other, to the righteousness and reasonableness of doing good, between the law's alarms and the gospel's comforts, for as Charles L. Cohen remarks "A superfluity of the Gospel contributes to laxity, while an overdose of the Law leads to despair" (Kaufmann, *Pilgrim's Progress* 18; Cohen 87). In mid-century these differences in part sort out between a Puritan commitment to the First Table of the Decalogue (the first to fourth commandments relating to one's duties to God) and an Anglican commitment to the Second Table (the final six commandments expressing one's duties to others), between obedience to higher powers and brotherly love, between rules dictated by revelation and those deduced by unaided natural reason (McGee ix–x, 67, 70, 189). They sort out also into two very different uses of the term *works*, both deriving as Christopher Hill notes from Calvin, for whom "works are not a means whereby a man can persuade himself he is saved when he doubts it, but are the necessary and actual fruits of the faith of an honest man engaged about a worldly job."[8] Once salvation has been attained, the fortunate soul leaves behind the Calvinistic, predominantly negative assumptions of human perceptual capacities and takes on new awareness and newly vitalized energy. Combining as they do both gifts and opportunities, the "good works" that follow from the second covenant contrast radically with the damning "works" of the first.

As the century advances, these rival claims become increasingly insistent even within Puritanism, and good works—and the reason, nature, and virtue that support them—register more and more largely in Puritan conduct, and hence the different understandings of the nature of charity even between parts I and II of *Pilgrim's Progress*. In miniature, the chief adjuncts of part I are Faithful and Hopeful, while those of part II are Mercy and Greatheart. Christian's interactions with other professors enact spiritual charity, that which aims at benefiting the souls of the recipients—what he calls "heart-holiness" and "Conversation-holiness in the world" (83)—while part II insists upon distinctly practical communal nurturing. It is in terms such as these that Isabel Rivers describes *Pilgrim's Progress* as "defin[ing] the crucial religious conflict of late seventeenth-century England and defend[ing] the position that lost," a conflict for her between Nonconformity and Conformity, between "what can loosely be called the religion of grace (the descendant of Reformation protestantism, represented by the majority of the Nonconformists) and the religion of reason (usually termed by contemporaries 'latitudinarian' or 'moral religion' and by modern historians 'Anglican rationalism' or 'moralism')." The end of the century saw a virtual eclipse of Calvinism and the rise of a much more accommodating relationship between religion and the world or between religion and human nature. The emerging system conflates grace and virtue, faith and works, religion and happiness; it compounds reason and morality not faith and self-sacrifice.[9] Economically, as the century advances, even the principle of good works gives way to the Puritan ethic of good *work*, spiritual calling to practical vocation (Walzer 211).

Of two Bunyan treatises taking up the question of good works—*Christian Behaviour* of 1663 and *A Holy Life* of 1684—the earlier judges them secondary and often neglected by contrast with prioritized faith, whereas the later urges their zealous practice: "Not that works do save us, but faith, which laieth hold on Christs righteousness for justification, sanctifies the heart, and makes men desirous to live in this world, to the glory of that Christ, who died in this world to save us from death" (ix:346). In *Christian Behaviour*, "for a *Work* to be rightly *Good*," it must have the Word for its authority, must flow from faith, must be both rightly timed and rightly placed, and must be done willingly, cheerfully, with simplicity and charity, according to what a man hath (iii:18, 20). The performer of each such work should regard the honor of God, the edification of neighbors, and the expediency or inexpediency of the action itself (iii:20). Its uses recommend James 2.18, to "shew us your faith by your works" (iii:56–57), with the added benefit that those who do good works also provoke others to do good works (iii:53–54, and similarly 58,

51–52). Although "Good Works do flow from Faith," they are not a contractual matter, not properly causes of desired effects, but rather effects of the divine causes operating within the believer. The early Bunyan would endorse William Perkins's definition of a good work as "a worke commanded of God, and done by a man regenerate in faith, for the glorie of God in man's good," and Bunyan emphasizes, as Perkins does, the contrast between Protestant and Roman Catholic performance of such works (George and George 47).

By *A Holy Life* of 1684, Bunyan admits some claims of *living in this world* and moves beyond theory into practice by distinguishing between justification before God and before one's fellows, and attaching the latter now emphatically to visible good works: "He then that would have Forgiveness of Sins, and so be delivered from the Curse of God, must believe in the Righteousness and Blood of Christ: but he that would *shew* to his Neighbours that he hath truly received this Mercy of God, must do it by *good Works*" (IX:251). The Epistle of James is insisted upon to distinguish "doers of the word" from self-deceiving "hearers only" (1.22), to deplore those who *say* they have faith but have no works (2.14, 17; similarly 2.20 and 2.26), and to honor works justifying and making faith perfect (2.24, 22).

Bunyan's usual verb phrase for the relation of good works to grace or faith is *flow from*, and his preferred imagery for the cause/effect relationship of faith and works is that of fruit or harvest (e.g., Offor I:750, 751; X:168, 169, 175) on the authority of Matthew 7.20, "By their fruits shall ye know them." The grace of the second covenant into which one is "adopted" transmutes into graces or "fruits" of daily life, "thy bed fruits, thy Midnight fruits, thy Closet fruits, thy Family Fruits, thy Conversation Fruits," and some possible causes of fruitfulness include "time, Seasons, Sermons, Ministers, Afflictions, Judgments, Mercies . . . awakenings, reproofs, threatnings, comforts . . . Patterns, Examples, Citations, Provocations" (*The Barren Figtree* V:30–31, and see Greaves, *John Bunyan* 148).

Parts I and II of *Pilgrim's Progress* attach these differing constellations of meaning to the word *works*. The covenant of law, uncompromising, just, and retributive, governs part I and foregrounds a presumed sinner, while the second covenant dominates the second part. Its superceding, redemptive law of mercy, forgiveness, grace, and love reaches outward from the unique, severely tested individual toward the containing community and its networks of nurture and service. In complementary bifurcations, Perkins distinguishes faith and love as a twofold summary of the

Scriptures in *The Arte of Prophesying* (338), and John Milton organizes his comprehensive *Treatise on the Christian Doctrine* upon a division between "Faith, or the Knowledge of God,—and Love, or the Worship of God" (*Prose* 6:128). In the words of *Christian Behaviour*, it is the difference between "Spirituals" for part I and "Temporalities" for part II (III:43), between the threat of works and the display of good works, and between the cause of faith and the effects of love.

Besides affirming these dominant assumptions, each part of *Pilgrim's Progress* raises questions about good works flowing (or not flowing) from faith. Part I's Talkative is a hearer and sayer not a doer: "his Religion is to make a noise therewith" (78, and see III:58), and Christian and Faithful condemn him for the "fruitlessness" of his empty profession (79–80), while they themselves are never shown in practical actions for others. Their *saying*, as we saw in Chapter 4, is in effect their *doing* as well. 1 Corinthians 4.20—"For the kingdom of God is not in word, but in power"—governs their separation of Talkative's presumptuous human words from their own fully empowered divine Word.

Part II also complicates the interaction of word and deed, especially through a distinction between pardon by word and pardon by deed (190). As initially presented, these terms occur as a mystery on which presumably the family meditate as they travel. Later Greatheart develops the distinction into a rehearsal of Bunyan's treatises on justifying and imputed righteousness (e.g., x:176–96 and Offor 1:300–312). As Greatheart explains, Christ grants salvation not simply by the word or promise of forgiveness—the pardon of part I—but by "perform[ing] Righteousness to cover you, and spil[ling] blood to wash you in." Such "Pardon by the deed done, is Pardon obtained by some one, for another that hath need thereof" (209); it governs part II. Greatheart moves beyond these large principles of covenantal theology to consider Christ's two natures and several righteousnesses, also a favorite topic of numerous Bunyan treatises. Although part II is generally remarkable for its narrative and theological simplicity, this Greatheart discourse so much compresses large areas of Puritan theology as to elude all but the thoroughly initiated. Both Greatheart here and part II generally package materials presumed to be familiar, and in this as in other matters lose the narrative intensity of part I and of *Grace Abounding* based on struggle, triumph, crisis, or even ardent propagandizing.

For the less than fully initiated modern reader, *A Holy Life* sorts out some of the complexities of Greatheart's explication by recognizing "a twofold Faith of Christ in the World," the two agreeing as to Christ's justifying righteousness but differing as to their application (IX:252, and see 257). What was sufficient for salvation for the earlier purposes of part I—here labeled "the first faith"—is now seen as "the *non-saving* faith, stand[ing] in speculation and naked knowledg of Christ, and so abid[ing] idle" (252). By contrast, the second faith "truly seeth, and receives him, and so becometh Fruitful" (252). Such "second Faith" for our purposes governs part II of *Pilgrim's Progress*, also published in 1684. Now faith is required to move the soul to good works, and to reject not only Old Testament legalism but also easily accomplished works: "There are Works that cost nothing, and Works that are chargeable: And observe it, The unsound Faith will chuse to it self the most easie works it can find. For example, there is Reading, Praying, hearing of Sermons, Baptism, Breaking of Bread, Church fellowship, Preaching, and the like: and there is mortification of Lusts, Charity, Simplicity, open-Heartedness, with a liberal Hand to the Poor, and their like also. Now the unsound Faith picks and chuses, and takes and leaves, but the true Faith does not so" (IX:254). Bunyan's 1684 position recognizes that reading and hearing the Word, the theological priorities of part I and *Grace Abounding*, may themselves be merely self-indulgent if they are not transmuted into generous action (IX:254).

   A Holy Life not only endorses the proposition of James 2.17, that "Faith, if it hath not Works is dead, being alone," but proceeds to the encouragement of Titus 2.14: "And when men have said all they can, they are the truly redeemed, *that are zealous of good works*" (IX:346). In the late Bunyan's view, the keeping of divine commandment and covenant reduces essentially to "loving the Brethren" (IX:260). Within the dominant travel metaphor, where part I emphasized the *Way*, part II emphasizes *walking*, and that walking literalizes the New Testament injunction to "walk in newness of life" (Romans 6.4 and see 7.6). Part II's adjustment of priorities answers to changes in Bunyan's own personal covenantal experience, but also—and conveniently—to his assumption of ministerial oversight of a diverse, digressive, occasionally unruly flock. The success of Bunyan's new "profession" depends upon fellowship and peace, and such converts as he himself once was test the limits of a community's good will and stability.

COVENANTAL THEOLOGY, even in its origins, was an ingenious strategy for balancing ardently embraced but irreconcilable Puritan aspirations:

> Flowing from the piety, from the tremendous thrust of the Reforma-
> tion and the living force of the theology, came a desire to realize on
> earth the perfect church order, cleansed of corruption and purified
> of all unregeneracy. At the same time, springing from the traditions
> of the past, from the deep and wordless sense of the tribe, of the
> organic community, came a desire to intensify the social bond, to
> strengthen the cohesion of the folk. And finally, prompted by the
> newer political and economic forces, fathered by the disruptive im-
> pulses which even then were smashing the last segments of medieval
> unity, came the powerful sense of the individual, of the supreme
> importance of the will, of the motives which were producing in
> England the theories of constitutional limitation and government
> by consent. (P. Miller, *New England Mind* 440)

These are conflicts not just between ideals and reality but between the individualistic and the sociopolitical, between New and Old Testament authorities, and between a Reformation retrospective and a vision of progress (Johnson 20). For Arthur E. Barker, the polarizing conflict—what he calls "the Puritan dilemma"—pits reformation against liberty and faith against progress, a conflict that for him translates into public policy tensions "between God's will and free will, righteousness and un-restrained activity, fate and individual responsibility" (20). Along similar lines, Diane McColley translates the Puritan revolution's battle cries for truth and liberty into the domestic categories of purity and charity: "For the individual, the problem is whether it is possible to consort with 'pub-licans and sinners' and keep one's constancy to God; for the church, it is whether strict and immutable forms of government and observance are necessary to avoid error and corruption, or whether discipline may be ac-commodated to the conditions of men with the general guidance of scrip-ture and the Holy Spirit" (166). In view of such divergences, the wonder is not that Puritanism flowered for such a brief time but that the system held together as long as it did. In England that duration was underwritten by Cromwellian politics, and for the middle decades of the seventeenth century, Boyd Berry's memorable image recognizes a theological ideal in-separable from the political history of its real context: "dreams of a single walk with God danced in polarized and polarizing heads with visions of a massed army in good order" (206).

We have seen part I of *Pilgrim's Progress* as expressive of purity and reformation—and Reformation—and part II as expressive of liberty and charity. Part I's theology still hopes to realize the contradictory vision just outlined, while part II shows the system unraveling. That unraveling occurs just at the intersection of regeneration and generation, of the atemporal conversion of the individual with time-defined family and church continuities. For Bunyan, the model moves beyond the dilemma with its disjunctive, equally pressuring, and coextensive alternatives, to a historical and cultural causal linearity. Puritanism, both when it enjoyed political power and when it did not, was driven by intense hopes for the future. When the Restoration erased immediate millennial expectations, its followers were obliged, among other things, to redefine their future in terms of their own progeny, and this entailed a number of adjustments as important as those we have seen in epistemology and theology.

Whether we assume a six-year separation between the publication of the two parts of *Pilgrim's Progress* or fourteen or more years between their writing,[10] key differences between the two texts are distinctly generational. Churches as well as the individuals that make them up are subject to a maturing process, and by 1684, of course, the heroic dissenters of the mid-century had significantly aged. In youth, sectarian churches, like Bunyan himself, could be vitalized by political persecutions in line with the principles outlined by Roger Bainton that "a segregated community thrives on persecution. It needs something like the ghetto for the preservation of its own morale. Contact with the outside and fraternization insidiously induce conformity."[11] But in the aftermath of the Civil War and monarchic restoration, faced with official Acts of Indulgence and Toleration, faced too with ameliorating economics and comforts, it is inevitable, in Roger Sharrock's words, "that the sect founded by converts to produce more holy individuals should, in mingling them together, produce a communal life of a new type: the inner purity so earnestly sought gives place, without any necessary hypocrisy, to the cultivation of certain outward marks of conformity to the type." These designs, writ large in history, are encoded in Bunyan's double text, and part II especially bespeaks a people settling into a longed-for stability and more comfortable religious practice. Commentators describe part I as enacting a crisis theology while part II reflects "a less heroic age" and becomes "an interesting commentary on the capacity of middle age, whether in an individual or a community, to reduce an overwhelming spiritual experience to more manageable proportions" (Newman 237, 241; Sharrock, *John Bunyan* [1968] 138, 141, 153). Thus contextualized, the theology that fuels part I appears not just tormented but dangerously destructive, and part II a wholesome and normative "progress."

Despite certain kinds of advancement, the changes are generally recognized as encoding the recurring paradox of Christian history, that the more vigorous the institution, the less vigorous the faith. Decline appears inevitable when individualized moral and spiritual capacity tries to adjust to the institutionalized forms and constraints its own evolution entails. In brief, church mediation turns into church power, and theology into politics. When the early Protestant doctrine of the priesthood of all believers gives way to institutionalized religious practice and then to newly "purified" or "Puritanized" institutional practice, its intense and vital "progress" lapses into the relaxed and mechanical, its progressive inward revelation into a religion outwardly expressed in ritual and good works. The church becomes not just a convenient and stable institution for religious practice but a system for social and personal control, homogenizing its members and demanding regularly ratified loyalty to itself and outwardly expressed conformity (George and George 27–28). The two parts of *Pilgrim's Progress* demonstrate the corollary that a restrictive church membership based on individual purity limits the minister's authority, while a more comprehensive—particularly second-generational—membership policy magnifies the ministerial office (Morgan, *Visible Saints* 143). Hence, part II's presentation of a dominant Greatheart, a submissive congregation or "family," insistent church practices, and enhanced expressive things and acts.

Such cultural declension is variously underwritten by the Bible and not just in the displacement of traditional typology by new tropic transactions. It is no accident that the biblical authorizations of recent arguments, as for example those on good works, rest not upon the mainstream Pauline thought that dominated discussion of the biblical Word and traditional typology but upon the minor epistles of James and Peter. *A Holy Life* explains why some late Pauline epistles may be grouped along with these. When the apostles departed from converted territories they left lesser evangelists to continue the work of Christ in the world, but upon that exchange "usually there did arise some bad Spirits among those people, where these were left for the furtherance of the Faith" (IX:261). Specifically, Paul's epistles to Timothy and Titus advise "how to carry it towards their disturbers . . . not only Doctrinally, but also by shewing them by his example and practice, what he would have them do" (IX:262). The doctrine of *A Holy Life*, 2 Timothy 2.19—"And, Let every one that nameth the name of Christ depart from iniquity"—calls for a reactive negation of evil rather than active affirmation of good. It inscribes a truth that requires not *proof* but *practice* (IX:298), not the stuff of Puritan sermons but the outward demonstration of good through works.

John S. Coolidge's *The Pauline Renaissance in England: Puritanism and the Bible* has much to say of the basic antithesis between regeneration and generation in Paul's thinking about the Church, "the latent difficulty of adopting to a historical situation a set of conceptions describing a peculiar eschatological one" (84, 94). Paul's principles of edification apply to the individual's struggle for spiritual maturity and perfection but not to the ongoing history and quantitative increase of the Church. Not only can Pauline edification not sustain generational continuity or ecclesiastical institution, it "positively militates against the historical extension of the Church beyond a single generation of converts to Christ" (78). Seventeenth-century Puritan theology appropriated Paul's discussion of the covenant with Abraham, however, to affirm the church as a present living process and to relegate its temporal continuity to the old dispensation. It made generation and regeneration correspond to old and new dispensations and also to the visible and invisible churches. In sum, "generation establishes the historical identity of the visible Church, regeneration the timeless identity of the invisible" (95). For many Puritans, the issue of succeeding generations hinged upon whether to affirm or reject baptism of infants. To reject is to insist that the church's identity resides in the individual, the spontaneous, and the present or timeless, while to baptize infants asserts the church's secular and thus temporal identity (149–50). On this subject we have no late Bunyan views, but the early Bunyan judged infant baptism to be irrelevant to salvation in *Doctrine of the Law and Grace Unfolded* (II:182), and Bunyan, the Open Communion Baptist controversialist of 1672–74, did not insist upon even adult baptism as a condition of church entrance.

Generationally as ethically, the challenge is how to translate the excitement and energy of initial achievement into continuity. Moral and spiritual exclusivity set Puritans apart from the unregenerate, but not of course from their own children. Transferring the faith from elders to juniors entails an inevitable slippage or dilution, the more troubling when church members of the first generation perceive themselves as declining in both grace and good works. The fact that prosperity threatened separatist membership as earlier persecutions had not adds to the difficulty. For whatever reason, an increasingly secularized church practices a theology of contracted sensibility with "gestures replacing feelings; taste subduing zeal; pride elbowing out humility; intellect playing a game; divided souls acting a part their ancestors have forced on them."[12] This constellation of change may explain why for Bunyan, as for Puritanism generally, the strict fire-and-brimstone theology of original sin gradually gave way to a more ameliorative emphasis upon Christ and saving grace and why, under various historical pressures, covenantal theology expanded beyond the contrasting covenants of works and grace and into such devices as New England's Halfway Covenant of 1662, a strategy extending the covenant to the institutions of family, church, and state, and allowing personalized grace to give way to grace by genealogical succession. By analogy with the salvation of Abraham's seed along with the patriarch, the American extension of the covenant offered a spiritual insurance policy for a believer's underage children. When the Halfway Covenant becomes, in Alan Simpson's words "just a halfway house between a church from which all but the saint had been excluded and one in which all but the flagrant sinner was admitted," conformity and something like a parochially arranged religious establishment are just a step away (34–36).

As younger generations were unable to carry on the taxing faith of their fathers, New Englanders evolved what Perry Miller calls "federal theology." Its ecclesiastical theory recognizes grace as inherently capricious, chaotic, and anarchic and seeks to build a law-abiding society out of voluntary subjection and outward conduct presumed to mirror inward rectitude. It makes piety a civic duty (*New England Mind* 462), and the mere obedience to an external order that ensues leaves behind immediate individualized confrontation with God and a covenant of grace in favor of a covenant of works of increasing conformity and subsiding energy. When, in Edmund Morgan's nice phrase, theology becomes the handmaid of genealogy, however, the group is also contracting to give external obedience rather than faith and to receive external, temporal prosperity rather than salvation.[13] When religious experience does not prove hereditary, the organization and habit of second-generation church members displace the spiritual openings and progressive revelation of the first, and professions of obedience replace professions of faith and conversion narratives, shaking the very foundations of sectarian community.

English sectarians concentrated their energies on educating their young to offset original ignorance as well as original sin and thereby extend the family, and also the church, into times to come, believing that covenantal theology increased the likelihood of their children's salvation even if its promise was merely conditional. Puritan views of childhood, the future, and education contrasted sharply with Anglican ones. Seventeenth-century conservative Anglicans, according to Leah Marcus, saw children as representing an idealized, innocent past lost to adulthood, symbolically linked with an idealized England predisposed toward a medieval, preindustrial, and agrarian world, closed, static, and collective. Such assumptions underscore what Marcus calls "cultural despair." By contrast, contemporary Puritans viewed children as the best hope of a generational future, grounded in progress, individualism, and commercial enterprise. Anglicans saw children starting out good and becoming bad, while Puritans saw them starting out bad and (potentially) becoming good.[14]

On the instruction of children, as on so many other matters, Bunyan's early and late views miniaturize differences between the theoretical convert and the ameliorative minister. In *I Will Pray With the Spirit* of 1662, Bunyan urges his audience to teach their children, "thine sweet babes" (!), to pray not by teaching them set prayers, but rather by

> tell[ing] their Children what cursed Creatures they are, and how they are under the wrath of God by reason of original and actual sin: also to tell them the nature of God's wrath, and the duration of the misery. . . . Learn therefore your Children to know their wretched state, and condition; tell them of hell fire, and their sins, of damnation, and salvation: the way to escape the one, and to enjoy the other (if you know it your selves) and this will make tears run down your sweet babes eyes, and hearty groans flow from their hearts; and then also you may tell them to whom they should pray, and through whom they should pray; you may tell them also of Gods promises, and his former grace extended to sinners, according to the word. (II:268–69)

Children, like adults, says Bunyan, should pray from conviction of sin, and the early Bunyan thinks that "to be busie in learning children forms of prayer, before they know any thing else, it is the next way to make them cursed hypocrites, and to puff them up with pride" (II:269).

In contrast, the ministerial Bunyan of 1686 proffers sugar-coated instruction in his *Book For Boys and Girls*:

> Wherefore good Reader, that I save them may,
> I now with them, the very *Dottril* [dotard] play.
> And since at Gravity they make a Tush,
> My very Beard I cast behind the Bush,
> And like a Fool stand fing'ring of their Toys;
> And all to shew them, they are Girls and Boys. (vi:190–91)

This volume in fact supplies memorizable versions of such "set prayers" as "Upon the Ten Commandments" (I), "Upon the Creed" (X), and "Upon the Lord's Prayer" (IV). These verses certainly seem to recommend the memorization earlier condemned, the more so as they immediately follow elementary instruction in consonants, vowels, names, and numbers.

The early *Doctrine of the Law and Grace Unfolded* shatters the claims of genealogical salvation in the most vigorous and biblically authorized terms:

> Again, some men think, that because their parents have been religious before them, and have been indeed the people of God, they think if they also do as to the outward observing of that which they learned from their forerunners, that therefore God doth accept them. . . . They do think that because they do spring from such and such, as the Jews in their generations did, that therefore they have a priviledge with God more then others, when there is no such thing: but for certain, if the same faith be not in them, which was in their forerunners, to lay hold of the Christ of God, in the same spirit as they did, they must utterly perish, for all their high conceits that they have of themselves. (ii:179–80)

This early Bunyan opts for Pauline edification and the timeless gospel targeted upon a community of adults who have knowingly and painfully chosen the Christian life. The later Bunyan, however, wields the scriptural ideal as a goal toward which church members work rather than as a standard of measurement against which they inevitably fall short. In this vein, Christiana's children are welcomed within the Wicket Gate with the familiar "Suffer the little children to come unto me" of Matthew 19.14, Mark 10.14, and Luke 18.16 (189), while Mercy—here reconstituting Christian's first-generation experience—is left outside and requires intercession by other than generational means. When the entrance is to church membership rather than to the Interpreter's awakenings, Christiana and all with her are joyfully welcomed to House Beautiful as adjuncts of Christian rather than through their own claims or merits.

Including children within a congregation necessarily lowers the level of spiritual intensity, and when the church leaves behind the primary task of mediating salvation to desperate sinners, it becomes instead a system for passing along gospel tenets and hopes to posterity and for perpetuating itself, even while it is defining itself according to past achievement rather than future goals. When the minister's role shifts from conversion and controversy, often among the antagonistic and recalcitrant, to instruction of the meek, it loses its intellectual edge, as expansive proselytizing or evangelical zeal gives way to contained self-interest. *Come, and Welcome, to Jesus Christ* (1678) distinguishes two targets of spiritual and ministerial attention as "two Sorts of sinners" coming to Christ: "First, *Him that hath never, while of late, at all, began to come. Secondly, Him that came formerly, and after that went back; but hath since bethought himself, and is now coming again*" (VIII:304). Bunyan judges the former an easier ministerial task, for a ministry primarily targeting the second group must wrestle not with grace, faith, adoption, and imputed righteousness but with hypocrisy, backsliding, and spiritual enervation, and hence the late Bunyan's emphasis on false professors.

Bunyan treatises from 1663 and 1683 consider sin in the family context, and that twenty-year interval magnifies their declensional differences. In the earlier *Christian Behaviour*, the father assumes an exemplary, authoritarian role analogous to the pastor. His highest priority is his family's spiritual state and his utmost endeavor is "to encrease Faith where it is begun, and to begin it where it is not" (III:22). Subjection and moderation, order and harmony, are the household watchwords; provision, correction, and spiritual instruction define parents' relation to children, and obedience and honor that of children to parents. This work grounds good relations with neighbors in godly conversation, courtesy and clarity, humility, discountenancing sin, and circumspect speech, and recognizes that bad relations grow out of covetousness, pride, and uncleanness (44).

A Holy Life of 1683 still holds the father and mother spiritually responsible for their household, but it assumes parental frailty, flexibility, hypocrisy, and self-indulgence, as in this sample: "Consider with thy self, whether thou hast done such duty and service for God in this matter, as, setting common frailties aside, thou canst with good Conscience lift up thy face unto God" (IX:323). It calls upon professors to depart especially from all *appearance* of sin. "What a man is at home, that he is indeed. . . . And a good report from those most near, and most capable of advantage to judge, is like to be truer than to have it only from that which is gotten by my observers abroad" (IX:322). Such comments show more flexible, less rigid assumptions and expectations than governed *Christian Behaviour*, for now faith, reprobation, and grace have given place to "conduct" and "report" and "observers abroad," behavior before a merely human audience. In a radical socialization of the kind of burden Christian carried at the beginning of his journey, the individual's moral decline ripples through the social fabric of "spectators" so that the lapsed professor drags others down with him. Against such error Bunyan exclaims, "Better no professor than a wicked professor: better open profane, than a hypocritical namer of the name of Christ: And less hurt shall an one do to his own soul, to the poor ignorant world, to the name of Christ, and to the Church of God" (IX:342–43).

   A Holy Life's subcategories of sinfulness include "family-iniquity" or "house-iniquity"; "Constitution-sin" (the sin specific to an individual temperament); "the iniquity of the times"; and iniquities of divisive opinions, of hypocrisies, and of the closet (IX:319, 312, 315, 329). In the strongest contrast with *Christian Behaviour*, *A Holy Life* specifies household iniquities as quarreling, wantonness, and disorderly children and servants (IX:319). In the first, husband and wife not only fail to maintain peace within their threshold but sometimes secretly cherish and fuel such discord (319). Unlike the domestic order and harmony envisioned in *Christian Behaviour*, Bunyan now finds the children of even professing parents to be irreverent, disrespectful, saucy, and malapert. So far has the fifth commandment been left behind that modern children act "as if the relation was lost, or as if they had received a dispensation from God to dishonour, and disobey Parents" (IX:320). No wonder the late Bunyan and Puritanism found it appropriate to approach a younger generation thus declined with carrots rather than birches! Adult children are said to be equally and shamefully guilty of lording it over their ancient and exhausted parents.

◄◙| IV |◙►

Christian Behaviour assumes an enacted ideal within the compelling present, while *A Holy Life* contextualizes advice within historical change, specifically "the iniquity of the times." It sees its era—1683—as a time of "dangerous *Lethargy*" and superfluous naughtiness (IX:257). To professors who complain of spiritual deadness in duties, barren ministers, and a withdrawn God (IX:317), Bunyan counters with the righteousness of

God's anger against self-serving professors who have polluted his name, his Word, and his ordinances and too often converted only temporarily and halfheartedly (256, 281). He details the causes of declension—also called "returning, or falling away again into iniquity" (286)—as weak original conversion, withdrawn or forgotten conversional influences, and grace weakened and overpowered by corruption—later listed as unbelief, hardness of heart, polluted sense and reason, and pride (286, 296, and see VIII:49).

As with earlier collections of evidence, Bunyan projects declension upon both typological individuals and church history. While the Bible commends Noah, Lot, and Christ for standing apart from the dominant evil of their eras, Moses had to "preadmonish" Israel against a spiritual falling off amongst the plenty of Canaan (*Genesis* Offor II:494), and in *A Holy Life* even the strongest scriptural figures of faith—Moses, Job, Daniel, and Paul—found themselves "assaulted with corruptions, or attended with very hard service for God, of their weakness, and insufficiency, as to a compleatness of doing the will of God" (IX:293–94). *An Exposition . . . of Genesis* reads a declension in Noah, who had been uniquely singled out for salvation because of his stand against the iniquity of his era, yet who after he left the ark lapsed from preaching into drunkenness (Offor II:494). The similarly chosen Lot committed incest; David murdered; and Peter swore and lied. The commentary on Genesis 11.1–2 recognizes a pattern of decline when closed and persecuted societies lapse into wider social intercourse and worldly comforts:

> Hence note, That the first and primitive churches were safe and secure, so long as they kept entire by themselves; but when once they admitted of a mixture, great Babel, as a judgment of God, was admitted to come into their mind. . . . So long as the church endured hardship, and affliction, she was greatly preserved from revolts and backslidings; but after she had turned her face from the sun, and had found the plain of Shinar; that is, the fleshly contents that the pleasures, and profits, and honours of this world afford; she forgetting the word and order of God, was content with Lot, to pitch towards Sodom; or, with the travellers in the text, to dwell in the land of Babel. (Offor II:501)

Bunyan generalizes the pattern as "A right resemblance of the degenerators' course in the days of general apostasy, from the true apostolical doctrine, to the church of our Romish Babel" (Offor II:501).

What *A Holy Life* specifies as the "iniquity of the times" (IX:315) does not exactly make participation in history a sin; it objects to an idolatry of one's own time and place rather than a prevailing specific practice, to preferring the temporal self over the eternal divine will. Against the model of earlier believers who cried out, as does Christian in *Pilgrim's Progress* part I, "What must I do to be saved?" modern professors, "if they will acknowledge that such things were with them once, they do it more like images and rejected Ghosts, than men. They look as if they were blasted, withered, cast out and dryed to powder, and now fit for nothing, but to be cast into the fire, and burned. The godliness from which they are departed, and the iniquity unto which again they have joyned themselves, has so altered, so *metamorphosed*, and changed their heart, and mind, and ways" (IX:290). Even the virtues appropriate to the later era are openly time-based: "an enduring to the end, a continuing in the word of Christ, and also a keeping of the word of his patience" (IX:347). Decline, exhaustion, perseverance, and repining over lost glory set the new tone and show the middle age, or even old age, of faith rather than the youth of the urgent Christian of part I or of *Grace Abounding*.

Christiana's narrative refers often to changing times. "Notwithstanding the Command of the King to make this place for Pilgrims good," they find the Slough of Despond "rather worse than formerly" (187). Pilgrims' enemies have muddied the clear spring at Hill Difficulty and reinforced the threatening lions before House Beautiful (214, 218). "Spots and Blemishes," overgrown grasses, and briars and thorns disfigure the Way (277, 218, 295–96). In an echo of Hebrews 11.13, now "there are many that go upon the Road, that rather declare themselves Strangers to Pilgrimage, then Strangers and Pilgrims in the Earth" (276). Some of the new threats are not of discovery but of endurance and target not the individual professor but the sect. Thus in an updated guise, Simple, Sloth, and Presumption "began to villifie his Servants, and to count the very best of them meddlesome, troublesome busie-Bodies: Further, they would call the Bread of God, *Husks*; the *Comforts* of his Children, *Fancies*, the Travel and Labour of Pilgrims, things to no purpose" (214). Even they have been hanged by the time of the family's travel, their threats transformed into the "cautionary" discourses of engraved markers and memorial song, as have those of Formality and Hypocrisy as well (213, 215).

Part II's conflicts are often less between the traveler and psychospiritual threats than between the traveller and normative indifference. The coinciding diminution of sectarian persecutions adjusts the tone toward greater comforts but also toward a certain fin-de-siècle ennui. At House Beautiful Prudence comments upon the declining times: "*Mercie* in our days is little set by, any further then as to its Name: the Practice, which is set forth by thy Conditions, there are but few that can abide" (228). Persevering in good works is harder than beginning to do them, for as even *Christian Behaviour* observes "man by nature, is rather a hearer than a doer," and "we are subject to be weary of well-doing, *Gal.* 6.9" (III:52).

The chief danger for part II, however, is worldliness, what the posthumous *Christ, A Complete Saviour* anatomizes as the "four things in the world that have a tendency to lull an awakened man asleep": (1) "the bustle and cumber of the world, that will call a man off from looking after the salvation of his soul"; (2) "the friendship of this world, to which, if a man is not mortified, there is no coming for him to God by Christ"; (3) "the terrors of the world, if a man stands in fear of them"; and (4) "the glory of the world, an absolute hinderance to convictions and awakenings, to wit, honours, and greatness, and preferments" (Offor 1:219).

Evangelist easily defined the threats of Mr. Worldly Wiseman in part I, but worldliness more dangerously infiltrates the value system of the sequel. Vanity Fair in part II strikingly contrasts the two eras: "In *those* days we were afraid to walk the Streets, but *now* we can shew our Heads. *Then* the Name of a Professor was odious, *now*, specially in some parts of our Town (for you know our Town is large) Religion is counted Honourable" (275). Although, as the gloss tells us, "Persecution [is] not so hot at Vanity Fair as formerly" (275), in fact prosperity poses a much greater and more insidious threat. Vanity Fair's new tolerance matches advances in its manufactures and trade. The sociological further displaces the soteriological when, by their good works and fruitfulness, the female pilgrims gain blessing for their cause among the townspeople and when, by defeating the local monster, Greatheart and the males achieve "Reverend Esteem and Respect" (278). The Enchanted Ground lures overwearied victims away from denying the flesh and into stasis and loss of the Way (296–97). The greatest enemy of pilgrims is Madam Bubble, a seductress, a witch, a goddess, whose body, purse, and bed signal the claims of the flesh and the world (301–2, and see the world again as bubble in *Christ, A Complete Saviour* Offor 1:223). Her offers of feasting, joy, and wealth lead the unwary into "Commending, and then preferring the excellencies of this Life." She appeals, interestingly, not just to a pilgrim's self-indulgence, but also to his hopes for his children's inherited prosperity (302).

Part II gathers evidences of decline and "the iniquity of the times" into what emerges as the comprehensive tone of the sequel, the diminished spiritual intensity and interiority and the compromises with worldliness that mirror late developments in the culture and sectarian history through which Bunyan lived. Charles II, James II, and Parliament's political manipulations of tolerance and presecution created a series of unexpected effects among the sectarian victims, as Declarations of Indulgence in 1662, 1672, 1687, and 1688 alternated with official persecutions of varying intensity and application, the most fierce of which were encompassed in the so-called Clarendon code of the 1660s. Bunyan's jailings from 1660 to 1672 and again for six months during 1677 mirror something of this rhythm. Although it was in place only briefly, the Declaration of Indulgence of 1672 consolidated sectarian groups, and as Gerald Cragg remarks: "The results of a decade of persecution had been inconclusive; the results of a few months of freedom were irrevocable" (20). When the Declaration of Indulgence was quickly displaced by the renewed persecution of the Test Act of 1673, the new, less than ruthless repression confirmed sectarian convictions and spiritual resources by pressuring them to rediscover depths of meaning in their beliefs. It also increased the separateness of separatist communities by increasing the victims' dependence on each other.

In its later allowed phase, however, the Puritanism we are considering fell victim to a reactionary lethargy and tepidity. As it turned out, the congregations' growth in self-assurance and outward prosperity entailed complacency and spiritual deterioration, a laxer corporate life, a slackening of discipline, a lowering of spiritual direction and intensity. As Cragg describes it, "A cooler faith connived at doctrinal aberrations which an earlier generation would have hotly condemned," and "a buoyant certainty no longer fortified the dissenters against the corroding influences of a new age."[15] What persecution failed to achieve came about in fact through tolerance. By the century's end, the Puritanism epitomized in *Pilgrim's Progress* part I and etiolated in *Pilgrim's Progress* part II had run its course in line with the patterning of church history outlined earlier, vital interiority giving way to a vigorous, then less vigorous institution, inward spiritual intensities dissolving into a variety of outward, progressively weakened ripples overwhelmed by the indifference and material prosperity of a new age.

Bunyan does not go so far as Milton did when, with the Restoration, he denounced his contemporaries for eagerly choosing a captain to lead them back to Egypt in a reversal of the advance of a previously Chosen

People on the stage of English history (*The Ready and Easy Way, Poems* 898–99). Bunyan sees something of the same reversal or declension, the same apostasy, but addresses it with less vehemence, less desperation. Indeed, we read his response chiefly in the sharp contrast between the energy and intensity present in part I and absent from part II, as well as in the incidental conforming and comfortable details that have entered the narrative in their place. A consideration of one final Bunyan work will place the kinds of contrast we have been considering in a differently formatted relation to each other and show that, from the historical vantage, a holding action is perhaps the best that can be hoped for to counter the pressures toward decline arising from within and without, from professors and succeeding generations.

The Holy War of 1682 was published in the interval between parts I (1678) and II (1684) of *Pilgrim's Progress* and its title page, like theirs, invokes the authority of Hosea 12.10—"I have used Similitudes"—to explain the operating procedures.[16] It exploits the artful trappings of battle epic to develop its salvation narrative as "emphatically a political transaction" (xx). In this work, two modes of salvation enact the contrasting theologies, psychologies, and socializations of parts I and II of *Pilgrim's Progress*. Its first half features a salvational siege by Emanuel's army; its second, a secure town falling under siege from Diabolus's army. The first miniaturizes conversion morphology, the progress or antiprogress of returning to original perfection. The second figures a holding action, a quest for patience and perseverance in faith, continuity not conversion, peaceful generation not militant regeneration. No longer looking to return to a stabilizing past, it sees before it only a highly uncertain future.

In the first military action, Diabolus deactivates Mansoul's most prominent citizens—Captain Resistance, Lord Innocence, Lord Understanding, and Mr. Conscience—and replaces them with Lords Wilbewill, Prejudice, Forget Good, Illpause, and Incredulity. To regain Mansoul, Shaddai sends his captains, Boanerges (son of thunder [Mark 3.17] = "powerful preaching," xxxi), Conviction, Judgment, and Execution, figures of Thunder, Sorrow, Terror, and Justice (36–37, 258n.). This army variously echoes Mosaic law and Old Testament prophecy and history (xxvi, xxviii). It parlays, uses battering rams, and wields slings, guns, and other engines; the password is "Ye must be born again" (50). Eventually son Emanuel's irresistible army—under captains Credence, Goodhope, Charity, Innocent, and Patience, supported by Promise, Expectation, Pitiful, Harmless, and Sufferlong (68)—wins over Eargate and sets its standard upon Mount

Hearwell (87). The restored town leadership—Conscience, Understanding, and a now-redeemed Wilbewill—trust their petitions for life not to Mr. Good-deed (99) but to the son of Repentance, Mr. Desires-awake.

The ensuing peace exercises the categories we have seen at work in the second part of *Pilgrim's Progress*: celebratory feasting, music, and riddles (115–16); an economically flourishing community (117, 244); and the leadership of Lord Understanding as mayor, Mr. Knowledge as recorder, and Mr. Experience as captain of the guard. Emanuel draws up a formal charter (a group covenant) for the town and appoints Conscience as the secondary teacher to the Holy Ghost. The latter echoes the earlier regime in presenting high and supernatural things, remembrance, and things to come (139); while Conscience treats "all terrene & domestick matters," later "all things humane and domestick," essentially the "Moral Vertues . . . Civil and Natural duties" (140, 142). The new regime is threatened not by external enemies but by communal dejection, weakness, and disease, and by too much material prosperity or "Carnal Security" (150). As the first battle militarized the psychodrama of conversion, the second half emphasizes defensive mobilization, provisioning (148), and rebuilding and reorganizing under Mr. Godspeace.

The new dispensation is chronologicalized as progress, as threatened decline, and as a hoped-for holding action. For many months, Mr. Godspeace's sweet-naturedness presides over the happiest of communities, but all too soon the idealized community deteriorates "into great and grievous slavery and bondage" (149–50) through a combination of complacency and pride. When Mr. Carnal Security, the son of Self-conceit and Fear-nothing, convinces the town that it is impregnable, its citizens cease their service to Emanuel, who withdraws to his father's court. Of course, Mr. Godspeace follows. Mansoul is undermined by Lord Lasciviousness, Lord Covetousness, Lord Anger, Lord Murder, and Mr. Mischief (161), who become spies, Covetousness disguising himself as Mr. Prudent-thrifty, Lasciviousness as Harmless-mirth, and Anger as Good-zeal. The enemy's new goal is less to defeat the town than to make Mansoul destroy herself (218), and toward this end they exploit the town's thriving market in order to "so cumber *Mansoul* with abundance, that they shall be forced to make their Castle a *Warehouse* instead of a Garrison fortified against us" (217), "to choak *Mansoul* with a fulness of this world, and to surfeit her heart with the good things thereof" (217).

Mansoul's second dispensation arrives essentially at the point where *Pilgrim's Progress* part II also finds itself, in a fragile holding action against insidious worldly encroachments. Emanuel tries to reempower the Holy Ghost against the Doubters, but Diabolus then gathers an army of Blood-men or persecutors, characterized by anger, scorn, grudging, and jealousy. Emanuel is able to capture and redirect the Bloodmen, but new problems arise in Evil-questioning, Fooling, Letgoodslip, Clip-promise, and especially again Carnal-sense. An emerging new leadership features Captain Patience and Lord Self-denial, but the tentative ending of *The Holy War* makes clear that the town continues under threat. Emanuel's last words are "Hold fast till I come."

Pilgrim's Progress part II, written two years after *The Holy War*, concludes a bit—but only a bit—more positively. Despite the sequential deaths of heroic elders, a loosely defined hopefulness attaches to future generations and the capable leadership of such figures as Greatheart. In an intriguing reflexive and open-ended narrative gesture, Bunyan bids farewell to his present readers with the generational continuity of Christian's four sons' families and the prospect of additional reenvisionings of Christian pilgrimage in an indeterminate future. In what turned out to be teasing silence, the compound of his first conversional and salvational myth with its temporal, familial, ecclesiological sequel echoes as the promise if not of action at least of later discourse: "Shall it be my Lot to go that way again, I may give those that desire it, an Account of what I here am silent about; mean time I bid my Reader *Adieu*" (311).

Notes

INTRODUCTION

The headnote is from Cohen 4.

1. F. Harrison xxi, 39; Talon, *John Bunyan* 13, 169, and on the original publication of *Pilgrim's Progress* see 166ff. and Appendix C. The quotation is from Stone 160.

2. Sir Charles Firth, quoted in Sharrock, *Casebook* 102; Hill, *Intellectual Consequences* 84; Hill, *World Turned* 406; *Coleridge* 476; [Isaac] Disreali and Thomas Adams, quoted in Sadler 135; Forrest and Greaves 31; J. A. Froude, quoted in Davie 77.

3. See McCombs 98; Forrest and Greaves vii; Godber 9. Since there were two ninth editions (1683 and 1684), the number of editions in Bunyan's lifetime may also be reckoned as twelve (F. Harrison xxi and Talon, *John Bunyan* 13). It had been translated into Welsh, French, and Dutch even within Bunyan's lifetime, according to Bottrall 100. For a full discussion of the reception of Bunyan's work, see Keeble, " 'Of him.' " Editions of *Pilgrim's Progress* vary widely in content and intent. Smith (1923), for example, claims to present "Bunyan's classic narrative shorn of the doctrinal theology belonging to the seventeenth century" ("Note," n.p.), while that of Scott (1828) devotes sometimes entire pages to theological explications of the running text. Forrest and Greaves's *Reference Guide* notes a jigsaw puzzle version dating from 1790 (23).

4. Leverenz 18–19; Hill, *Some Intellectual Consequences* 7, 88; Hill, *Century* 163; Blumenberg xvii–xviii; Foucault 42, 55, 51–52, 57; Rivers 45, 47; and Cragg, *Puritanism* 249. Hill's *Experience* describes a gradual secularization of politics during the revolutionary decades (292–93 and 296).

5. Earl Miner's "Restoration mode" describes a shift from lyric to narrative as preferred medium of expression, from heroic to diurnal, and from the private or selectively social to the public and historical as standard of value (vii, xiv, xvii, 12, 13). On early poetry and late prose see also Matthew Arnold's "The Study of Poetry" (1880). Malcolm M. Ross describes a descent from symbol to metaphor to cliché during this century of disintegration as well as revolution (182, 91).

6. Blumenberg 243, 146, 145; Hill, *Century* 17, 263, 253; Braudel 251, 256, 183, 206, and passim. Keith Thomas sees the change as partly a matter of new technology, but more importantly of new aspirations, new faith in human initiative and capacity—from the old magical beliefs to a combination of "the growth of urban living, the rise of science, and the spread of an ideology of self-help" (665).

7. Greaves, "Conscience" 31–32; and Sharrock, " 'When at the first' " 84–85. See also note 10 of Chapter 1 below and note 10 of the Conclusion.

8. Similarly Talon, *John Bunyan* 259–60.

9. Talon, *John Bunyan* 54, 87, vi, v, 122. Greaves, *John Bunyan* 49. But cf. G. Campbell, "Fishing" 150–51. See also G. Harrison 11; Winslow 1–2; and Brittain 15, 320. These last two are especially readable biographies developing full political and cultural contexts for the details of Bunyan's life and work; Brittain's is also an illustrated guidebook to Bedfordshire sites.

10. Davie 9; Hill, *Century* 69; Bush 294, 296. On the forms and subject matters of contemporary religious controversy, see Keeble, *Literary Culture* esp. chap. 1; and Cragg, *Puritanism* chap. 8. McCombs itemizes the Restoration laws and pamphlets relating to Nonconformity and Toleration (793–95).

11. See also Cohen 7.

12. Greaves, *John Bunyan* 11, 25, 156, 159, 29, and 56–57. Walzer concisely analyzes Calvinistic ideology and process, with emphasis not just on its assumptions of original sin and predestination but on communal organization, participation, and obedience (chap. 2). Coleridge famously describes Bunyan as more Lutheran than Calvinist (*Coleridge* 476n.).

13. *Miscellaneous Works* II:7; Sharrock, " 'When at the first' " 85; Talon, *John Bunyan* 121; Cragg, *Puritanism* 204; and similarly Greaves, "Conscience" 36–37, 41–42, 43; Kaufmann, "Spiritual Discerning" 131. See also Shepard, *God's Plot* 21–22.

14. Damrosch 52, 183, 54; and see Cragg, *Puritanism* 89.

15. Hill, *Society and Puritanism* 13, and see 20. See also Cragg, *Puritanism* viii. For further definitions of *Puritan*—and recognition of the problem of definition—see George and George 5–8 and 397–407. The Protestantism before 1640 (including the Puritanism) which the Georges anatomize is separated by a chasm from Roman Catholicism on the right and a vigorously condemned Anabaptism on the left (393). Bunyan, reflecting the Puritanism of the 1660s to 1680s, has crossed over the latter chasm. The Georges speak too of fear and avoidance in their period of what they call "the disaster of separatism" (397), but for Bunyan that disaster has already happened. Two commentaries define *Puritan* by contrast with *Anglican*—see works by New and McGee (esp. McGee 246–47).

16. Collinson 6. For further definitions, see Sasek 17–18 and Emerson 44, 46. For brief anthologies of Royalist views of Puritans and Puritan self-images, see Lamont and Oldfield 71–82 and 98–122.

17. Greaves, "Nature" 257; Walzer 31; and Milton, *Poems* 743. See further, Walzer, 10, 13–16, 199, 300; Keeble, *Literary Culture* 12–15; and Packer 11–12.

18. *Grace Abounding*, 171, 149, 65, 79 (but see also xvi); *Minutes* 15; or *Church Book* 15; Tindall 101, 12–13, 227. See also Forrest and Greaves ix-x; *Grace Abounding*, 83, 86; Winslow 116; and Sharrock and Forrest's introduction to *The Holy War*, xi.

19. Hill, *Tinker* 8, 10, and chap. 5; Talon, *John Bunyan* 43–44. See also Sadler 14; and *Miscellaneous Works* 1:xliii–xliv.

20. Hill, *God's Englishman* 79. See also Hill, *Experience* chap. 9 and 294–95; Hill, *Century* 95, 108; and Walzer chap. 8, esp. 286.

21. Walzer 142; Plum 97, 51–52, 66, 98–99. See also Talon, *John Bunyan* 189 for encodings of dissent and persecution in *Pilgrim's Progress*.

22. For the Bible and Foxe as books Bunyan had with him in the Bedford jail, see McCombs 787, 791. Sharrock describes Bunyan's copy of *Actes and Monuments*, surviving in the library at Bedford with his autograph on the title page of each of the three volumes, as the black-letter edition of 1641, adorned with fearsome but inspiring woodcuts—"Bunyan" 106. Bunyan may have been inspired by accounts in this edition of historical "Actes" as recent as 1621 and also by its included "Treatise of afflictions and Persecutions of the faithfull preparing them with patience to suffer martyrdome"—Haller, *Elect Nation* 228, 227, and chap. 7 passim. *Actes and Monuments* was required by law to be placed in English churches throughout much of the century, but see Hill, *Century* 83 and *Intellectual Origins* 178–80. For some Bunyan uses of *The Book of Martyrs* see 97, 260, 344n.; *Grace Abounding* 84, 122, 153n.; 1:314, 358; 11:239, 247; 111:xxxv and xxxviii; VIII:98, 203, 383–84, 412; IX:309, 345; Offor 11:45, 77, 78, 700, 716–17, 724, 729; Offor 111:530–32, 534. For a rare use of Luther, see Offor 11:228.

23. For Bunyan as author of sixty books, see *Grace Abounding* 175 and more largely F. Harrison.

CHAPTER 1

The headnote is from Daniells 153.

1. Sharrock, *John Bunyan* (1966), 12; Sharrock, *Casebook* 18. See also Damrosch 150; and Batson 47.

2. *Coleridge's Miscellaneous Criticism* 30; *Coleridge's Essays* 46. The whole of Hosea 12.10 reads: "I have also spoken by the prophets, and I have multiplied visions, and used similitudes, by the ministry of the prophets."

3. Fletcher 23, 32, 130, 276, 30, 73, 360, 368; and Robertson 286. Nellist argues for *Pilgrim's Progress* as deconstructing the allegorical mode. For Damrosch Christian's phrase "I thought in my mind" (81–82) "perfectly captures Bunyan's

sense of an allegory that bodies forth interior states but never forgets their interiority" (168). Baird collects Bunyan's uses of *allegory, similitude,* and related
diction (14–18), and see Chapter 8 below.

4. Furlong 106–7. Kaufmann distinguishes four kinds of characters: sincere wayfarer, insincere wayfarer, biblical wayside character, and wayside "memorial"
(*Pilgrim's Progress* 94).

5. Van Ghent 30. Harding equates Faithful with "that aspect of faith, or *pistis,*
which is more loyalty to one's own inner experience than faith or belief in something as yet unseen"; "a personification of all the inferior and repressed aspects
of Christian himself, but in their positive aspect"; a personification of "what was
lacking in Christian's conscious personality" who brings "the vision of the Self
nearer to conscious realization" (188). For Talon in *John Bunyan,* Christian and
Faithful "make their way towards the same goal but not the same destiny" (150)
and Hopeful is insubstantial and inconsistent (200–201).

6. James Turner and Philip Edwards collapse the travel sequence into comparable stasis by viewing Vanity Fair and the City of Destruction as the same place,
only differently apprehended ("Bunyan's" 106 and "Journey" 114). For a list of
occasions where pilgrims do quite properly step out of the Way and risk or suffer
harm when they do not, see Turner 93 and for interiors turning into exteriors 95.

7. For other Bunyan alignments of sleep with sin, see *Some Gospel Truths Opened*
1:13 and *A Few Sighs From Hell* 1:344, 354. Characteristically in part II of *Pilgrim's
Progress,* God speaks through dreams (e.g., 273).

8. Knott, *Sword* 140. Knott links travel in the Way with the journeys of Abraham
and the Israelites, 140–41. Keeble outlines the numerous layers of simultaneous
forward progress in *Pilgrim's Progress* part I (*Literary Culture* 264, and see 268–72).

9. Walzer 278. The *footman* of *Prison Meditations* 261 is an image from racing,
according to its recent editor, Graham Midgeley (VI:321). The twelve instances
of *footmen* in the KJV Bible refer to soldiership, though Jeremiah 12.5 emphasizes
their running rather than fighting capacity.

10. Greaves reviews the evidence for dating *The Heavenly Footman,* and therefore also *Pilgrim's Progress* part I, in the late 1660s—"Conscience" 31–32. In *John
Bunyan* Talon insists that not *The Heavenly Footman* but Bunyan's *The Strait Gate*
was the work Bunyan abandoned in favor of the allegory (167), and see his Appendix B, "When Was *The Pilgrim's Progress* Written?"

CHAPTER 2

The headnote is from L. Edwards 3.

1. Kahler 2–4; and see Honig 24, 188; Aristotle 10; and N. Frye 341, 52.

2. N. Frye 71; Clifford 11; and note the subtitle of Fletcher, *Allegory: The
Theory of a Symbolic Mode.* Fletcher locates allegory between the mimetic and the

mythic. In Auerbach's terminology *figura* serves as a comparable middle term between *littera-historia* and *veritas* and is roughly equivalent to *spiritus* or *intellectus
spiritalis* or "phenomenal prophecy." Figura is historical, symbol magical—*Scenes*
47, 57.

3. *Coleridge* 474; Honig 113, 47, 49; and Nellist 133.

4. Lewis, *Allegory* 44–45. *Princeton Encyclopedia of Poetry and Poetics* attributes
to the increasing influence of Aristotle's *Poetics* the conception of poetry as an
imitation of nature that expresses the general and the typical rather than the specific and particular (14), a shift that largely left behind the sense of all literature
as allegory.

5. J. Campbell 36, 38, 35, 37. For mythic readings of *Pilgrim's Progress* part I,
see Lindsey chaps. 20 and 21; Harding; and Honig 72–87.

6. Morgan, *Visible Saints* 66; Perkins 168–69; and Berry 9. Morgan details the
conversional stages thus:

> First comes a feeble and false awakening to God's commands and a pride
> in keeping them pretty well, but also much backsliding. Disappointments
> and disasters lead to other fitful hearkenings to the word. Sooner or later
> true legal fear or conviction enables the individual to see his hopeless and
> helpless condition and to know that his own righteousness cannot save him,
> that Christ is his only hope. Thereafter comes the infusion of saving grace,
> sometimes but not always so precisely felt that the believer can state exactly
> when and where it came to him. A struggle between faith and doubt ensues,
> with the candidate careful to indicate that his assurance has never been
> complete and that his sanctification has been much hampered by his own
> sinful heart. (91)

See also Greaves, *John Bunyan* 50, 69, and subheadings of chap. 3; Knott, *Sword*
142; Cohen chap. 3. Watts notes that Perkins's "teaching on the self-confirming
value of perpetual doubt" defined normative Evangelical religious experience for
the ensuing three centuries (173–74).

7. Winslow 146; and Baxter, quoted in Damrosch 38. See also Kaufmann, *Pilgrim's Progress* chap. 1.

8. Offor III tip-in. James Turner describes Bunyan's *Mapp* as "an artistic concordance of Threats and Promises" ("Bunyan's" 108). Burke discusses Bunyan's *Mapp*
as being simultaneously bisymmetrical, rectilinear, and circular (243). G. Campbell argues for Bunyan's *Mapp* as directly derivative from Perkins's *Chain* in "Fishing" 141, 145–46.

9. Webber 33 (noting that *walk* contrasts with Donne's comparable Anglican
emphasis upon *change*); Watkins 114; and Ebner 67.

10. In *Justification By an Imputed Righteousness* Bunyan dramatizes Acts 16.30–
31 and Paul's response to the similar query from the Roman keeper of the prison:
"When he began to shake under the fears of everlasting burnings, yet then his heart

was wrapped up in ignorance as to the way of salvation by Jesus Christ; 'What must I do to be saved?' He knew not what; no, not he. His condition, then, was this: he neither had righteousness to save him, nor knew he how to get it. Now, what was Paul's answer? Why, 'Believe on the Lord Jesus Christ,' look for righteousness in Christ, 'and thou shalt be saved'" (Offor 1:315). See also *The Strait Gate* v:72; *Good News For the Vilest of Men* xi:69; *A Holy Life* ix:289–90; and *Mr. Bunyan's Last Sermon* Offor 11:756.

11. The psychoanalyst provides a modern analogue of the Herald, and Newey's psychological reading of *Pilgrim's Progress* outlines Christian's incipient insanity including such symptoms of neurosis as withdrawal from family, violent outbursts, obsession with death, and "a paralysis of will due to irresistible compulsions which have no direction in which to flow" ("Bunyan" 35). Newey aligns Christian's psychological journey with Jung's process of individuation (38). See also *The Holy War* 106, 107–8, 146 and *The Greatness of the Soul* ix:173.

12. Fish, *Self-Consuming Artifacts* 240, 245–46; but cf. Knott, *Sword* chap. 6, and Newey, "Bunyan" 42.

13. Leverenz 107. At the family level, Puritan patriarchy is marked by ambivalence: "the need for strong fathers, the need to limit their strength; resentment of the social compromises eroding the father's proper authority, yet resentment of tyrannical or corrupt authority; sons expressing ambition, yet needing identity; fathers commanding reverence, yet needing love" (69). Puritan discourse regularly overlaps the parental father and the divine one, an ambivalence absorbing seventeenth-century political confrontations as well.

14. Morgan, *Puritan Family* 162–66. A number of Edward Taylor's contemporaneous poems show the basic Puritan model of the soul, whether male or female, as the Bride of Christ, but as Porterfield points out (chap. 2) for many males this "Puritan bride-consciousness" (50) raised serious gender role difficulties.

15. Keeble, "Christiana's Key" 17; and Bercovitch 16. On Christian as edifying text, see also Damrosch 184; and Lewalski, "Typological Symbolism" 82. On the pillar "to keep [Absalom's] name in remembrance upon earth," see *An Exposition . . . of Genesis* (Offor 11:452).

CHAPTER 3

The headnote is from *The Geneva Bible* ii verso.

1. Berry 146. Nuttall speaks similarly of the "yeast-like quality" of Bible reading in the mid-seventeenth century—*Visible Saints* 44.

2. Kaufmann, *Pilgrim's Progress* 152. Similarly, for Damrosch: "Despite its insistence on direct apprehension of the Word, this kind of [Puritan] faith is absolutely inseparable from hermeneutics, the task of interpretation" (67).

3. Coolidge 142, 145; Knott, *Sword* 34–35, 47. For the Epistle to the Romans as

the key and gist of Puritan theology, see Haller, *Rise of Puritanism* 87. Knott's first chapter traces Reformation attitudes toward "The Living Word."

4. Bunyan uses *gospelize* also in III:9 and Offor II:607 and 501; *gospeller* in IX:351, XI:54 and 82, and Offor I:238 and 587; and *gospelly* (adjective) in III:9, VIII:316, IX:203, Offor II:248, 309, 346, and 425. See also *Christian Behaviour* III:9 and *Ebal and Gerizzim* VI lines 99, 451, 514, and see 325n.; and J. N. King 15.

5. *Some Gospel Truths Opened* I:16, 97. Elsewhere Quakers are "fond hypocrites" and "painted hypocrites" who are "horribly deluded" and "wolves in sheep's clothing" and Ranters are "foaming dogs." Bunyan condemns both for claiming God within themselves and for failing to acknowledge sin (*A Vindication of Some Gospel Truths Opened* I:145, 45, 113, 30, 138). *Peaceable Principles and True* asserts that "Anabaptists, Independents, Presbyterians, and the like" are invariably divisive or "factious" titles, deriving from Hell or Babylon (Offor II:649).

6. See also *A Few Sighs From Hell* I:381–82; *Differences in Judgement About Water Baptism* Offor II:640, 641; and *Solomon's Temple Spiritualized* Offor III:477, 467. For background of this issue, see Shapiro 75; and Hill, *Century* 78–79.

7. Lowance vii, viii, 39; Watkins 97; Kibbey 32. See also Caldwell 91–96, 136–40.

8. *Grace Abounding* 12, 17. Bunyan specifies Genesis 8.22 as among his earliest spiritual openings:

> These words were some of the first, with that of 'the bow in the cloud,' that prevailed with me to believe that the scriptures were the word of God.
>
> For my reason tells me, they are, and have continued a true prophecy, from the day that they were related.

(*An Exposition . . . of Genesis* Offor II:486)

9. Stranahan 333, 336. Stranahan's "event" describes a spiritual opening, when "[Bunyan's] life had 'caught up' with a particular experience described in the Bible" (343), and Knott extends such textual "events" to Bunyan's miscellaneous prose as well in "'Thou must live'" 153–70. Bruss finds even in the modal verbs of *Grace Abounding* an intense consciousness of obligation (50), and in a related vein Webber can remark, "Unless he is careful to keep it in its place, Bunyan does not use language; it uses him" (45).

10. Sibbes, quoted in Nuttall, *Holy Spirit* 24. Generally Nuttall proposes that the doctrine of the Holy Spirit provides the fundamental difference between Protestantism and Roman Catholicism (5). See also Knott, *Sword* 4.

11. Case, *Mount Pisgah*, quoted in Kaufmann, *Pilgrim's Progress* 26; and G. Campbell, "Fishing" 137.

12. Christopher 110–11, 121, 118. Luther (*Works* 31.349) is cited from Christopher 111. See also Knott, *Sword* 18, 132. Wallace offers a deft summary: "Revelation, according to Calvin, never takes place without a word. There is never a genuine sign given without a voice which at some stage in the event comes from God to man. The word may be spoken in various ways. It may be put in the mouth of some

figure in a dream. It may be spoken by an angel. It may come directly as if from heaven itself. It may be heard, as in the New Covenant, from the lips of one who preaches. However it comes, the voice must be there or it would not be revelation according to the true biblical pattern. Revelation in the Bible is never a dumb event" (72). For the Holy Ghost as illuminator and explicator of Bible riddles, see *The House of God* VI:284. R. A. Marcus discusses St. Augustine's twofold theory of signs in which Christ serves both as the teacher within who guides the mind to relate signs to significance and also as the Word, that is the sign of what God signifies (61–91).

13. Milton, *Prose* 6.581; and see Perkins 338.

14. Abundant information on Ramus of both introductory and scholarly sorts is to be found in P. Miller, *New England Mind* Book II; and Ong. Milton's textbook, *The Art of Logic* (*Prose* vol. 8), presents a fairly representative version of Ramistic logic. See further Berry 86–87; and Swaim, *Before and After* chap. 3.

15. Stranahan 338; and Fish, *Self-Consuming Artifacts* 243. On the glosses in *Pilgrim's Progress*, see also Damrosch 156; Keeble, *Literary Culture* 146–51; Cunningham 219–20; and Van Dyke 158, 166. For Cunningham, glosses generally are symptoms of deconstructive textuality and Bunyan's glosses "devotedly aimed at propping rather than contradicting the texts they refer to," but with nonetheless undermining effects (235).

16. For additional references to Lot and/or his wife, see Offor II:80, 471, 493, 494; III:62; VIII:43, 217; and IX:316. Alpaugh considers "Remember Lot's Wife" as the model for reading and interpreting in *Pilgrim's Progress* (308, 309).

17. Coolidge xiii, 142; *Ebal and Gerizzim* VI:118; and *Paul's Departure and Crown* Offor I:725. See also *Saved by Grace* VIII:216–17; *Solomon's Temple Spiritualized* Offor III:477; and Greaves, *John Bunyan* 154.

18. Kaufmann, *Pilgrim's Progress* 81, 85; and Van Dyke 173. See also Luxon 449 and 452. A tablet at the Church of St. John the Baptist in Bedford claims that its rectory was Bunyan's own Interpreter's house—Brittain 143, 146.

19. Sadler 129, 130. Knott sees three stages of instruction in Interpreter's house (biblical texts), House Beautiful (scriptural and extrascriptural tradition of heroic faith), and Delectable Mountains (Christian vision and scriptural mystery)— "'Thou must live'" 166.

20. *Of the House of the Forest of Lebanon* notes that the armor of Ephesians 6 is wholly spiritual and defensive; that the battle against Antichrist is defensive rather than offensive (Offor III:526); and that Ephesians makes no provision for arming warriors' backs, a point specified in *Pilgrim's Progress* part I (56). *The House of God* equates Sword and Word invoking the two-edged sword coming out of Christ's mouth VI:283, but cf. 302. See *The Holy War* for a parody of the Ephesians armor, 34–35, and Knott, *Sword* 155.

21. Kaufmann follows Harold Golder in finding five uses of the phrase "the shadow of death" in the Bible, but an exhaustive Bible concordance discovers

twenty: ten in Job (3.5, 10.21, 10.22, 16.16, 24.17 [twice], 28.3, 34.22, 38.17), four in Psalms (23.4, 44.19, 107.10, 107.14), two in Jeremiah (2.6, 13.16), and one each in Isaiah (9.2), Amos (5.8), Matthew (4.16), and Luke (1.79) (*Pilgrim's Progress* 160). *Paul's Departure and Crown* calls the author of the Book of Job "the penman of the Word" (Offor 1:735); and *An Exposition . . . of Genesis* speaks of "that blessed book of Job; which book, in my opinion, is a holy collection of those proverbs and sayings of the ancients, occasioned by the temptation of that good man" (Offor 11:425). Golder examines the episode in the light of the romance tradition and finds such motifs as the unheeded warning, the resisted temptation to return, assault by demons, the useless sword, the sword bridge (i.e., narrow passage), and the sudden contrast with light. To the early Bunyan, he suggests, the Old Testament was a romance (68).

22. Stewart 17. See also J. Turner, *One Flesh* 63–64. Turner summarizes the tradition thus: "The myth of Eden is thus transformed by the Song of Songs into an erotic dream, by the New Testament into a marital 'ordinance', and by Reformation bibliolatry and primitivism into the 'first institution' of marriage and the standard of perfection that should regulate its practices and emotions" (77). From the frequency of citations, Talon infers Bunyan's preference of the Song of Solomon over other books of the Bible on the grounds of its beauty, poetry, and melody (*John Bunyan* 115). On the sensuousness of Eden, see also Van Dyke 184–85; and Keeble, *Literary Culture* 261–62, 281.

CHAPTER 4

The headnotes are from Bush 296 and P. Miller, *New England Mind* 335–36.

1. Cragg, *Puritanism* 204; and Watkins 6. See also Cohen 86. Bunyan discusses Romans 10.17 in *Defense of the Doctrine of Justification By Faith* Offor 11:304.

2. Perkins 341–42. See also Haller, *Rise of Puritanism* 65. On the importance of *The Art of Prophesying* see v:xxvii, and Mitchell 99.

3. On the two poles of Bunyan's preaching see Talon, *John Bunyan* 109, 111, 260; and Sadler 34–35. Berry records the larger historical patterns in an appendix, "The Increased Reference to Christ in Puritan Preaching," generalizing from his count of sermons before Parliament that "from 1640 through 1645, sermons referring to Old Testament topics and themes clearly outnumbered sermons referring to New Testament topics, Christ, and the Apocalypse. But beginning with 1646, sermons addressed to the latter topics outnumbered sermons on the former *in every single year*" (277; Berry's italics). For an American analogue, see Elliott 13–14, 127, and 129.

4. Berry describes contemporary theological works as characteristically "profoundly repetitious" and extremely augmented (4 and 282n.). On sermon delivery modes see v:xxii-xxiv, and Mitchell 14–15.

5. Morgan, *Visible Saints* 27, 28, and see 99; Nuttall, *Holy Spirit* 75–76. On prophesying, see also Watts 306–7; Walzer 128; van Beek 45–46; and Hill, *Society and Puritanism* 47. The Scriptures governing prophesying are 1 Corinthians 14.29–31.

6. Kaufmann, *Pilgrim's Progress* 240; Lewalski, *Protestant Poetics* 152, 458n., 148; and Lewalski, *Donne's Anniversaries* 85.

7. Hall 57, 72, 77, 38, 84. Fisch credits Hall with deriving from Psalms an authentically Hebraic imaginative structure much followed in seventeenth-century literature based on "schematic use of the Rule of Three: composition, analysis, and colloquy" (48–49, 51). See also Hambrick-Stowe 161–75.

8. Baxter 163, 143, 166, 144, 29. See also Knott, *Sword* chap. 3; and Martz 332. Martz links Baxter with Bunyan's practice, 172–73.

9. Fish, *Self-Consuming Artifacts* 250. Newey sees memory in *Pilgrim's Progress* part I displacing the wrestlings with the Word of *Grace Abounding*—" 'With the eyes' " 211. On Puritan memory as exercised in sermons, see Cragg, *Puritanism* 217–18. For a quick review of a number of classical views of memory see Caplan 196–246. See also Yates esp. chap. 10.

10. Berry 8–9. For additional sermon models Bunyan inherited, see Mitchell 95, 111–12; and Cragg, *Puritanism* 210.

11. Glanvill, quoted in *Miscellaneous Works of John Bunyan* v:xxix; and Herbert 235. *The Fear of God* is a 130-page treatise on a two-word text, "Fear God," Revelation 14.7; indeed, from its second page on, the treatise confines itself almost exclusively to the one word *fear*.

12. F. Harrison 26–27, xvii–xviii. See also G. Campbell, "Fishing" 140. According to Stranahan, the first complete Bible concordance by Alexander Cruden in 1737 acknowledges Powell's "small concordance" as one of several predecessors (338n.). Contemporaries sometimes inveighed against the "concordance" method of sermon preparation (e.g., Joseph Glanvill, v:xxxii), but Robert Wickens's *A Compleat and Perfect Concordance* (1655) likens the use of a concordance "to the top of Pisgah, which, though itself was barren and rocky, yet it was able to show the discoveries of the whole land of Canaan"—cited in J. Turner, "Bunyan's" 109. See also Weintraub 237.

13. *The Desire of the Righteous Granted* Offor 1:764ff.; *Some Gospel Truths Opened According to Scripture* 1:109, 113; *I Will Pray With the Spirit* 11:272, 281; *The Saints' Knowledge of Christ's Love* Offor 11:28–40; *Of Antichrist and His Ruin* Offor 11:42, 45; *A Fear of God* IX:90, 102, 118, 123, 130; and *Christ, A Complete Saviour* Offor 1:238–39. Two-thirds of a late work, *Paul's Departure and Crown*, are given over to applications under the defining formulae: "A Reason why Christians should so manage their time and the work that God hath appointed them to do for his name in this world, that they may not have part thereof to do when they should be departing this world, it is because . . ." (Offor 1:730) and "If thou wouldst be faithful to do that work that God hath allotted thee to do in this world

for his name, then labour to . . ." (732). Changes in the subtitles of first and later editions of *A Few Sighs From Hell* shift attitudes toward applications: Thus, *Also A brief Discourse touching the profitableness of the Scriptures for our Instruction in the way of Righteousness, according to the tendancy of the said Parable* (i.e., Dives/Lazarus) becomes *With a Discovery of the Usefulness of the Scriptures, as Our Safe Conduct for avoiding the Torments of Hell* (on "profitableness" see esp. 1:323–31). In a prefatory letter to this work, I.G. (John Gibbs, 1:xxxix) commends Bunyan's applications as being particularly "natural" (1:242). The second edition of *A Few Sighs*, apparently the work of Bunyan himself, transfers some thirty pages of applications of the parable into the commentary on one of its verses (1:228).

14. Bercovitch 29; Keeble, *Literary Culture* 240, and see 242; and Sasek chap. 3, esp. 41, 56. See also Tindall 166, 167; and Berry 205.

15. Leverenz 138. His psychological approach presses the distinction between form and style:

> Puritan sermons appear to be paradigms of the obsessive style. They offer compulsive patterns of external order, rigid arrangements of 'doctrine, reasons, and uses' in a thicket of numbers and quotations, with no space for private opinion or loose feelings. They call for patriarchal deference, invoke the one true text continuously, endlessly repeat their litany of 'shoulds,' and take minute care to make precise distinctions within a grand either-or frame of polarity. Yet Puritan sermons are at the same time capacious, supple, and vivid in their similes, with a practical sense of social roles. The double appeal of Puritan language is nowhere more expansively set than in the flexibility of sermon imagery speaking through the rigidity of sermon form. (138)

Leverenz notes a tendency of Puritan sermons to generate a number of small similes rather than develop (or overdevelop) a long one, saying "Puritan style sets bounds to metaphoric fantasies even in the act of making them" (146).

16. Murdock 49. In a Puritan commonplace, a good style is like a pane of glass and a bad style like a stained glass window (Murdock 182).

17. F. Harrison 64. Mitchell generalizes from *Mr. John Bunyan's Last Sermon* that "His preaching and exposition of Scripture was heavy and dull" (257). Offor considers *Israel's Hope Encouraged* very close to the original sermon delivery, as is *The Resurrection of the Dead* (Offor 1:577, 11:83, and see v:xxvi). The subtitle of *The Acceptable Sacrifice* identifies it as *Being the Last Works of That Eminent Preacher, and Faithful Minister of Jesus Christ, Mr. John Bunyan of Bedford*, but it is a last work prepared for the press rather than a last oral presentation.

18. Evangelist is regularly seen as a portrait of John Gifford, whose ministry Bunyan attended beginning in 1651. See *Grace Abounding* 25, 37; and, for example, E. W. Bacon 72, 74. *A Holy Life* speaks of Timothy as an *Evangelist*, and defines that status as "inferior to Apostles and extraordinary Prophets, and above ordinary

Pastors and Teachers" (IX:261). The content of Greatheart's discourse on Christ in part II (209–12) is sermonic, indeed along the precise lines of Bunyan's first work *Some Gospel Truths Opened*, but its format is dialogic or catechismic not sermonic.

CHAPTER 5

The headnote is from Clarke's *Lives of Sundry Eminent Persons*, quoted in Watkins 1.

1. Nuttall, *Visible Saints* viii and chapter titles; and similarly Morgan, *Visible Saints* 34–35.

2. Hambrick-Stowe 93–94, 103–4, 136; and Walzer 223. Hambrick-Stowe describes, for New England at least, the admission of new members as reenacting the first founding of a Church and thus reaffirming the original congregational covenant (129). On "closet" duties, see *A Holy Life* IX:329.

3. McGiffert, in Shepard, *God's Plot* 20; and Watkins 227, 237–38, 28.

4. McGiffert, in Shepard, *God's Plot* 25. On the experience meeting, see also Caldwell 76–78.

5. Haller, *Rise of Puritanism* 95–96. On biography, autobiography, and ministerial biography, see esp. chap. 3; and Sharrock, Introduction, *Grace Abounding* xxvii–xxx. Van Beek's glossary of Puritan vocabulary lists some forty-two compounded *self-* words (117–20, and see 7–8, 68–69). In America at least, pious biographers exploited accounts of the first generation of Puritans as a device for stimulating the second generation to emulate their father's glories—see Murdock esp. 128–29.

6. Damrosch 39, 24; and Leverenz 109. See also Hambrick-Stowe 95–96; and McGiffert, in Shepard, *God's Plot* 19–20. J. O. King says of the structured discourse of conversion narrative: "Prescription is not opposed to experience; prescription is language with which to order and craft experience" (49).

7. Keeble, *Literary Culture* 236, 237; Webber 51; Starr 13–14, 16, 17; Bercovitch 24; Bruss 34; and Ebner 48. On the required similarity among conversion narratives, see Carlton 27–29. Starr lays down the general principle for spiritual autobiographies: "the greater the attention paid to events before conversion, the less emphasis given to what happens afterwards, and vice versa" (46).

8. Morgan, *Visible Saints* 41–43, 88–93; Caldwell 72, 67–68; Watkins 37, 51; Watts 169–79, 317–18; and Shea 91. See also Cohen chap. 5, esp. 135. On "Visible Saints" see Morgan 113; "Saints" is a recurrent Pauline usage.

9. Caldwell 81, 45, 54; Cragg, *Puritanism* 166; Bottrall 109; Hambrick-Stowe 151. See also McGee 195–96.

10. *Minutes* 19, 24—a transcription of *The Church Book of the Bedford Meeting 1650–1821*. For selections from this work, see Appendix A of *Grace Abounding*, ed. Sharrock, and for discussion of it, White 1–19. Brittain finds "the story of Chris-

tianity in miniature" in the Church Book's history of the community's vigor, persecution, internal controversy, and rituals (144). She speaks also of *Grace Abounding* as the *record* of Bunyan's life and *Pilgrim's Progress* as its *interpretation* (299).

11. *The Barren Figtree* also draws the distinction: "It is one thing to be IN *the Church*, or in a Profession; and another to be OF *the Church*, & to belong to that Kingdom, that is prepared for the Saint, that is so indeed" (v:15 and similarly *The Strait Gate* v:99).

12. Sharrock, *Casebook* 14; and Watkins 102. Ebner comments similarly (59) and distinguishes the features of Baptist, Presbyterian, Anglican, and Quaker autobiography (13). See also *Grace Abounding* xxx; Batson 13–14; and Damrosch 125, 154. William James's *Varieties of Religious Experience* presents the autobiographical Bunyan as an instance of "The Sick Soul" and the later Bunyan as "The Divided Self" (chapter headings).

13. Spengemann 32, 5, 4. For him the defining three-stage pattern emerges so late in *Grace Abounding* "that it seems more an afterthought than a preconceived design, and so offhandedly that it seems far less important to the narrator than the specific experiences it purports to explain" (46). See also Matthews 4.

14. Martz, quoting the Jesuit Luis de la Puente 34, 35; and Fisch 52, 50–51. Contrary to Martz and Perry Miller's later datings, Hambrick-Stowe finds formal meditation important to the earliest Puritan practice in America and essentially constant throughout the second half of the seventeenth century (viii–ix, 38–39).

15. Bercovitch 27, 37; and similarly Berry 127.

16. Berry 209, 81–83; and MacCallum 166, 167. Berry remarks that in *Grace Abounding* Bunyan "pictures his world in essentially circular terms, with the repetition of temptations (the circle of despair in which for much of the book he represents himself as languishing) and repetition of God's mercies." "We may well conclude," he continues, "that Bunyan somehow desired to run in circles" (194, and similarly 224). In a related argument, Rosenblatt can see in loops "the approximation of simultaneity through the abrogation of chronological precedence" (37).

17. Milton's *The Art of Logic* explains the two matters thus:

Aristotle in *De anima* 2.4 distinguishes the *end of which* and the *end for which*. The end of which is the end of the action or of the operation. The end for which is the end of the thing done or made. . . . Again, the end is first in the mind of the efficient cause, but last in the action and in the effect. But while it is still only in the mind of the efficient cause and has not been achieved, it does not yet truly exist; and since it does not yet exist, how can it be a cause? So while it is commonly said that the end, inasmuch as it moves the efficient cause—persuasively, as it were—to prepare matter and induce a form in it, is the cause not only of the effect but of the causes themselves and is the best of the causes, this is said improperly and out of a certain preconception.

(*Prose* 8.237, 236.) For a useful and engaging overview of Ramus and Puritanism, see P. Miller, *New England Mind.*

18. On differences between Christian and Faithful, and between Christian and Hopeful, see Talon, *John Bunyan* 198–201. Talon finds parallels between Hopeful's narration and *Grace Abounding* (201), as does Tindall (40).

19. Several other treatises offer similar listings of false professors. *Some Gospel Truths Opened* offers four categories: the profane scoffer, the formal professor, the legal righteous man or woman, and those whose hearts are set upon the world (1:90–91, and similarly 99); and *Justification By an Imputed Righteousness* distinguishes the legalist, the believer in civility, the formalist, and the vicious and debauched (Offor 1:333). The subtitle of *The Barren Figtree* (1673) promises *The Signs also by which such miserable Mortals may be known*, including anger, mockery, lust, loss of God's controlling influence, hardheartedness, and willfulness. On the backslider see *Saved by Grace* VIII:206–7; on the hypocrite, *A Treatise on the Fear of God* IX:130–32; and on the covetous, *A Discourse Upon the Pharisee and the Publicane* X:129. For Bunyan the two titular figures of this last treatise comprehend the whole of humanity (X:111).

20. Van Dyke 181. *Come, and Welcome, to Jesus Christ* offers an expansive "application" based on the precedent of St. Peter's "little faith" (Matthew 14.31) (VIII:362–64). Here often "little faith" reflects the proper fears of "an awakned, sensible, considering people" (363). A related anecdote in *Seasonable Counsel* recommends that a man going to London with a large amount of money should commit the money to the care of another powerful figure (God) also going to London and thus escape robbery by highwaymen (Offor II:701).

CHAPTER 6

The headnote is from Bradstreet 167.

1. Houlbrooke 97. According to Latt, seventeenth-century women "were praised for being upholders of what may be called the virtues of restraint. Rather than actively working in the political or theological worlds, women were expected to correct the world's immorality by being static *exempla*" (43). See also MacLean. Counters to the usual anti-Eve arguments are concisely offered, 91. In his *Exposition . . . of Genesis*, Bunyan necessarily rehearses the usual views of Eve's weakness and folly (see esp. Offor II:428–29, 438, 439), but commenting on Genesis 5.2, he presents the broader, New Testament view: "For the Holy Ghost . . . counteth not by male and female, but 'ye are all one in Christ Jesus.' Ga. iii.28. Wherefore, women are not to be excluded out of the means of salvation; nay, they have, if they believe, a special right to all the promises of grace that God hath made to his saints in all ages" (Offor II:455).

2. See also Hill, *Century* 143; Woolley; Mendelson esp. 189–90; and Clark esp.

47–51. A radically altering attitude toward women may be gleaned from the titles alone of other books of the 1680s: *The Wonders of the Femall World, or A general History of Women In Two Books. Wherein by many hundreds of Examples, is shewed what Woman hath been from the first Ages of the World to these Times, in respect of her Body, Senses, Passions, Affections, her Virtues and Perfections, her Vices and Defects . . . To which is added, A Discourse of Female Pre-eminence* and *Haec et Hic, or The Feminine Gender more worthy than the Masculine. Being a Vindication of the ingenious and innocent Sex from the biting Sarcasms, bitter Satyrs, and opprobrious Calumnies, wherewith they are daily, though undeservedly, aspersed by the virulent Tongues and Pens of malevolent Men; with many examples of the rare Virtues of that noble Sex, in which they have not only equalled, but excelled, most of the other Sex* (cited in Ford 137).

3. Perkins 418, 419, 425; and *Christian Behaviour* iii:27. Schlatter sees Perkins as typical of Puritan positions (chaps. 1 and 2, esp. 9).

4. Johnson 23, 37–38. On Gataker, see George and George 270, and Johnson 94–100; and on marriage manuals, Powell chap. 4, Appendix D.

5. In *Tinker* Hill evidences Bunyan's continuing defensiveness on the issue of family abandonment (226–30), generalizing that "the revisions, and Part II, were written at least in part in order to give the husband the last word in this proxy matrimonial brawl" (229) and that "absolute devotion to any human being was, for [Bunyan], sinful servitude" (230).

6. Brown charts the details of Bunyan's pedigree and progeny (tip-in between 20–21). In summary, Bunyan was the father of six children, five of whom survived his lifetime: four by his first wife (m. 1647, d. 1658): Mary (b. 1650, blind); Elizabeth (b. 1654, m. 1677); John; Thomas (m. early 1680s, entered ministry 1692); and two by his second wife Elizabeth (m. 1659, d. 1692): Sarah (m. 1686); Joseph. Talon guesses that Christiana was suggested by his second wife, and Mercy by his first (*John Bunyan* 203). When Bunyan adds a defense against accusations of womanizing to the fifth edition of *Grace Abounding*, he professes in the strongest terms his shyness of women and his absolute fidelity to his wife (94, and Appendix C, "Extracts from *The Narrative of the Persecution of Agnes Beaumont in 1674*," 176–80; but cf. 88). For religious and political backgrounds, and especially the conditions of prison life, see Cragg, *Puritanism* chaps. 1 and 4. Greaves labels as "one of [Bunyan's] profoundest insights" the principle expounded in *Seasonable Counsel* of "the necessity for Christians to suffer *actively* for righteousness by *willingly* embracing affliction" ("Conscience" 40; Greaves's italics).

7. Stone 22, 93, 104. See Hill's review of this study, "Sex, Marriage" 188–209. Stone's social history is profitably supplemented by MacFarlane's social anthropology.

8. Sharrock, *John Bunyan* (1968), 140, 144, 148, 141; Sharrock, *John Bunyan* (1966), 43–44, 50, 46, 47; Sharrock, *Casebook* 19; and Knott, "Bunyan" 211. For Newman, "progress" for "the isolate 'masculine'" in part I is an expedition, while

"progress" for "the visceral 'feminine' " in part II signifies improvement and cultivation (239, 240).

9. Messer-Davidow 79, 80, 90; and see Armstrong and Tennenhouse 15.

10. J. Turner, "Bunyan's" 93, 104. E. W. Bacon calls attention to architectural
not just atmospheric or interpretational changes (137).

11. Rybczynski 40, 62, 74–75, 77. See also Braudel esp. chap. 4; Fastnedge
chaps. 1 and 2; and Trevelyan 2.192–97. Bunyan's Emblem XII, "Upon Over-much
Niceness," chides sacrificing the soul's interests to over-attention to the body
and household affairs (vi:209–10), and see also XVI, "Upon Apparel" (213–24).
As to Bunyan's own property, a deed of gift of December 1685 leaves his wife
"all and singuler my goods, chattels, debts, ready mony, plate, rings, household
stuffe, aparrel, vtensiles, brass, peuter, beding, and all other my substance" (Offor
1:cxii). Offor's edition includes drawings of a Bunyan chair, cabinet, box of scales
and weights, apple-scoop, jug, and pair of knives (1:cxix, cxx, lxxix). See also
Winslow vii; and Talon, John Bunyan 193.

12. Snyder 52, 46, 48. Van Dyke praises part II as "richer than its predecessor
in what is usually called human interest" and sees its focus as "on the individual
and the instinctual rather than on the universal and the abstract" (187, 188).

13. J. Miller 49, 83, 71–72, 39, 41, 60. And see Chodorow 169. Compare Whitehead: "Religion is what the individual does with his own solitariness. It runs
through three stages, if it evolves to its final satisfaction. It is the transition from
God the void to God the enemy, and from God the enemy to God the companion" (16).

14. Sharrock, John Bunyan (1968) 153, and similarly John Bunyan (1966) 53;
and Knott, "Bunyan" 223–24. Van Dyke recognizes the paradox that the deaths
of part II are not "a progressive abandonment of individuality," for serially the
characters "are never more vividly individualized than in their grand ceremonial
relinquishments of personality" (196). Hill's Tinker contrasts Mr. Badman's quiet
death with the heroic deaths endorsed in Foxe's Book of Martyrs (239); and Houlbrooke indicates that in this period wills were typically made or amended at the
deathbed especially by those with relatively little property (202). Paul's Departure
and Crown depicts the death process of the faithful as attended by peace, angels,
and good works (Offor 1:741–42, and see 2 Timothy 4.6–8). It interprets crossing
over Jordan as a type of death (742). See also Saints' Privilege and Profit Offor
1:678–79.

15. Thickstun 104, and similarly 35. Thickstun denies Christiana the potential "to achieve a metaphoric transformation into the representative Christian
believer" and labels her an essentially secondary participant in the covenant of
grace (25). For her part II "humanizes" the fiction, but by this she means only
makes it carnal rather than spiritual (24). She develops the parallels of Mercy and
the biblical Ruth in detail (92–93).

16. Edwards 5–6; and see also Pearson and Pope 6.

17. Thus Bunyan can, for example, ask the readers of his *Doctrine of the Law and Grace Unfolded* to "pray for me to our God, with much earnestness, fervency, and frequently, in all your knockings at our fathers door" (II:19). For a convert's knocking and fears about reception at the door, see also *Come, and Welcome* (VIII:271, 340, 343–58, and 362).

18. Kaufmann, *Pilgrim's Progress* 94–95; see also Iser 17 and Quilligan 129–30.

19. Bercovitch 14; Bercovitch's italics. For other Bunyan mirrors, see *The Doctrine of the Law and Grace Unfolded* II:13–14; Emblems LXVIII and XLVIII ("Upon the Image in the Eye" and "Upon a Looking-Glass" VI:266, 250); *The Advocateship of Jesus Christ* XI:204; and more generally II:157; XI:47; Offor I:647 and lxxviii; Offor III:555. Forrest traces the mirror as a reflector of material things to Plato; as a medieval metaphor for the spotless Virgin and thence transferred to Christ; as an icon of *Veritas*; and as a Puritan metaphor for the Word or conscience (122–24). McGee, however, argues that Puritans did not seek an imitative relationship to Christ as did Anglicans (107–13).

CHAPTER 7

1. V. Turner 177, 132, 147–48, 200. See also Turner's distinction between rituals of hierarchy and rituals of humility (200), and Weintraub 241–42.

2. Hambrick-Stowe 93–94, 103–4, 136, 144; Morgan, *Puritan Family* 136–37; Cragg, *Puritanism* 130–31; and Dent, quoted in Greaves, *John Bunyan* 125.

3. Kaufmann, "Spiritual Discerning" 178; Sharrock, *John Bunyan* (1966) 43; Sharrock, *John Bunyan* (1968) 138; Sharrock, "Life and Story" 64; Furlong 117, 114, 124; Knott, "Bunyan" 208, 216; and St. Augustine, cited in R. Frye 102. Hill calls part II more ecumenical and more tolerant than part I, but tolerant only of godly Protestants: "Bunyan's hostility towards Catholics and persecution had if anything hardened since Part I" (*Tinker* 200).

4. Newman 241. See also Leverenz 122 and 110. G. Campbell calls *Pilgrim's Progress* "a religious work rather than a theological work" ("Theology" 257).

5. Guibbory 14, 12. The pattern options are discussed, 5–30. Hill calls Providential history "one of the casualties of the revolutionary decades" (*Experience* 293). On the Renaissance displacement of a cyclical view of history by a linear one, see also Thomas 430–32. See also Hill, *Some Intellectual Consequences* 59–60; and Berry 9. The latter calls attention to the characteristic Puritan collapse of time: "Puritans most heavily emphasized the stable arrangements made by God at the creation and the final fixity of the end, rhapsodizing upon paradise lost and paradise regained; there was no Aristotelian 'middle' to human history, to theology, or to their art."

6. *Solomon's Temple Spiritualized* applies the metaphor from the Song of Solomon in detail: "These are feasting times: the times in which our Lord used to

have his spouse into his wine-cellar, and in which he used to display with delight his banner over head in love. *Ca.* ii.4,5. The church of Christ, alas! is of herself a very sickly puely thing; a woman; a weaker vessel; but how much more must she needs be so weak, when the custom of women is upon her, or when she is sick of love? Then she indeed has need of a draught, for she now sinks, and will not else be supported. 'Stay me with flagons,' saith she, 'and comfort me with apples, for I *am* sick of love.' *Ca.* ii.5" (Offor III:494). Solomon's Temple recurs in *The Holy City* III:117.

7. Tindall concludes generally that "Bunyan cherished a deep and natural hatred of both king and government, like any normal Baptist of the time" and that he professed loyalty in order to hide his true political views from all but an inquisitive elect (137), but Tindall ignores Bunyan's most explicitly political work *Of Antichrist and His Ruin*. See also Hill, *Tinker* chaps. 25 and 26 and passim. Among the most specific historical references in all of Bunyan, *Of Antichrist* mentions various European countries (Offor II:48), the Spanish Inquisition (50), and Henry VIII and his children who became rulers—Edward, Mary, and Elizabeth (50). The Antichrist (Roman Catholicism) must be destroyed, among other causes, because "she has *bepuddled* the word of God" (77; Bunyan's italics). As Hill notes: "Everybody was against Antichrist; so his name could be extended from Pope to bishops, to the whole hierarchy of the state church, to the King and royalists who defended them" (*Experience* 22). Indeed Nuttall locates the assumption that the Anglican Church had fallen unto Antichrist as foundational to the separatist movement of the mid-century (*Visible Saints* 56–67). On Bunyan's relation to seventeenth-century politics, see Greaves, "Conscience" 39–41.

8. Nuttall, *Holy Spirit* 91. See also Watkins 229; Greaves, *John Bunyan* 135; and Hambrick-Stowe chaps. 4, 5, and 6. *A Confession of My Faith* similarly distinguishes confessions of faith in the two media of word and life (Offor II:607).

9. Tindall 43. For Tindall, Book I targets Anglican enemies and part II quarrels with other Baptists, especially T. S. [Thomas Sherman], whose sequel to part I of *Pilgrim's Progress* paid corrective attention to matters of church organization and discipline, the ordinances, and the general rather than the particular call (164 and see 64–65).

10. G. Campbell, "Theology" 253. Gathered churches, including Bunyan's Bedford one, pledged at entrance to unite in the fellowship even "though they agree not in judgment in all outward things" (*Minutes* 19, 17). See also Greaves, *John Bunyan* 135–45; Nuttall, *Visible Saints* 117–21; and Greaves, "Conscience" 143.

11. Sharrock, *John Bunyan* (1966) 343–44n.; Sharrock, *John Bunyan* (1968) 144; and Sadler 97–98. See *The Story of Susannah*, in *Apocrypha* 349–53, and 2 Samuel 11.2–4.

12. *The Water of Life* glances at contemporary life, for example the effects of popular watering spas at Epsom, Tunbridge, and Bath (Offor III:543 and 558); *The Saints' Privilege and Profit* mentions Bath as well (Offor I:652).

13. Sibbes, quoted in Knott, *Sword* 45. It is a point of some interest that John Gifford, Bunyan's pastor, first came to Bedford to practice medicine (Brittain 147–48).

14. *Pilgrim's Progress* 345; Sharrock, *John Bunyan* (1968) 154; Sharrock, *John Bunyan* (1966) 51; and cf. Talon, *John Bunyan* 161–62; and Sutherland, *English Literature* 333.

15. John Field, quoted in Morgan, *Visible Saints* 14, and similarly 29 and 55–56; and *A Case of Conscience Resolved* Offor 11:662. Samuel Mather's definition of the *covenant* extends our earlier definitions of *church*:

> A solemne and publick promise before the Lord, whereby a company of Christians, called by the power and mercy of God to fellowship with Christ, and by his providence to live together, and by his grace to cleave together in the unitie of faith, and brotherly love, and desirous to partake together in all the holy Ordinances of God, doe in confidence of his gracious acceptance in Christ, binde themselves to the Lord, and one to another, to walke together by the assistance of his Spirit, in all such wayes of holy worship in him, and of edification one towards another, as the Gospel of Christ requireth of every Christian Church, and the members thereof.

Quoted in P. Miller, *New England Mind* 435.

16. On the vocabulary describing *Puritans*, see further Keeble, *Literary Culture* 41–44; Watts 1–2; and van Beek chap. 4. *Nonconformist* derives too from Romans 12.2: "Be not conformed to this world, but be ye transformed by the renewing of your mind." Among his other vices, Mr. Badman threatens to become an informer and turn in his wife's conventicle to the authorities (129), and for further illustration of the danger and process of informing, see 130ff. For biblical backgrounds, see also the subsection "Readiness of enemies to destroy the Apostle and his doctrine," in *Paul's Departure and Crown* (Offor 1:726).

17. Tindall 59; and Keeble, "Christiana's Key" 14.

18. P. Miller, *New England Mind* 375–83, 435–44, 447. Miller describes the church covenant as "a fascinating scheme for securing rectitude in a community without sacrificing cohesion" (443). On pilgrim diversity, see also Keeble, *Literary Culture* 232–35. Bunyan grounds a developed metaphor comparing pilgrims with various instruments upon the Book of Revelation (253 and Revelation 8.2, 14.2–3); and see Sharrock, *John Bunyan* (1966) 46 and 52 and *John Bunyan* (1968) 141.

19. Offor 111:505. On the mediatorial office see also *Christ, A Complete Saviour* (Offor 1:620ff.); *The Saints' Privilege and Profit* (Offor 1:663ff.); and Greaves, *John Bunyan* 134–35.

20. Talon, "Space" 165; Talon, *John Bunyan* 191, and similarly 307.

21. Although Thickstun, I believe, goes too far in building her argument so exclusively upon this brief occasion in *Pilgrim's Progress* part II (chap. 3), it is true that the assault is a sexual one, especially as the two ill-favored ones propose

by it to "make women of you [Christiana and Mercy] for ever" (195). Thickstun endorses the Reliever's insistence on blaming Christiana the victim, an error I think in view of Bunyan's *Come, and Welcome, to Jesus Christ* which examines an occasion of sexual assault from Deuteronomy 22.25–27 to develop an analogy between "a betrothed damsel" walking in a field who meets a stronger man who forces himself upon her, and the seeker after Christ upon whom the devil forces blasphemous thoughts. Bunyan recalls the righteous God of the Old Testament who passes judgment upon the violent aggressor but lays no sin at the door of the innocent victims who "abhor such wicked leudness" (VIII:266).

22. Greaves, "Conscience" 39. Hill fully backgrounds this controversy in "Bunyan and the Woman Question," in *Tinker* 296–303. Brittain says that *A Case of Conscience Resolved* responded to a request from a group of London not Bedford women (374). For some contemporaneous conflicts between ministers and female church members in America, see Ulrich 219–23. She argues that winning the confidence of the women in his church was a key factor in ministerial stability, and although they lacked formal power within the church structure, women in fact wielded significant influence (223). See also Porterfield 7, 9. For separate women's prayer meetings in New England, see Hambrick-Stowe 140–41.

CHAPTER 8

1. Van Dyke 196; and see Fish, *Self-Consuming Artifacts* 72.

2. Hall 72, 31; and Lewalski, *Protestant Poetics* 152. Bunyan seems to emphasize the place rather than the content of memorial occasions when he asks in the preface to *Grace Abounding*: "Have you never a Hill *Mizar* (see Psalm 42.6) to remember? Have you forgot the Close, the Milk-house, the Stable, the Barn, and the like where *God* did visit your Soul?" (3). Two promising Bunyan titles, *Profitable Meditations* (1661) and *Prison Meditations* (1663) are in fact texts outside the formal traditions of meditation. Kaufmann acknowledges that occasional meditation is more appropriate to part II than part I of *Pilgrim's Progress*, but he does not explore the matter beyond noting that by and large Christian learns through action and Christiana through reflection (*Pilgrim's Progress* 188) and that Christiana's leisure differs from Christian's compulsive urgency.

3. Baxter 135–36, 144. For Bunyan's concordancing of *rest*, see *An Exposition . . . of Genesis* Offor 11:424.

4. Miller, Introduction, *Images* 3–4; and Bradstreet 195. Bradstreet's meditations were intended to instruct her son rather than simply record her private thoughts. She gravitates regularly toward Ecclesiastes and "all is vanity" and toward variations on "Whom the Lord loveth he chasteneth," a repeated lesson of the Book of Proverbs.

5. For Bunyan's version of Adam naming the animals, see *An Exposition . . . of Genesis* Offor 11:427.

6. God is to be known by his works, providences, judgments, and Word according to *Instruction For the Ignorant*; by his Word, the book of creatures, and the book of providences according to *The Saints' Knowledge of Christ's Love* (Offor II:13); by the four books of the creatures, God's remembrance, the law, and life according to *The Resurrection of the Dead* (see Daniel 7.10 and Revelation 20.11–12); and by the books of creatures, conscience, Lord's remembrance, law, and gospel according to *A Few Sighs From Hell* (1:338, and cf. Revelation 22.19). As *Resurrection* works it out, the book of God's remembrance is something like the conversion narrative from God's point of view, a record of *all* sins and *all* saving occasions and spiritual struggles; the book of the law is essentially the Ten Commandments; and the book of life is that wherein all the Elect are recorded as well as "the nature of Conversion, of Faith, Love &c." and noble and Christian acts or "the Testimony of the Saints against sin and Antichrist" (III:274, 276). As such, it includes the whole record of good works. The latter is also called "The Book of the Word of the Lord" (III:277, and for an overview see III:lii).

7. Lewalski's *Protestant Poetics* links the form of occasional meditation with Bacon's essays and its encouragements with Calvin (151–52, 164); Talon links emblems with Theophrastan characters (218–19); Freeman links emblems with metaphysical conceits (7); and Sadler (like Freeman) links emblems with allegory (112, 128). J. Paul Hunter points out that for seventeenth-century Puritans "Emblems become substitutes for icons. Unable to create objects to symbolize spiritual truths (because such action would usurp a divinely reserved prerogative), they permit themselves to isolate and interpret objects and events created by God" (29n.). From the ninth edition on, about half of Bunyan's emblems (50) are also accompanied by visual emblems. The title of the first edition, *A Book For Boys and Girls; or, Country Rhimes for Children*, becomes *A Book For Boys and Girls: or Temporal Things Spiritualized* in the edition of 1701, and *Divine Emblems: or, Temporal Things Spiritualized, Fitted for the Use of Boys and Girls. Adorned with cuts suitable to every subject* in the ninth edition of 1724.

8. Freeman 227, 212, 213, 223. See also Daly 72, 74. L. Marcus discusses and contextualizes Bunyan's *A Book For Boys and Girls* (52–53), and see Tindall 282, 43n. Sadler's chap. 7 provides the most expansive commentary on the literary qualities of Bunyan's emblems in *A Book For Boys and Girls*, especially their varied verse forms and special sound effects (114–16).

9. Foucault passim; and Van Dyke 193–94, 197. Ross finds seventeenth-century Puritans confusing the ornamental with the sacramental and describes the descent of symbol to metaphor to cliché in the seventeenth century as "evidence of a radical transformation in the Christian apprehension of reality, evidence of a shift in value so drastic that it must finally force a re-formation of value, a new kind of firmament" (80).

10. On the spider emblem, see Sadler 125–27; and Sharrock, "Bunyan" 105–16. The latter finds the robin and spider to be Bunyan's most striking and original contribution to the emblem genre (115–16). In *Pilgrim's Progress* Kaufmann traces

other spiders in the tradition of occasional meditation. Hall's two spider items in *Occasional Meditations* equate the spider with the spiritual enemy. Bunyan's Emblem XVII again claims the authority of Proverbs 30.28 for its spider (VI:219, and similarly *The Resurrection of the Dead* III:257). Other Bunyan spider emblems occur in *A Discourse of the House of God* (VI:304); *Light For Them That Sit in Darkness* (VIII:156–57); and *The Holy City* (III:95). For some other Bunyan chickens, see V:44 and Offor I:302.

11. Bunyan's catechism proceeds through the knowledge of God, the worship of God, and a series of applications. In his introduction to *Instruction For the Ignorant*, Greaves details the history, and indeed the politics, of catechizing in the 1670s. Church and state authorities agreed "that the principal cure for the evils besetting the Church of England was catechizing, especially of children, in order to 'imprint' their minds," a practice aimed especially at bringing back Dissenters to the Anglican fold (VIII:xxxi). He speaks of "the contest of catechisms [as] warfare for the souls of men" (xxxi–xxxii). Bunyan's doctrinal questions concur with other contemporary catechisms, but Bunyan is less polemical, includes humanizing personal and experiential touches, and shows a unique and expansive concern with self-denial (viii, xxxvi). Talon I believe overstates a keen insight in generalizing that in part II "Catechism takes the place of allegory" (*John Bunyan* 161). On household catechizing and the repetition of remembered sermons, see Cragg, *Puritanism* 139; and on catechizing in New England, see Morgan, *Puritan Family* 98–100.

12. Mark 4.33–34 describes Christ speaking the Word to the multitude in parables, "as they were able to hear it," but expounding the doctrine privately to his disciples without parables, a text examined in *An Exposition . . . of Genesis* Offor II:485. *Genesis* describes one text as "words . . . also under Moses's veil" (485). For a full consideration of Bunyan's tropic vocabulary, see Baird 14–22. Korshin finds that seventeenth-century speakers generally interchanged the vocabulary relating to this matter (6, 86, 102).

13. Hobbes 2:65; Black chap. 3. Hobbes would of course condemn many of Bunyan's similitudes as deriving from "mean conversation and experience of humble or evil Arts" (64).

14. Mather 52–59, 73–74. The cited portions of this work are dated July-August 1667. In two additional points Mather remarks: "Similitudes not understood are Riddles and Clouds of Darkness upon the Understanding: But if once interpreted and understood, they are like bright Candles, they give a clear Light" (63); and a parable is "a *Sacred* Similitude," authored by God, set apart, made into an ordinance (59).

15. Korshin 31, 34; and Hunter 101, 98, 99. Korshin dates to mid-century a slow secularization overtaking typology and a broadening into varied genres (5). For him the new like the old typology is "linked indissolubly to prophecy" (35). In a related vein, Joan Webber notes a contemporary Anglican preference for such Old

Testament characters as Adam, who includes all men, and a Puritan preference for "Biblical characters wholly immersed in history" (24).

16. For some Bunyan usages of *antitype*, see *An Exposition . . . of Genesis* (Offor 11:420, 467); and note the distinction between type and antitype (i.e., Christ) in *The Defense of the Doctrine of Justification By Faith* Offor 11:316. Hill reads Bunyan's biblical commentary, and *Genesis* in particular, as "a way of discussing the [politically] undiscussable," that is as "designed to convey points to which the censor might have objected if put directly" (*Tinker* 323).

CONCLUSION

1. Ross 19, 182, 91; see also Hill, *Some Intellectual Consequences* 65; *Intellectual Origins* 188; and *Tinker* 56.

2. Shapiro studies the increasing compatibility seventeenth-century theologians discovered between natural and revealed religion, between natural law and revelation, and the increasing use of metaphors drawing upon the book of nature as by-products of attempts to prove the existence of God by natural means. Her examination of changing seventeenth-century views on the relation of truth to natural phenomena, and thus also on the relation of knowledge (logic) and opinion (rhetoric), generally credits Bacon with publicizing the idea of translating experience from the realm of opinion (Ramus's contingent truth) to the arena of science (experimental truth) (94, 16). See also Blumenberg 205; and Cragg, *From Puritanism* esp. chaps. 5 and 6.

3. Pooley 101, 107, 108, 109, 91, 94; and see Hill, *Tinker* 134. Sutherland judges *The Holy War* a comparative failure because Bunyan succeeds in this ambition, treating his themes with overly sophisticated embroideries (*English Literature* 337).

4. Hill, *Experience* 293. Walzer admirably traces Calvinism transmuting into Hobbesianism (passim).

5. Batson 47, 53. For Newman the language of part I is "denuded" and "plain to the point of boldness" (237), and what Bunyan gains in solidity of metaphor, he loses in numinousness of language (241). Newman also finds in part II "an imaginative revitalization of the English common tongue," a dismantling of myth to expose the limits of metaphor and reinstate language as "miraculous, poetic and potential" (241).

6. Damrosch 8, 10, and see 180; see also Lewis, *English Literature* 319.

7. On covenant, see Fisch 106 and chap. 7; Greaves, *John Bunyan* 51–52; and Coolidge 112 and 109. Noting six repetitions of the word *Covenant* in Genesis 9, Bunyan defines "the everlasting Covenant" as one in which "the parties on both sides are faithful, perfect, and true" (*An Exposition . . . of Genesis* Offor 11:492).

8. Morgan, *Visible Saints* 67; and Hill, *God's Englishman* 224. See also Hill, *Some*

Intellectual Consequences 71; and Haller, *Liberty* 18–19. In *Pilgrim's Progress* part II Greatheart and the other males at Vanity Fair "entred into a Covenant" to fight the analogue of the beast of Revelation (278).

9. Rivers 45, 69; see also Hill, *Century* 253 and Shapiro 104–5, 107, 109.

10. Although a number of Bunyan commentators proffer his second imprisonment of 1677 for the writing of *Pilgrim's Progress* part I, Bunyan's earliest editor Charles Doe and his earliest biographer George Cokayne specify the first imprisonment (Offor III:765–66; *Grace Abounding* xlii, 172). A several-year interval would be necessary for the text to have undergone the conflicting responses described in the verse "Apology" (2). Recently Roger Sharrock, who has discussed this issue on earlier occasions, has reviewed it with some fullness in " 'When at the first' " (84–85). Recently too Hill has dated the writing of the first part of *Pilgrim's Progress* in the late 1660s on the basis of internal political evidence and changes in the second edition (also 1678) (*Tinker* 123, 197–98, 226).

11. Bainton 109. Davies describes Puritanism as "a resistance movement . . . not a religion or form of worship that would flourish, except in times of danger" (534).

12. Hill, *Some Intellectual Consequences* 76; and Simpson 36. On Bunyan's late and altered attitudes, see *Tinker* 148–49, 309, 310.

13. Morgan, *Puritan Family* 186, 9. For similar English entrance compromises favoring the second generation, see Watts 389–91; but cf. *The Holy City* III:175. On American practice see further Hambrick-Stowe 246–53; Elliott 60 and 113n.; and Caldwell Epilogue. She calls attention to particular second-generation fears of being an Esau, that is the supplanted rather than the chosen son (189).

14. L. Marcus 43, 243; see also McGee 256, 258.

15. Cragg, *Puritanism* 20, 66, 156–57, 255–56, and see 257–58. Similarly, Watts chap. 3 and 264, 391–93; Keeble, *Literary Culture* chap. 1; and Hill, *Century* part 3. In *Experience* Hill remarks, "The period after 1660 . . . was for many ordinary people one of unheroic passive opting out from the church they nominally adhered to" (296).

16. On *The Holy War* as the great Puritan epic, see also Introduction xxiv, xxv; Tillyard 406; and Knott, *Sword* 154. On parallels between *The Holy War* and English politics and economics, see Introduction xx–xxv, xxviii; Brittain chap. xvii; and J. Turner, "Bunyan's" 99.

Works Cited

Alpaugh, David J. "Emblem and Interpretation in *The Pilgrim's Progress.*" *English Literary History* 33 (1966): 299–314.

The Apocrypha. Trans. Edgar J. Goodspeed. Chicago: University of Chicago Press, 1938.

Aristotle. *On the Art of Poetry.* Trans. S. H. Butcher. New York: Liberal Arts Press, 1948.

Armstrong, Nancy, and Leonard Tennenhouse, eds. *The Ideology of Gender: Essays on Literature and the History of Sexuality.* New York: Methuen, 1987.

Auerbach, Erich. *Mimesis: The Representation of Reality in Western Literature.* Reprint. Garden City: Doubleday Anchor Books, 1957.

——— . *Scenes from the Drama of European Literature.* Reprint. New York: Meridian Books, 1959.

Bacon, Ernest W. *Pilgrim and Dreamer: John Bunyan: His Life and Work.* Exeter: Paternoster Press, 1983.

Bacon, Sir Francis. *Essays, Advancement of Learning, New Atlantis, and Other Pieces.* Edited by Richard F. Jones. New York: Odyssey Press, 1937.

Bainton, Roland H. *The Reformation of the Sixteenth Century.* Reprint. Boston: Beacon Press, 1970.

Baird, Charles W. *John Bunyan: A Study in Narrative Technique.* Port Washington: Kennikat Press, 1977.

Bamber, Linda. *Comic Women, Tragic Men: A Study of Gender and Genre in Shakespeare.* Stanford: Stanford University Press, 1982.

Barkan, Leonard. *Nature's Work of Art: The Human Body as Image of the World.* New Haven: Yale University Press, 1975.

Barker, Arthur E. *Milton and the Puritan Dilemma 1641–1660.* Toronto: University of Toronto Press, 1942.

Batson, E. Beatrice. *John Bunyan: Allegory and Imagination.* London: Croom Helm, 1984.

Baxter, Richard. *The Saints' Everlasting Rest.* N.p.: Fleming H. Revell Company, Epworth Press, 1962.

Bercovitch, Sacvan. *The Puritan Origins of the American Self*. New Haven: Yale University Press, 1975.

Berger, Harry, Jr. *The Allegorical Temper: Vision and Reality in Book II of Spenser's Faerie Queene*. Reprint. N.p.: Archon Books, 1967.

Berry, Boyd M. *Process of Speech: Puritan Religious Writing and Paradise Lost*. Baltimore: The Johns Hopkins University Press, 1976.

Black, Max. *Models and Metaphors: Studies in Language and Philosophy*. Ithaca: Cornell University Press, 1962.

Bloom, Edward A. "The Allegorical Principle." *English Literary History* 18 (1951): 163–90.

Blumenberg, Hans. *The Legitimacy of the Modern Age*. Trans. Robert M. Wallace. Cambridge: MIT Press, 1983.

Bottrall, Margaret. *Every Man a Phoenix: Studies in Seventeenth-Century Autobiography*. London: John Murray, 1958.

Bradstreet, Anne. *The Complete Works of Anne Bradstreet*. Edited by Joseph R. McElrath, Jr., and Allan P. Robb. Boston: Twayne Publishers, 1981.

Braudel, Fernand. *The Structures of Everyday Life: The Limits of the Possible*. Vol. 1 of *Civilization and Capitalism: Fifteenth to Eighteenth Century*. Rev. trans. Sian Reynolds. New York: Harper and Row, 1979.

Brittain, Vera. *In the Steps of John Bunyan: An Excursion into Puritan England*. London: Rich and Cowan, [1950].

Brown, John. *John Bunyan (1628–1688): His Life, Times, and Work*. Reprint. N.p.: Archon Books, 1969.

Bruss, Elizabeth. *Autobiographical Acts: The Changing Situation of a Literary Genre*. Baltimore: The Johns Hopkins University Press, 1976.

Burke, Kenneth. *The Rhetoric of Religion: Studies in Logology*. Boston: Beacon Press, 1961.

Bush, Douglas. *English Literature in the Earlier Seventeenth Century 1600–1660*. New York: Oxford University Press, 1945.

Caldwell, Patricia. *The Puritan Conversion Narrative: The Beginnings of American Expression*. Cambridge: Cambridge University Press, 1983.

Campbell, Gordon. "Fishing in Other Men's Waters: Bunyan and the Theologians." *John Bunyan: Conventicle and Parnassus: Tercentenary Essays*. Edited by N. H. Keeble. Oxford: Clarendon Press, 1988. Pp. 137–51.

——— . "The Theology of *The Pilgrim's Progress*." *The Pilgrim's Progress: Critical and Historical Views*. Edited by Vincent Newey. Totowa: Barnes and Noble Books, 1980. Pp. 251–62.

Campbell, Joseph. *The Hero with a Thousand Faces*. Reprint. New York: Meridian Books, 1956.

Caplan, Harry. "Memoria: Treasure-House of Eloquence." *Of Eloquence: Studies in Ancient and Mediaeval Rhetoric*. Edited by Anne King and Helen North. Ithaca: Cornell University Press, 1970. Pp. 196–246.

Carlton, Peter J. "Bunyan: Language, Convention, Authority." *English Literary History* 51 (1984): 17–32.

Chodorow, Nancy. *The Reproduction of Mothering: Psychoanalysis and the Sociology of Gender.* Berkeley and Los Angeles: University of California Press, 1978.

Christopher, Georgia B. *Milton and the Science of the Saints.* Princeton: Princeton University Press, 1982.

The Church Book of the Bedford Meeting 1650–1821. Facsimile ed. Introduction by G. B. Harrison. London: J. M. Dent and Sons, 1928.

Clark, Alice. *Working Life of Women in the Seventeenth Century.* London: George Routledge and Sons, 1919.

Clifford, Gay. *The Transformations of Allegory.* London: Routledge and Kegan Paul, 1974.

Cohen, Charles L. *God's Caress: The Psychology of Puritan Religious Experience.* New York: Oxford University Press, 1986.

Coleridge, Samuel Taylor. *Anima Poetae, From the Unpublished Note-Books of Samuel Taylor Coleridge.* Edited by Ernest Hartley Coleridge. Boston: Houghton Mifflin and Company, 1895.

——— . *Coleridge on the Seventeenth Century.* Edited by Roberta F. Brinkley. Durham: Duke University Press, 1955.

——— . *Coleridge's Essays and Lectures on Shakespeare and Some Other Old Poets and Dramatists.* London: J. M. Dent, 1907.

——— . *Coleridge's Miscellaneous Criticism.* Edited by Thomas M. Raysor. London: Constable and Co., 1936.

Collinson, Patrick. *English Puritanism.* The Historical Association, General Series 106. London, 1983.

Coolidge, John S. *The Pauline Renaissance in England: Puritanism and the Bible.* Oxford: Clarendon Press, 1970.

Cragg, Gerald R. *From Puritanism to the Age of Reason: A Study of Changes in Religious Thought within the Church of England 1660–1700.* Cambridge: Cambridge University Press, 1950.

——— . *Puritanism in the Period of the Great Persecution 1660–1688.* Cambridge: Cambridge University Press, 1957.

Cunningham, Valentine. "Glossing and Glozing: Bunyan and Allegory." *John Bunyan: Conventicle and Parnassus: Tercentenary Essays.* Edited by N. H. Keeble. Oxford: Clarendon Press, 1988. Pp. 217–40.

Daly, Peter M. *Literature in the Light of the Emblem: Structural Parallels between the Emblem and Literature in the Sixteenth and Seventeenth Centuries.* Toronto: University of Toronto Press, 1979.

Damrosch, Leopold, Jr. *God's Plot and Man's Stories: Studies in the Fictional Imagination from Milton to Fielding.* Chicago: University of Chicago Press, 1985.

Daniells, Roy. *Milton, Mannerism and Baroque.* Toronto: University of Toronto Press, 1963.

Danielou, Jean, S.J. "The Problem of Symbolism." *Thought: A Review of Culture and Idea*, September 1950: 423–40.

Dante. *Literary Criticism of Dante Alighieri*. Trans. and ed. Robert S. Haller. Lincoln: University of Nebraska Press, 1973.

Davie, Donald. *A Gathered Church: The Literature of the English Dissenting Interest, 1700–1930*. New York: Oxford University Press, 1978.

Davies, Horton. *Worship and Theology in England from Andrewes to Baxter and Fox, 1603–1690*. Princeton: Princeton University Press, 1975.

Davis, Nick. "The Problem of Misfortune in *The Pilgrim's Progress.*" *The Pilgrim's Progress: Critical and Historical Views*. Edited by Vincent Newey. Totowa: Barnes and Noble Books, 1980. Pp. 182–200.

Dutton, A. Richard. "'Interesting, but Tough': Reading *The Pilgrim's Progress.*" *Studies in English Literature* 18 (1978): 439–56.

Eagleton, Terry. *Literary Theory: An Introduction*. Minneapolis: University of Minnesota Press, 1983.

Eberle, Eliza, ed. *The Pilgrim's Progress*. New Haven: J. H. Benham, 1855.

Ebner, Dean. *Autobiography in Seventeenth-Century England: Theology and the Self*. The Hague: Mouton, 1971.

Edwards, Lee R. *Psyche as Hero: Female Heroism and Fictional Form*. Middletown: Wesleyan University Press, 1984.

Edwards, Philip. "The Journey in *Pilgrim's Progress.*" *The Pilgrim's Progress: Critical and Historical Views*. Edited by Vincent Newey. Totowa: Barnes and Noble Books, 1980. Pp. 111–17.

Elliott, Emory. *Power and the Pulpit in Puritan New England*. Princeton: Princeton University Press, 1975.

Emerson, Everett H. *English Puritanism from John Hooper to John Milton*. Durham: Duke University Press, 1968.

Fastnedge, Ralph. *English Furniture Styles from 1500 to 1830*. Harmondsworth: Penguin Books, 1955.

Firth, Sir Charles. Introduction to *Pilgrim's Progress* (London 1898). *Bunyan: The Pilgrim's Progress: A Casebook*. Edited by Roger Sharrock. London: Macmillan, 1976.

Fisch, Harold. *Jerusalem and Albion: The Hebraic Factor in Seventeenth-Century Literature*. New York: Schocken Books, 1964.

Fish, Stanley E. *The Living Temple: George Herbert and Catechizing*. Berkeley and Los Angeles: University of California Press, 1978.

———. *Self-Consuming Artifacts: The Experience of Seventeenth-Century Literature*. Berkeley and Los Angeles: University of California Press, 1972.

Fletcher, Angus. *Allegory: The Theory of a Symbolic Mode*. Ithaca: Cornell University Press, 1964.

Ford, Worthington Chauncey. *The Boston Bookmarket: 1679–1700*. Reprint. New York: Burt Franklin, 1972.

Forrest, James F. "Mercy With Her Mirror." *Philological Quarterly* 42 (1963): 121–26.

Forrest, James F., and Richard L. Greaves. *John Bunyan: A Reference Guide*. Boston: G. K. Hall and Co., 1982.

Foucault, Michel. *The Order of Things: An Archaeology of the Human Sciences*. Reprint. New York: Vintage Books, 1973.

Fraser, Antonia. *The Weaker Vessel*. Reprint. New York: Vintage Books, 1985.

Freeman, Rosemary. *English Emblem Books*. London: Chatto and Windus, 1948.

Frei, Hans W. *The Eclipse of Biblical Narrative: A Study in Eighteenth and Nineteenth Century Hermeneutics*. New Haven: Yale University Press, 1974.

French, Marilyn. *Shakespeare's Division of Experience*. New York: Summit Books, 1981.

Frye, Northrop. *Anatomy of Criticism: Four Essays*. Princeton: Princeton University Press, 1957.

Frye, Roland M. *God, Man, and Satan: Patterns of Christian Thought and Life in Paradise Lost, Pilgrim's Progress, and the Great Theologians*. Princeton: Princeton University Press, 1960.

Furlong, Monica. *Puritan's Progress*. New York: Coward, McCann and Geoghegan, 1975.

Fussell, Paul. *The Great War and Modern Memory*. New York: Oxford University Press, 1975.

Geertz, Clifford. *The Interpretation of Cultures: Selected Essays*. New York: Basic Books, 1973.

The Geneva Bible: A Facsimile of the 1560 Edition. Introduction by Lloyd E. Berry. Madison: University of Wisconsin Press, 1969.

George, Charles H., and Katherine George. *The Protestant Mind of the English Reformation 1570–1640*. Princeton: Princeton University Press, 1961.

Gilligan, Carol. *In a Different Voice: Psychological Theory and Women's Development*. Cambridge: Harvard University Press, 1982.

Godber, Joyce. *John Bunyan of Bedfordshire*. Bedfordshire County Council, 1972.

Golder, Harold. "Bunyan's Valley of the Shadow." *Modern Philology* 27 (1929): 55–72.

Greaves, Richard L. "Conscience, Liberty, and the Spirit: Bunyan and Nonconformity." *John Bunyan: Conventicle and Parnassus: Tercentenary Essays*. Edited by N. H. Keeble. Oxford: Clarendon Press, 1988. Pp. 21–43.

———. *John Bunyan*. Courtenay Studies in Reformation Theology 2. Appleford: Sutton Courtenay Press, 1969.

———. "The Nature of the Puritan Tradition." *Reformation Conformity and Dissent: Essays in Honour of Geoffrey Nuttall*. Edited by R. Buick Knox. London: Epworth Press, 1977. Pp. 255–73.

Guibbory, Achsah. *The Map of Time: Seventeenth-Century English Literature and Ideas of Pattern in History*. Urbana: University of Illinois Press, 1986.

Hadyn, Hiram. *The Counter-Renaissance*. Reprint. Gloucester, Mass.: Peter Smith, 1966.

Haec et Hic, or The Feminine Gender more worthy than the Masculine. Being a Vindication of the ingenious and innocent Sex from the biting Sarcasms, bitter Satyrs, and opprobrious Calumnies, wherewith they are daily, though undeservedly, aspersed by the virulent Tongues and Pens of malevolent Men; with many examples of the rare Virtues of that noble Sex, in which they have not only equalled, but excelled, most of the other Sex. London, 1683.

Hall, Joseph. *Bishop Joseph Hall and Protestant Meditation in Seventeenth-Century England: A Study with the Texts of The Art of Divine Meditation (1606) and Occasional Meditations (1633)*. Edited by Frank L. Huntley. Binghamton: Medieval and Renaissance Texts and Studies, 1981.

Haller, William. *The Elect Nation: The Meaning and Relevance of Foxe's Book of Martyrs*. New York: Harper and Row, 1963.

———. "'Hail Wedded Love.'" *A Journal of English Literary History* 13 (1946): 79–97.

———. *Liberty and Reformation in the Puritan Revolution*. New York: Columbia University Press, 1955.

———. *The Rise of Puritanism, or The Way to the New Jerusalem as Set Forth in Pulpit and Press from Thomas Cartwright to John Lilburne and John Milton 1570–1643*. Reprint. New York: Harper Torchbooks, 1957.

Hambrick-Stowe, Charles E. *The Practice of Piety: Puritan Devotional Disciplines in Seventeenth-Century New England*. Chapel Hill: University of North Carolina Press, 1982.

Harding, M. Esther. *Journey into Self*. New York: David McKay Co., 1956.

Harrison, Frank Mott. *A Bibliography of the Works of John Bunyan*. Oxford: Oxford University Press, printed for the Bibliographical Society, 1932.

Harrison, G. B. *John Bunyan: A Study in Personality*. Reprint. N.p.: Archon Books, 1967.

Herbert, George. *The Works of George Herbert*. Edited by F. E. Hutchinson. Oxford: Clarendon Press, 1941.

Hill, Christopher. *The Century of Revolution 1603–1714*. Second ed. Reprint. New York: W. W. Norton and Company, 1982.

———. *The Experience of Defeat: Milton and Some Contemporaries*. New York: Viking, 1984.

———. *God's Englishman: Oliver Cromwell and the English Revolution*. Reprint. New York: Harper and Row, 1972.

———. *Intellectual Origins of the English Revolution*. Oxford: Clarendon Press, 1965.

———. "Sex, Marriage and Parish Registers." *The Collected Essays of Christopher Hill*. Vol. 3. Amherst: University of Massachusetts Press, 1986. Pp. 188–225.

———. *Society and Puritanism in Pre-Revolutionary England*. Second ed. Reprint. New York: Schocken Books, 1972.

———. *Some Intellectual Consequences of the English Revolution*. Madison: University of Wisconsin Press, 1980.

———. *A Tinker and a Poor Man: John Bunyan and His Church, 1628–1688*. New York: Alfred A. Knopf, 1989.

———. *The World Turned Upside Down: Radical Ideas During the English Revolution*. Reprint. Harmondsworth: Penguin Books, 1975.

Hobbes, Thomas. *Answer to Davenant's Preface to Gondibert*. *Critical Essays of the Seventeenth Century*. Vol. 2. Edited by J. E. Spingarn. Bloomington: Indiana University Press, 1968. Pp. 54–67.

Honig, Edwin. *Dark Conceit: The Making of Allegory*. Reprint. New York: Oxford University Press, 1966.

Houlbrooke, Ralph. *The English Family 1450–1700*. London: Longman, 1984.

Hunter, J. Paul. *The Reluctant Pilgrim: Defoe's Emblematic Method and Quest for Form in Robinson Crusoe*. Baltimore: The Johns Hopkins University Press, 1966.

Iser, Wolfgang. *The Implied Reader: Patterns of Communication in Prose Fiction from Bunyan to Beckett*. Baltimore: The Johns Hopkins University Press, 1974.

Johnson, James Turner. *A Society Ordained by God: English Puritan Marriage Doctrine in the First Half of the Seventeenth Century*. Nashville: Abingdon Press, 1970.

Kahler, Erich. "The Persistence of *Myth*." *Chimera* 4 (Spring 1946): 2–11.

Kaufmann, U. Milo. *The Pilgrim's Progress and Traditions in Puritan Meditation*. New Haven: Yale University Press, 1966.

———. "Spiritual Discerning: Bunyan and the Mysteries of the Divine Will." *John Bunyan: Conventicle and Parnassus: Tercentenary Essays*. Edited by N. H. Keeble. Oxford: Clarendon Press, 1988. Pp. 171–87.

Keeble, N. H. "Christiana's Key: The Unity of *The Pilgrim's Progress*." *The Pilgrim's Progress: Critical and Historical Views*. Edited by Vincent Newey. Totowa: Barnes and Noble Books, 1980. Pp. 1–20.

———. *The Literary Culture of Nonconformity in Later Seventeenth-Century England*. Leicester: Leicester University Press, 1987.

———. "'Of him thousands daily Sing and talk': Bunyan and His Reputation." *John Bunyan: Conventicle and Parnassus: Tercentenary Essays*. Edited by N. H. Keeble. Oxford: Clarendon Press, 1988. Pp. 241–63.

Kibbey, Anne. *The Interpretation of Material Shapes in Puritanism: A Study of Rhetoric, Prejudice, and Violence*. Cambridge: Cambridge University Press, 1986.

King, John N. *English Reformation Literature: The Tudor Origins of the Protestant Tradition*. Princeton: Princeton University Press, 1982.

King, John Owen, III. *The Iron of Melancholy: Structures of Spiritual Conversion in America from the Puritan Conscience to Victorian Neurosis.* Middletown: Wesleyan University Press, 1983.

Knott, John R., Jr. "Bunyan and the Holy Community." *Studies in Philology* 80 (1983): 200–25.

——. *The Sword of the Spirit: Puritan Responses to the Bible.* Chicago: University of Chicago Press, 1980.

——. " 'Thou must live upon my Word': Bunyan and the Bible." *John Bunyan: Conventicle and Parnassus: Tercentenary Essays.* Edited by N. H. Keeble. Oxford: Clarendon Press, 1988. Pp. 153–70.

Korshin, Paul J. *Typologies in England 1650–1820.* Princeton: Princeton University Press, 1982.

Lamont, William, and Sybil Oldfield, eds. *Politics, Religion and Literature in the Seventeenth Century.* London: J. M. Dent and Sons, 1975.

Latt, David J. "Praising Virtuous Ladies: The Literary Image and Historical Reality of Women in Seventeenth-Century England." *What Manner of Woman: Essays on English and American Life and Literature.* Edited by Marlene Springer. New York: New York University Press, 1977. Pp. 39–64.

Leavis, Q. D. *Fiction and the Reading Public.* London: Chatto and Windus, 1965.

Leverenz, David. *The Language of Puritan Feeling: An Exploration in Literature, Psychology, and Social History.* New Brunswick: Rutgers University Press, 1980.

Lewalski, Barbara K. *Donne's Anniversaries and the Poetry of Praise: The Creation of a Symbolic Mode.* Princeton: Princeton University Press, 1973.

——. *Protestant Poetics and the Seventeenth-Century Religious Lyric.* Princeton: Princeton University Press, 1979.

——. "Typological Symbolism and the 'Progress of the Soul' in Seventeenth-Century Literature." *Literary Uses of Typology from the Late Middle Ages to the Present.* Edited by Earl Miner. Princeton: Princeton University Press, 1977. Pp. 79–114.

Lewis, C. S. *The Allegory of Love: A Study in Medieval Tradition.* Reprint. New York: Oxford University Press, 1958.

——. *English Literature in the Sixteenth Century Excluding Drama.* Oxford: Clarendon Press, 1954.

Lindsey, Jack. *John Bunyan: Maker of Myths.* Reprint. New York: Augustus M. Kelley Publishers, 1969.

Lowance, Mason I., Jr. *The Language of Canaan: Metaphor and Symbol in New England from the Puritans to the Transcendentalists.* Cambridge: Harvard University Press, 1980.

Luxon, Thomas H. "Calvin and Bunyan on Word and Image: Is There a Text in Interpreter's House?" *English Literary Renaissance* 18 (1988): 438–59.

MacCaffrey, Isabel G. *Spenser's Allegory: The Anatomy of Imagination.* Princeton: Princeton University Press, 1976.

MacCallum, H. R. "Milton and Sacred History: Books XI and XII of *Paradise Lost.*"

Essays in English Literature from the Renaissance to the Victorian Age Presented to A. S. P. Woodhouse. Edited by Millar MacLure and F. W. Watt. Toronto: University of Toronto Press, 1964. Pp. 149–68.

McColley, Diane K. *Milton's Eve.* Urbana: University of Illinois Press, 1983.

McCombs, Charles F. "*The Pilgrim's Progress:* John Bunyan, His Life and Times, 1628–1928." *Bulletin of the New York Public Library* 32 (1928): 786–809. Updated in *Guide to the Research Collections of the New York Public Library.* Edited by Sam Williams. Chicago: American Library Association, 1975.

MacFarlane, Alan. *Marriage and Love in England: Modes of Reproduction 1300–1840.* Oxford: Basil Blackwell, 1986.

McGee, J. Sears. *The Godly Man in Stuart England: Anglicans, Puritans, and the Two Tables, 1620–1670.* New Haven: Yale University Press, 1976.

MacLean, Ian. *The Renaissance Notion of Woman: A Study in the Fortunes of Scholasticism and Medical Science in European Intellectual Life.* Cambridge: Cambridge University Press, 1980.

Madsen, William G. *From Shadowy Types to Truth: Studies in Milton's Symbolism.* New Haven: Yale University Press, 1968.

Marcus, Leah S. *Childhood and Cultural Despair: A Theme and Variations in Seventeenth-Century Literature.* Pittsburgh: University of Pittsburgh Press, 1978.

Marcus, R. A., ed. *Augustine: A Collection of Critical Essays.* Garden City: Anchor Books, 1972.

Martz, Louis L. *The Poetry of Meditation: A Study in English Religious Literature of the Seventeenth Century.* New Haven: Yale University Press, 1962.

Mather, Samuel. *The Figures or Types of the Old Testament.* Introduction by Mason I. Lowance, Jr. New York: Johnson Reprint Corporation, 1969.

Matthews, William. "Seventeenth-Century Autobiography." *Autobiography, Biography, and the Novel: Papers Read at a Clark Library Seminar by William Matthews and Ralph W. Rader.* Los Angeles: William Andrews Clark Memorial Library, 1973.

Mendelson, Sara Heller. "Stuart Women's Diaries and Occasional Memoirs." *Women in English Society 1500–1800.* Edited by Mary Prior. London: Methuen, 1985. Pp. 181–210.

Messer-Davidow, Ellen. "The Philosophical Bases of Feminist Literary Criticisms." *New Literary History* 19 (1987): 65–103.

Miller, Jean Baker. *Toward a New Psychology of Women.* Boston: Beacon Press, 1976.

Miller, Perry. *The New England Mind: The Seventeenth Century.* Reprint. Boston: Beacon Press, 1961.

———. Introduction. *Images or Shadows of Divine Things by Jonathan Edwards.* New Haven: Yale University Press, 1948.

Milton, John. *Complete Poems and Major Prose.* Edited by Merritt Y. Hughes. New York: Odyssey Press, 1957.

———. *Complete Prose Works of John Milton*. General editor Don M. Wolfe. 8 vols. New Haven: Yale University Press, 1953–82.

Miner, Earl. *The Restoration Mode from Milton to Dryden*. Princeton: Princeton University Press, 1974.

The Minutes of the First Independent Church (Now Bunyan Meeting) at Bedford 1656–1766. Edited by H. G. Tibbutt. Publications of the Bedfordshire Historical Record Society. Vol. 55. Bedford: The Society, 1976.

Mitchell, W. Fraser. *English Pulpit Oratory from Andrewes to Tillotson: A Study of Its Literary Aspects*. New York: Russell and Russell, 1962.

Morgan, Edmund S. *The Puritan Family: Religion and Domestic Relations in Seventeenth-Century New England*. Rev. ed. New York: Harper Torchbooks, 1966.

———. *Visible Saints: The History of a Puritan Idea*. New York: New York University Press, 1963.

Murdock, Kenneth B. *Literature and Theology in Colonial New England*. Cambridge: Harvard University Press, 1949.

Nellist, Brian. "*The Pilgrim's Progress* and Allegory." *The Pilgrim's Progress: Critical and Historical Views*. Edited by Vincent Newey. Totowa: Barnes and Noble Books, 1980. Pp. 132–53.

New, John F. H. *Anglican and Puritan: The Basis of Their Opposition, 1558–1640*. Stanford: Stanford University Press, 1964.

Newey, Vincent. "Bunyan and the Confines of the Mind." *The Pilgrim's Progress: Critical and Historical Views*. Edited by Vincent Newey. Totowa: Barnes and Noble Books, 1980. Pp. 21–48.

———. "'With the eyes of my understanding': Bunyan, Experience, and Acts of Interpretation." *John Bunyan: Conventicle and Parnassus: Tercentenary Essays*. Edited by N. H. Keeble. Oxford: Clarendon Press, 1988. Pp. 189–216.

Newman, S. J. "Bunyan's Solidness." *The Pilgrim's Progress: Critical and Historical Views*. Edited by Vincent Newey. Totowa: Barnes and Noble Books, 1980. Pp. 225–50.

Nussbaum, Felicity. "By These Words I Was Sustained: Bunyan's *Grace Abounding*." *English Literary History* 49 (1982): 18–35.

Nuttall, Geoffrey F. Introduction to *John Bunyan* by Richard Greaves. Appleford: Sutton Courtenay Press, 1969.

———. *The Holy Spirit in Puritan Faith and Experience*. Oxford: Basil Blackwell, 1946.

———. *Visible Saints: The Congregational Way 1640–1660*. Oxford: Basil Blackwell, 1957.

Ong, Walter J., S.J. *Ramus, Method, and the Decay of Dialogue: From the Art of Discourse to the Art of Reason*. Cambridge: Harvard University Press, 1983.

Packer, J. I. Introduction. *Introduction to Puritan Theology: A Reader*. Edited by Edward Hindson. Grand Rapids: Baker Book House, 1976.

Pearson, Carol, and Katherine Pope. *The Female Hero in American and British Literature*. New York: R. R. Bowker Company, 1981.

Perkins, William. *The Works of William Perkins*. Edited by Ian Breward. The Courtenay Library of Reformation Classics. Appleford: The Sutton Courtenay Press, 1970.

Plum, Harry G. *Restoration Puritanism: A Study of the Growth of English Liberty*. Reprint. Port Washington: Kennikat Press, 1972.

Pooley, Roger. "Plain and Simple: Bunyan and Style." *John Bunyan: Conventicle and Parnassus: Tercentenary Essays*. Edited by N. H. Keeble. Oxford: Clarendon Press, 1988. Pp. 91–110.

Porterfield, Amanda. *Feminine Spirituality in America: From Sarah Edwards to Martha Graham*. Philadelphia: Temple University Press, 1980.

Powell, Chilton Latham. *English Domestic Relations 1487–1653: A Study of Matrimony and Family Life in Theory and Practice as Revealed by the Literature, Law, and History of the Period*. Reprint. New York: Russell and Russell, 1972.

Princeton Encyclopedia of Poetry and Poetics. Edited by Alex Preminger et al. Enlarged ed. Princeton: Princeton University Press, 1974.

Quilligan, Maureen. *The Language of Allegory: Defining the Genre*. Ithaca: Cornell University Press, 1979.

Rivers, Isabel. "Grace, Holiness, and the Pursuit of Happiness: Bunyan and Restoration Latitudinarianism." *John Bunyan: Conventicle and Parnassus: Tercentenary Essays*. Edited by N. H. Keeble. Oxford: Clarendon Press, 1988. Pp. 45–69.

Robertson, D. W., Jr. *A Preface to Chaucer: Studies in Medieval Perspectives*. Princeton: Princeton University Press, 1962.

Rosenblatt, Jason P. "Structural Unity and Temporal Concordance: The War in Heaven in *Paradise Lost*." *Publications of the Modern Language Association* 87 (1972): 31–41.

Ross, Malcolm M. *Poetry and Dogma: The Transfiguration of Eucharistic Symbols in Seventeenth Century English Poetry*. New Brunswick: Rutgers University Press, 1954.

Rybczynski, Witold. *Home: A Short History of an Idea*. Harmondsworth: Penguin Books, 1987.

Sadler, Lynn Veach. *John Bunyan*. Twayne's English Authors Series. Boston: Twayne Publishers, 1979.

Sasek, Lawrence A. *The Literary Temper of the English Puritans*. Baton Rouge: Louisiana State University Press, 1961.

Schlatter, Richard B. *The Social Ideas of Religious Leaders 1660–1688*. Reprint. New York: Octagon Books, 1971.

Schucking, Levin L. *The Puritan Family: A Social Study from the Literary Sources*. Trans. Brian Battershaw. London: Routledge and Kegan Paul, 1969.

Scott, Thomas, ed. *The Pilgrim's Progress*. Hartford: Silas Andrus, 1828.

Scott, Sir Walter. Review of Southey's edition of *Pilgrim's Progress*. *Pilgrim's*

Progress: A Casebook. Edited by Roger Sharrock. London: Macmillan Press, 1976.

Shapiro, Barbara. *Probability and Certainty in Seventeenth-Century England: A Study of the Relationships between Natural Science, Religion, History, Law, and Literature.* Princeton: Princeton University Press, 1983.

Sharrock, Roger, ed. *Bunyan: The Pilgrim's Progress: A Casebook.* London: Macmillan Press, 1976.

———. "Bunyan and the English Emblem Writers." *Review of English Studies* 21 (1945): 105–16.

———. *John Bunyan.* London: Macmillan, 1968.

———. *John Bunyan: The Pilgrim's Progress.* London: Edward Arnold, 1966.

———. "Life and Story in *The Pilgrim's Progress.*" *The Pilgrim's Progress: Critical and Historical Views.* Edited by Vincent Newey. Totowa: Barnes and Noble, 1980. Pp. 49–68.

———. " 'When at the first I took my Pen in hand': Bunyan and the Book." *John Bunyan: Conventicle and Parnassus: Tercentenary Essays.* Edited by N. H. Keeble. Oxford: Clarendon Press, 1988. Pp. 71–90.

Shea, Daniel B., Jr. *Spiritual Autobiography in Early America.* Princeton: Princeton University Press, 1968.

Shepard, Thomas. *God's Plot: The Paradoxes of Puritan Piety: Being the Autobiography and Journal of Thomas Shepard.* Edited by Michael McGiffert. Amherst: University of Massachusetts Press, 1972.

———. *Thomas Shepard's Confessions.* Edited by George Selement and Bruce C. Woolley. Publications of the Colonial Society of Massachusetts Collections 58. Boston: The Society, 1981.

Simpson, Alan. *Puritanism in Old and New England.* Chicago: University of Chicago Press, 1955.

Smith, Edith F., ed. *The Pilgrim's Progress.* Boston: Atlantic Monthly Press, 1923.

Snyder, Susan. *The Comic Matrix of Shakeapeare's Tragedies: Romeo and Juliet, Hamlet, Othello, and King Lear.* Princeton: Princeton University Press, 1979.

Spengemann, William C. *The Forms of Autobiography: Episodes in the History of a Literary Genre.* New Haven: Yale University Press, 1980.

Stannard, David E. *The Puritan Way of Death: A Study in Religion, Culture, and Social Change.* New York: Oxford University Press, 1977.

Starr, G. A. *Defoe and Spiritual Autobiography.* Princeton: Princeton University Press, 1965.

Steiner, George. Introduction. *Homer: A Collection of Critical Essays.* Edited by George Steiner and Robert Fagles. Twentieth-Century Views. Englewood Cliffs: Prentice-Hall, Inc., 1962.

Stewart, Stanley E. *The Enclosed Garden: The Tradition and the Image in Seventeenth-Century Poetry.* Madison: University of Wisconsin Press, 1966.

Stone, Lawrence. *The Family, Sex and Marriage in England 1500–1800.* Abridged ed. New York: Harper Torchbooks, 1979.

Stranahan, Brainerd P. "Bunyan's Special Talent: Biblical Texts as 'Events' in *Grace Abounding* and *The Pilgrim's Progress.*" *English Literary Renaissance* 11 (1981): 329–43.

Sutherland, James. *English Literature of the Late Seventeenth Century.* Oxford: Clarendon Press, 1969.

————. *A Preface to Eighteenth Century Poetry.* Oxford: Clarendon Press, 1948.

Swaim, Kathleen M. *Before and After the Fall: Contrasting Modes in Paradise Lost.* Amherst: University of Massachusetts Press, 1987.

Talon, Henri. *John Bunyan: The Man and His Works.* Trans. Barbara Wall. Cambridge: Harvard University Press, 1951.

————. "Space and the Hero in *The Pilgrim's Progress:* A Study of the Meaning of the Allegorical Universe." *Bunyan: The Pilgrim's Progress: A Casebook.* Edited by Roger Sharrock. London: Macmillan Press, 1976.

Thickstun, Margaret O. *Fictions of the Feminine: Puritan Doctrine and the Representation of Women.* Ithaca: Cornell University Press, 1988.

Thomas, Keith. *Religion and the Decline of Magic.* New York: Charles Scribner's Sons, 1971.

Thrall, William F., and Addison Hibbard. *A Handbook to Literature.* Edited by C. Hugh Holman. Rev. ed. New York: Odyssey Press, 1960.

Tillyard, E. M. W. *The English Epic and Its Background.* New York: Oxford University Press, 1954.

Tindall, Willliam York. *John Bunyan: Mechanick Preacher.* Reprint. New York: Russell and Russell, 1964.

Trevelyan, G. M. *The Age of Shakespeare and the Stuart Period.* Vol. 2 of *Illustrated English Social History.* Reprint. Harmondsworth: Penguin Books, 1964.

Turner, James. "Bunyan's Sense of Place." *The Pilgrim's Progress: Critical and Historical Views.* Edited by Vincent Newey. Totowa: Barnes and Noble Books, 1980. Pp. 91–110.

————. *One Flesh: Paradisal Marriage and Sexual Relations in the Age of Milton.* Oxford: Clarendon Press, 1987.

Turner, Victor W. *The Ritual Process: Structure and Anti-Structure.* Chicago: Aldine Publishing Company, 1969.

Ulrich, Laurel Thatcher. *Good Wives: Image and Reality in the Lives of Women in Northern New England 1650–1750.* New York: Alfred A. Knopf, 1982.

van Beek, M. *An Enquiry into Puritan Vocabulary.* Groningen: Wolters-Noordhoff n. v., 1969.

Van Dyke, Carolynn. *The Fiction of Truth: Structures of Meaning in Narrative and Dramatic Allegory.* Ithaca: Cornell University Press, 1985.

Van Ghent, Dorothy. *The English Novel: Form and Function.* Reprint. New York: Harper Torchbooks, 1961.

Wallace, Ronald S. *Calvin's Doctrine of the Word and Sacrament*. Edinburgh: Oliver and Boyd, 1953.

Walton, Geoffrey. *Metaphysical to Augustan: Studies in Tone and Sensibility in the Seventeenth Century*. London: Bowes and Bowes, 1955.

Walzer, Michael. *The Revolution of the Saints: A Study in the Origins of Radical Politics*. Cambridge: Harvard University Press, 1965.

Watkins, Owen C. *The Puritan Experience*. London: Routledge and Kegan Paul, 1972.

Watts, Michael R. *The Dissenters*. Oxford: Clarendon Press, 1978.

Webber, Joan. *The Eloquent "I": Style and Self in Seventeenth-Century Prose*. Madison: University of Wisconsin Press, 1968.

Weintraub, Karl J. *The Value of the Individual Self and Circumstance in Autobiography*. Chicago: University of Chicago Press, 1978.

White, B. R. "The Fellowship of Believers: Bunyan and Puritanism." *John Bunyan: Conventicle and Parnassus: Tercentenary Essays*. Edited by N. H. Keeble. Oxford: Clarendon Press, 1988. Pp. 1–19.

Whitehead, A. N. *Religion in the Making*. Reprint. Cleveland: Meridian Books, 1960.

Willey, Basil. *The Seventeenth-Century Background: Studies in the Thought of the Age in Relation to Poetry and Religion*. London: Chatto and Windus, 1934.

Williams, Sam P., ed. *Guide to the Research Collections of the New York Public Library*. Chicago: American Library Association, 1975.

Winslow, Ola E. *John Bunyan*. New York: Macmillan Co., 1961.

The Wonders of the Femall World, or A general History of Women In Two Books. Wherein by many hundreds of Examples, is shewed what Woman hath been from the first Ages of the World to these Times, in respect of her Body, Senses, Passions, Affections, her Virtues and Perfections, her Vices and Defects . . . To which is added, A Discourse of Female Pre-eminence. London, 1683.

Woolley, Hannah. *The Gentlewoman's Companion; or A Guide to the Female Sex: Containing Directions of Behaviour, in All Places, Companies, Relations, and Conditions, from their Childhood down to Old Age*. London, 1675.

Yates, Frances A. *The Art of Memory*. London: Routledge and Kegan Paul, 1966.

Index

A NOTE ON THE AUTHOR

Kathleen Swaim, professor of English at the University of Massachusetts, Amherst, specializes in Milton and related seventeenth-century topics. Her publications include *Before and After the Fall: Contrasting Modes in Paradise Lost*, *A Concordance to Milton's English Poetry* (with William Ingram), and several dozen essays, including the 1984 winner of the Milton Society of America's Hanford Best Essay Prize.